V&R unipress

Marek Świstak

Regional Policy in China

Development and Strategic Challenges

With 25 figures

V&R unipress

MIX
Papier aus verantwortungsvollen Quellen
FSC www.fsc.org FSC® C083411

Bibliographic information published by the Deutsche Nationalbibliothek
The Deutsche Nationalbibliothek lists this publication in the Deutsche Nationalbibliografie; detailed bibliographic data are available online: https://dnb.de.

This publication was financially supported by the Jagiellonian University in Kraków, Poland.

The publication was co-funded under the program "Excellence Initiative – Research University" at the Jagiellonian University in Kraków, Poland.

Printed and bound by CPI books GmbH, Birkstraße 10, 25917 Leck, Germany
Printed in the EU.

Vandenhoeck & Ruprecht Verlage | www.vandenhoeck-ruprecht-verlage.com

ISBN 978-3-8471-1523-6

For Sylwia

Contents

Abbreviations

AIIB	Asian Infrastructure Investment Bank
AMR	Academy of Macroeconomic Research
BRI	Belt and Road Initiative
CC CPC	Central Committee of the Communist Party of China
CDB	China Development Bank
CMC	Central Military Commission
CPC	Communist Party of China
EU	European Union
FDI	Foreign Direct Investment
FYP	Five-Year Plan
GDP	Gross Domestic Product
GMS	Greater Mekong Subregion
MOR	Ministry of Railways
NBS	National Bureau of Statistics of China
NDB	New Development Bank
NDRC	National Development and Reform Commission
NPC	The National People's Congress
NPM	New Public Management
NRP	National Reform Programs
P CPC	Politburo of the Communist Party of China
PG	People's Government
PRA	People Representative Assembly
PRC	People's Republic of China
SASAC	State-owned Assets Supervision and Administration Commission of the State Council
SC	State Council
SCO	Shanghai Cooperation Organization
SEZ	Special Economic Zone
SME	Small Medium Enterprises
SPC	Supreme People's Court
TBNA	Tianjin Binhai New Area
USA	United States of America

USSR	Union of Soviet Socialist Republics
VAT	Value Added Tax
WDS	Western Development Strategy
WRDLG	Western Region Development Leading Group
WTO	World Trade Organization
YREB	Yangtze River Economic Belt

Lists of tables, diagrams, graphs and maps

Tables

Diagrams

Graphs

Maps

Introduction

Undoubtedly, the current situation of the People's Republic of China (PRC) is conducive to shaping regional development policy. This is not just a redundant action taken by the Middle Kingdom but a specific necessity, taking into account the priorities of high-ranking members of the Communist Party of China (CPC). These undoubtedly include the CPC's continued leadership of the nation, social peace, and respect for hierarchy in the spirit of Confucian values. Naturally, the PRC's policy aims are much more complex. In the past four decades, China has significantly caught up with its economic backwardness thanks to continued strong economic growth. Rejecting the "perpetual revolution", the goal has been to ensure constant economic growth, and thus improve welfare. However, the situation, from the point of view of regional development, has also caused many negative phenomena, which, ultimately not covered by a properly targeted policy, may contribute to the intensification of the challenges facing China, and thus undermine its intention to play a key role in the world, not only in the economy and politics.

China aspires to become the country with the largest economy and the greatest development potential, thus establishing itself as a center of power. This requires the ability to modernize, especially in the economic, social, political, and technological dimensions. This intention may become fleeting if such significant development disproportions in the territorial system are still present in the economic landscape. Competitiveness is not built at the level of an abstract state, but in a specific local dimension, specific industries, or even specific programs and investments that build the foundations for being competitive. The dynamics of socio-economic change since the end of the 1970s make it clear that the Middle Kingdom skillfully uses globalization, and also applies adaptation mechanisms, mainly in the economic dimension. It is therefore important to pay attention to how this economic growth admired by others and the resulting increase in living standards are presented not only from the point of view of the entire country but also its individual components (e.g., regions). Therefore, in this book, I reflect on the PRC's activities in the field of regional development, in which the intervention of the state and its organizational units (units below the state level) meets the influence of market mechanisms (including the forces of concentration and deconcentration). Thus, I am convinced that a full understanding of China's (possible) return to the role of a world power is not possible without reflection on the country's internal challenges including regional policy.

China's regional policy (hereinafter interchangeably regional development policy) is therefore an extremely interesting example of the coexistence of public intervention and the use of market mechanisms, accompanied by political centralization and economic decentralization. The dynamically developing Middle Kingdom, increasingly connected with the world economy, increases its influence on the dynamics of global GDP growth as well as the directions and pace of economic development in the world. From the perspective of regional policy, this process is very complex, as it results from many determinants, also located outside the Middle Kingdom. In this book, I take a different perspective, looking at China's development from the perspective of that country's internal policies, such as the regional development policy. The identifiable challenges of the Middle Kingdom are also problems resulting from the internal situation of the country, which is also mentioned in this book. In other words, the key to understanding the transformation of contemporary China is to recognize the internal factors affecting how both the state (and its constituent units) and the economy function.

Taking into account the specific characteristics of the Middle Kingdom, rooted in Asian values, cultural differences, and systemic experiences, I reflect on the extent to which regional policy, which is a derivative of state capitalism, shows universal features, and to what extent it is unique to the PRC. The legitimacy of the above results from observing the shaping of regional policy in other latitudes, e. g., in Europe. It is widely believed that it is very difficult to transfer solutions in the field of regional policy from one latitude to another. Meanwhile, the problems faced regarding regional policy are often universal in nature. It is true that they often result from a unique set of interdependent factors, the characteristics and classification of which occupy the minds of many researchers in the fields of economics, management sciences, geography, sociology, and political science. In the following considerations, I use the paradigms of political science to the greatest extent, but I also use concepts from the fields of economics, management sciences, and law. Meanwhile, the repertoire of methods used to influence regional development is explored, as is the extent to which it requires specific adaptation to the place where it is applied. Hence, an element of reflection on China's regional policy is a reflection on the extent to which Chinese solutions can constitute unique ideas and to which they are universal.

Here, I propose to look at regional policy from the perspective of public policy[1]and institutional theory[2]. Hence, the book focuses on the policy process and the way of creating it, not only the agreement of development priorities, but also the ways of making decisions. The proposed approach may contribute to a better understanding not only of the essence of public policy, which is regional policy, but also the determinants of its success in an authoritarian political system and an economic system that is partly based on the free market and partly subordinated to the state. This approach makes it possible to answer the questions about how and why regional policy was shaped, how it is implemented and what its effects are. Analyzing the activity of regional policy from the institutional perspective is justified due to the fact that the actions taken and the allocation of resources are a derivative of the functioning and transformation of the institutional system of the PRC understood as long-term principles and practices[3].

The analytical approach based on public policy takes into account in particular how public policy steers public tasks. For the purposes of this book, the policy process is viewed as a set of public policymaking mechanisms[4]. In relation to the PRC's regional policy, this concept is therefore treated as a set of mechanisms shaping actions and activities which contribute to the implementation of policy and the achievement of goals. With regard to regional policy, but also other policies, decisionmakers are burdened with the need to make decisions based on a limited amount of knowledge and information, which is a big challenge for the Middle Kingdom due to its vast territory and the size of its population. It is not only about limitations related to the temporal perception of socioeconomic and political phenomena that affect this policy. We are talking here, on the operational level, about understanding the limitations and circumstances of the instruments with which public policy tries to solve public problems. A methodological orientation based on public policy broadens our knowledge of the conditions necessary for effective control of regional policy, as it also takes into

1 For a research approach based on public policy, see: Michael E. Kraft, Scott R. Furlong, *Public Policy. Politics, Analysis, and Alternatives*, Los Angeles-London-New Delhi-Singapore-Washington 2015, pp. 34–169; Michael Howlett, *Designing Public Policies. Principles and Instruments*, London-New York 2011, pp. 13–80; William N. Dunn, *Public Policy Analysis*, New York 2015, pp. 14–98; Peter Knoepfel, Corinne Larrue, Frédéric Varone, Michael Hill, *Public Policy Analysis*, Bristol 2007, pp. 3–15.

2 Peter Hall, Rosemary C.R. Taylor, *Political science and the three new institutionalisms*, "Political Studies", 1996, vol. 44, no. 5, pp. 936–957.

3 James G. March, Johan P. Olsen, *Institutional Perspectives on Political Institutions*, "Governance" 1996, vol. 9, issue 3, pp. 247–259.

4 John A. Chandler, *Public Policy and Private Interest: Ideas, Self-Interest and Ethics in Public Policy*, Oxon-New York 2017, pp. 5–8; Andrew Heywood, *Political Science*, Warszawa 2009, p. 494.

account the complexity of relations within the public management of regional policy in the People's Republic of China.

To look at China's regional development policy from the perspective of its formulation, implementation, and adaptation, it is necessary to present the basic assumptions underlying this work at the outset. First, due to the specificity of regional policy as an activity that involves public intervention and an attempt to control market mechanisms, and the characteristics of China's socio-economic development model, the political and economic dimensions have been integrated into the work to capture the dynamism/stagnation of the processes of politics and economic change. This allows us to capture the interaction of different economic governance models and different forms of public intervention. Second, it was assumed that any analysis of regional policy in China cannot ignore the influence of political culture and legitimacy on its formulation, implementation, and effects. In this book we use a systemic analysis; it was also assumed that changes, stability, and adaptation in individual power structures and in the system as a whole must be taken into account in the context of discussing individual aspects of regional policy. Therefore, the subject of the present study is neither Chinese political culture (including cultural aspects) nor mechanisms of legitimizing power in the Middle Kingdom, as it goes beyond the accepted framework for research on these topics. This does not mean that they are completely neglected in the context of the problems, shaping, and effects of regional policy.

Taking the above into account, the aim of this work is to answer the following research questions:

1. To what extent have the achievements of economic reforms in the last four decades influenced the shape and results of regional policy in China?
2. Do growing disproportions and inequalities have a destabilizing effect on the authoritarian mode of governance and the system implementing regional policy?
3. To what extent does Chinese political centralism[5] determine the implementation of regional development activities?
4. What is the impact of hierarchical regional policymaking on the way and results of its implementation?
5. Does the Chinese regional policy implementation system have a sufficient level of adaptation, allowing it to be shaped within a heterogeneous socio-economic structure, in different geographic conditions and with a varied quality of life of the inhabitants?

5 Art. 2 of the Constitution of the PRC, http://www.npc.gov.cn/zgrdw/englishnpc/Constitution/2007-11/15/content_1372963.htm (access: 9/11/2021).

6. Do the instruments of regional policy based on bureaucratic relations enable reflection and learning in the field of regional development with regard to changing socio-economic conditions?

These research questions lead to the formation of the following hypotheses of the following hypotheses:

1. The evolution of the socioeconomic development model towards increasing the importance of market mechanisms is conducive to shaping regional policy and influences its results in China.
2. Significant development disproportions in the Middle Kingdom - despite many years of regional development policy - still pose a challenge not so much to the authoritarian system of exercising power, but to the socio-economic development of the country as a whole, in particular, achieving its long-term development goals and establishing a dominant position in the world economy.
3. Chinese political centralism is the main feature of the implementation of regional development measures.
4. The hierarchical shaping of regional development activities dominates the organization of policy, but complementary actions based on a bottom-up approach can also be identified, which also contribute to the results of the policy in question.
5. The Chinese system of regional policy implementation ensures adaptability in relation to the heterogeneous socioeconomic structure of the country, as well as economic and international challenges.
6. The dominant position of the CPC and hierarchical bureaucratic relations in the application of regional policy instruments affect China's limited ability to reflect and learn in the face of changing socioeconomic conditions.

The purpose of this book is to reflect on China's regional development policy, though not in a static view of its regional development, but rather with a view to capturing the dynamic aspects of shaping regional policy (including its implementation) in an authoritarian political system. Another important aspect is to establish to what extent regional policy is able to adapt to changing economic and social conditions. Observations of the regional development policy in the Middle Kingdom indicate a change in its function along with an increase in the statehood of this country. Hence, in this book I explore the importance of regional policy in the broader dimension of the country's political system in order to identify its essence and evolution. I also assume that research on the functions of regional policy is the most intellectually rewarding, and therefore desirable.

In this work I adopt the approach proposed by Giliberto Capano, Michael Howlett and M. Ramesh[6], i.e., perceiving regional policymaking in three dimensions. First, it is an institutional dynamic because power arrangements change over time, creating a political mix. Public policy is dynamic, responding to the challenges that pose problems. Dynamics is not only a function of time, but also a function of features of the institutional architecture of a given public activity and of the instruments used. The management of public affairs is therefore more related to the temporal moment of equilibrium than to a fixed and stable construct. Secondly, it is a strategic dimension – politics is the product of actions and interactions of the most important actors of politics, guided by specific goals (e.g., within the CCP and state institutions)[7]. The strategic dimension is at the same time the ability of the authorities to change the arrangements within a given policy, and at the same time the need to respond to systemic challenges. Third, there is capacity, which is the extent to which policy findings can be successful in addressing important public goals.

The cultural diversity and political experiences of the Middle Kingdom make us pay attention to the specificity of the functioning of the public sphere. It is about capturing not only the policymaking process, but also evaluating its results in the light of the non-Western development paradigm. It is assumed that the shaping of regional policy is a derivative of managing the public sphere. The shaping of the regional development policy can be seen in the light of how governance drives the way the authorities create activities related to regional development through the effective allocation of public funds[8]. Francis Fukuyama[9] believes that governance manifests itself in the ability of a government to make and enforce rules and provide services, whether or not the nature of power is democratic. This approach excludes democratic accountability from the concept of governance and thus extends the application of this analytical category to countries outside the democratic regime. The reason for this approach, according to Fukuyama, is the lack of sufficient empirical confirmation that democracy and good governance reinforce each other. Skepticism in this respect leads the cited author to the conclusion that it is a theory that requires further research.

According to Fukuyama, the quality of governance differs from the results that governance is expected to achieve. Public management is concerned with the

6 Giliberto Capano Michael Howlett, M. Ramesh (eds.), *Varieties of Governance. Dynamics, Strategies, Capacities,* London 2015, pp. 8–9.

7 Anna L. Ahlers, Gunter Schubert, *Effective Policy Implementation in China's Local State,* "Modern China" 2015, vol. 41, no. 4, pp. 372–405.

8 Konrad Raczkowski, *Zarządzania publiczne. Teoria i praktyka*, Warszawa 2015, p. 33.

9 Francis Fukuyama, *What is governance?*, "Governance: An International Journal of Policy, Administration, and Institutions" 2013, vol. 26, no. 3, p. 350.

efficiency of the administration (agents) in fulfilling the wishes of the principals, and not with the very goals set by the aforementioned principals. Thus, whatever the nature of the political regime, a government is an organization that can perform its functions better or worse. An authoritarian regime can be well governed like democracy, and it can also be maladministered. Separating public management from its normative dimension, which boils down to what it is supposed to serve, is not easy. It is not clear, for example, whether there is a well-governed state that increases the level of general well-being of its inhabitants at the high cost of the poorest social strata or one that maintains social peace with the military or allows for the devastation of the environment in which its inhabitants live.

I assume with regard to the regional development policy that these patterns of public management are reflected in the process of formulating and executing this public activity[10]. In the case of China, a country with a large area and a large population, disaggregation of public authority should be taken into account. The aforementioned Fukuyama[11] proposes a division according to the function, region, and level of government in this regard. The rationale is that you cannot look at management problems on just one level. Many of them arise from the interaction between different levels of power. A weak national government can reduce the efficiency of local government, and vice versa. For example, in relation to China, it is widely believed that local authorities are more corrupt than higher authorities. In fact, we do not know if it is true or not. The level of corruption varies depending not only on the level of government, but also on the region and function or even area of social life (in this case, a specific policy).

An attempt to capture the specificity of the shaping of regional policy in the Middle Kingdom by identifying the model of public management is not enough. It is also important to specify the subject scope of this work and the time frame. I am reflecting on the regional development policy of the People's Republic of China and more precisely on regional policy as one of the public policies. This book is problematic in nature, focusing on selected issues that affect the results of the regional policy of the Middle Kingdom; hence no strict time limit has been adopted. However, the text refers to China's regional policy, which has been shaped over the last four decades – until 2022.

The specificity of regional policy requires a short presentation of key concepts that characterize the main threads of the public action analyzed here. Regional policy is an example of collective public action solving very complex problems,

10 Andrzej Zybała, *Państwo i społeczeństwo w działaniu. Polityki publiczne wobec potrzeb modernizacji państwa i społeczeństwa*, Warszawa 2013, pp. 40–41.

11 Francis Fukuyama, *What is governance?…*, pp. 344, 364, Bob Jessop, *The State: Past, Present, Future*, Cambridge-Malden 2016, pp. 167–168.

among which are, for example: development disproportions, social inequalities, unemployment, poverty, lack of structural adjustment, low development potential, innovation, and competitiveness deficit[12]. However, complex problems are not simply reducible to individual components. This happens because there is a specific interaction between the components that creates the dynamics of the problem. The regional policy fully reflects the specificity described, as the main axis of its activities is to eliminate disproportions and support development (increasing competitiveness, supporting prosperity). As specific relationships exist between these elements, the results of regional policy are far from what is expected from it. To define the focus of regional policy, it is essential to clarify the concept of region. The region as an element of regional policy can be treated as a conventionally separated or homogeneous area, distinguished from adjacent areas by certain natural or acquired features. Approaches to the concept of a region results from the science on which it is defined. The region is very often defined from the point of view of economics, political science, administration studies, sociology, geography. In economic sciences, a region is constituted by features related to human activity. In this perspective, the region is referred to as the center of economic activity and is the place where the individual engages in production and production processes. Therefore, the classification of regions is made by distinguishing the specificity of the management (e.g., mining, industrial, agricultural region) and based on the analysis of economic dependencies that exist in connection with human activity in a given area[13].

For the PRC, the region is considered as the area that results from the formal administrative division of the country at the level of the provincial government. The choice is not perfect in a given country as diverse as China and its local characteristics. Many individual provinces are units as large and diverse as entire countries in other latitudes of the world. The huge area and extremely diverse space pose a challenge to the correct interpretation of the ongoing processes of concentration and distraction. In theory, the main factor in the identification of regions is the homogeneity of the studied space in relation to the heterogeneous environment, but in research practice an important point of reference is the availability of data; hence, in this book provincial-level units are treated as regions. Therefore, when identifying the spatial differentiation of China's development, provincial-level units are the basic unit of measurement. Constructions such as "economic regions" or "macroregions" are also used as an analytical unit, meaning in both cases groups of provinces that do not constitute a formal ter-

12 Niles Hansen, Benjamin Higgins, Donald Savoie, *Regional Policy in a Changing World*, New York-London 1990, p. 282.
13 Jan Wiktor Tkaczyński, Marek Świstak, *Encyklopedia polityki regionalnej i funduszy europejskich*, Warszawa 2013, p. 454.

ritorial unit, but due to the similar specificity of regional development, are identified as groups of provinces with a similar level and trajectory of development. Here we are talking here about the eastern, central, and western economic regions (macroregions). The division into three economic regions also has a traditional dimension – it is widely used by the Chinese in empirical research and political discussions and therefore seems to be a reasonable starting point, especially when referring to current political discussions, where more synthetic conclusions are necessary.

Regional policy is considered as one of the public activities, an inherent part of which is interference with the functioning of the free market[14]. Regional policy is a part of economic policy that aims to stimulate economic and social development in the regions by public authorities, and in particular to improve the geographical distribution of economic activity[15]. At the same time, as far as the regional policy of the PRC is concerned, its aim is to reduce development disparities and increase the competitiveness and potential of the weaker regional economies[16]. From the macroeconomic perspective, the above requires that regional policy be treated as a sectoral policy constituting an element of the overall economic policy.

Development treated as a process is the result of actions taken by public authorities and is contextual in nature. This means that its evaluation should be carried out in the broader dimension of development goals, benchmarks and an assessment of the degree to which goals have been achieved. Development refers to increasing level of competitiveness, optimizing the use of resources, sustainability and associating it with progress. Jacek Szlachta defines regional development as a systematic improvement of the competitiveness of companies and the standard of living of the inhabitants, as well as an increase in the economic potential of the region[17]. The element related to the treatment of development as a process is also highlighted by Andrzej Klasik, who defines the development of the region in the context of sustainable growth of the economic potential, its competitive strength, and the level and quality of life of its inhabitants[18]. The "development" category is therefore a process of transformations, changes,

14 Lieselotte Klein, *The European Community's Regional Policy*, "Built Environment" 1981, vol. 7, pp. 182–188.

15 Norbert Vanhove, *Regional Policy: A European Approach*, New York 2018, p. 57.

16 Bolesław Woś, *Rozwój regionów i polityka regionalna w Unii Europejskiej oraz w Polsce*, Wrocław 2005, p. 46; Tomasz Grzegorz Grosse, *Polityka regionalna Unii Europejskiej. Przykład Grecji, Włoch, Irlandii i Polski*, Warszawa 2004, p. 7.

17 Jacek Szlachta, *Główne problemy polityki rozwoju regionalnego Polski na przełomie XX i XXI wieku*, [in:] Ryszard Bartoszkiewicz (ed.), *Strategiczne wyzwania dla polityki rozwoju regionalnego Polski*, Warszawa 1996, p. 16.

18 Andrzej Klasik, *Strategia konkurencyjna regionu*, [in:] Andrzej Klasik, Florian Kuźnik (ed.), *Zarządzanie strategiczne rozwojem lokalnym i regionalnym*, Katowice 2001, pp. 48–51.

transition to states or forms that are in some respects more perfect, subordinated to the dignity of the human person, and meeting the requirements resulting from axioms, natural law, and superior values. In this sense, development may not necessarily mean complexity; moreover, complexity does not have to be the only attribute of development[19]. Regional policy has often been treated as a structural policy[20] aimed at a key change in the management structure and the stimulation of economic development in a given area by optimizing the use of resources[21].

An important aspect of development to which most specialists pay attention to is competitiveness[22]. We are talking here about the increase in regional competitiveness. Michael Storper defines competitiveness as the ability of the economy to attract and maintain companies with a stable or increasing market share, maintaining or improving the living standards of those who participate in it[23]. Janne Huovari, Aki Kangasharju and Alane Aku perceive competitiveness in a similar way, treating regional competitiveness as the ability of regions to attract and support economic activity so that the inhabitants have a relatively good economic condition[24].

The above approaches to regional policy indicate several features of development. First, development is not segmental, but a process. This way of thinking very well reflects public action based on public policies, in which a great deal of attention is paid to the political process in governance. Development is therefore to be of a permanent nature, not only occurring in short periods of time. Its manifestation increases the level of competitiveness, understood as increasing the ability to compete. Second, development is also a process whose aim is not to increase competitiveness in principle, but to increase competitiveness so that there is also an increase in the quality of life of the inhabitants.

In this book the official transcription of Chinese *pinyin* names and terms is used.

In closing, I wish to emphasize that I am personally responsible for any shortcomings in this book. Hence the appeal to potential readers for understanding and constructive criticism.

---

19 Franciszek Piontek, Barbara Piontek, *Teoria rozwoju*, Warszawa 2016, pp. 9, 16, 18.

20 Tomasz Dorożyński, *Rola polityki Unii Europejskiej w usuwaniu regionalnych dysproporcji gospodarczych. Wnioski dla Polski*, Łódź 2012, p. 9.

21 Bolesław Winiarski (ed.), *Polityka Gospodarka*, Warszawa 2006, p. 61.

22 David L. Barkley, *Evaluations of Regional Competitiveness: Making a Case for Case Studies*, The Review of Regional Studies 2008, vol. 38, pp. 121–143.

23 Michael Storper, *The Regional World: Territorial Development in a Global Economy*, New York 1997, p. 20.

24 Janne Huovari, Aki Kangasharju, Alane Aku, *Constructing an Index for Regional Competitiveness*, Pellervo Economic Research Institute, Working Paper no. 44, Helsinki, 2001, p. 1.

Chapter 1. Socioeconomic Development Model: evolution and current situation

1.1. The economic situation in light of development challenges

China is an example of a country that has made very significant progress in terms of the level and dynamics of economic development in the last four decades. This arouses great interest not only from observers of the international situation, but also from the countries themselves, especially highly developed countries. In the West, knowledge of the model of China's socioeconomic development is still insufficiently understood. The list of achievements is significant; it suffices to mention the highest rate of economic growth in the world in recent years, the drastic reduction of the scale of poverty, and the dynamic expansion of the national infrastructure. A key aspect in the success or failure of a regional policy is how it both affects and is affected by the overall economic situation of a country. Hence the need to define the general economic situation in the People's Republic of China. The last four decades have seen continuous economic growth linking state intervention with the use of market mechanisms while maintaining an authoritarian political system. It is therefore justified to find an answer to the question of what the economic development of the Middle Kingdom is built around, whether the role of the state is the decisive factor or whether market mechanisms are.

Contrary to appearances, this is not a purely academic question, as it also has a practical dimension. Today, the influence of the state on the economy can be observed in countries with even the most free-market economies; this is even greater in countries with an authoritarian political system. Some define it as the influence of the state on the economy[1], others as the role of institutions in economic growth[2] – institutions understood as the rules of the game in society,

1 Douglas North, *Understanding the Process of Economic Change*, Princeton 2005, pp. 81–126, Daron Acemoglu, James A. Robinson, *Why Nations Fail: The Origins of Power, Prosperity and Poverty*, London 2012, pp. 7–95.

2 Daron Acemoglu, Simon Johnson, *Understanding Institutions*, "Journal of Political Economy" 2005, vol. 113, no. 5, pp. 949–995.

and in the economic dimension, in the economy. Institutions defined in this way influence the structure of economic incentives in a society. We are talking, for example, about the structure of ownership or the nature and efficiency of market mechanisms. On the other hand, efficient market mechanisms are those that ensure the proper level of allocation of economic effects. Economic institutions that facilitate and encourage the accumulation of growth factors, innovation, and efficient allocation of resources help to improve the economic situation and, in the long run, to maintain prosperity[3].

One thing is certain: states exert considerable influence on the economic sphere. The nature of the state's influence on the economy and the economy on the state is the key to answering the question posed earlier. In a word: it is about determining to what extent what is happening in China is a manifestation of the "invisible hand of the market", and to what extent, the "visible hand of the state". The international experience shows the occurrence of both phenomena, while in China the voluntary influence of the state on the economy and other manifestations of social life is considered crucial.

Table 1. The pace of China's economic development compared to selected countries

Country	Year reaching USD 2,000 GDP per capita	Year reaching USD 8,000 GDP per capita	Number of years when GDP per capita was achieved	Average annual GDP growth
Netherlands	1827	1960	133	1.0
Great Britain	1839	1957	118	1.2
Australia	1848	1955	107	1.3
USA	1860	1941	81	1.7
France	1896	1962	93	1.5
Germany	1874	1962	88	1.6
Mexico	1950	2008	58	2.4
Hong Kong	1950	1977	27	5.3
Singapore	1950	1979	29	4.9
Japan	1951	1968	17	8.5
Turkey	1955	2007	52	2.7
Taiwan	1965	1985	20	7.2
South Korea	1969	1989	20	7.2
Malaysia	1969	2002	33	4.3
Thailand	1976	2005	29	4.9
China	**1995**	**2011**	**16**	**9.1**

3 Daron Acemoglu, Simon Johnson, James Robinson, *Institutions as the Fundamental Cause of Long-Run Growth*, "NBER Working Paper" May 2004, no. 10481, pp. 1–2.

Table 1 *(Continued)*

Country	Year reaching USD 2,000 GDP per capita	Year reaching USD 8,000 GDP per capita	Number of years when GDP per capita was achieved	Average annual GDP growth
World	1950	2004	54	2.6

Source: Ross Garnaut, Ligang Song, Cai Fang, *Reform and China's Long-Term Growth and Development*, [in:] Ligang Song, Ross Garnaut, Cai Fang (eds.), *Deepening Reform for China's Long-term Growth and Development*, Canberra 2014, p. 9.

In the discussion on the economic achievements of the Middle Kingdom, attention should be paid to the pace of changes. The speed with which the PRC is catching up with developed world is undoubtedly remarkable. Measuring the rate of economic development with GDP per capita, there is no doubt that China in the twentieth and twenty-first centuries is the undisputed leader. By 1995, China had a GDP per capita of $ 2,000. They quadrupled production over the next 16 years, which translated to $ 8,000 in GDP per capita, surpassing these two breakthrough levels of production in less time than any other country in history. It is worth mentioning that in the case of the old economic powers it took much longer: it took the USA 81 years, Great Britain 118 years, and Germany 88 years. It is comparable only with the countries of East Asia that are geographically close to China: Korea (20 years) and Japan (17 years).

The transformation of socioeconomic development is undoubtedly a success, considering that the GDP of the Middle Kingdom currently accounts for approximately 24% of the global value of such an indicator (Table 2). This allows us to conclude that China is an example of a country that was becoming an economic superpower at the beginning of the twenty-first century. Importantly, in four decades, from a relatively undeveloped, politically and economically isolated country, China has become one of the main actors in global trade. China's global GDP ($ 12.2 trillion) now ranks second after the US ($ 19.3 trillion) and ahead of Japan ($ 4.8 trillion). When we take into account GDP measured in purchasing power parity, China is ahead of the US, thus becoming the largest economy in the world[4]. Considering only these data, it is difficult to say whether China is the first economy in the world. However, if you look at the macroeconomic data of the last 40 years, China's growth dynamics is impressive.

4 *China Overtakes the US as the World's Largest Economy*, p. 3, https://www.iimk.ac.in/libportal/reports/China-Overtakes-US-Worlds-Largest-Economy-White-PaperEuromonitor-Report.pdf (access: 09/11/2021).

Table 2. Transformation of China's economic position compared to various world economies

Country	**1978**	**1988**	**1998**	**2008**	**2016**	**2018**	**2019**
Total GDP (billion USD, current prices)							
China	149	312	1029	4598	11 190	13 894	14 342
United States	2356	5252	9089	14 718	18 624	20 580	21 427
Japan	1013	3071	4032	5037	4949	4954	5 081
Germany	737	1395	2243	3752	3477	3949	3845
World	8542	19 153	31 346	63 433	75 936	86 408	87 751
GDP at purchasing power parity (million USD, current prices)							
China	no	no	3053	10 113	21 411	21 730	23 460
United States	no	no	9089	14 718	18 624	20 580	21 427
Japan	no	no	3166	4456	5369	5230	5459
Germany	no	no	2081	3122	4030	4514	4659
World	no	no	43 017	82 629	120 848	129 250	135 669
GDP growth year on year (in%)							
China	11.7	11.2	7.8	9.7	6.7	6.8	6.1
United States	5.6	4.2	4.4	-0.3	1.5	3.2	2.3
Japan	5.3	6.8	-1.1	-1.1	0.9	0.3	0.7
Germany	3.0	3.7	2.0	1.1	1.9	1.5	0.6
World	4.0	4.6	2.5	1.8	2.5	3.1	2.5
GDP *per capita* (in USD, current prices)							
China	156	284	829	3471	8117	9976	10 261
United States	10 587	21 483	32 949	48 401	57 589	62 996	65 280
Japan	8882	25 052	31 903	39 339	38 972	39 159	40 246
Germany	9446	17 863	27 341	45 699	42 233	47 639	46 258
World	no	no	7 216	12 212	16 234	11 381	11 435

Source: own study based on: Marek Świstak, *Ewolucja chińskiego modelu rozwoju społeczno-gospodarczego w supranarodowej perspektywie Unii Europejskie*, [in:] Marek, Świstak, Jan Wiktor Tkaczyński (eds.), *Azjatycki model polityki rozwoju społeczno-gospodarczego. Wybrane aspekty w świetle standardów i doświadczeń Unii Europejskiej*, Kraków 2019, p. 96; The World Bank, https://databank.worldbank.org/data/reports.aspx?source=2&series=NY.GDP.MKTP.CD,NV.AGR.TOTL.ZS,NV.IND.TOTL.ZS,NV.IND.MANF.ZS,NV.SRV.TETC.ZS,NV.SRV.TOTL.ZS# (access: 09/11/2021).

Data show that in the period 1978–2019 the average growth rate of China's GDP was 8.57%, and in some years it reached a double digit value, while, for example, in the USA this average is less than 3%. The dynamics of growth is incredible if you compare it with the average growth – calculated for the entire world economy on the basis of World Bank data – which is, similar to the USA, around 2.8%. Therefore, it can be assumed that, since the end of the 1970s, China has been developing three times faster than the entire world economy and the economy of the United States. Regardless of any surprise at the size and pace of development, it is difficult to hide the fact that we are dealing here with a unique case of a country rapidly catching up with its economically developed competitors.

Does this mean that the Chinese citizen becomes as wealthy as an American or a European? The data clearly show that the statistical wealth of Chinese citizens is still about half of the same figure for citizens of other countries of the world. From this perspective, China is still a long way from developed countries such as the US or Japan, not to mention Germany. Analyzing the above data, it should be pointed out that the process of catching up with the most competitive economies in the world is still in the implementation phase. It was easier for China to achieve the high development dynamics necessary to catch up with western countries, starting from the low level of $ 156 (GDP *per capita* for 1978). Approaching the level of development in the economies of the Western world can reduce the growth dynamics of the Chinese economy, as evidenced by the experience of economic transformation in the countries of Central and Eastern Europe, including Poland. Some GDP data show some slowdown in China's economic growth, especially in recent years. It is possible that this tendency may be clearer in the long run, and the Chinese themselves describe this state as "the new normal".

The scale of economic development, measured by GDP per capita, is also noteworthy. In less than 40 years, the Chinese statistically increased their standard of living by $ 10,105, which is perhaps not spectacular when you consider the same figures for the United States ($ 54,693). However, if you look at the Chinese income catching up in percentage terms, it should be stated that in the period 1978–2019, China increased its GDP per capita by 6577%, the USA by 616%, and Germany by 489%. Taking into account the size of the country in question (1.4 billion inhabitants), it can be undoubtedly stated that the way China has caught up with more developed countries is unparalleled in the contemporary world. In this case, the popular saying that a small organism can do more, bearing in mind, for example, its flexibility or adaptability, does not work. China proves that a large entity can also demonstrate the ability to adapt to the challenges it faces.

1.2. The role of the state in the Chinese economy

The economic phenomenon of China, especially in the light of the development experiences of Western countries, focuses the discussion on the extent to which the Middle Kingdom in the economic dimension is an example of a free market, and to what extent it is a centrally planned economy. There is currently no consensus on how to name the Chinese economy. This is so not only for theoretical reasons, but also because China is experiencing a constant economic transformation, which complicates the formulation of unambiguous conclusions. The belief that answers should be sought somewhere between free market capitalism and a centrally planned economy is beyond doubt. Anna Zaorska points out that the development model in China can be called hybrid capitalism due to the confusion of many elements and solutions used in the past in connection with solutions typical of the modern economy. However, treating Chinese capitalism as state-led is also not fully in line with reality, mainly because the term does not apply to all the characteristics of the model[5].

Ian Bremmer notes that in the case of state capitalism, the state is the leading actor in economic relations. In this perspective, governments manipulate markets for political ends. The government uses various types of state-owned enterprises, treated as key economic entities, to manage resources in the economy, for example, to create and maintain jobs. Existing private enterprises are only admitted to the market to the extent that they are unable to dominate entire sectors, especially those considered key by the government. The authorities use the market to create prosperity that meets the expectations of policymakers. The reasons for this are not economic factors (maximization of economic growth), but factors of a political nature (power maximization, legitimization, maintenance of power). The role of the state is visible not only in internal economic relations but also in relation to foreign capital. In this respect, the policy of the Chinese government aims to protect strategic sectors to which foreign capital access is highly regulated, such as telecommunications, shipbuilding and petrochemicals[6]. Observing the behavior of other highly developed countries, it can be concluded that such practices are quite common. Hence, the protection of strategic sectors of the economy by the state cannot constitute a reference point in deciding on state capitalism. It is only a complementary element in the possible saturation of the economy with elements of state intervention.

Joshua Kurlantzick also refers to the role of the state in the economy[7], for whom the essence of state capitalism comes down to the fact that the government sees itself as an entity that has a direct role to play in managing the economy and shaping corporate governance. The cited author also refers to the ownership structure in the economy, pointing out that of the 42 largest companies in China, only three are examples of fully private capital. The ownership structure is not everything. The state affects the economy through various types of public policy, which can be reduced to providing various subsidies in many areas of the

5 Henryk Chołaj, *Chiny a świat. Współczesny chiński model ekonomiczny*, Warszawa 2014, p. 103.
6 Ian Bremmer, *The End of the Free Market: Who Wins the War Between States and Corporations?*, London 2010, pp. 46–82.
7 Joshua Kurlantzick, *State Capitalism: How the Return of Statism is Transforming the World*, New York 2016, pp. 16–88.

economy[8]. We can talk here about supporting endogenous innovations, protection, and consolidation of domestic companies operating in the largest industries, reducing trust in foreign capital as the main instrument of the export industry, building a social security system, reducing income inequalities, and implementing antipoverty programs.

Barry Naughton points out that at present it is difficult to classify the socioeconomic system of the Middle Kingdom as socialism, mainly because the mechanism of redistribution and responsiveness of the system is insufficiently present in the PRC's economic model. This researcher draws attention to four constitutive components of socialism as a socioeconomic system[9]:

1. Capability: the government controls a large proportion of an economy's resources, thereby influencing economic performance.
2. Intention: the deliberate exercising of power over the economy in order to obtain results different from those that the market would give without intervention.
3. Redistribution: benefiting the less well-off, e.g., through social security policy, redistribution that benefits the poor.
4. Responsiveness: the mechanism of the population's influence on the shape of economic and social policy.

The most general definition of socialism, to which almost all researchers could contribute is connected with the socialization of the means of production. This socialization refers to the authorities' ability to influence economic performance in an economy. The influence of the state on the economy, in turn, comes down to the scale of public ownership in the economy. There is no doubt that the scale of public ownership in China has declined significantly since the 1990s. This is despite the fact that the Chinese state has not fully accepted privatization and the role of private property in the economy. The gradual increase in the acceptance of private property in the economy is reflected in the provisions of the Chinese constitution, especially its subsequent amendments. Based on article 6 of the constitution, the economic system in Chinese socialism is based on social ownership of the means of production[10]. The amendment to the constitution of

8 Axel Dreher, Andreas Fuchs, *Rogue Aid? An Empirical Analysis of China's Aid Allocation*, "The Canadian Journal of Economics" 2015, vol. 48, no. 3, pp. 988–1023; *An Assessment of China's Subsidies to Strategic and Heavyweight Industries*, Capital Trade Incorporated, pp. 16, 115–116, https://www.uscc.gov/sites/default/files/Research/AnAssessmentofChina'sSubsidiestoStrategicandHeavyweightIndustries.pdf (access: 09/11/2021).

9 Barry Naughton. *Is China Socialist?*, "Journal of Economic Perspectives" 2017, vol. 31, no. 1, pp. 3–4.

10 Article 6 of the PRC Constitution, http://www.npc.gov.cn/zgrdw/englishnpc/Constitution/2007-11/15/content_1372963.htm (access: 09/11/2021).

April 12, 1988 also allows the nonpublic sector in the economy, which complements the economy based on public ownership of the means of production. At the same time, the amendment to the constitution of March 15, 1999 stated that the nonpublic, individual and private sector, operating within the limits set by law, constitute an important component of the socialist market economy.

The state is still the owner of key sectors for the Chinese economy, such as energy, transport, telecommunications, financial services (including banks), insurance, water management, and education, science and technology. Meanwhile, private property, taking into account the industries in which private companies operate in China (as of 2005), plays an important role in production (43.5% of entities), services and gastronomy (26% of entities), and agriculture (6.3% of entities)[11]. State ownership is actually slightly more widespread in the service sector than in industry. State ownership is concentrated in capital-intensive sectors. For example, state ownership of industrial assets in 2014 was 39%, which was significant compared to the state's share of revenues (34%) and employment (18%)[12].

Chinese state-owned enterprises (SOE) make up the majority of companies listed on the Fortune Global 500 (FG500) list. In 2000, there were nine Chinese state-owned enterprises, and in 2017, already 75 of the 102 state-owned companies were from China. The state-owned enterprise sector in China is highly developed. According to the State-owned Assets Supervision and Administration Commission of the State Council (SASAC), the assets of Chinese state-owned enterprises in 2017 reached 151,711 billion yuan, and sales of products and services amounted to more than 52.2 billion yuan[13].

There is a complex ownership taxonomy in China. In other words: it is not easy to identify the importance of SOEs in the economy. According to OECD criteria, we can deal with three forms of ownership: (1) state, (2) collective, and (3) private (private entity, foreign capital). The problem is that there are also intermediate, mixed forms. In 2003, business entities of mixed capital accounted for about 40% of the entire economy[14]. One should also pay attention to the dispersed shareholding of companies operating in China, which *de facto* makes it even more difficult to recognize whether we are dealing with public or private capital. An

11 Son Ngoc Chu, Ligang Song, *State Control, Entrepreneurship and Resource Allocation*, [in:] Ligang Song, Ross Garnaut, Cai Fang (eds.), *Deepening Reform for China's Long-term Growth and Development*, Canberra 2014, p. 88.

12 Barry Naughton. *Is China Socialist…*, p. 8.

13 Karen Jingrong Lin, Xiaoyan Lu, Junsheng Zhang, Ying Zheng, *State-owned enterprises in China: A review of 40 yearsof research and practice*, "China Journal of Accounting Research" 2020, vol. 13, no. 1, p. 32.

14 Xinhua, 混合所有制经济已占 40% 5–10 年后将达到80%, November 25, 2003, http://news.southcn.com/china/zgkx/200311250786.htm (access: 09/11/2021).

illustration of the issue may be the shareholding structure of one of the largest Chinese companies operating in the financial sector – Ping Aa Insurance[15].

Table 3. Ten largest shareholders of Ping An Insurance in 2012

Shareholder	Status	Assets (in %)
Shenzhen Investment Holdings Co., Ltd.	State	6.07
Shum Yip Group Ltd.	State	2.27
Yuan Trust Investment Co., Ltd.	Domestic non-state	4.08
Linzhi New Horse Investment Development Co., Ltd.	Domestic non-state	4.03
Linzhi Jingao Industrial Development Co., Ltd.	Domestic non-state	3.46
Shenzhen Wuxin Yufu Industrial Co., Ltd.	Domestic non-state	2.22
Gongbujiangda Jiangnan Industrial Development Co., Ltd.	Domestic non-state	1.76
The Hongkong and Shanghai Banking Corporation Ltd.	Foreign	7.76
HSBC Insurance Holdings Ltd.	Foreign	4.58
All Gain Trading Ltd.	Foreign	1.04

Source: *Annual Report 2012,* Ping An Insurance, 2012, p. 83, https://www1.hkexnews.hk/listedco/listconews/sehk/2013/0327/ltn201303271176.pdf (access: 09/11/2021).

In 2012, the structure of the company was of mixed ownership, so-called because neither state- nor non-state shareholders owned a controlling interest in the company. Only 8.34% of shares in the capital group belonged to the state. Moreover, the shareholding structure was very fragmented. Therefore, the analysis of Ping An Insurance's ownership status for 2012 does not provide an answer as to who is the actual parent entity. In addition, it should be added that the current ownership structure changed in 2020; the status of shareholders allows us to say with some caution that it is rather a private enterprise[16].

As already mentioned, the economic importance of the public sector is decreasing: in 1998, state sector companies accounted for 46.5% of the added value

15 A capital group that provides financial products and services, operating in such segments as insurance, banking, trust, securities, other assets, management and technology. The company offers life, property and accident, pension and health insurance. The banking segment operates in the areas of loans and brokerage, wealth management and credit cards. The securities segment provides brokerage, trading, investment banking and asset management services. Source: Ping An Insurance Group, https://www.forbes.com/companies/ping-an-insurance/#8856a605c7b0 (access: 09/11/2021).

16 *Annual Report 2019*, Ping An Insurance, 2020, p. 114, http://www.pingan.cn/app_upload/images/info/upload/a74ffb10-16be-4415-b9b3-a365225049fe.pdf (access: 09/11/2021).

of the Chinese economy, while in 2003, only 36.7%[17]. It is also visible in the number of enterprises broken down by ownership type: in 2010, there were 249,622 state-owned entities, while in 2017 there were 325,800 of them. The share of gross industrial production in the private sector exceeded the share of the public sector in 2010 and amounted to approximately 30%[18].

Table 4. The number of enterprises in China by ownership in 2010–2017

Description	2017	2015	2013	2010
Total number of enterprises	18 097 682	12 593 254	8 208 273	6 517 670
Number of private enterprises	16 204 143	10 677 612	7 059 996	5 126 438
Number of state-owned enterprises	325,800	291 263	220 508	249 622
Number of enterprises of collective ownership	249 946	253 199	212 585	269 565
Number of foreign capital enterprises	111 628	99 693	85 896	98 412
Other companies	1 093 062	1 169 757	545 448	683 952

Source: National Bureau of Statistics of China, 2022.

Despite the decline in the number of SOEs and the changing economic performance of these entities, it has been shown that state-owned enterprises achieve worse financial results than private enterprises. The main reason is the lower production efficiency. Government interventions in public enterprises have consequently led to lower productivity rates and overemployment compared to non-state-owned enterprises[19]. When trying to solve the dilemma of the extent to which the Chinese economy is saturated with elements of the free market and with elements of state intervention, it should be noted that not only is the ownership status important, but also the forms of management and control of the state, which can be reduced to two basic dimensions: first, the scale of supervision over private property exercised by the state; second, a situation in which a state-owned enterprise is managed by a private company and benefiting from it[20]. Although the vast majority of China's human resources today are self-employed or work in private enterprises, the government has retained control over many upstream sectors, large producers of goods and machinery. For example, sectors such as oil and gas are structured to generate monopoly rents. In

17 *OECD Economic Surveys: China 2005,* 2005, https://read.oecd-ilibrary.org/economics/oecd-economic-surveys-china-2005_eco_surveys-chn-2005-en#page82 (access: 09/11/2021).
18 Son Ngoc Chu, Ligang Song, *State Control…,* p. 87.
19 Karen Jingrong Lin, Xiaoyan Lu, Junsheng Zhang, Ying Zheng, *State-owned enterprises in China…,* p. 33.
20 Grzegorz Kołodko, *Czy Chiny zbawią świat?,* Warszawa 2018, p. 135.

addition, the government has retained control of all land and almost all financial institutions. In an increasingly market-oriented environment, it becomes easier and easier to "earn" on this control, generating large streams of income. The Chinese government therefore owns a relatively small fraction of overall production assets, but the assets it owns often give it a monopoly position (land, natural resources, transport, and communications) or are strategically placed at a higher level in the production system (semi-finished products and production equipment)[21].

1.3. The main features of the Chinese model of Socioeconomic development

The above-described manifestations of the state's influence on the economy in China can be boiled down to the statement that the Chinese government has virtually no means of production. Furthermore, by easing ownership restrictions, it can take advantage of the supply and demand mechanisms present in a free market economy, and on this basis, it can influence the productivity of the economy[22]. The state retains far-reaching control over economic processes, for example, by setting certain prices, investments by public enterprises, and some forms of direct intervention[23]. However, this does not change the fact that the government still has a strong ownership position in the economy. Thanks to an appropriate tax policy, the government is constantly increasing the share of income under its control.

Another element that constitutes socialism is the intention of the state to influence the economy. There is no doubt that for almost four decades, efficiency in creating economic growth has been a key element in legitimizing China's government. Ensuring continued growth of the Chinese economy is of interest to the Chinese political elite. In China, the intention of the state to influence the economy can be illustrated by the functioning of bureaucratic structures and the central planning system, as evidenced by, for example, the Five-Year Plans. Until recently, bureaucratic structures were held accountable primarily for achieving the goals of economic growth, to the extent that this determined the promotion of local or regional administrative staff. Focusing so much attention on economic growth resulted in inertia in the implementation of other activities, also im-

21 Barry Naughton, *Is China Socialist* ..., p. 8.
22 Yanrui Wu, *Is China's economic growth sustainable? A productivity analysis*, "China Economic Review" 2000, vol. 11, issue 3, pp. 278–296.
23 Grzegorz Kołodko, *Czy Chiny zbawią świat?...*, pp. 152–153.

portant from the point of view of long-term development[24]. This is the case with environmental issues. At the local and regional level, economic factors have often taken precedence over ecological factors.

Undoubtedly, the central planning system in China plays an important role in the context of the intentional influence of the state on the economy, for three reasons. First, central planning defines the development vision of the People's Republic of China. Planning is an element that integrates the activities of various state institutions while achieving relatively uniform goals. Plans are also an instrument for coordinating public affairs management in such a populous country. Secondly, the aforementioned planning makes it possible to define binding goals for the authorities at various levels of Chinese administration. As part of strategic planning, there are the so-called mandatory targets, e.g., in recent years regarding the level of environmental protection or social welfare. Third, strategic planning is a set of interrelated sectoral and territorial plans (individual units of territorial division). The National Five-Year Plan is only the beginning of a nationwide planning process. Coordination of sectoral and territorial plans is a challenge due to their large number, which will be discussed later in this study. In 2016, the State Council approved at least 50 sectoral plans related to the 13th Five-Year Plan for 2016–2020[25].

The issue of redistribution is another of Barry Naughton's premises in deciding on the socialist nature of the Middle Kingdom. The question is whether, given the fast pace of growth and development, we are also dealing with a process of redistribution of the national income to the least privileged social groups. Taking into account only the Gini coefficient, it can be concluded that the measures taken to reduce social disproportions had a very moderate effect. This is because the concentration (inequality) ratio in the distribution of income[26] has generally shown an upward trend since the beginning of the reforms in the late 1970s. It achieved the highest values in 2008–2010 (average 43.35%). Since 2010, the ratio has shown a downward trend and in 2016 it amounted to 38.5%[27].

It should be noted that China's efforts to improve the distribution and supply of public goods have produced only modest results. In the same period as incomes increased, the income disparity in China widened significantly. The de-

24 Hongbin Li, Li-An Zhou, *Political Turnover and Economic Performance: The Incentive Role of Personnel Control in China,* "Journal of Public Economics" 2005, vol. 89, no. 6–7, pp. 1743–1762.

25 Chen Ling, Barry Naughton, *An Institutionalized Policy-making Mechanism: China's Return to Techno-Industrial Policy,* "Research Policy" 2016, vol. 45, no. 10, pp. 2138–2152.

26 The zero value of the coefficient indicates full uniformity of the distribution. An increase in the value of the coefficient means an increase in the inequality of distribution.

27 *GINI index – China,* The World Bank, https://data.worldbank.org/indicator/SI.POV.GINI (access: 09/11/2021).

velopment challenge of China's transformation is growing social inequalities. Rapid economic growth has not been accompanied by an adequate increase in household income and consumption. Inequalities can be observed especially in terms of income diversification of urban and rural residents (Table 5). Slightly less than half of the population of the PRC live in villages (41.48%)[28]. The highest income difference between urban and rural residents was recorded in 2007 (3.33 to 1). Recent years have brought some stabilization in terms of income differentiation. There is no doubt that the incomes of city dwellers are growing faster than those of rural residents. Between 2013 and 2019, the income of urban residents increased by 15,891 yuan, while in the countryside, it increased by only 6,591 yuan.

Table 5. Income differentiation of inhabitants of rural and urban areas in China

Year	1978	1995	2000	2007	2014	2017	2019
Ratio	2.6	2.7	2.8	3.3	2.75	2.17	2.64

Source: own study based on: Tomasz Kamiński, *Sypiając ze smokiem. Polityka Unii Europejskiej wobec Chin*, Łódź 2015, pp. 153–154 National Bureau of Statistics of China 2022.

Income inequality is not only China's experience, but it also occurs and is increasing in developed countries, including the US and European countries. For example, it can be observed that in 1980 10% of the richest people in the USA and Canada accounted for 34% of the national income, in Europe 32%, and in China 27%. Meanwhile, in 2016, this share grew to 37% in Europe and to 46% in the United States and Canada. In China, the richest 10% of citizens accounted for 41% of national income (graph 1). This confirms the global trend of increasing disproportions between the richest and the poorest.

Naturally, this is not the only indicator that can be used to measure the level of social stratification. However, this undoubtedly illustrates the real departure of the PRC from the propaganda ideals of the socialist state, one of the characteristic elements of which is, after all, the lack of significant material differences in society. However, such large development disparities are also a source of social discontent in China.

The government perceives the problem of the stratification of society and since the nineties has been implementing actions aimed at reducing development disproportions. In recent years, the government has begun to give preference to western and central regions in the investment process[29]. Implementation of the

28 *China Statistical Yearbook 2020*, National Bureau of Statistics of China, http://www.stats.gov.cn/tjsj/ndsj/2018/indexeh.htm (access: 09/11/2021).

29 Ravi Kanbur, Xiaobo Zhang, *Fifty Years of Regional Inequality in China: A Journey Through Central Planning, Reform, and Openness*, "Review of Development Economics" 2005, vol. 9, no. 4, p. 101.

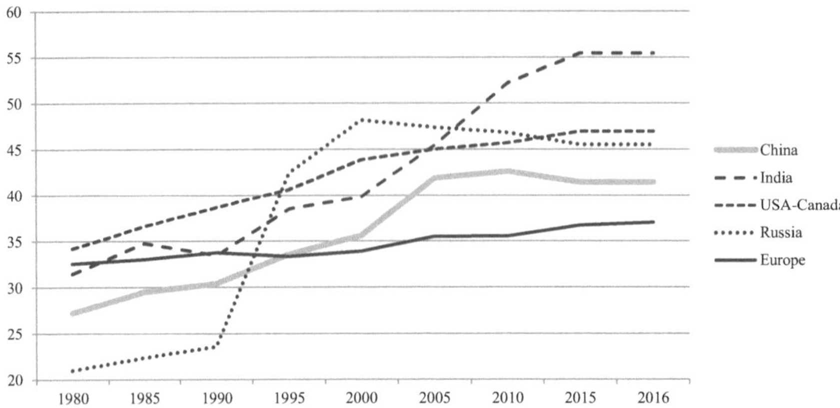

Graph 1. Change in income inequality: China compared to selected countries in 1980–2016 – the share of the richest 10 % in the total income of a given country (%). Source: own study based on: Facundo Alvaredo, Lucas Chancel, Thomas Piketty, Emmanuel Saez, Gabriel Zucman, *World Inequality Report 2018*, p. 10, https://wir2018.wid.world/files/download/wir2018-full-report-english.pdf (access: 09/11/2021).

so-called development strategy of the western regions is an example[30]. Actions to support the western regions include subsidies aimed at expanding the infrastructure of roads, railways, airports, and securing energy needs through the construction of hydroelectric plants and gas pipelines. The government is also trying to attract foreign investment by introducing tax incentives and ensuring perpetual usufruct of land to potential investors. The state provides financial support to investors active within the country and undertakes particularly intensive attempts to transform local state-owned enterprises.

Income stratification is one thing, but in the context of redistribution, the scale of activities aimed at redirecting the generated income towards less developed groups is also important. At present, China is far from implementing the welfare state model, although some transformation has been noted in the last three decades. Probably the strategy of the PRC, which focused first on lifting the country from economic nonexistence, and then on the implementation of certain prosocial solutions referring to the redistribution of national income, played a role here. It is not true that redistributive measures were not taken, as the claims that China is an example of socially sustainable development are unfounded. The Chinese labor market, which incurs to the greatest extent the costs of the economic transformation of the People's Republic of China, illustrates this. The competitiveness of the production of Chinese factories (and, more broadly, enterprises) is largely attributed to the low labor costs of Chinese workers. Very

30 Minjia Chen, Yongnian Zheng, *China's Regional Disparity and Its Policy Responses*, "China & World Economy" 2008, vol. 16, no. 4, pp. 21–24.

difficult working conditions, no respect for the provisions of labor law, and no social protection are just some examples. From around the 1990s, China began to realize the need to make efforts to redistribute national income to the benefit of less performing social groups and territories.

In the last ten years, there has been an expansion of social security, especially in the field of health insurance and protection against poverty. There are about 1 billion people, or nearly 70% of the Chinese population, currently insured under one of the three major health insurance systems, two of which were introduced in 2003 and 2007, respectively. The government's goals are ambitious, as they include insuring more than 90% of the population in the next few years. Since 2007, households have been protected against falling below defined poverty lines by the Minimum Living Standard Program[31].

Despite the changing situation in terms of increased redistribution, the scale of public investment in the social sphere is still modest. In 2014, public expenditure on education amounted to 3.6% of GDP, on health protection 1.6% of GDP, and on public construction 0.8% of GDP[32]. All the figures cited are strikingly low compared to international standards. There are many factors behind the enormous progress made in expanding social security in China. One of the most important reasons is the government's adoption of social security as a national priority, supported by an increased amount of special fiscal measures. Between 2003 and 2007, a total of 1,950 billion yuan was allocated to social security, which represented about 11.6% of the state budget.

The responsiveness of the socialist system raises doubts[33], but if the government seeks to implement socialist ideals, it should develop mechanisms by which society can influence economic and social policy. In countries with a democratic system, such a mechanism can be undoubtedly considered, inter alia, universal, competitive elections. The nation has the opportunity, most often every four years, to allow political groups to exercise power that will fully meet the expectations of society, handing over responsibility and at the same time having meaningful consequences. In this way, the legitimacy of power with respect to citizens is renewed. Since China is an authoritarian country, such a mechanism does not exist there. It does not change the fact that, pursuant to the provisions of Art. 1 of the constitution – the PRC is a socialist state, a democratic dictatorship

31 Aidi Hu, Valérie Schmitt, *China*, International Labor Organization, 2017, https://www.usp2030.org/gimi/ShowCountryProfile.action;jsessionid=D41r8zQbPIpXhYXtNn2R2rJBr72l_7jtDhXGRY0HxoPmNs!.2021gUs (access: 09/11/2021).

32 Barry Naughton, *Is China Socialist…*, p. 15.

33 Marek Świstak, *Polityka rozwoju społeczno-gospodarczego a wyzwania rozwojowe Chin*, [in:] Marek Świstak, Jan Wiktor Tkaczyński (eds.), *Azjatycki model polityki rozwoju społeczno-gospodarczego. Wybrane aspekty w świetle standardów i doświadczeń Unii Europejskiej*, Kraków 2019, pp. 117–146.

of the people, led by the working class and based on an alliance of workers and peasants[34]. Thus, the constitutional provisions make the people the subject of power.

The problem is that democratic mechanisms in the form of competitive elections are indeed practiced but at the lowest levels of government. This applies to some towns and districts of large cities, mainly during the elections of deputies to The National People's Congress (NPC) at the municipal or county level in a situation where voters vote directly for their candidates. However, the indirect election procedure dominates, which virtually excludes candidates from competing for certain positions. This is because it is conducted in accordance with the guidelines of the CPC, which manages personnel and "collectively delegates power". The competition between candidates is strictly limited. Voters at the bottom of the social status are prevented from voting for senior officials. The experiments carried out in this area were negatively evaluated by the Chinese political elite. Mostly due to the fact that this would challenge the leadership role of the central government in relation to local authorities, which, seeking support at the local level, would contest the implementation of top-down policies[35]. The result is that citizens have a low level of confidence in authority. This is mainly due to the lack of public access to information on how to elect and appoint party government officials. The sense of participation in the process of shaping power is low, as is the bond with the Communist Party of China[36].

Responsiveness is not only the influence of society on policymaking in a general sense. They are also influential in creating a political consensus on issues of individual policies, including economic and social policy. Here we are dealing not so much with the responsiveness of the government as with its activities aimed at formulating a political consensus, in which the mass membership of 86 million people in the CPC and the administrative structures of the Chinese meritocracy plays an important role[37]. State factors shape public opinion also through the control of the media, contributing to the fight against voices critical of the official moves of the authorities. Undoubtedly, in the Middle Kingdom, it was possible to achieve a political consensus[38] around the postulate of economic development, which has been the main political task of the Chinese authorities

34 Article 1 of the PRC Constitution, http://www.npc.gov.cn/zgrdw/englishnpc/Constitution/2007-11/15/content_1372963.htm (access: 09/11/2021).

35 Yan Yilong, Bai Gang, Zhang Leyong, Ou Shujun, He Jianyu, *China's Great Way. The Communist Party of China and Chinese Socialism,* Toruń 2018, pp. 73–74.

36 Ibid, p. 69.

37 Christine Wong, Valerie J. Karplus, *China's War on Air Pollution: Can Existing Governance Structures Support New Ambitions?,* "The China Quarterly" 2017, vol. 231, pp. 662–684.

38 On the ways of achieving political consensus, see Wang Shaoguang, Fan Peng, *The Chinese Model of Consensus Decision-Making: A Case Study of Healthcare Reform,* Beijing 2013.

since the end of the 1970s. In this regard, the Chinese authorities responded to the desire for development also among the poorest social strata by promoting state capitalism. Even if we treat the invoked capitalism as the actions of a state that pursues its own interests in the market, the recovery of millions of Chinese people from the state of extreme poverty cannot go unnoticed. Thus, the current legitimacy of power is unquestionable as long as the state ensures uninterrupted economic growth and contributes to the increasing economic wellbeing of its citizens. China is already at such a stage of economic transformation that there are more and more questions not only about maintaining growth (which is an important task), but also about how it is consumed. In other words: it is about how the state should react to development deficiencies in the spatial dimension i. e., with regard to regional development. In this light, the responsiveness of the Chinese authorities leaves much to be desired.

Referring to the issue of (not) meeting Naughton's criteria with regard to the socialist character of the Chinese system, it should be stated that the first two conditions are met: the Chinese authorities have the ability and intention to create the economy. The state controls a significant part of economic resources, thus influencing the results of management, and also performs intentional actions to influence the economy, e. g., through an extensive central planning system and its subordinate planning system at lower administrative levels. The current socioeconomic system, however, does not meet the premises of redistribution and responsiveness. China is certainly far from a welfare state with wide-ranging efforts in the field of social security. The policies implemented in this area still leave much to be desired, taking into account the very large stratification of incomes of the inhabitants of the Middle Kingdom. It is similar to the expansiveness of the political system: the election mechanism has almost no, or actually a very small, influence on the shape of implemented policies. The development of Chinese state capitalism only to some extent replaces the aforementioned gap. One thing is certain: The success of Chinese state capitalism will determine the political future of the PRC.

The policy of socioeconomic development can be analyzed with guidelines known as the Beijing Consensus. However, this concept is not used by the Chinese, who seem to distance themselves from it, contrasting themselves with a different development model in the Western world, i. e., the Washington Consensus. It also results from the belief that the Chinese development path is very specific, which may not be useful at other latitudes. The question therefore arises whether the Consensus, as the set of features of the Chinese development model that makes up the Beijing Consensus, contradicts the Washington Consensus, or is a supplement or modification to it. In order to find this out, it is necessary to consider what the Washington Consensus is about from an economic point of view. In 1989, the English economist John Williamson presented a compact list of

economic guidelines that became known as this Consensus. They concern the following issues[39]:
- Fiscal deficit: Introduce fiscal discipline and avoid a large state budget deficit in relation to gross domestic product.
- Appropriate priorities for public spending: Reorientation of the public spending policy and giving preference to pro-development spending on education, health care, and infrastructure.
- Tax reform: Widening the tax base, i. e., improving tax collection, reducing the marginal tax thresholds (especially direct taxes).
- Interest rates: Maintaining moderate real interest rates.
- Exchange rate: Maintaining a uniform exchange rate at a level that ensures the competitiveness of exports and the balance of payments.
- Trade policy: Liberalization of trade, including the elimination of various quantitative restrictions, the reduction of tariffs, and the pursuit of their uniformity.
- Foreign direct investment: Liberalization of the flows of foreign direct investment, removal of barriers to their entry into domestic markets, and their equal treatment in comparison to investments of domestic enterprises.
- Privatization: Maintaining an appropriate ownership structure, i. e., privatization of state-owned enterprises in order to increase their efficiency and allowing foreign capital to participate in this process.
- Deregulation: Reducing the role of the state in the functioning of markets, supporting the competitiveness of its participants. State regulations should focus on issues related to national security, environmental protection, consumer protection, and supervision over financial institutions.
- Property rights: The state should ensure the protection of property in all its forms (material, legal, and intellectual).

The concept of the Washington Consensus has made a tremendous impact not only among economists or international institutions such as the World Bank and the International Monetary Fund but also among politicians. Later, the economic guidelines were slightly modified, e. g., toward taking into account the postulate of environmental protection or supervision over financial institutions and the banking system. The Consensus has also been criticized[40], mainly because of its

39 John Williamson, *What Washington Means by Policy Reform,* [in:] John Williamson (ed.), *Latin American Adjustment: How Much has Happened,* Washington 1990, pp. 7–20.

40 Hansjoerg Herr, *Underdevelopment and Unregulated Markets: Why Free Markets do not Lead to Catching-Up,* "European Journal of Economics and Economic Policies-Intervention" 2018, vol. 15, pp. 219–237; Fidel Aroche Reyes, *The death of development theory: From Friedrich von Hayek to the Washington consensus,* Journal of Post Keynesian Economics 2018, vol. 41, pp. 509–525.

neoliberal nature. This narrative referred to the lack of alternatives to the[41] so-called golden rules of capitalism that relate to rapid liberalization, deregulation, privatization, and opening up to the world with a simultaneous restrictive monetary and fiscal policy. The economic problems of Asian and Latin American countries were used as examples of a failed application of the golden rules of capitalism. The arguments that modern developed countries owe their position not only to the market, but to countless state interventions in industry, trade, and financial policy have not been ignored. It indicated that the Washington Consensus had benefited mainly the most affluent countries and contributed to an increase in economic diversification in the world.

The Beijing Consensus is not a uniform recommendation. This is despite the fact that the term first appeared in 2004 and was used by Joshua Cooper Ramo[42]. It is more a set of general thoughts on the basis of China's development experiences in the last forty years than clearly defined guidelines for conducting economic policy. Therefore, not all of its implied postulates can be treated as a one-to-one projection for an alternative to the Washington Consensus. The Consensus discussed here is rather a set of assumptions. Analyzing the position of Joshua Cooper Ramo, the following elements can be identified[43]:

- innovation-based development, stimulating the creation of added value faster than the accumulation of economic problems in a country undergoing transformation;
- an alternative way of measuring development: managing the economic contradictions of a developing country requires other than GDP per capita measures of development; it is proposed to focus on sustainable development and equality;
- self-determination of China and other countries in relation to the US – searching for its own path of development, contesting external pressure, mainly prescriptions resulting from the Washington Consensus; globalization on its own terms[44].

China is believed to have prospered by ignoring the economic guidelines of the Washington Consensus. In fact, China followed eight of the ten guidelines set out

41 An example is the position of the Margaret Thatcher government in Great Britain – see Ha-Joon Chang, Ilene Grabel, *Reclaiming Development from the Washington Consensus*, "Journal of Post Keynesian Economics" 2004, vol. 27, pp. 273–291.

42 Joshua Cooper Ramo, *The Beijing Consensus*, The Foreign Policy Center, May 2004, http://www.chinaelections.org/uploadfile/200909/20090918021638239.pdf (access: 09/11/2021).

43 Ibid, pp. 11–13. See also: *The Beijing Consensus: An alternative approach to development*, World Foresight Forum, April 2011, issue brief no. 2, pp. 2–4, https://hcss.nl/sites/default/files/files/reports/WFF02_Issue_Brief_The_Beijing_Consensus02.pdf (access: 09/11/2021).

44 Examples include the maintenance of a large sector of state-owned enterprises, low labor costs and a low yuan, export subsidization.

in this Consensus. It is pointed out here that in the case of China, deregulated and market-based decision making is not the only way of economic growth and integration with the global economy. Thus, the Chinese development model is based on illiberal state capitalism, in which the economy is dominated by a strong state, and state-owned enterprises operating in sectors important for state development, such as energy, utilities, transport, and heavy industry. The private sector plays only a supporting role and is heavily influenced by the political elite[45].

The discussion around the not uniform range of economic guidelines resulting from the Beijing Consensus has also provoked a reaction from the (co-) makers of the Washington Consensus. John Williamson, referring to individual issues of the Beijing Consensus, as well as the overall development model of China, points to the continuing validity of the guidelines resulting from the Washington Consensus[46]. First, it addresses the recommendation of a gradual transformation process rather than shock therapy. States that are in transition do not always have the ability to apply such a strategy, mainly because economic change is accompanied by violent processes that result in the violation of existing social ties, creating political uncertainty. There is therefore a need for swift action in the spirit of liberalism, as fundamental economic changes require it to maintain political stability.

Secondly, basing the development model of a country undergoing economic transformation mainly on innovation is not possible and is like inventing the circle. A state that allocates funds to innovative solutions in its country may thus waste its already limited resources. Meanwhile, in the early stages of development, the practice of many countries showed the effectiveness of the strategy of imitation, which is also experienced by China. It is possible to purchase technology from abroad at a lower cost than to develop it using internal resources.

Third, Williamson points to the continued validity of the guideline with regard to maintaining macroeconomic stability (stable prices), which has not been the subject of controversy in Beijing's economic policy.

Fourth, the opening of the economy to capital and external competition is also not a subject of controversy in this case. According to Williamson, the only doubts are the method of determining the yuan exchange rate and its amount. In practice, Beijing has used its own currency's undervalued exchange rate as its main tool for generating large current account surpluses. Measuring the openness of the economy with the ratio of exports to GDP, China is the most open

45 Stefan Halpe, *The Beijing Consensus: How China's Authoritarian Model Will Dominate the Twenty-First Century*, New York 2010, pp. 114–115; Yasheng Huang, *Capitalism with Chinese Characteristics: Entrepreneurship and the State*, New York 2008.

46 John Williamson, *Beijing Consensus versus Washington Consensus*, [in:] Robert E. Looney (ed.), *Handbook of Emerging Economies*, Yorkshire 2014, pp. 178–182.

large economy in the world. Therefore, it can be concluded that the above-mentioned elements prove the application of the guidelines resulting from the Washington Consensus.

Fifth, with regard to market liberalization, which is the area of greatest discrepancy between the two consensuses, it must be said that the state plays a much greater role in the Chinese economy than the Washington Consensus implies. Critical arguments relate to the liberalization of the financial system, as it is recognized that optimal decisions should be taken at a decentralized level while maintaining the liberalization of the internal market and privatization. In the latter case, it is worth noting that in the years 1998–2009 private capital companies achieved almost twice as much profit as state-owned enterprises[47]. Certain market liberalization efforts in China are clearly identifiable. For example, at the end of the 1990s, China had already liberalized the prices of most goods. Thus, in 1978, three-quarters of the products in China were produced by state-owned enterprises, while in 2010 they accounted for less than a quarter of the products[48].

Comparing the Chinese model of economic development with that proposed by the West, it should be stated that the thesis that the Beijing Consensus and the Washington Consensus are mutually exclusive is not fully confirmed. On a high level of generality, it can be argued that the Beijing Consensus is contrary to the golden principles of capitalism. Meanwhile, observation of the practice of China's economic policy does not allow for such an unambiguous conclusion. It should be added that solutions to China's economic practice do not constitute a model that could be said to be a proven scientific theory. In contrast, they are a set of non-accidental, flexible[49] actions, although undertaken in specific circumstances, reflecting the size of the country, the moment of development, and the activity of the environment. The Washington Consensus was formulated in a similar context to support the economic changes in Latin America at the end of the twentieth century.

The Chinese development model is still in the process of being shaped; it draws on the guidelines of the Washington Consensus, but also complements this model with solutions that are modified depending on the circumstances (e.g., partial liberalization of the internal market, partial privatization of the binding property law). The Washington Consensus was not formulated with the aim of maximizing the pace of catching up with the developed world, but rather as a compromise composed of relatively universal guidelines aimed at stimulating

47 *China 2030: Building a Modern, Harmonious, and Creative High-Income Society*, World Bank, Development Research Center of China's State Council Washington 2012, pp. 244–246.

48 John Williamson, *Beijing Consensus versus Washington Consensus…*, p. 6.

49 Yang Yao, *Political Economy Causes of China's Economic Success*, [in:] Ross Garnaut, Ligang Song, Cai Fang (ed.), *China's 40 Years of Reform and Development: 1978–2018*, Acton 2018, p. 79.

economic growth. As a kind of agreement, it does not contain solutions considered at that time controversial or unacceptable. Therefore, from an economic point of view, both compromises should be treated as complementary. However, the gap between economic liberalization and the lack of pro-democratic reforms from the Western point of view seems irreconcilable, not for economic reasons, but for the values of the Euro-Atlantic community[50]. It should be emphasized that in its original form, the Consensus does not refer to the political system because, as Williamson claims, overcoming, for example, a debt crisis is possible regardless of the shape of the political system[51]. Both sides are aware that cooperation is more profitable for mutual development than fierce competition. However, it is difficult to predict for how long this condition may persist.

1.4. The level and dynamics of regional development in the context of factors determining the diversification of China's modernization

Among the many approaches[52] identifying the factors determining the diversification of the PRC's development in the regional perspective, the following should be mentioned: (a) geographic, (b) market, (c) political. Due to the purpose of this study, the last two factors will be of particular interest. In spatial arrangement, the determinants of structuring the management results in China are geographic conditions[53] and long-term processes[54]. Historically, Chinese civilization, originating from the middle of the Yellow River[55] in the Loess Plateau, has gradually moved eastward. Pressure from the north tribes caused China to relocate its economic center from the north to the more fertile south. The political and economic center of China shifted to the east, leaving the western part of the country on the periphery of development in the long term.

50 In this context, it is worth paying attention to the so-called Asian values. For more on this topic, see Adam W. Jelonek, *Wartości azjatyckie – jako platforma polityczna i przedmiot badań socjologicznych*, "Azja i Pacyfik" 2004, vol. 7, pp. 9–24.

51 Yang Yao, *Political economy causes of China's economic success…*, p. 9.

52 Rong Sheng, Shi Lin Liu, *Evolution on Regional Disparities in China from 2000 to 2012: Evidence from 74 Cities within Three Mega-Urban Regions along Yangtze River*, "Qual Quant" 2018, no. 52, pp. 1989–2006.

53 Shuming Bao, Gene Hsin Chang, Jeffrey D. Sachs, Wing Thye Woo, *Geographic Factors and China's Regional Development under Market Reforms, 1978–1998*, "China Economic Review" 2002, vol. 13, no. 1, pp. 89–111.

54 Fernand Braudel, *Historia i trwanie*, Warszawa 1999, Yehua Dennis Wei, *Regional Development in China: States, Globalization and Inequality*, London-New York 2000, p. 94.

55 Henry Kissinger, *O Chinach*, przeł. Magdalena Komorowska, Wołowiec 2014, p. 27.

The eastern coast, which lies on the Pacific Ocean, currently consists of the most important port cities in the world. Tianjin, Shanghai, Hangzhou, and Hong Kong. Coastal provinces benefit from better access to major world markets. Meanwhile, the western part of China is the Tibetan Plateau, located in a relatively inaccessible area, and the deserts of Central Asia. In this situation, it may not be entirely surprising that the western provinces developed much slower than the eastern ones, and foreign investors concentrated their activities almost exclusively in the eastern coastal areas. The northern and western parts of the country are a base for raw material and energy and a source of cheap labor. These provinces are characterized by poor infrastructure, lower level of entrepreneurship, and distance from seaports, which means they face greater problems with attracting foreign investments[56].

When describing the specificity of China's current economic position, one should take into account the huge development disparities within the country, mainly between the three main economic regions (eastern, central and western), individual Chinese provinces (regions), within the province and between the city and the countryside[57]. This is because the inhabitants of the richest cities, and thus the provinces, have an average standard of living characteristic of highly developed countries. The existing disproportions (for 2018) in terms of regions (although not only these) are significant. The region with the highest level of development (the city of Beijing) reaches 215% of the average GDP *per capita* for China, while the least developed area (Gansu province) is only 48.02%, which translates into a difference in the level of development reaching four times (exactly 4.47 to 1). This means that the development range is as high as 166 points[58].

The same value, for example, for Poland is 84.9 points, while the disproportion in the level of development between the richest and the poorest regions in Poland is slightly more than twice (2.26 to 1)[59]. Therefore, the development gap in China between the poorest and the richest regions is almost more than twice that of Poland (GDP per capita). However, the nature of the development differentiation of Chinese regions is much smaller than, for example, in the regions of the EU-28 member states. The development disproportions in terms of GDP per capita calculated for 281 regions of the EU member states are almost twice as large (8.44

56 Maciej Walkowski, *Chińska strategia rozwoju społeczno-ekonomicznego. Implikacje dla Unii Europejskiej*, Poznań 2018, p. 195.

57 Jiangang Peng, Jing He, Zhangfei Li, Yu Yi, Nicolaas Groenewold, *Regional Finance and Regional Disparities in China*, "Australian Economic Papers" 2010, vol. 49, no. 4, pp. 301–302.

58 National Bureau of Statistics of China, 2021, http://data.stats.gov.cn/english/easyquery.htm?cn=E0103 (access: 09/11/2021).

59 Data for 2018. In relation to Poland, it is about Mazovia and the Lublin region. See *Preliminary estimates of gross domestic product by region in 2018*, Central Statistical Office, https://stat.gov.pl/obszary-tematyczne/rachunki-narodowe/rachunki-regionalne/wstepne-szacunki-produktu-krajowego-brutto-w-Przekrój-regionow-w-2018-roku,8,2.html (access: 09/11/2021).

to 1) than the corresponding value for China. This is clearly illustrated by the disproportion in standard of living between Luxembourg (245.34% of the EU average) and the Bulgarian planning region of Severozapaden, which has only 29.06% of GDP per capita compared to the EU average (100%).

Table 6. Developmental spread in China versus the EU-28 and Poland in regional terms – the ratio of the richest to the poorest regions using the example of GDP per capita and average income per capita

Country	PKP *per capita*	Year	Per capita income	Year
China	4.47	2018	3.71	2018
EU-28	8.44	2017	4.31	2016
Poland	2.26	2018	1.82	2016

Source: own study based on: National Bureau of Statistics of China, 2021; Eurostat, 2021; *Preliminary estimates of gross domestic product by region in 2018,* Central Statistical Office, https://stat.gov.pl/obszary-tematyczne/rachunki-narodowe/rachunki-regionalne/wstepne-szacunki-produktu-krajowego-brutto-w-Przekrój-regionow-w-2018-roku,8,2.html (access: 09/11/2021).

With regard to the average per capita income, which reflects to a greater extent the differentiation in the purchasing power of the inhabitants of individual regions, the spread between the inhabitants of the regions with the highest and lowest incomes in national currency in the case of China is almost four times (3.71 to 1), with this disproportion being lower than the achieved economic growth calculated per person (let us recall: 4.47). For example, for EU regions, the income gap is very large, as it significantly exceeds the values recorded for China (3.71 to 1).

The difference in average income between the inhabitants of the EU's highest-income regions with those in the lowest-income regions is well over four times (4.31 to 1). Taking into account the deficiency of the above comparison, mainly related to the use of the average, which may slightly distort the picture, it should be stated that although in China the differentiation of development is perceived as the cost of the development of the country as a whole, the data indicate that this does not exceed the trends between the regions of the Member States of the European Union. The available data on regional differentiation in Chinese regions in terms of GDP *per capita* have not changed radically since 2000. Data published by the Chinese statistical office show that since 2000, when data are available, the average spread of the richest and poorest regions (in terms of GDP *per capita)* is 5.54 to 1. Only in three years has it exceeded the value of 6.0 (in 2006–8.61, in 2004–10.73, in 2002–10.85), and in recent years it has fluctuated at the level of 4.5 to 1 (2007 and 2018)[60].

60 Own calculations based on: National Bureau of Statistics of China, http://data.stats.gov.cn/english/easyquery.htm?cn=E0103 (access: 30/06/2021).

Table 7. List of units at the provincial level according to the level of development in terms of economic regions in 2013 and 2018

Region	GDP per capita (in RMB)	Relation to the national average (in %)	Income per capita of a city in a given region (in RMB)	Income per capita of a village in a given region (in RMB)	City / village income	GDP per capita (in RMB)	Relation to the national average (in %)	Income per capita of a city in a given region (in RMB)	Income per capita of a village in a given region (in RMB)	City / village income
Year	**2018**					**2013**				
Eastern coastal regions										
Beijing	140 211	215	67 990	26 490	2.6	94 648	200	44 564	17 101	2.6
Tianjin	120 711	185	42 976	23 065	1.9	100 105	211	28 980	15 353	1.9
Hebei	47 772	73	32 977	14 031	2.4	38 909	82	22 227	9 188	2.4
Liaoning	58 008	89	37 342	14 656	2.5	61 996	131	26 697	10 161	2.6
Shanghai	134 982	207	68 034	30 375	2.2	90 993	192	44 878	1 908	23.5
Jiangsu	115 168	176	47 200	20 845	2.3	75 354	159	31 585	13 521	2.3
Zhejiang	98 643	151	55 574	27 302	2.0	68 805	145	37 080	17 494	2.1
Fujian	91 197	140	42 121	17 821	2.4	58 145	123	28 174	11 405	2.5
Shantung	76 267	117	39 549	16 297	2.4	56 885	120	26 882	10 687	2.5
Guangdong	86 412	132	44 341	17 168	2.6	58 833	124	29 537	11 068	2.7
Hainan	51 955	80	33 349	13 989	2.4	35 663	75	22 411	8802	2.5

Table 7 *(Continued)*

Region	GDP per capita (in RMB)	Relation to the national average (in %)	Income per capita of a city in a given region (in RMB)	Income per capita of a village in a given region (in RMB)	City / village income	GDP per capita (in RMB)	Relation to the national average (in %)	Income per capita of a city in a given region (in RMB)	Income per capita of a village in a given region (in RMB)	City / village income
Year	**2018**					**2013**				
Central regions										
Jilin	55 611	85	30 172	13 748	2.2	47 428	100	21 331	9781	2.2
Heilongjiang	43 274	66	29 191	13 804	2.1	37 697	80	20 848	9369	2.2
Inner Mongolia	68 302	105	38 305	13 803	2.8	67 836	143	26 004	8985	2.9
Anhui	47 712	73	34 393	13 996	2.5	32 001	68	22 789	8850	2.6
Jiangxi	47 434	73	33 819	14 460	2.3	31 930	67	22 120	9089	2.4
Henan	50 152	77	31 874	13 831	2.3	34 211	72	21 741	8969	2.4
Hubei	66 616	102	34 455	14 978	2.3	42 826	90	22 668	9692	2.3
Hunan	52 949	81	36 698	14 093	2.6	36 943	78	24 352	9029	2.7
Shanxi	45 328	69	31 035	11 750	2.6	34 984	74	22 258	7949	2.8

Table 7 *(Continued)*

Region	**GDP per capita (in RMB)**	**Relation to the national average (in %)**	**Income per capita of a city in a given region (in RMB)**	**Income per capita of a village in a given region (in RMB)**	**City / village income**	**GDP per capita (in RMB)**	**Relation to the national average (in %)**	**Income per capita of a city in a given region (in RMB)**	**Income per capita of a village in a given region (in RMB)**	**City / village income**
Year	**2018**					**2013**				
Western regions										
Guangxi	41 489	64	32 436	12 435	2.6	30 741	65	22 689	7793	2.9
Chongqing	65 933	101	34 889	13 781	2.5	43 223	91	23 058	8493	2.7
Sichuan	48 883	75	33 216	13 331	2.5	32 617	69	22 228	8381	2.7
Guizhou	41 244	63	31 592	9 716	3.3	23 151	49	20 565	5898	3.5
Yunnan	37 136	57	33 488	10 768	3.1	25 322	53	22 460	6724	3.3
Tibet	43 398	67	33 797	11 450	3.0	26 326	56	20 394	6553	3.1
Shaanxi	63 477	97	33 319	11 213	3.0	43 117	91	22 346	7092	3.2
Gansu	31 336	48	29 957	8 804	3.4	24 539	52	19 873	5589	3.6
Qinghai	47 689	73	31 515	10 393	3.0	36 875	78	20 352	6462	3.1
Ningxia	54 094	83	31 895	11 708	2.7	39 613	84	21 476	7599	2.8
Xinjiang	49 475	76	32 764	11 975	2.7	37 553	79	21 091	7847	2.7
Average China	**65 253**	**100**	**37 750**	**15 228**	**2.6**	**47 396**	**100**	**25 279**	**9253**	**3.4**

Source: own study based on: National Bureau of Statistics of China, 2022.

In terms of the spatial dimension, the country is developing unevenly. High levels of development can be seen in eastern coastal provinces, while western and, to a lesser extent, central provinces suffer from low GDP *per capita,* income levels or underinvestment in infrastructure[61]. The data included in Table 8 partially confirm the above observations. There is no doubt that the PRC is developing threefold spatially, as the division in terms of development trends in three economic regions (macroregions) – eastern, central, and western – is clearly visible. The above division is not of an administrative nature, but one which merely serves to illustrate the development trends in a country of over 1.4 billion citizens. Among the many distinctions of the three macroregions indicated, attention should be paid to the level of development (GDP per capita), income per capita that the inhabitants of a given province have, and the phenomenon of concentration or deconcentration of production, and thus growth. Although the majority of the inhabitants of the Middle Kingdom currently live in the city, the standard of living in these areas, traditionally considered less developed not only in China, also determines the state of development in spatial terms.

Table 8. Development diversity of economic regions by area, population, and level of development (2018)

Economic region	**Surface**		**Population**		**GDP**		***GDP per capita (in RMB)***
	(in km^2)	**(in %)**		**(in %)**	**(in million RMB)**	**(in %)**	
Eastern	1 072 322	11.1	581 090 000	44.6	50 631 119	55.4	92 847
Central	2 902 000	30.0	461 220 000	30.1	24 138 336	26.4	53 042
Western	5 690 000	58.9	354 220 000	25.3	16 701 291	18.3	47 650
Together	9 664 322	100	1 396 530 000	100	91 470 746	100	65 253

Source: own study based on: National Bureau of Statistics of China, 2022.

Data for 2018 indicate that the most developed eastern economic macroregion, inhabited by 41.6% of the population, generates more than half of the GDP of the PRC (55.4%), while occupying only 11.1% of the country's territory. Central provinces, inhabited by 30.1% of the country's population and accounting for only 26.4% of GDP, are in a worse situation. This group also includes the western region provinces, which occupy 58.9% of the Country are inhabited by 25.3% of Chinese citizens and generate only 18.3% of the country's GDP[62]. The above data confirm the uneven concentration of economic growth, mainly in the area of highly developed eastern provinces. The country has a significant concentration

61 Eva Minarcíková, *EU-China Cooperation on Regional Policy,* "Perspectives in Science" 2016, vol. 7, p. 34.

62 Own calculations based on data of the National Bureau of Statistics of China, 2022.

of growth in the eastern area, which covers a very small part of the Middle Kingdom. The concentration of growth is reflected in a very high GDP *per capita* ratio in relation not only to the national average but also to the average for central and western macroregions. Table 8 confirms that almost all of the 11 provinces included in the eastern macroregion (except Liaoning, Hebei, and Hainan) have a level of development expressed in GDP *per capita* above the average for the entire country. In the case of the western macroregion, 10 out of 11 provinces are below the national average. This clearly highlights the significant development differences between individual macroregions.

The remarks noted above reflect the current state of affairs, but there is no doubt that the differentiation of development or its equalization has been shaped in the long term. Economic globalization, along with Chinese reforms of opening up to the world, especially in the 1990s, led to an increase in regional disparities. China's opening up to the world resulted, among others, in the inflow of foreign direct investment. The Chinese authorities, adopting the new development strategy, placed great emphasis on the role of market mechanisms in the allocation of resources and efficiency of production, and the decentralization of economic decision making[63]. The influx of investments led to the modernization of Chinese production and management technologies. Geographical allocation of foreign investments strongly influenced the model of regional development in China. The influx of foreign investments was mainly directed to provinces and large cities on the east coast, i. e. Guangdong, Fujian, Shanghai and Tianjin, even exceeding the national average.One of the manifestations of this situation was the very high growth in industrial production in the eastern provinces, much higher than in the rest of the country. This trend continued until the beginning of the 2000s. It did not change until the second half of the 2000s, when off-coast regions experienced higher industrial production growth than coastal provinces. The change in this trend is attributed to state intervention to support the development of western provinces[64].

During the last two decades, the development trends of Chinese regions, taking into account the dynamics of GDP growth, also show some positive phenomena. In the period 2000–2018, the average annual GDP growth rate for the entire country was 13.02%, which, taking into account the results achieved by highly developed countries, is admirable. Positive tendencies refer to the faster catching up by some regions lagging behind in development compared to the national average. In the more developed eastern regions, the average annual GDP

63 Minjia Chen, Yongnian Zheng, *China's Regional Disparity and its Policy Responses,* "China & World Economy" 2008, vol. 16, no. 4, p. 18.

64 Yanrui Wu, Ning Ma, Xiumei Guo, Growth, *Structural Change and Productivity Gaps in China's Industrial Sector,* [in:] Ligang Song, Ross Garnaut, Cai Fang (eds.), *Deepening Reform for China's Long-Term Growth and Development,* Canberra 2014, pp. 455–456.

growth in the indicated period was 12.89%, while in the regions considered poorer – the central provinces – there was a higher growth rate (13.26%) in relation to not only the national but also to the eastern economic region. The negative phenomena include the low growth dynamics of the western economic region, which in the analyzed period – admittedly only slightly – is below the growth dynamics for the national average (12.91%). The data of the Chinese statistical office allow us to say with some caution that despite the considerable development disproportion between the three economic regions, the trends of recent years indicate the possibility of a convergence process. The dynamics of GDP growth shows faster growth in the provinces of the western and central regions compared to the eastern economic region in the 18 years for which the analysis was carried out (2000–2018). The above trend is also confirmed by the 2018 data: the poorest provinces (the western economic region) increased by 8.91%, while the national average was 7.86%, and the provinces included in the central regions showed a relatively high level of growth for Chinese conditions (7.41%), compared to the eastern economic region (7.27%)[65]. The analysis of the above data allows us to conclude that, despite the positive phenomena concerning the dynamics of economic growth, there is no clear tendency to equalize the standard of living, measured by the rate of GDP growth, between the richest and the poorest regions.

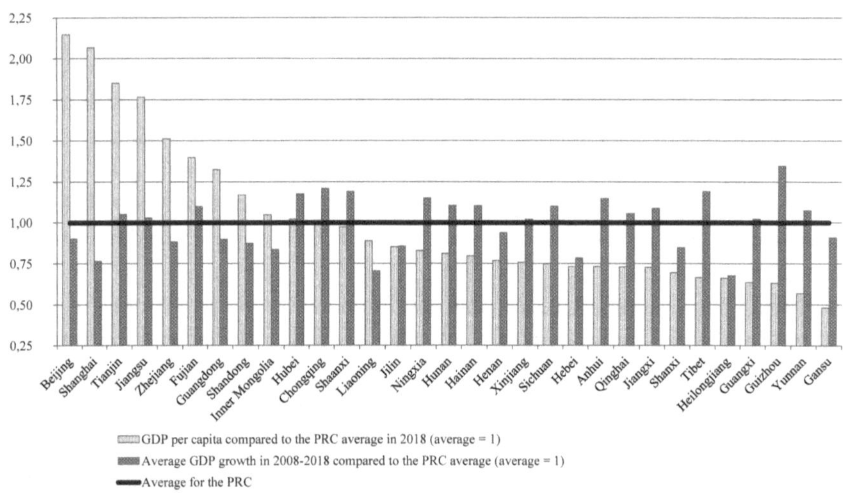

Graph 2. Average GDP growth in 2008–2018 and GDP per capita level in relation to the 2018 average for the PRC (average = 1) in regional terms. Source: own study based on: National Bureau of Statistics of China 2022.

65 Calculations own based on data of the National Bureau of Statistics of China, 2021.

An important element of the development diversification of Chinese regions is an attempt to answer the question not only about the current state of affairs, but also about the prospects for changing the level of development of both economic regions and the provinces which are currently lagging behind the more developed ones. It is also justified by the fact that the assignment of a given province to a given economic region is of an arbitrary nature. Analyzing only macroregions in the context of development diversification may not reflect the full picture.

Graph 2 shows that the five richest regions, with per capita GDP above 1.50 relative to the national average (1.0), are well outside the reach of the least developed regions. To be able to talk about the process of catching up with the richest regions by less developed areas (reaching below 0.75 of the national average GDP per capita), they would have to develop much faster than the richest regions. Areas with GDP growth above the national average (exceeding 1.0) have moderate chances of catching up with the richest regions. Among the 11 regions whose GDP *per capita* is less than 0.75 of the national average[66], this condition is met by seven regions. It should be noted that their GDP growth rate in 2010–2018 only slightly exceeds the average for the PRC and amounts to 1.01. Some exceptions are Tibet (1.19) and the province of Guizhou (1.35). However, the level of development (measured by GDP *per capita*) of the remaining provinces, respectively 0.67 and 0.63 of the national average, is still low. The catching-up process, if current trends continue, must be counted in decades. Another important phenomenon resulting from the above chart is the fact that the richest regions, such as Beijing, Shanghai, Tianjin, Jiangsu, Zhejiang, develop with moderate dynamics, i. e., lower than the national average (0.88 on average).

This is a different phenomenon from that often observed in developed countries, where highly developed regions present high dynamics of economic growth, which is the cause of divergence at the national level. Despite the faster growth of the regions that are lagging behind in development in the years 2008–2018, the level of development is still low compared to the average of the whole country, not to mention the richest regions. Graph 2 shows the potential for smoothing development in both macroregions and individual provinces, but if the trends analyzed above prove to be permanent, the process will spread over decades. The above reservation is also important because in a situation of a significant slowdown in economic growth or an economic crisis - looking at historical experience - regions with the highest level of development lose the most in terms of growth dynamics. Then the convergence process may take place not because of catching up with the leaders by less developed regions, but because of the stagnation of the regions with the highest level of development.

66 They are: Hebei, Anhui Qinghai, Jiangxi, Shanxi, Tibet, Heilongjiang, Guangxi, Guizhou, Yunnan, Gansu.

The consequence of such drastic development disproportions is significant migration inside China, which results, on the one hand, in "washing away" the rural population, and on the other, with the urbanization problems of Chinese cities (low standard of living[67]). For if in 1983 the number of rural immigrants amounted to 2 million, in 2006 it reached 132 million[68]. However, the labor force in the Chinese countryside is still very high compared to developed countries. This is favored by the *hukou* registration system, used since the 1950s[69], which in practice limits the possibility of employment for a citizen to the place of birth. The *hukou* prevents migrant workers living in cities but registered in their localities from using public services. Including, among others, access to education or health care, the right to acquire real estate, handling administrative matters in offices and courts, the amount of pension received, and even work for a lower salary[70].

67 Stefano Bartolini, Francesco Sarracino, *The Dark Side of Chinese Growth: Declining Social Capital and Well-Being in Times of Economic Boom,* "World Development" 2015, Vol. 74, pp. 333–351.

68 Cai Fang, *The Formation and Evolution of China's Migrant Labor Policy,* [in:] Xibao Zhang, Shenggen Fan, Arjan de Haan (eds.), *Narratives of Chinese Reforms: How Does China Cross the River?*, Singapore 2010, pp. 71–74, 81–90.

69 Kam Wing Chan, Li Zhang, *The Hukou System and Rural Urban Migration in China: Processes and Changes,* "The China Quarterly" 1999, vol. 160, pp. 818–855.

70 Maciej Walkowski, *Chińska strategia rozwoju społeczno-ekonomicznego…*, p. 202; Joanna Wardęga, *Nierównomierna modernizacja a przeobrażenia struktury społecznej w Chińskiej Republice Ludowej,* "Krakowskie Studia Międzynarodowe" 2015, vol. 12, no. 3, p. 59.

Chapter 2. Regional policy in the political and administrative system

2.1. The system of central authorities in the context of regional policy

The political system of the PRC can be considered partially centralized and hierarchical, with some autonomy in the application of local solutions. The special role of the CPC in the political system of the PRC causes the State to identify itself with the Party and the Party with State institutions. A reading of the PRC's constitution, as well as the CPC's constitution, leaves no doubt that we are dealing with a unitary country of a centralized nature. Centralization based on the significant domination of central state institutions is one of the distinguishing features of socialist states, especially those that adopted communism in the style of the Union of Soviet Socialist Republics (USSR). Taking into account both the size and population of the PRC, it is practically impossible to effectively manage the country only from the central level, so administrative structures below the central government are necessary. As a result, the central government is not the only entity that formulates national policies, but is certainly their important enforcer. Both state organs and local units of the CPC are obliged to loyally follow orders from Beijing (one party, one authority, one ideology[1]). The central government has mechanisms to effectively enforce the submitted directives. The CPC itself is not a unitary entity, but an institution in which different factions clash. The factional struggle is also reflected at the local level.

The size of the central government determines the importance of the national administration system. The structure of the government affects the administrative efficiency of the state. Hence, the size and complex structure of the government administration determines the effectiveness of policymaking, which determines social stability, progress, and economic development. Despite the fact that in the PRC we are dealing with a one-party authoritarian system, and with it a

1 Lucian W. Pye, *The Spirit of Chinese Politics*, Cambridge, Massachusetts, London 1992, p. 16.

large degree of top-down central control and initiative, local administrative structures, including those in the CPC, have many possibilities to shape policies, including regional policy, and to control them or hinder their implementation[2]. Thus, local administrative structures can influence the ability of the entire political system to achieve the desired results[3]. Therefore, it is necessary to analyze the central authority system in the context of regional policy. It is an attempt to capture the process of shaping the regional policy as a whole, and not only from the point of view of the relationship between the central government and the local government.

With regard to regional policy, an inseparable element of which is public intervention, it should be noted that in the case of China, the economic activity of the state varies depending on the period on which we focus our attention. State interference in the economy depends not only on the degree of economic development at a given time, but also on the perception of the scope of tasks of public authority and, more broadly, the political system. Analysis from the perspective of the political system is justified precisely by the role of the state in the economy, which can be reduced to three dimensions[4]: (a) an economic actor who is directly involved in socioeconomic activities; (b) a political decision-maker who allocates resources, implements public policies, influences economic activity; (c) a regulator – by the legislative function, administration, regulation of economic relations. Although it is possible to observe the influence of the state (including the region) on the economy, using the characteristics of its structure and size, there is no consensus among experts[5]on the desired nature of the state. The main two paradigms revolve around the nature of state activity. In the first case, the growing economic importance of the state (including the region) may push private economic initiatives to the periphery of the economy and thus contribute to a decline in economic growth. In the second case, it is the public authority (including regions) that, thanks to its active policy, stimulates growth, for example, by implementing public investment in infrastructure, education, or health protection.

2 Bob Hudson, David Hunter, Stephen Peckham, *Policy Failure and the Policy-Implementation Gap: Can Policy Support Programs Help?*, "Policy Design and Practice" 2019, vol. 2, no.1, pp. 3–5.

3 Jessica Teets, William Hurst, *Introduction: The politics and patterns of policy diffusion in China,* [in:] Jessica Teets, William Hurst (eds.), *Local Governance Innovation in China: Experimentation, Diffusion, and Defiance,* Oxon–New York 2014, pp. 12–21; Krzysztof Trzciński, *Czym jest stabilność polityczna państwa?*, "Przegląd Politologiczny", no. 2, pp. 37–47.

4 Guo Qingwang, Jia Junxue, *Structural Reform in China's Regional Governments*, vol. 1, Hong Kong 2013, p. vii.

5 Mark Pauly, *Income Redistribution as a Local Public Good,* "Journal of Public Economics" 1973, vol. 2, pp. 25–58.

2.1.1. State Council: The National People's Congress

Article 85 of the Constitution of the PRC states that the State Council is the executive body of the highest state authority (administration), which in the PRC is The National People's Congress (NPC)[6], composed of about 3,000 delegates elected under the procedure of multistage indirect elections from the people's representatives in provinces, autonomous regions, special administrative regions, and cities, as well as in the armed forces. The term of office of the NPC is five years, and the body meets only once a year, in early March. The deliberations usually last about two weeks. This makes the NPC a nominal legislative authority, mainly because in practice it only authorizes laws and various decisions, and does not constitute a forum in which decisions on matters important to the state are shaped. Outside of deliberations, the powers of the NPC are exercised by the Standing Committee, assisted by special committees working under its leadership[7]. The NPC and the Standing Committee have the power to amend the constitution, enact decrees, interpret laws, ratify treaties, appoint ambassadors, and approve economic plans and the state budget[8].

An important role in the political system is played by the President of the PRC, elected by the NPC, who serves as the head of state. The President is usually the Secretary General of the CPC. The fact that the same person holds both positions makes the President a real leader of the state with a decisive voice in political affairs. This is also confirmed by formal powers, for example, with regard to the promulgation of laws, and the appointment and dismissal of the prime minister, deputy prime ministers, members of the State Council, ministers, chairmen of government committees and the Chief Auditor and Secretary General of the State Council. The Vice-Chairman of the PRC acts as an assistant to the Chairman. The scope of his duties depends mainly on the scope of the power of attorney granted to him by the Chairman. This post is filled in elections by the NPC. In the event of a vacancy in the position of Chairman, his duties shall be taken over by the Vice-Chairman of the People's Republic of China[9].

When analyzing the power of the constitutional organs of the state, it should be emphasized that the CPC plays a dominant role in the Chinese political system for at least two reasons. First, as an organization with about 86 million members, it is treated as a representation of the broad masses of society. The political

6 Constitution of the PRC, http://www.npc.gov.cn/zgrdw/englishnpc/Constitution/2007-11/15/content_1372963.htm (access: 09/11/2021).

7 Marek Bankowicz, *Political systems. Academic textbook*, vol. 2: *Systems of modern states*, Kraków 2020, pp. 367–369.

8 Article 62 of the PRC Constitution, http://www.npc.gov.cn/zgrdw/englishnpc/Constitution/2007-11/15/content_1372963.htm (access: 09/11/2021).

9 Marek Bankowicz, *Political systems...*, p. 373.

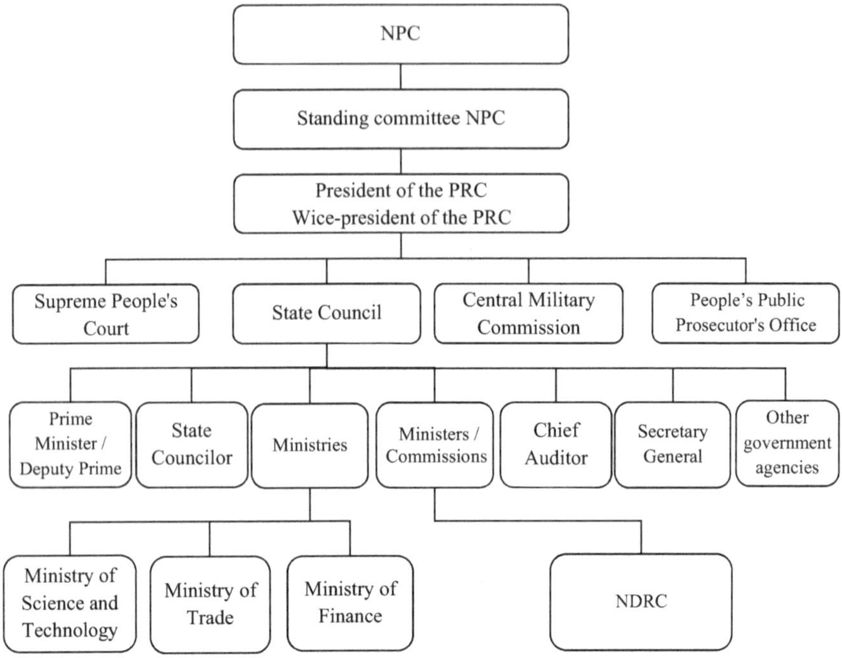

Diagram 1. The system of central authorities in the PRC in the context of regional policy. Source: own study based on: constitution of the PRC, http://www.npc.gov.cn/zgrdw/englishnpc/Constitution/2007-11/15/content_1372963.htm (access: 20/04/2022).

leadership of the CPC is explained in state doctrine with the help of the theory of three representations. It serves to justify the CPC's leading role in the country, which represents: (a) the progressive productive forces of the PRC; (b) the progressive culture of China; (c) the basic interests of the masses of the Chinese people. Thus, there is harmonization that ensures political agreement. Second, the CPC is the governing body of the state organs. The CPC's committees at every level of government play a decisive role in exercising state power, which is not only the foundation of the country's existing institutional order but also a specific method of governing. It is assumed that the political future of the PRC is the future of the CPC and its ability to maintain leadership in the long term. It is supposed to be a remedy for incessant conflicts over power, which can be noted, for example, in Western democracies. From this perspective, the above leads to the lack of a consistent policy or the lack of its implementation as a result of constant changes at the helm of government. Alternating power through elections is not desirable, as all political forces would be focused on trying to win the next election. The main instrument to legitimize the Chinese authorities is the current achievements in the field of socioeconomic development. Leadership competences and leadership skills are indicated to be greater than in western countries. The key challenge is how to justify minority leadership over the majority. The answer lies in the gradation of the representative nature of power that emerged according to the advancing legal order from the bottom to the top of the governance structure[10].

As mentioned above, the State Council is the highest body of state administration, which operates through various ministries, and at the same time has no attribute of state power, as it is exercised exclusively by the NPC. The Prime Minister is responsible for the work of the government. Members of the government are responsible for the matters assigned to them. The government exercises uniform leadership in the work of local state administration bodies at various levels throughout the country and formulates a detailed division of tasks and competences between the central government and state administration bodies in provinces, autonomous regions, and cities directly under the central government. In the area related to regional policy, the following competences should be indicated[11]:

- Adoption of administrative measures, issuing administrative regulations, and issuing decisions and orders in accordance with the constitution and other laws.
- Formulating the tasks and responsibilities of the ministries and committees of the State Council, exercising uniform leadership over the work of ministries and commissions, and managing any other national administrative work that does not fall within the competence of ministries and commissions.
- Exercising uniform leadership in the work of local state administration bodies at various levels throughout the country and formulating a detailed division of tasks and competences between the central government and administration bodies of provinces, autonomous regions, and cities directly subordinate to the central government.
- Preparation and implementation of the country's economic and social development plan and the state budget.
- Managing and administering economic affairs, and urban and rural development.
- Managing and administering education, science, culture, public health, physical culture, and family planning.

10 Yan Yilong, Bai Gang, Zhang Leyong, Ou Shujun, He Jianyu, *Great Way of China...*, pp. 10–20; Christine Wong, Valerie J. Karplus, *China's War on Air Pollution: Can Existing Governance Structures Support New Ambitions?*, "The China Quarterly" 2017, vol. 231, pp. 662–684; Thomas Heberer, *Representation in a context across political orders and the Chinese case*, "Journal of Chinese Governance" 2019, vol. 4, issue 4, pp. 339–361.

11 Art. 89 of the Constitution of the PRC, http://www.npc.gov.cn/zgrdw/englishnpc/Constitution/2007-11/15/content_1372963.htm (access: 09/11/2021).

- Directing and administering civil affairs, public security, judicial administration, supervision, and other related matters.
- Amendment or revocation of improper directives and ordinances issued by ministries or government committees.
- Change or revocation of improper decisions and orders of local state administration bodies at various levels.
- Approving the geographic division of provinces, autonomous regions and cities directly under the central government, and approving the establishment and geographic division of autonomous prefectures, counties, autonomous counties and cities.
- Deciding on the number and types of administrative bodies and – in accordance with the law – appointing or dismissing administrative officials, training them, assessing the performance of their tasks, and rewarding or punishing them.

2.1.2. The National Development and Reform Commission

The NDRC is an agency of the State Council, and its tasks include matters related to the shaping – i.e., planning, implementation and monitoring – of activities related to the broadly understood regional policy, including in particular[12]:
- Formulating and organizing the implementation of national economic and social development strategies, medium- and long-term plans, and annual plans. The Commission is responsible for special planning at national level, regional planning, spatial planning, and national development planning. The institution presents draft laws and regulations regarding national economic and social development, economic restructuring, and openness to the world.
- Proposing general development goals and related policies to accelerate the construction of a modern economic system and to foster quality development. Organizing and conducting major strategic plans, major policies, major projects and other projects and supervision, presenting appropriate corrective actions.
- Monitoring and forecasting macroeconomic and social development trends and presenting macrocontrol policy proposals. Coordinating integrated macroeconomic policy and conducting a macroeconomic response study. The Commission is also responsible for formulating and organizing the implementation of appropriate pricing policies, and formulating lists of the few

12 *Zhineng peizhi he nei she jigou* (职能 配置 与 内设 机构), https://www.ndrc.gov.cn/fzggw/bnpz/ (access: 20/04/2022).

core commodities, service prices, and important government-administered fee standards.
- Conducting and coordinating comprehensive work related to the reform of the economic system and presenting appropriate reform proposals.
- Proposing strategies and plans, ensuring balance and creating a policy of structural optimization in the use of foreign capital and foreign investment. The Belt and Road Initiative.
- Being responsible for the overall management of state investments. Organizing funds for the implementation of investments.
- Promoting the implementation of regional development strategies, new urbanization strategies and major policies, and organizing the formulation of relevant regional plans and policies.
- Organizing and formulating a comprehensive industrial policy. Coordinating major issues in the development of major industries and coordinating relevant development plans and major policies.
- Promoting the implementation of an innovation-based development strategy. Collaborating with relevant departments to develop plans and policies to spread innovation and entrepreneurship, and to propose policies to develop innovation and foster a new pace of economic development.
- Promoting the implementation of the sustainable development strategy, building and reforming ecological development, and coordinating the protection and restoration of the ecological environment, and the protection and comprehensive use of energy resources.
- Collaborating with relevant departments to develop strategies and plans to support the coordinated development of economic and defense construction and to coordinate key issues. Organizing and preparing plans for the mobilization of the national economy, and coordinating and organizing the implementation of relevant works of national economic mobilization.

It should be noted that the NDRC works in cooperation with other institutions in order to perform the tasks assigned to it. An example is the Ministry of Trade, which cooperates in establishing the rules for foreign capital access to the Chinese market, including issuing guidelines and incentives for investing in the central and western regions of China. The situation is similar to that of the Ministry of Finance, which is responsible for planning the entire state budget, including activities entrusted to the NDRC, and for fiscal planning. The cooperation with the NDRC also includes the National Health Commission, in the field of demographic policy, including fertility, and the National Food and Materials Reserve Office, in order to secure strategic food resources. The NDRC also cooperates with the National Energy Agency in the field of shaping energy security, including coordination of energy policy with the country's development planning.

The internal organizational structure of the NDRC is very extensive (Diagram 2), taking into account the tasks of the basic organizational units. Units dealing with strategy and planning: organizing, formulating, and promoting National Reform Programs (NRP), including building a uniform planning system throughout the country, are very important for this institution. Other units deal with researching and monitoring the macroeconomic situation, as well as undertaking activities related to economic functioning. Separate departments deal with reforms of the investment and finance system, including the organization of central funds for the construction of large infrastructure projects approved by the government, and the development of strategies for the use of foreign capital for the implementation of large investment projects. From the point of view of cooperation with the region, an important element is the organizational unit defined as the Regional Economic Department, which promotes the implementation of regional development strategies. The faculty focuses in particular on supporting revitalization, implementing strategies in the regions of western China, revitalizing the north-eastern part of the country, and promoting coordinated development. A separate unit deals with the implementation of the Belt and Road Initiative (the so-called New Silk Road).

The Department of Integrated National Economy deals with the formulation and implementation of annual plans for socioeconomic development. Its tasks include monitoring, analyzing, and forecasting the macroeconomic situation, presenting political proposals for building a modern economy and promoting high-quality development. It also organizes and formulates a catalog of national reserve materials. Meanwhile, the Department of Coordinated Economic Development and National Defense is engaged in formulating strategies and plans to support the coordinated development of economic and defense construction and coordinating important defense-related issues. In this regard, it coordinates and organizes the implementation of national activities related to economic mobilization in the event of a public emergency. Other units deal with the rural economy, industry, innovation, and advanced technologies (including the development of digital industry), coordinating the implementation of social development strategies, supporting employment, including social security, and controlling the prices of key goods, services and the means of production[13].

13 Ibid.

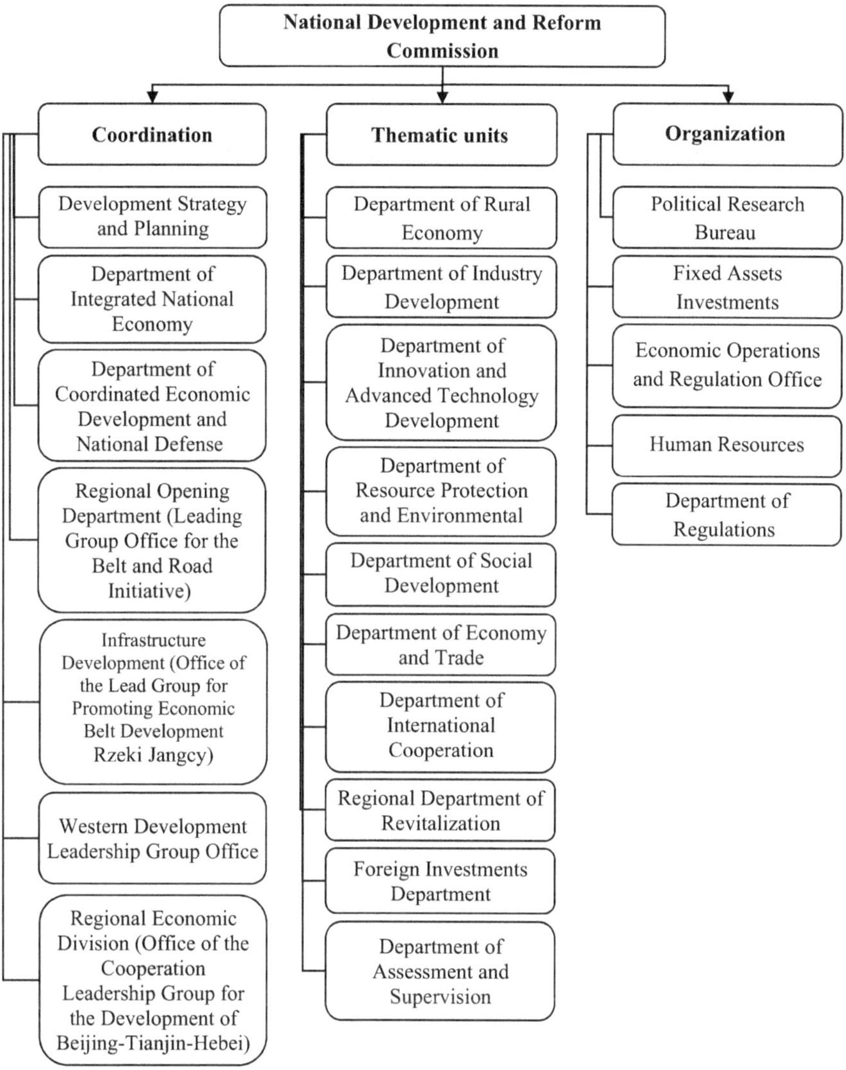

Diagram 2. Organizational structure of the National Development and Reform Commission. Source: own study based on: *Zhineng peizhi he nei she jigou*, (职能配置与内设机构), https://www.ndrc.gov.cn/fzggw/bnpz/ (access: 20/04/2022).

2.2. The territorial system of the state in the light of regional development

China is a unitary country with a centralized character; therefore, the central government only partially shares power with territorial structures[14]. From historical experience, one of the main challenges is to maintain the unity of the state and its organizational units in a situation of transformation of the political system on the one hand and socio-economic diversification, on the other. The historical experiences of the PRC in the field of decentralization and the current differentiation (including economic, social, spatial, cultural) have led to internal particularisms and the emergence of centrifugal forces. As a consequence, there have been many internal political breakdowns and civil wars[15]. Hence, decentralization tendencies are present in the political system as long as they do not begin to dominate particularisms and centrifugal forces, thereby disturbing social peace. Similarly, manifestations of centralization, which, according to the authorities, are associated with the expected social peace, occur to the extent that problems related to the control of the state, including territorial structures, do not dominate, and the system ensures a minimum level of adaptability.

It should be recalled that the constitution, with regard to the division of power into central and subnational components (regional, intermediate, local), refers to the principle of central government leadership[16] and the full involvement of territorial structures in the policy of central government. This indicates that the Chinese political system is very centralized in the legal and formal sense. In practice, however, subnational authorities can shape their own public policies based on local conditions and preferences, as long as it supports the social stability and economic growth expected by the center[17]. Hence, the asymmetry of various types of solutions, which are still dominated by political centralization in many areas, but at the same time – for China – by far-reaching economic decentralization. This is accompanied by the reflection that it is impossible to treat decentralization as a remedy for all problems, and centralization as a cause of the misfortunes of contemporary China. Reflection should therefore move towards thinking about the level at which to make decisions and implement specific solutions so that the implementation of regional policy is also optimal. It de-

14 Pei Li, Yi Lu, Jin Wang, *Does flattening government improve economic performance? Evidence from China*, "Journal of Development Economics" 2016, vol. 123, pp. 18–37.

15 Scott Morton, Charlton Lewis, *Chiny. Historia i kultura*, Kraków 2007, pp. 113–245.

16 The principle of democratic centralism contained in Art. 3 of the Constitution of the PRC, http://www.npc.gov.cn/zgrdw/englishnpc/Constitution/2007-11/15/content_1372963.htm (access: 20/04/2022).

17 Jae Ho Chung, *Centrifugal Empire: Central-Local Relations in China*, New York 2016, pp. 3–14.

pends on many factors, including the specificity, organizational culture, and institutional structure of the Chinese political system. The Chinese system of territorial governance is hierarchical, that is, lower-order units are generally subordinate to higher-order units. According to Art. 95 of the Constitution territorial structures can be divided into four levels[18]:

- provincial: provinces (22 units), autonomous regions (5 units), municipalities (4 units), special administrative regions (2 units),
- prefecture: prefectures (districts), autonomous prefectures, prefecture-level cities (333 units in total),
- county: counties, autonomous counties and county-level cities, districts under the jurisdiction of cities; this level also includes the flag in Inner Mongolia (2844 units in total),
- township: townships, towns, towns of ethnic minorities, offices of quarters within larger cities (38,741 units in total).

The four-tier administrative division is not completely uniform, because there are many exceptions which are the result of ethnic or economic differences (e.g., in the provinces – autonomous regions – separate cities). Administrative division is also influenced by the structures of the CPC, as differences in party hierarchies affect formal relationships between individual administrative units. The party is not a homogeneous creation, but an environment in which different factions clash. These factional games are also reflected at the local level. At the regional level, China is divided into 22 provinces[19] and five autonomous regions (Guangxi, Inner Mongolia, Tibet, Xinjiang, Ningxia). The formal status of the latter does not differ much from the other provinces, but they are inhabited by dense groups of ethnic minorities, and honoring their status in this way is supposed to create the appearance of special treatment of the rights of ethnic minorities[20]. Autonomous regions inhabited by ethnic minorities in fact enjoy less administrative autonomy, as the central government is suspicious of politically sensitive regions such as Tibet and Xinjiang. This does not change the fact that these areas are a source of basic raw materials and the provincial authorities are dependent on significant financial aid from the central government. The next units with provincial status are the so-called separate cities, directly subordinate to the central government, i.e., Beijing, Tianjin, Shanghai, and Chongqing. To this must be added two Special Administrative Regions: Hong Kong and Macao; these regions, controlled by the central government, have some autonomy in decision-making due to incomplete

18 See also *China Statistical Yearbook 2021*, China Statistics Press 2022; Marta Dargas, *Idee i zasady konstytucyjne chińskiego porządku prawnego*, Warszawa 2017, pp. 228–229.
19 The Chinese authorities treat Taiwan as the twenty-third province.
20 Michał Bogusz, Jakub Jakubowski, *Komunistyczna Partia Chin i jej państwo. Konserwatywny zwrot Xi Jinpinga*, Warszawa 2019, p. 137.

integration within the Chinese Communist Party's control system[21]. It is difficult to speak of a uniform pattern of functioning of individual provinces, as well as of autonomous regions and separated cities. For the purposes of this publication, it has been assumed that the 31 provincial-level units include 22 provinces, five autonomous regions, and four municipalities[22] (Beijing, Tianjin, Shanghai, Chongqing).

The prefecture level of administration developed in China's political system after 1949 with the aim of reducing the administrative burden on the higher level, i. e., the provinces. Rapid urbanization has led to almost all cities in China now becoming prefecture-level units, established as centers of growth that affect their surroundings, mainly the surrounding rural areas. These are cities that due to their mainly economic potential have received special status, and are directly administered by the provincial authorities, not the prefecture. For this reason, they are often included in the first provincial level. As they are subordinate to the provinces and not directly to the central government, they are classified by convention at the prefectural level (diagram 3). Cities separated by prefectures are often important industrial centers, often separated industrial zones crucial for the regional development of the province. These cities receive special administrative privileges from the central government for economic development and regulation, making them more independent from provincial authorities[23]. Although in accordance with the provisions of the Chinese constitution we can distinguish four levels of territorial structures, informally, the fifth level consists of local committees (urban and rural). However, they are not official state structures.

The rulers of individual administrative units are representatives of central government in the field, acting as local people's governments (with a three- or five-year term of office). People's congresses and people's governments are es-

---

21 Regarding the status of Hong Kong and Macao, the constitutional principle of "one country – two systems" applies, which implies a certain degree of autonomy, albeit under the supervision of the Beijing authorities. The goal of the authorities in Beijing is to fully unify special administrative regions. Rao Geping, Wang Zhenmin, *Hong Kong's 'One Country, Two Systems' Experience under the Basic Law: Two Perspectives from Chinese Legal Scholars*, "Journal of Contemporary China" 2007, vol. 16, no. 52, pp. 341–358; Lo Shiu Hing, *Comparative Political Systems: The Cases of Hong Kong and Macau*, "Journal of Contemporary Asia" 1995, vol. 25, no. 2, pp. 254–271; *The Practice of the "One Country, Two Systems" Policy in the Hong Kong Special Administrative Region*, http://ls.chineseembassy.org/eng/ci/t1164027.htm (access: 20/04/2022).

22 These are municipalities directly under the central government. They have the same administrative rank as provinces and special urban management privileges.

23 Dirk Schmidt, Sebastian Heilmann, *Provincial- and Municipal-Level Governments*, [in:] Sebastian Heilmann (ed.), *China's Political System*, Lanham-Boulder-New York-London 2017, p. 85.

tablished in provinces, townships directly under the central government, counties, cities, towns, townships, national townships[24].

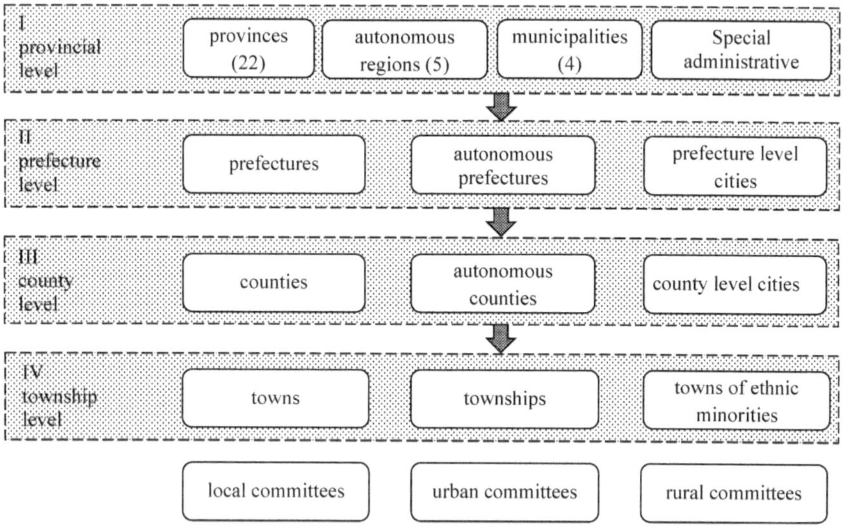

Diagram 3. The layout of territorial structures in the PRC from the perspective of regional policy. Source: own study based on: Tony Saich, *Governance and Politics of China*, London-New York 2015, p. 157; *China Statistical Yearbook 2020*, China Statistics Press, 2021; *An Overview of Spatial Policy in Asian and European Countries*, http://www.mlit.go.jp/kokudokeikaku/international/spw/general/china/index_e.html (access: 09.04.2022); Susan V. Lawrence and Michael F. Martin, *Understanding China's Political System*, [in:] Camelia L. Jacoby (ed.), *China's Political System Features, Institutions, and Leaders*, New York 2014, p. 12; Guo Qingwang, Jia Junxue, *Structural Reform in China's Regional Governments*, vol. 1, Hong Kong 2013, p. 17.

The functioning of territorial structures in China is regulated by the constitution (Articles 95–111) and the Act of June 1, 1972, on the organization of local assemblies of people's representatives and local people's governments at all levels. Power in territorial structures is exercised by the People's Representatives' Assembly (PRA). The assemblies of provinces, autonomous regions and separate cities, as well as prefectures and autonomous prefectures, are elected in indirect elections in which lower-level members of the PRA participate. The term of office of the PRA at the provincial level is five years, and at the lower level, three years. County, city, township, and district PRAs are formed via direct elections, and active and passive voting rights are granted to citizens from the age of 18. Such a system means that the elections of higher-level PRAs e.g., provinces, is not competitive.

24 Article 95 of the PRC Constitution, http://www.npc.gov.cn/zgrdw/englishnpc/Constitution/2007-11/15/content_1372963.htm (access: 20/04/2022).

The executive body within individual administrative units is the People's Governments (PG) elected by the PRA at a given level of local structures (Article 105 of the Constitution). The local PGs are also local state administration bodies. At the head of a local structure is – depending on the level – the provincial governor, the president of the autonomous region, and the mayor, who also presides over the local PG. Local authorities at or above the provincial level, within the limits of their authority provided for by law, manage in their administrative areas matters in the field of the economy, education, science, culture, public health, physical culture, urban and rural development, finance, civil matters, public security, nationality matters, judicial administration, supervision and family planning. The PGs of cities implement the resolutions of the PRAs at the appropriate levels, as well as the decisions and orders of state administrative bodies at the next higher level, and conduct administrative work in their administrative areas. The PGs of provinces and townships directly subordinate to the central government decide on the establishment and geographical division of cities (Articles 107–108 of the constitution).

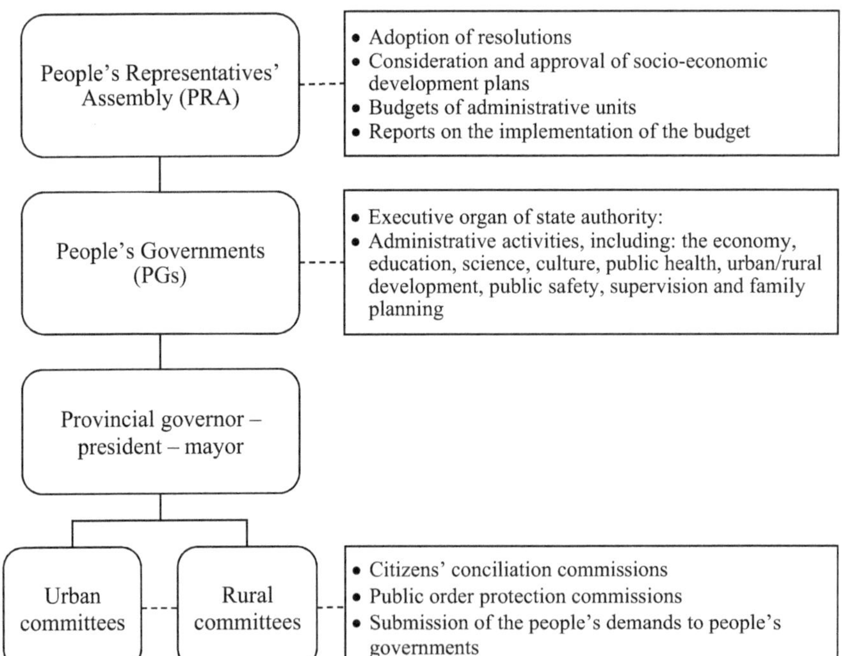

Diagram 4. A typical structure of a local authority and its main tasks. Source: Own study based on: Marta Dargas, op. cit., pp. 168–171.

Units of the administrative division are hierarchical to some extent (Diagram 4). This is because the upper-level PG may cancel the decisions of the lower administration (Article 108 of the Constitution). The local administration is therefore subject to both the appropriate level and the higher-level people's assembly. This double dependence causes a lack of self-governance in a formal sense[25]. This is confirmed by the organization of, for example, public finances of local authorities. As a rule, a given level of local government influences the shaping of finances at a lower level of government, which, of course, additionally complicates the relations between the various levels of administration. This is often referred to as "lower-level governance", which is why there is no fully unified system of public finance at the local level, encompassing the relationship between central government and local authorities, and local authorities themselves. The central policy of the State Council plays a dominant role in financial relations. Hence, in relation to the territorial structures of the PRC, it is more appropriate to speak of "local authority", which does not have the characteristics of self-government. Chinese style local authority covers all government entities, with the exception of the central government, from provinces to below that level, bearing in mind the close relationship between provincial governments and the central government[26].

City committees and village committees are the lowest level of local authorities The chairman, vice-chairman, and members of each committee are elected by residents. The relations between the inhabitants and committees of villagers, as well as grass-roots organs of state power, are defined by law. Citizens' committees set up residents' committees for mediation, public safety, public health, and other matters to manage public affairs and social services in their area. They also mediate in civil disputes, assist in maintaining public order, and convey opinions and demands of residents, or present the suggestions of the PG (Art. 111 of the Constitution).

According to the law, villages are not part of the state structure, but are "autonomous" and jointly administer the land. This autonomy is also sometimes misunderstood in the administrative practice of local structures, most often as "autonomy under the leadership of the township". Hence, the villages are closely monitored by the townships. Townships oversee village finances, decide on rural development plans, approve the results of rural elections, appoint party secretaries in villages, and monitor the fulfillment of tasks in areas such as birth planning, economic development, and the fight against religious cults. Pursuant to the 1988 Act on City Committees, villages are guaranteed administrative self-governance, and elections to rural committees are held every three years. Here,

25 Jan Rowiński, Wojciech Jakóbiec, *System konstytucyjny Chińskiej Republiki Ludowej*, Warszawa 2006, p. 73.

26 Jianxing Yu, *Introduction: Local Governance in China-Past, Present, and Future*, [in:] Jianxing Yu, Sujian Guo (eds.), *The Palgrave Handbook of Local Governance in Contemporary China*, Singapore 2019, p. 7.

unlike the local PRA, elections are by definition competitive because every inhabitant of the village who has turned 18 has the right to vote and be elected. Practice shows frequent interference of the commune in the selection and nomination of candidates for elections in the countryside and the election results. Townships sometimes oppose the selection of undesirable candidates or arrest candidates selected by the village. It happens that representatives are removed due to the fact that the peasants did not have "sufficient qualifications to choose the right people"[27].

In recent years, self-governance at the level of local committees has been gradually reduced. An example is the opinion of the Central Committee of the Communist Party of China (CC CPC) and the State Council on the establishment and improvement of the system, mechanism and policy for the integration of towns and villages of May 25, 2019[28], which envisaged strengthening the position of local party structures at the expense of local committees. The solution aimed at combining the function of the chairman of the local committee with the position of the local secretary of the CPC, under the pretext of improving the mechanism of managing rural areas or introducing the rule of law at the local level, is undoubtedly an example of centralization and a departure from practicing elements of democratization at the lowest administrative level. The CPC's analogous dominance is also expected to apply to collective economic organizations and economic cooperatives. In this context, the only instrument of a bottom-up initiative bearing the characteristics of self-governance may be the announcement of increasing the importance of the consultation system at the local level, especially in rural areas.

Townships strengthen their supervision over villages by stricter control over the finances and development of villages. Expenditure in the countryside above a certain amount must be approved by the township authorities. This is to prevent poor financial management and embezzlement on the part of rural cadres and further indebtedness of the village. However, many cadres and villages consider it a violation of rural autonomy. In addition, increasing interference and pressure from townships significantly has decreased the enthusiasm of the rural cadres. At the same time, the resistance of the villages has increased, making their administration increasingly difficult[29].

It should be noted that the contemporary shape of China's territorial system naturally reflects, albeit to a limited extent, a centuries-old tradition, but the

---

27 Thomas Heberer, *Local Cadres,* [in:] ibid, p. 167.

28 Zhonggong zhongyang gu persuyuan guanyu jianli jianquan chengxiang ronghe fazhan tizhi jizhi he zhengce tixi de yijian (中共中央国务院关于建立健全城乡融合发展体制机制和政策体系的意见), http://www.gov.cn/zhengce/2019-05/05/content_5388880.htm (access: 09/11 /2021).

29 Ibid.

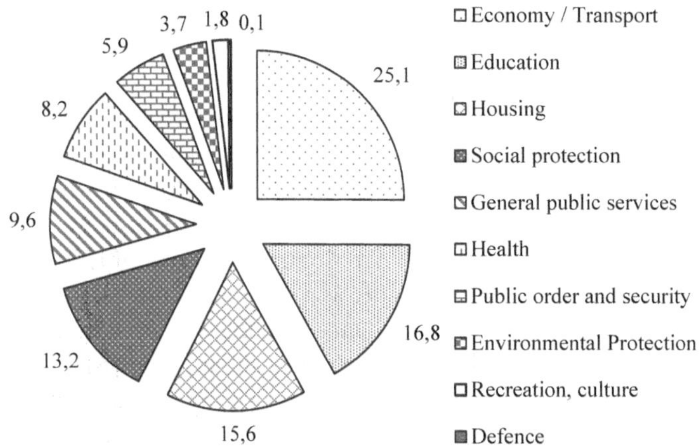

Graph 3. Percentage distribution of expenditure of all levels of subnational government in China (2016). Source: Own study based on: *2019 Edition of the World Observatory of Subnational Finance and Investment, Country Profiles*, The World Observatory on Subnational Government Finance and Investment, 2019, p. 173, http://www.sng-wofi.org/publications/SNGWOFI_2019_report_country_profiles.pdf (access: 20/04/2022).

practical shape of the tasks of individual administrative structures in the last four decades is the aftermath of economic reforms. The real functioning of territorial structures is based on the calculation of economic growth and the solving of ad hoc problems. Autonomous regions and cities are an example of this; individual units receive their autonomy. However, in practice, it does not play a major role in the daily administration of such a large country. The authorities at each level of the territorial structure are universal and are responsible for the provision of public services and local affairs, and above all for economic growth. Either way, subnational authorities complete the executive functions of central government. The implementation of policies within their jurisdiction is the primary responsibility of these authorities. The largest budgetary position of all subnational authorities relates to economic growth (Graph 3).

2.3. Province: subject or object of regional policy?

When analyzing the role of provincial authorities in China's regional policy, attention should be paid to the political and formal position of the governors and provincial secretaries of the CPC. The leaders of provincial authorities do not emerge through competitive election procedures, but through intra-party selection. In practice, provincial governors are very geographically mobile – moving a governor from one province to another may be a punishment for poor performance or a reward for exceptionally good performance in managing a given province. The political mobility of provincial leaders is determined not only by political movements within the CPC, but also by the economic performance of provincial leaders. The worse the economic performance, the more likely a provincial leader is to be demoted[30]. Provinces often provide the human resources from which later members of the CPC's central bodies, such as the Political Committee or the Executive (Permanent) Committee, come. The role of the leaders is significant considering that in 2020 only five governors were simultaneously members of the Politburo of the Communist Party of China (P CPC). The appointment of the provincial leader as a member of the P CPC may also be a way to increase the degree of compliance with the directives resulting from the central policy (political control). Experience shows, referring to the principal agent theory, that, for example, the governor of a given province, who is a member of the P CPC, takes the central guidelines more into account than the interests of the province to which he is entrusted with managing[31]. This makes these particular governors important political players. Regardless of this, provincial leaders have an administrative rank similar to that of government ministers.

Given the dual presence of the CPC and government bodies at every level of the Chinese political hierarchy, it must be recognized that power in the province belongs to the CPC committee secretary and the governor. They have the right to approve and direct provincial policies, allocate resources, and regulate the conduct of economic activity[32]. A governor may be removed or promoted before the end of his term of office, and he may run for another term depending on his performance or other political considerations. In practice, the term of office of the highest official in the provincial government ranges from three to five years on average[33]. Changes in the positions (fluctuations) of the governor and provincial secretary of the CPC are not very frequent and take place in the year of the meeting of the CPC Congress or within one year of the meeting. In the period 2000–2013, the CPC Congress meetings were held in 2002, 2007 and 2012. In 2002, there were 12 changes, in 2003 17 changes, in 2007 17 changes, in 2008 19 changes, in 2012 nine changes, and in 2013 24 changes. Throughout the period, the average turnover of key personnel in 31 provinces amounted to 35.94%, ranging from

30 Bo Zhiyue, *Economic Performance and Political Mobility: Chinese Provincial Leaders*, "Journal of Contemporary China" 1996, vol. 5, p. 12.
31 Sheng Yumin, *Economic Openness and Territorial Politics in China*, New York 2010, pp. 123, 136–138.
32 Charles J.P. Chen, Zengquan Li, Xijia Su, Zheng Sun, *Rent-Seeking Incentives, Corporate Political Connections, and the Control Structure of Private Firms: Chinese Evidence*, "Journal of Corporate Finance 2011", vol. 17, no. 2, pp. 229–243.
33 Hongbin Li, Li-An Zhou, *Political Turnover and Economic Performance…*, pp. 1743–1762.

3.23% in 2009 to as much as 77.42% in 2013[34]. It is worth adding that in recent years, changes in the positions of governor and provincial secretary of the CPC have occurred much more often, which has been attributed to the anti-corruption campaign carried out under the slogan of fighting "tigers and flies", but is in fact a manifestation of factional confrontation within the party[35].

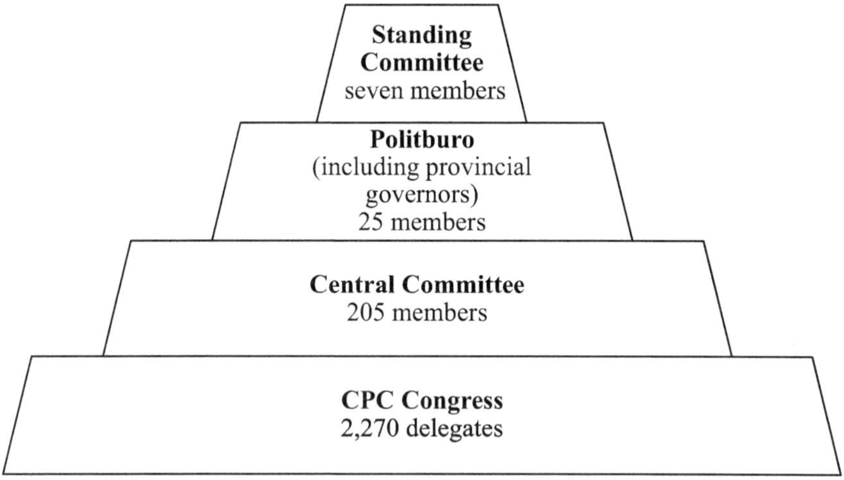

Diagram 5. The CPC hierarchy at the national level and the political position of the provincial governor in 2012. Source: own study based on: Susan V. Lawrence, Michael F. Martin, *Understanding China's Political System*, [in:] Camelia L. Jacoby (ed.), *China's Political System Features, Institutions, and Leaders*, New York 2014, p. 27.

The CPC's Department of Organization in Beijing decides on the appointments and promotions of all provincial party secretaries and governors, and routinely transfers provincial leaders from provinces to provinces or to nonprovincial positions in Beijing to ensure that they do not form regional political forces. For the same reason, the CPC also tries to keep military districts from coinciding with provincial boundaries. Beijing's influence on provinces includes the prerogative of sending the Party's Central Disciplinary Control Commission to the provinces

34 Danlu Bu, Chenyu Zhang, Philip T. Lin, Fang Hu, *Political Uncertainty, Institutions and Accounting Conservatism: Evidence from the Provincial Leader Turnover in China*, "Spanish Journal of Finance and Accounting" 2020, vol. 49, no. 4, pp. 406.

35 Jiaqi Liang, Laura Langbein, *Linking Anticorruption Threats, Performance Pay, Administrative Outputs, and Policy Outcomes in China*, "Public Administration" 2018, vol. 97, no. 1, pp. 177–194; Siqin Kang, Jiangnan Zhu, *Do People Trust the Government More? Unpacking the Distinct Impacts of Anticorruption Policies on Political Trust*, "Political Research Quarterly" 2021, vol. 74, no. 2, pp. 434–449; Elizabeth Quade, *The Logic of Anticorruption Enforcement Campaigns in Contemporary China*, "Journal of Contemporary China" 2007, vol. 16, no. 50.

to investigate corruption allegations and to send the Bureau of General Audit to the provinces to check the accounts[36].

Apart from the provincial government structure described above, the core of the regions are provincial committees of the Communist Party of China. They play an important role in all aspects of politics, economy, culture[37]and social development at the provincial level. They are responsible for recommending candidates for the main leaders of congresses and governments in the regions. In recent years, provincial party committees have been increasingly involved in the work of popular congresses in provinces. In many provinces, the provincial secretary of the CPC also serves as chairman of the standing committee of the Provincial People's Congress[38].

As in other unitary countries, Chinese provinces have neither their own constitutions nor, as already mentioned, the authority to appoint their leaders. However, the provinces, with the consent of the central authorities, shape the local fiscal policy, so they have their own sources of income. This makes provincial expenditure a significant part of total public expenditure and therefore also government expenditure. This applies to areas such as education, health, unemployment insurance, social security, and welfare. Lower-level administrations (counties, townships) also participate in the above-mentioned expenses. Beijing's central government often tries to impose its will on the provinces. The central ministries maintain their offices in the provinces, but the officials working there report to both the Beijing home ministry and the provincial leadership. In the event of a conflict of priorities, directors of such offices prioritize the interests of the provincial leadership, largely because it is the provincial leadership that controls the allocation of personnel. However, China has a unitary political system, not a federal one, so in a conflict situation, Beijing ultimately has the upper hand. Another important prerogative of a province is the right to make its own laws, which must comply with national law. In practice, local law interprets or extends national law[39].

Although each province formally has the same administrative rank, their different characteristics affect the political weight that they carry. The variation between provinces and even within provinces, is enormous[40]. Some of them, due to the area they occupy and the number of people inhabiting them or their

---

36 Susan V. Lawrence, Michael F. Martin, *Understanding China's Political System…*, p. 13.

37 On the subject of cultural policy, see Dikun Xie, Ye Chen (eds.), *Chinese Dream and Practice in Zhejiang – Culture*, Singapore 2019.

38 Zhiyue Bo, *Governing China in the Early 21st Century: Provincial Perspective*, "Journal of Chinese Political Science" 2002, vol. 7, pp. 165–166.

39 Susan V. Lawrence, Michael F. Martin, *Understanding China's Political System…*, p. 11.

40 Nicolaas Groenewold, Anping Chen, Guoping Lee, *Linkages Between China's Regions: Measurement and Policy*, Cheltenham, Northampton 2008, pp. 8–10.

access to natural resources, could constitute separate states. As many as six provincial-level units have over 70 million inhabitants: Hebei (75.5 million), Jiangsu (80.5 million), Shantung (100.4 million), Henan (96 million), Guangdong (113.4 million), Sichuan (83.4 million); in contrast, Tibet has a population of only 3.4 million and an area of 1.2 million sq km. In Shanghai, GDP per capita was 134,818 yuan, whereas in the poorest province, Gansu, it was 31,271 yuan. The economic power of provincial-level entities such as Shanghai and Guangdong makes them important centers for the central government. Shanghai is therefore an important source of income for public finances. Hence, there are comments[41] that Beijing, in the transformation process, was mainly interested in redistributing the wealth of Guangdong Province. Meanwhile, poor Tibet and other sparsely populated border provinces are also strategically important to the center. They occupy about 60% of the entire country, are inhabited by only 6% of the population, and are the homeland for many national minorities.

As already indicated, the provinces are very diverse in terms of population and level of socioeconomic development, as well as cultural development. Regional authorities not only provide various public services to citizens but also improve the efficiency of central government activities aimed at increasing the efficiency of state administration and public management. Compared to the central administration, regional authorities have limited powers. On the more important issues, they formulate the regional tax policy and are authorized to establish local law. The above reflects the shaping of competences in a unitary state, which are usually smaller than in a federal state. Regional authorities focus on the enforcement of their fiscal functions, such as resource allocation, income distribution, and stabilization of the local economy. Moreover, regional authorities are a good source of information on citizens' preferences and costs of public services in their area of administration. When taking great responsibility for the allocation of resources, they have an impact on the quality of public services, which can result in an increase in social security[42].

However, there is no doubt that at the regional level the responsibility for the allocation of resources depends on the preferences of the regional authorities, the economies of scale, the factors of production occurring in the region, and the amount of financing[43]. Chinese provincial leaders have been entrusted with significant powers over the allocation of resources such as credit, land, lawmaking, and the enforcement of power in entities under their jurisdiction. For

41 Tony Saich, *Governance and Politics of China…*, p. 159.

42 Guo Qingwang, Jia Junxue, *Structural Reform in China's Regional Governments…*, p. 4.

43 Ziyin Zhuang, Wei Zou, *Gonggong zhichu neng fou cujin jingji zengzhang* (公共 支出 能否 促進 經濟 增長), "Guanli Shijie" (管理 世界) 2003, no. 7, pp. 14–16.

companies interested in a good relationship with the provincial government, these prerogatives are crucial. The party secretary, who heads the provincial committee of the CPC, in practice represents the central government in the region, and his real political position is so significant that he dominates the governor. Governors usually deal with specific administrative matters in their jurisdiction. The governor is the administrative head of the organizational units of the provincial authorities, including departments, offices and committees. He is formally elected by the Provincial Assembly of People's Representatives for a five-year term, heads the Provincial People's Government, and is responsible for coordinating its work. The People's Government implements the decisions of the People's Representatives' Assembly and is accountable to it. According to the Chinese Constitution, the provincial-level People's Government is under the leadership of the State Council, which has the power to appeal against 'inappropriate' decisions made by provincial authorities. Relatively rarely, there are documented disputes over powers between the central government and provincial level authorities. Discrepancies are resolved quietly and informally before final decisions are announced[44]. Hence, formal and legal solutions are often secondary to the solutions practiced.

Practice shows that the business community is quite sensitive to changes in the positions of both the provincial governor and the secretary of the CPC, as this poses a threat to the relationships maintained so far. This is because political decisions determine the allocation of capital, as evidenced by the fact that in the past there has been massive investment in the same industries. As a result, local businesses can adapt their investment process to the personal change of provincial leaders as needed. Often, companies are able to shape economic activity in such a way as to gain the favor of the new authorities, e.g., by increasing the scale of investment, entrepreneurs are able to provide support for a newly appointed governor and develop good relations with the local authorities. The reverse is also true: if there is a high probability that a provincial governor will be removed, economic actors relying on the resources at the disposal of the provincial government refrain from developing extensive investment activities. This is because companies perceive the political change in key positions in the region as uncertainty and are therefore able to temporarily reduce their activity pending the appointment of new people to key positions[45].

In addition to the relationship between provincial authorities and entrepreneurs, the relationship between the provincial authorities and the central government is also important for the development of the province. Since eco-

44 Dirk H. Schmidt, Sebastian Heilmann, *Provincial- and Municipal-Level Governments…*, p. 88.
45 Danlu Bu, Chenyu Zhang, Philip T. Lin, Fang Hu, *Political Uncertainty, Institutions and Accounting Conservatism…*, pp. 395–426.

nomic reforms began in 1978, these relationships have become more complex, as provincial economic developments offer more opportunities for creative leadership than in the past. Provinces control enormous resources, which, from the point of view of economic development, slightly reduces the authority of the central authorities. The provinces have far more to gain from cooperative relations with the central government than from making efforts towards independence. In general, the provinces accepted the idea that each should develop its comparative advantages, but as part of a centralized program of economic reform[46]. In such an arrangement, apart from good relations with Beijing, what counts is the natural features of the province (e.g., and abundance of resources) and the political skills of the provincial leaders in building the region's competitiveness and improving the quality of life.

Due to the critical role of the provinces in the political system, their leaders constitute an important group that undertakes activities aimed at influencing the decision-making process at the central level. Often, these are activities aimed at a significant modification of the central policy. An opportunity for this is, for example, the annual congresses of the CPC during which provincial leaders try to include in central policies postulates in accordance with the needs of individual provinces (e.g., distribution of fiscal revenues). In turn, the provinces also play an important role for the central authorities in the process of incubating new solutions, e.g., in the form of experimentation. Often, reforms tried at the local or regional level have become the basis for formulating implementation at the level of the entire country. Provincial experiments precede final decisions in the decision-making process at the central level[47]. It also works the other way around; the attitude of the provincial authorities influences the pace of implementing the new centrally planned policy or specific political measures.

46 Tony Saich, *Governance and Politics of China…*, p. 160.
47 Ibid, pp. 164–166.

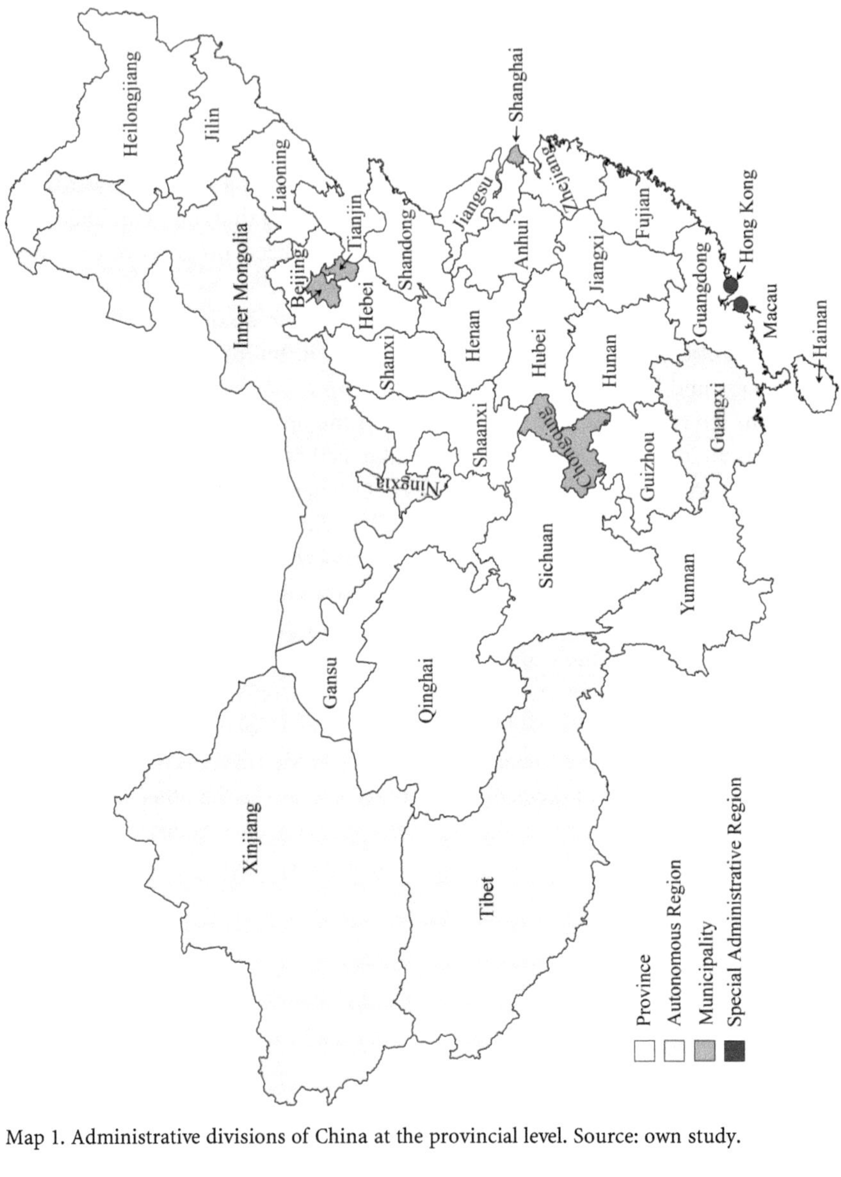

Map 1. Administrative divisions of China at the provincial level. Source: own study.

2.4. The systemic position of the county as an intermediate subnational authority

Counties are the oldest organizational units in the PRC administrative system, as they were established nearly two millennia ago. They are referred to as the cornerstone of Chinese statehood. Counties are an important element of the territorial structures of the state, especially in the relations between the state and society. The county jurisdiction covers counties and county-level cities, but also autonomous counties and urban districts. A county as an administrative unit most often consists of counties and county-level cities. Most often, counties cover an administrative unit inhabited by about 410,000 inhabitants.

Table 9. The structure of authorities at the county level in 2000–2019

Type of unit	2019	2009	2000
Counties	1323	1464	1503
County level cities	387	367	400
Districts level cities	965	855	787
Autonomous counties	117	117	116

Source: National Bureau of Statistics of China, National Data, 2022.

After 1978, the number of counties decreased due to the progress of the urbanization process (Table 9). It should be noted that at the same time the county-level administration system influenced subsequent waves of urbanization. The engine of the changes was not only urbanization, but also the economic growth of cities. The urbanization process influenced and still influences administrative changes through the creation of two types of units: county-level cities and cities. The above explains the numerical instability of counties starting in the 1980s. A decrease in the number of counties can also be noted in recent years – between 2000 and 2019, 180 counties disappeared. Between 1997 and 2015, 229 counties were transformed into districts (prefectures), including 47% of counties in eastern China.

Local cadres at the county level also include, apart from officials and county leaders, members of the party organs of the CPC. Activities of local staff at the county level are determined by: (a) guidelines from higher administration (central government, province); (b) limited local resources, mainly in the form of finance, industrial presence, or spatial size; (c) evaluation requirements, mainly relating to economic growth achievements. As for the organization of party cadres at the county level, it reflects the cadre system at the central or provincial level.

The decision-making body is the Standing Committee of the CPC which most often includes the party secretary, the mayor, the secretary for political and legal affairs (justice, including the prosecutor's office, courts, public safety), the vice-mayor (industry, rural development), director of the Organization Department of the CPC Committee, chairman of the Discipline Control Committee, commander of the local armed forces, and secretary responsible for the work of the Party Committee (diagram 6). Since the party secretary has the final say in key decision-making, he is, in fact, at the forefront of the local (in this case the district) political elite. The functions of the party secretary cover a wide range of tasks. He is responsible not only for the comprehensive development of the county, but also has to take care of the daily life of his subordinates, including solving family problems[48]. Party secretaries at a given administrative level are a kind of link between the supreme authority and the lower-level administration to ensure the proper implementation of both individual policies and laws. Although the CPC is not a monolith that can impose its will anytime, anywhere, it remains a source of power, ensuring that policy priorities are implemented from the top down. It allows the authorities to maintain a minimum level of control at all levels, down to the lowest level, i. e., communes and villages.

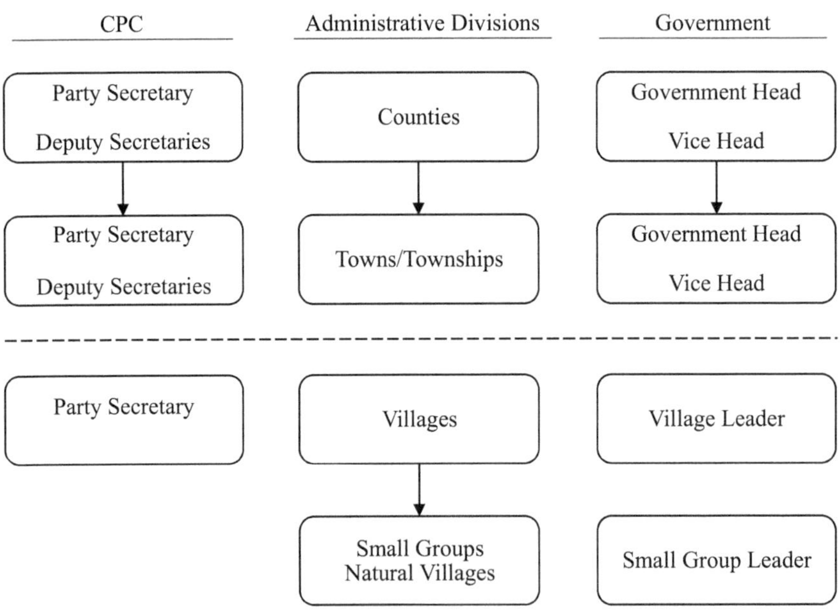

Diagram 6. Administrative and party structures at the local level in the PRC. Source: John James Kennedy, *Rural China: Reform and Resistance*, [in:] William A. Joseph (ed.), *Politics in China: An Introduction*, Oxford 2019, p. 320.

48 Thomas Heberrer, *Local Cadres…*, p. 163.

Counties have a certain level of independence, especially in tasks related to supporting economic growth. Due to enormous differences and unsustainable development, counties play a vital role in Chinese administrative management, often perform various tasks at their discretion, and are quite independent in developing the county's economy. In terms of how counties function, the issue of which of the subnational structures plays the leading role for this territorial unit remains a matter of debate. They are prefectures and provinces. The Chinese constitution stipulates that the counties are administratively under the provinces. The same document places the prefecture as the administrative unit between the province and the county. The problem is that the provincial oversight system is far from perfect. The provinces are very large; some of them contain more than a hundred units of this type in their area, and given the large number of people living in each unit, this prevents proper supervision. This forces the supervision of an indirect authority, which is the prefecture[49]. The local authority at this level has a wide range of tasks, including introducing economic regulations, market surveillance, social management, public services and environmental protection[50].

Table 10. Volume and structure of county expenditure in 1997–2005 (%)

Period	**Economic expenditures**	**Social expenditures**	**Maintenance**
1997–2005	14.22	27.54	21.16
1997–2001	12.78	27.19	21.89
2002–2005	15.65	27.90	20.25

Source: own study based on: Guo Qingwang, Jia Junxue, *Structural Reform in China's Regional Governments*, vol . 1, Hong Kong 2013, p. 62.

The specificity of counties' tasks can be presented by describing the size and structure of expenditure of the authorities at this level. It should be assumed that changes in the scope and targets of spending are key to understanding the direction of the evolution of this level of power. Expenditures of counties can be expressed in three categories: (1) economic, i. e., infrastructure, agriculture, forestry, hydrometeorology; (2) social, which includes education, social security; (3) maintenance, i. e., administration, public safety. Despite the fact that, as mentioned, economic growth has been a priority of the administration at all

49 Tao Chiu Lam, *The County System and County Governance*, [in:] Jae Ho Chung, Tao-chiu Lam (eds.), *China's Local Administration: Traditions and Changes in the Sub-National Hierarchy*, Oxon-New York 2010, pp. 169.

50 Jianxing Yu, *Local Governance in China – Past, Present and Future*, [in:] Jianxing Yu, Sujian Guo (ed.), *The Palgrave Handbook of Local Governance in Contemporary China*, Singapore 2019, p. 9; Ying Zhang, *Analysis of the History and Current Status of Country-to-District-Transformation*, "Legal System and Society" 2016, vol. 24, pp. 216–218.

levels for years, economic expenses are not the highest item in the budgets of counties: it is social expenditure, regardless of the time series in which the calculations are made. The analysis of shorter time intervals confirms a slight increase in economic expenses (from 12.78% in 1997–2001 to 15.65% in 2002–2005) at the expense of maintenance expenses (from 21.89% in 1997–2001 to 20.25% in 2002–2005).

When analyzing the county system as the level managing the implementation of public policies, including elements of regional policy, attention should be paid to two aspects. The first of them is the urbanization discussed above, which forces the transformation of units in two ways: (a) division of counties into county-level cities and (b) transformation of a county into a city. Experts[51] point out that cities should be created as subordinate units in relation to counties to maintain the integrity of the organizational hierarchy, any change to which would require a review of the Constitution of the People's Republic of China. Also, there is the problem of delimiting the tasks of individual administrative structures. The problem of urbanization concerns mainly the populations of coastal provinces, which are subject to the industrialization process, and thus rapid population growth in their area. The existing administrative structures do not fully meet the current needs. The second aspect is the efficiency of management at a given administrative level. The management crisis, also felt at the municipal level, has accompanied the process of economic and political reforms since 1978[52]. The challenges related to the management of local affairs are the result of the actions of the central government on the one hand, but also the deficiencies in the implementation of public policies or public services by the local authorities themselves. Distribution of local taxes, subsidies, minor embezzlement of funds in county and the general shape of public finances at the local level are just some of the key elements[53]. Problems related to the implementation of public activities, including tax collection at the local level or the indebtedness of local authorities, occurred due to the dictatorship of the supreme authorities[54]. The challenge is the lack of objective checks at the local level. Recent changes in the fiscal system, crucial for the functioning of authorities such as counties, contributed to the deterioration of their financial situation. This does not change the fact that the

51 Tao Chiu Lam, *The County System and County Governance…*, p. 172.

52 Christine Wong, *Overview of Issues in Local Public Finance in the PRC*, [in:] Christine Wong (ed.), *Financing Local Government in the People's Republic of China*, Oxford 1997, pp. 8–15.

53 Yinqiu Lu, *Local Government Financing Platforms in China: A Fortune or Misfortune?*, "IMF Working Papers" 2013, vol. 13, no. 243, pp. 3–22.

54 Zhuo Chen, Zhiguo He, Chun Liu, *The Financing of Local Government in China: Stimulus Loan Wanes and Shadow Banking Waxes*, "ADBI Working Paper Series" 2018, no. 800, pp. 1–62; Deng Yongheng, Randall Morck, Jing Wu, Bernard Yeung, *China's Pseudo-Monetary Policy*, "Review of Finance" 2015, vol. 19, no. 1, pp. 55–93.

system of fiscal transfers is still anti-equalizing, but nevertheless they constitute the foundation of governance at the local level. Fiscal transfers allowed poorer counties to settle arrears in payments or the salaries of local officials. However, a large part of the funds did not ultimately reach the most needy individuals.

2.5. The township in light of the tasks of local authorities

The township is the most basic administrative unit in the territorial structure of the Chinese state; rural cadres of that rank are called "parent officials" since they deal with almost all the needs of the inhabitants of their jurisdiction[55]. The vast majority of the population of townships are rural residents. Township authorities directly manage local affairs and perform tasks commissioned by higher authorities, including the central government. Townships have integrated management and complete leadership and assume full responsibility for all administrative matters within their jurisdiction. The functions of township are closely related to the daily life of the inhabitants and have the characteristics of social management. Changes in the number of townships provide convincing evidence of rapid urbanization in China. The reform of "merging townships" in 2005–2015 reduced this number by 5.3 thousand units. Townships are mainly divided into central and regular. Central townships are the seat of county-level authorities and have an advantage over regular townships in terms of economic and political development and resource allocation[56]. The scale of tasks performed by the administrative staff of the communes is evidenced by the fact that they have about 8 million employees[57]. Most often, the township administration consists of four departments: (1) civil matters, (2) police, (3) economic, and (4) culture. The People's Representative Assembly at the township level has the right to establish the budget and manage the commune's assets. The township PRA elects representatives to the political structures of the PRA at the county level[58].

The township authorities are responsible for carrying out various tasks. These tasks cover dozens of areas such as maintaining public order, ensuring economic development, maintaining irrigation facilities, birth planning, public safety, production and food safety, and preventing animal epidemics and diseases. An important role in the functioning of the township is played by the so-called hard political goals, most often related to economic development or maintaining

55 Yang Zhong, *Chinese Township Government: Between a Rock and a Hard Place*, [in:] Jae Ho Chung, Tao-chiu Lam (eds.), *China's Local Administration: Traditions and Changes in the Sub-National Hierarchy*, Oxon- New York 2010, p. 175.

56 Jianxing Yu, *Local Governance in China – Past, Present and Future* ..., p. 9.

57 Thomas Heberer, *Local Cadres...*, p. 166.

58 Yang Zhong, *Chinese Township Government: Between a Rock and a Hard Place...*, p. 177.

social stability, the achievement of which is obligatory. The practice of how townships function indicates, however, that the resources at their disposal (including financial ones) are often too small to carry out all tasks. Financially, communes are to a certain extent dependent on grants from counties. Township representatives indicate that achieving all goals at the same time is very difficult[59].

From the perspective of development policy, the tasks of the township can be viewed in a dichotomous system – in this light, townships are market participants and implementers of government policy[60]. The practice of the functioning of the township shows at least a partial justification of the above approach. Townships are a tool by which the central government of the PRC achieves its overarching goals, i.e., mainly economic growth. Townships act as a quasi-owner of the resources, and to a lesser extent a regulator or even a rent-seeker. Undoubtedly, townships are to some extent partners for business entities looking for new places to locate production and new ways of its implementation. Bureaucratic coordination, patronage, and even the use of price controls and social mechanisms are elements of building local institutions among market participants. The townships are also administrative structures through which central policies are implemented, as well as tasks defined by higher-level territorial structures (which will be discussed later).

The township is crucial in exercising power as the policy implemented at the national (central) or subnational level (province, prefecture, county) is implemented mainly by townships. The township officials (along with village officials) are the main staff for implementing policies established at the upper level of administration. This administration is also responsible for implementing the often unpopular central policies on the ground. Furthermore, townships are responsible for the consequences of their implementation and have to deal with them at the local level. It should be added that this is the implementation of policies in which townships are not involved in the formulation stage. Hence, communes often find themselves in a difficult situation, standing between the expectations of counties that supervise their activities and citizens who are often irritated by new requirements. Therefore, a huge responsibility rests on the townships, especially considering that they are the least powerful administration among the territorial structures of the PRC. Municipalities operate in a complex environment of vertical and horizontal relations between citizens and higher authorities[61]. It is not only about implementing policies imposed by higher-level

59 Thomas Heberer, René Trappel, *Evaluation Processes, Local Cadres' Behavior and Local Development Processes,* "Journal of Contemporary China" 2013, vol. 22, no. 4, pp. 1048–1066.

60 Graeme Smith, *Measurement, Promotions and Patterns of Behavior in Chinese Local Government,* "The Journal of Peasant Studies" 2013, vol. 40, no 6, pp. 1027–1050.

61 Yang Zhong, *Chinese Township Government: Between a Rock and a Hard Place...,* p. 180.

authorities or central authorities, but also about the need to cooperate with various types of stakeholders, including government agencies and enterprises.

The township cadre can by divided into three categories in regard to the level of (in)dependence of the township from the supreme authority (including the central government)[62]: (a) under the authority of the township, (b) under the authority of the upper level of administration, (c) under both the township and upper level of administration. The first case concerns the subordinate offices (*Kuai Kuai*) of the jurisdiction of township party committees chaired by the township party secretary. As in the case of a province or a county, it has the greatest power in its jurisdiction. The most common structures that report to the secretary are the office of party and general affairs, the office of economic development, the office of social affairs, and rural development offices. The mayor of the township usually supervises directly the bureau for party and general affairs, and his deputy, the other units. This is the part of the administration that reports directly to the township authorities and receives technical assistance from their counterparts at the county-level offices.

The second category of township administrative structures are offices under the jurisdiction of counties (*Tiao Tiao*), or substantively relevant offices of superior authorities. The offices strictly implement central policies at the local level. They concern, among others, industry and trade, national taxes, agricultural equipment, banking and financial institutions, postal administration, health, energy management, irrigation, transport. These structures are, in fact, controlled by the upper-level authorities because they determine the composition of the cadre, finances, and the allocation of material resources. This part of the local administration receives direct orders from the county level or from an even higher-level administration. The development of this category of administration at the county level is treated not only as a manifestation of centralism but, above all, as a lack of confidence in the local administrative cadre under the direct authority of the township. Two decades ago, China experienced a sharp increase in the number of such offices in the administrative structures of townships; 82% of the offices were *Tiao Tiao* in nature in Hubei province.

At this point, it is necessary to ask about the detailed reasons for creating an administration at the township level, which, *in fact,* is not a township due to the lack of influence of the township on its functioning. As it turns out, the answers go beyond thinking only about the superiority of centralism over decentralization solutions, although this has also played a role. It should be[63] pointed out that the tendency to concentrate power in townships has been counteracted. This was accompanied by the suspicion of the upper-level authorities that if it came to

62 Ibid.
63 Ibid, p. 182.

local officials to decide the priority of local and national interests, the former would prevail. There was also a belief that township cadres represented a low quality of human resources, often poorly educated, with low skills and competences to administer public affairs. The motivation of upper-level authorities and central agencies to expand their sectoral jurisdiction at the municipal level in order to secure the implementation of their own tasks is also very interesting.

The third category of township administration consists of offices that are subordinate to both the commune authorities and the county authorities (*Tiao Kuai*). An example is local tax offices, which are responsible to the county authorities in terms of personnel and budget. The only connection of these offices to the township is the fact that the township committee of the CPC has influence over party activists who are also employees in this office. There are also structures that show double administrative subordination, i. e., township and county. Examples include matters related to public order and safety as well as the functioning of the judiciary in the area of the township.

The cadre evaluation system, including that exercised over township personnel, is designed to force the implementation of top-down policies, and to a lesser extent to increase their effectiveness[64]. The cadre evaluation system relates to (a) program implementation, (b) the key cadre, and (c) the so-called principle of one veto. In the first case, the local cadre prepare a set of tasks and goals for a given year, which are planned to be implemented and achieved in the next year. The relevant upper-level authorities (in this case counties) accept the set goals and at the end of the year make an assessment of the degree of their achievement. The evaluation system is where the higher-level unit evaluates the lower-level unit. For example, the Laixi commune evaluation program measured 19 areas in 2008. Another evaluation system is based on the evaluation of the local cadre, which involves examining the achievements of individual management figures and other top officials in the township at the lower level of the village administration. The evaluation relates to the extent to which a cadre member acts in accordance with the policy of the upper level of government, is efficient, is actively solving problems, and is refraining from corruption. The third cadre evaluation system focuses on the so-called one veto principle – these are goals that must be achieved. If one of these goals is not achieved, all other local leadership achievements are void. Therefore, the management of the township cannot apply for promotion to upper-level positions. In this case, the objectives of the "veto" are set by the upper-level authorities (for townships, these are counties). Targets can therefore cover various issues such as environmental

64 Maria Edin, *State Capacity and Local Agent Control in China: CCP Cadre Management from a Township Perspective,* "China Quarterly" 2003, vol. 173, pp. 35–52.

protection, social sustainability and birth planning, no social unrest or petitions to higher administrations, and improvement of infrastructure in rural areas[65].

2.6. Multilevel governance of regional policy and interactions between central and subnational governments

The analysis of the prerogatives of individual units of the territorial division of the PRC allows the identification of only a part of the complicated system of dependencies, which is reflected in the tasks implemented under regional policy. From this point of view, it is important to identify interactions between the center, regions, intermediate structures, and local government. The main feature of the Chinese civil service[66] is its hierarchy; therefore, it is reasonable to specify that the relationship of individual units resembles the relationship of the principal to the agent. As already indicated, the supreme governments delegate tasks to the lower-level administration. The relationship between the center and the local authority goes beyond the simple scheme of delegating tasks to a lower level of administrative management. The principal – agent relationship means a truncated delegation of certain functions of the central authority in the form of appropriate powers (administrative, fiscal, personal), responsibilities and resources[67]. The relationship between the central and subnational government is the main element in the deepening of the reform of the administrative system. At present, there are still numerous problems in the division of power between governments at all levels, such as duplication of functions, improper segregation of tiers of power, mismatch between financial resources and prerogatives, insufficient normative empowerment, controversy over decentralization and centralization[68]. Local authorities have the task of implementing policies formulated at the level of superior authorities and in accordance with their guidelines, but at the same time, referring to local conditions.

The most striking example of China's modernization over the years is its development policy, including stimulating economic growth[69]. Therefore, at-

65 Thomas Heberer, René Trappel, *Evaluation Processes…*, pp. 1050–1064.

66 Derk Bodde, Clarence Morris, *Law in Imperial China: Exemplified by 190 Ch'ing Dynasty Cases*, Cambridge, 1973, pp. 122–231.

67 *2019 Report of the World Observatory on Subnational Government Finance and Investment – Key Findings*, OECD/UCLG, 2019, p. 19.

68 Ronghua Shen, Sheng Cao, *Modernization of Government Governance in China. The Great Transformation of China (China's Economic Transformation, Innovation and Development)*, Singapore 2020, pp. 101–146.

69 The concept of modernization in relation to China has a multidimensional character; it is also often used in the sociological dimension as a social change accompanied by various con-

tention should also be paid to local cadres. Their task is to solve local problems and ensure social stability. Therefore, categorizing them solely as agents of the regional or local authorities is a simplification. The aforementioned implementation of tasks concerned with promoting economic growth indicates that subnational authorities may also act as the principal. It is true that they act as agents from the point of view of the center, but at the local level they already act as superiors. It should be noted that the observed trend towards increasing the role of decentralization elements in the Chinese political or economic system is not the result of deep reflection on the improvement of the process of shaping public policies at the local level, but the country's transition to an economy based more on market mechanisms. Increasing the importance of the market in the Chinese modernization process has drawn attention to the fact that one of the most important stakeholders in this regard is subnational governments.

The shaping of regional policy is a derivative of the relationship between the central government and various levels of subnational authorities. In this context, it is necessary to consider the nature of these relations, which can be described as asymmetric decentralization. With respect to China, this concept should be treated in two ways. There are certain areas in which it is possible to identify solutions that determine the transfer of competences to a lower level. However, there are areas where this process does not take place. Thus, we are dealing with the presence of decentralization elements in the economic dimension, such as fiscal or partially administrative decentralization, but at the same time with the maintenance of control mechanisms in the political dimension, mainly through the Communist Party of China. The second dimension of asymmetric decentralization is related to the diversification of competences, e.g., of provinces, in the political, administrative, and fiscal areas. In other words: units representing the same administrative level (e.g., provinces) have different legal and organizational statuses. Examples include autonomous regions (Tibet, Inner Mongolia), separate cities (Beijing, Shanghai), and special administrative regions (Hong Kong, Macau). In light of the above, China only partially reflects the global tendency to decentralize public affairs management. It should be noted that decentralization is not linear, as there are reforms that aim towards (re)centralization, mainly because of the unexpected effects of decentralization. In practice, we never deal with complete centralization or decentralization in a pure form, but rather with a mixture of both. Therefore, it is about rational (optimal) proportions between what the center should be and what lower-level units should deal with and be responsible for. This, in turn, is a derivative of organizational experiences and historical traditions.

---

sequences. See Francis Soo, *China and Modernization: Past and Present. A Discussion*, "Studies in Soviet Thought" 1989, vol. 38, no. 1, pp. 3–5.

As part of global tendencies, power, responsibility, and resources have been decentralized in many countries. Few governments have retained all their powers at the central level since the 1970s. Although China is perceived as a highly centralized country, many authors[70] attribute China's economic success to a transformation, the core of which was local actors driving the official or informal use of decentralized resources in pursuit of regional interests and the promotion of economic development. China thus reflects global trends, only to a certain extent being an example of the nonlinearity of the process we are talking about here. The changes introduced in this area are rather step-by-step, which, depending on the effects, can be corrected, e. g., by increasing the role of the center in exercising local authority or reducing it.

The key to understanding the relationships of local governments with central government is the top-down responsibility behind asymmetric decentralization. The personnel appointment system involving local officials offers local cadres many political and material incentives to obey the authority of central government. In the context of political centralization in the CPC, the results-based nomination system is capable of motivating politically unelected local officials. As already noted, career advancement is determined by development achievements: The greater the economic growth, the greater the promotion opportunities for local leaders. Hence, one of the most important activities of local officials seeking career advancement is to promote local development, so much so that it is often seen as more important than obeying central policies or regulations. Political compliance, which was the only important criterion for clerical promotion before the reform, was replaced by economic performance and other competency-related indicators. This mechanism shapes the relationship between a local cadres and political incentives for local officials to achieve economic goals. At the same time, it should be emphasized that the responsibility for growth clearly differs from the situation we deal with in many liberal democracies, where local cadres rely on elections (for example, in the US or Germany). Meanwhile, the experiences of these countries show[71] that the incentives to win an election or reelection stimulated and inspired many politicians to promote local social and

70 Fulong Wu, *The Global and Local Dimensions of Place-Making: Remaking Shanghai as a World City,* "Urban Studies" 2000, vol. 37, no. 8, pp. 1359–1377; Henry Waichung Yeung, *Local Politics and Foreign Ventures in China's Transitional Economy: The Political Economy of Singaporean Investments in China,* "Political Geography" 2000, vol. 19, no. 7, pp. 809–840; Roger Gordon, Wei Li, *Chinese Enterprise Behavior under the Reform,* "American Economic Review" 1991, vol. 81, no. 2, pp. 202–206; Doug Guthrie, *Between markets and politics: Organizational Responses to Reform in China,* "American Journal of Sociology" 1997, vol. 102, pp. 1258–1304.

71 Alan Altshuler, *Bureaucratic Innovation, Democratic Accountability, and Political Incentives,* [in:] Alan Altshuler, Robert Behn (eds.), *Innovation in American Government,* Washington 1997, pp. 38–55.

economic development, as a result of the expectations of local residents and entire communities.

In the case of Chinese local administrative personnel, this is a top-down accountability system (Figure 7). The effectiveness of this kind of influence of the center on local authorities can be seen, for example, in a nature conservation survey conducted among residents and the local cadre in Shanxi province, one of the most polluted regions in China. In a survey conducted in 2006, 70% of citizens when asked whether the environment should be sacrificed for the sake of economic development answered "no", while as many as 91% of employees answered "yes". The cadres expressed more conflicting motivations than the citizens, as officials had to be in line with the political priorities set by the central government. Meanwhile, the central policy in the field of environmental protection[72] has changed, but nevertheless it shows very well the influence of the center on local administrative staff. Another aspect is the change in the behavior of local administrative staff in the event of a revision of the clerical appraisal indicators by higher-level authorities. An example is the focus on development in the Zhangjiang High Technology Zone in Pudong (Shanghai), where the change concerned a policy adjustment from attracting foreign investment to creating research and development institutions. This happened after their criteria had been changed by the central government from GDP growth to the number of prestigious R&D laboratories, world-famous universities, or engineering colleges that could be located there. The same was true for the preservation of traditional waterways and landscapes in Zhouzhuang (a canal village near Shanghai), which was maintained after changing the clerical evaluation indicators to increase the emphasis on environmental protection and promotion of the tourism industry[73].

The relations of the central government with local governments are an example of the alternating occurrence of phenomena related to centralization and decentralization. As part of political centralization, one should mention the control of political and administrative staff by the CPC. One of the determinants of this activity is the term of office or the definition of procedures and standards for the selection of personnel. The main goal of the central authorities in these relations is to strive for efficient implementation of public policies at the local

72 Qingzhi Huan, *Regional Supervision Centers for Environmental Protection in China: Functions and Limitations*, "Journal of Current Chinese Affairs" 2011, vol. 40, no. 3, pp. 139–162; Peter Zabielskis, *Environmental Problems in China: Issues and Prospects*, [in:] Zhidong Hao, Sheying Chen (eds.), *Social Issues in China. International Perspectives on Social Policy, Administration, and Practice*, vol. 1, New York 2014, pp. 157–280; Shuzhong Gu, Meie Xie, Xinhua Zhang, *Green Transformation and Development*, Singapore 2019, pp. 1–33, 55–76.

73 Shiuh-Shen Chien, *Economic Freedom and Political Control in Post-Mao China: A Perspective of Upward Accountability and Asymmetric Decentralization*, "Asian Journal of Political Science" 2010, vol. 18, no. 1, pp. 76–77.

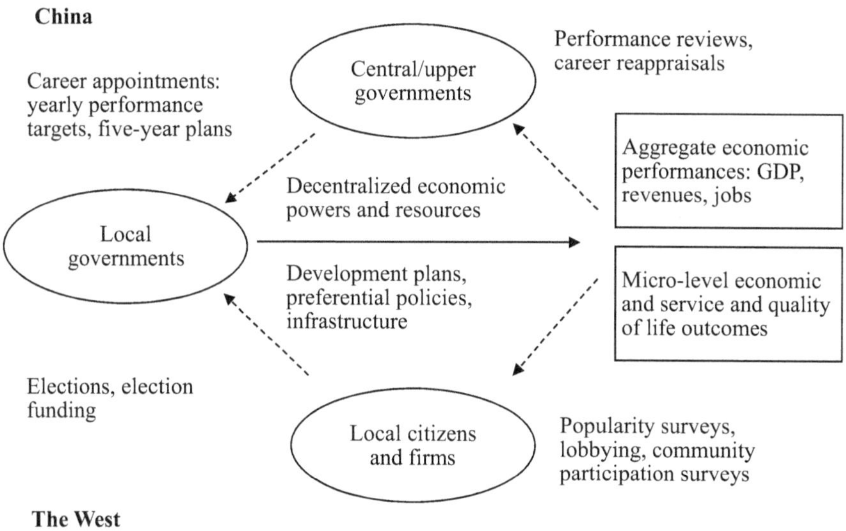

Diagram 7. "Top-down" and "bottom-up" accountability of local leaders in China and the West. Source: study own based on: Shiuh-Shen Chien, *Local Responses to Globalization in China – A Territorial Restructuring Process Perspective*, "Pacific Economic Review" 2008, vol. 13, no. 4, pp. 492–516.

level. As an example of decentralization, the progressing fiscal decentralization starts from the Deng rule Xiaoping[74], which boiled down to limiting the government's influence on interfering with local development. It should be noted that within the framework of limited decentralization, we can talk about cascading administrative relations. This has contributed to an increase in the incentive for local authorities to develop in the coastal regions of China.

Local government relations reforms focus mainly on adjusting vertical intergovernmental relations below the provincial level and redistributing bottom-up powers and responsibilities to better match the needs of economic and social development. Local government, as the dominant force in local governance in the present system, is largely constrained by vertical relationships regarding governance goals, development strategies, and modus operandi. Vertical relations can be divided into central – local, province – county, and county – township.

Relations between the central government and local governments cover aspects such as human resources and personnel management, tax matters and administration. These are referred to as "political centralization" and "administrative decentralization". It also creates space for innovation through the

74 Yu Jianxing, Lin Li, Yongdong Shen, *Rediscovering Intergovernmental Relations at the Local Level: The Devolution to Township Governments in Zhejiang Province*, "China Review" 2016, vol. 16, no. 2, pp. 1–26.

"authoritarian resistance" of local authorities to central reform. The features of political centralization are reflected in the management of central and local cadres[75]. The central government strengthens its absolute control over the core political and administrative cadres of higher-level authorities by leaving them under the supervision of the CPC, relocating positions and fixing terms, as well as establishing procedures and standards for the selection and appointment of cadres to ensure the smooth implementation of central policies and enforce obedience to local authorities. The central government – local government relations in the fiscal dimension have been characterized by a certain level of decentralization since the reform and the opening of the PRC to the world. It should be noted that the decentralized fiscal system, on the one hand, limits the interference of central authorities in the development of the local economy and society, and, on the other, it encourages local governments to develop local economies, with all the consequences. Decentralization also exists in administrative relations in the dimension of central government – local government. The cascade of administrative decentralization following the reform and opening up of the country has become a key method of adjusting the vertical relations between the center and local governments. Meanwhile, the path of development of developed coastal regions and the decentralization of economic and social power are an effective stimulus to motivate local governments to exercise power in the social and economic dimensions, thus driving regional economic growth that stimulates development. Moreover, relations at the central and local levels are characterized by great flexibility in supporting innovation by local authorities and create space and impetus for the transformation and reform of local authorities[76].

The relationships between the various levels of local government are also part of the vertical relationship between the levels of government in China, namely the relationship between provinces and counties, and counties and municipalities. Reforms of local government relations mainly focus on aligning vertical relations below the provincial level and on a bottom-up sharing of competences and responsibilities to better align with the needs of economic and social development. Yu Jianxing, Lin Li, and Yongdong Shen claim that relations between provinces should be adjusted because the dynamically developing economy of the district is hampered by the lack of spatial planning, as well as the unsatisfactory way of building infrastructure and troublesome procedures of obtaining approval of the supreme authorities for foreign investments. As a consequence, local authorities miss out on many opportunities to stimulate eco-

75 Andrew Mertha, *China's 'Soft' Centralization: Shifting Tiao / Kuai Authority Relations*, "The China Quarterly" 2005, vol. 184, pp. 791–810.
76 Jianxing Yu, *Local Governance in China-Past, Present and Future…*, pp. 12–13.

nomic growth[77]. Therefore, we are dealing with typical problems resulting from the excessive centralization of power, in which decisions are made at a distance from citizens, which makes it difficult to optimize the decisions taken.

There is some experience of decentralization in China that shows that this course of action is worth considering. The actions of the Zhejiang provincial government are a good example – it initiated a reform and transferred certain powers to the county level, and they took proactive measures to increase administrative efficiency. Interestingly, these activities did not involve decentralization of fiscal or personnel, which is already practiced in China[78], but administrative decentralization. The experiment was concerned with the gradual delegation of social and economic powers to local authorities. Such activities not only expanded local autonomy in socio-economic management, but also contributed to the intensification of economic growth in the area[79].

The assessment of the relationship between the central and regional governments is very difficult due to the diversity of the provinces themselves. Undoubtedly, Chinese regionalism weakens the influence of the central government, which reduces its control over numerous public policies, including the regional policy of lower-level governments. There are several areas where there are tensions between central government and local administrative structures. These include taxes, differences in the concept of development, and environmental policy. The Center has repeatedly accused local governments, especially townships, of embezzling taxes. The provincial governments have the ambition to pursue their own development policy by taking protectionist measures to defend their own market. Doubts from the center's perspective are also raised by the data transferred from the local level to the central level on public statistics, especially economic growth[80]. The credibility of Chinese official statistics is a separate topic; it should only be noted that there are opinions on overestimating and underestimating data on economic growth, as is the case with statistics on the labor market[81] and environmental protection[82].

77 Jianxing Yu, Lin Li, Yongdong Shen, *Rediscovering Intergovernmental Relations at the Local Level: The Devolution to Township Governments in Zhejiang Province,* "China Review" 2016, vol. 16, no. 2, pp. 1–26.

78 Hongbin Li, Li-An Zhou, *Political Turnover and Economic Performance…*, pp. 1743–1762.

79 Jianxing Yu, Xiang Gao, *Redefining Decentralization: Devolution of Administrative Authority to County Governments in Zhejiang Province,* "Australian Journal of Public Administration" 2013, vol. 72, no. 3, pp. 239–250.

80 Thomas Heberer, *Pomiędzy kryzysem a szansą: nowe społeczne wyzwania ze szczególnym uwzględnieniem wiejskich Chin* [in:] Karin Tomala (ed.), *Chiny, Przemiany państwa i społeczeństwa w okresie reform 1978–2000,* Warszawa 2003, p. 81.

81 John Knight, Shi Li, *Unemployment duration and earnings of re-employed workers in urban China,* "China Economic Review" 2006, vol. 17, no. 2, pp. 103–119; Carsten A. Holz, *The quality of China's GDP statistics,* "China Economic Review" 2014, vol. 30, pp. 309–338; Nomaan Majid, *The Great Employment Transformation in China,* International Labor Organ-

2.7. Financial aspects as an element of shaping regional policy at the local level

International experience shows that the decentralization of development activities has a positive impact on the provision of high-quality public services, including the results of regional policy. The negative aspects of decentralization should not be overlooked either. From the point of view of economic efficiency, the decentralization of power favors the development of competition between local governments and the improvement of the efficiency of public spending. However, from the point of view of social justice[83] excessive decentralization of power can lead to unbalanced economic growth between different regions, resulting in an imbalance in the level of public spending between local structures. Apart from the political dimension of decentralization, i.e., the transfer of certain decisions to a lower level of government, the financial subjectivity of local administrative units is of great importance here. This subjectivity can be identified as a degree of financial independence from the arbitrary decisions of the central government. In the relations between the center and local authorities, we are talking about the extent to which the central government may delegate power in the field of shaping finances to territorial structures and to what extent subnational governments can use revenues and shape expenses on their own. From the financial perspective, subjectivity can be reduced to four elements[84]: (1) resource allocation, (2) income distribution, (3) stabilization, (4) economic development. Each of these aspects is correlated with tasks related to regional policy. Furthermore, without exception, all the elements determine political stability also at the local level, which is one of the main functions of the Chinese political system. In the light of the above, ill-considered decentralization (including financial decentralization) may increase chaos, and centralization may cause stagnation (including in the economic dimension).

---

ization, 2015, p. 15, https://www.ilo.org/wcmsp5/groups/public/-edemp/documents/publication/wcms_423613.pdf (access: 11/04/2022).

82 Daniele Brombal, *Accuracy of Environmental Monitoring in China: Exploring the Influence of Institutional, Political and Ideological Factors*, "Sustainability" 2017, no. 9, pp. 1–18; Liu Qin, *Clear as Mud: How Poor Data is Thwarting China's Water Clean-Up*, "China Dialogue", May 18, 2106, https://www.chinadialogue.net/article/show/single/en/8922-Clear-as-mud-how-poor-data-is-thwarting-China-s-water-clean-up (access: 11/04/2022); Keith Bradsher, *China Asks Other Nations Not to Release Its Air Data*, "New York Times", June 5, 2012, https://www.nytimes.com/2012/06/06/world/asia/china-asks-embassies-to-stop-measuring-air-pollution.html?_r=0 (access: 11/04/2022).

83 Anna Szklarska, *Sprawiedliwość w czasach kryzysu*, Kraków 2015, pp. 29–35.

84 Feizhou Zhou, Mingzhi Tan, *Relationship between the Central Government and Local Governments of Contemporary China*, Singapore 2017, pp. 2, 6.

Naturally, China is difficult to compare with Western economies, e.g., countries with a federal administrative structure, where the constituent units of the state have greater freedom and thus also have greater financial resources. In 2016, the expenditure of subnational governments in federal states represented 46.9% of public expenditure and 16.8% of GDP. Meanwhile, in unitary countries, it was only 19.4% of public expenditure and 6.9% of GDP, which is well below the average of 24.1% of public expenditure and 8.6% of GDP among 106 countries with available data[85]. It should be noted that the share of local government in total public expenditure in the world depends on the level of development of a given country. In richer countries, a tendency can be observed to increase the expenditure of subnational authorities, while in poorer countries, the share of such authorities in public expenditure is relatively lower. Regardless of this, the tasks that have been set before China's subnational governments are very broad.

Table 11. Share of local governments in total public expenditure in the PRC (%)

Year	The level of expenses
1952	25.9
1962	38.4
1972	43.8
1978	52.6
1988	66.1
1998	68.5
2000	65.3
2004	74.1

Source: Ravi Kanbur, Xiaobo Zhang, *50 Years of Regional Inequality in China: A Journey Through Central Planning, Reform, and Openness*, "Review of Development Economics" 2005, vol. 9, no. 1, pp. 87–106.

Although China has a unitary organizational structure and belongs to middle income countries, the share of subnational governments in total expenditure is very high. The share of local governments in total public sector expenditure shows the increasing importance of this level of administration and is a good illustration of the size of the country. This is especially true for the economic growth process. Caring for development in centralized China is very often local. Therefore, local governments have considerable experience in supporting development investments, attracting capital, and creating jobs on this basis. The growing importance of subnational governments (regional, intermediate, local)

85 *2019 Report of the World Observatory on Subnational Government Finance and Investment...*, p. 10.

confirms that the expenditure of this sector in relation to GDP is at a fairly high level on an international scale. The spending of the Chinese subnational governments accounts for around 21.6% of GDP, while in Japan it is 15.5% of GDP and in Korea it is 13.9% of GDP (Graph 4).

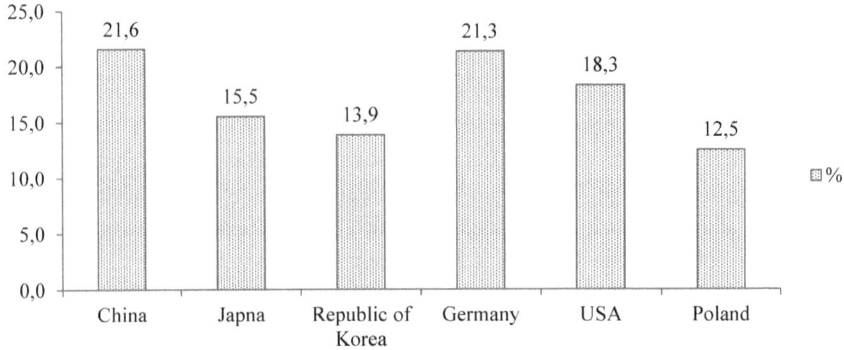

Graph 4. Expenditure of subnational authorities (regional, intermediate, local) as a percentage of GDP in 2017. Source: own study based on: *SNG expenditure by type, % of GDP*, World Observatory on Subnational Government Finance and Investment, https://www1.compareyourcountry.org/subnational-government-finance-and-investment/en/1/all/default (access: 09/04/2022).

Compared to other countries, also highly developed, it should be noted that although the Chinese subnational governments' spending constitutes a significant part of GDP, a significant amount comes from the central level. The financial independence of local authorities shows considerable limitations. This is because the expenditure of this level of administration is largely dependent on transfer payments from the central budget. In 2014, transfer payments represented 40.47% of their income. At the same time, the huge development leap that occurred in China thanks to the creation of state intervention and entrepreneurialism, including huge investments, mainly (but not only) in infrastructure, led to an increase in public debt – in 2014 it amounted to 7.86% of local expenditure[86]. A consequence is the large variation in the share of local authorities (in this case, municipalities) in public revenues and expenses.

86 Naoyuki Yoshino, Peter J. Morgan, *Central and Local Government Relations in Asia, Achieving Fiscal Sustainability*, Cheltenham-Northampton 2017, p. 250.

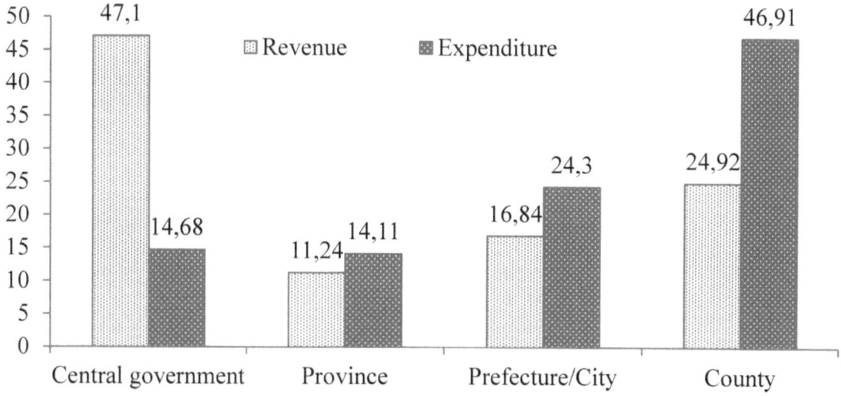

Graph 5. The difference between revenues and expenditure, total in 2016 – depending on the level of the administrative unit (%).[87] Source: own study based on: *OECD Economic Surveys: China 2019*, OECD Publishing, Paris 2019, https://doi.org/10.1787/eco_surveys-chn-2019-en (access: 11/04/2022).

When analyzing the differences between income and expenditure at the administrative level, it should be noted that counties are responsible for the largest part of expenditure. It is justified because of all levels of government taken into account in Graph 5, counties with townships constitute the administrations that provide direct services to citizens. It is worth noting that counties remain in a particularly unfavorable situation when it comes to income, as the share of these units in public income is only 24.92%, and in expenditure, as much as 46.91%. Naturally, the incomes at the central government's disposal are not consumed only by the central government, but the scale of the disproportions is illustrated by the still relatively high level of centralization of public finances in China. It should be clearly noted that as the level of subnational government decreases, the difference between the share of income and expenditure grows. When comparing the situation of the provinces with counties or prefectures, where the difference between expenditure and revenues reaches 3–8%, it should be stated that they maintain the most balanced situation of public finances among all levels of administration. Provinces are becoming a kind of intermediary in shaping public expenditure, including within the framework of regional policy.

The sources of income in the example of counties very well illustrate the level of emancipation of local authorities. Only 38.5% of their income is constituted by their own taxes, i. e., income relatively independent of the central government, which allows them to carry out their tasks. Among other subnational authorities, private companies have the highest share in public taxes. The tax system, like the administrative one, is hierarchical, and local authorities do not have the power to

87 Data refer to general budget accounts and exclude transfers.

Graph 6. Financial transfers as sources of income for counties in China in 2016 (billion RMB). Source: own study based on: *OECD Economic Surveys: China 2019*, OECD Publishing, Paris 2019, https://doi.org/10.1787/eco_surveys-chn-2019-en (access: 11/04/2022).

independently establish taxes[88]. Another source may be nontax income, which in 2016 alone amounted to slightly over 12.5% of the counties' budget. Therefore, it accounts for only 51% of the counties' budget; the remaining recharges are mainly funds fully under the control of the central government. We are talking here about taxes on general transfers (25.9%) or only specific transfers (22.9%). Thus, almost half of the local government's budget is made up of resources, the transfer of which is fully dependent on the central government. In this context, it should be noted that the dependence of county government on transfers from the center is still quite high.

The main source of income for counties are nontax revenues and VAT, which account for approximately 25% and 21% of the budget, respectively. Local taxes, such as land tax, city building tax, contract taxes, and property tax, provide around 23% of budget revenues. It should be noted, prefectures and counties receive income from the sale of land use rights over a period of 30 to 70 years. Under the Chinese constitution, urban land is owned by the state, and rural land is jointly owned by rural communities. The law provides subnational governments at all levels with powers to control and regulate land use, the conversion of rural to urban areas, and the sale of land rights to developers, within the limits established by the national agricultural land protection policy. Land is often used as collateral in commercial banks, and the net proceeds from the sale of the land must be earmarked for investment. In some provinces and municipalities, rev-

88 *2019 Edition of the World Observatory of Subnational Finance and Investment, Country Profiles…*, p. 173.

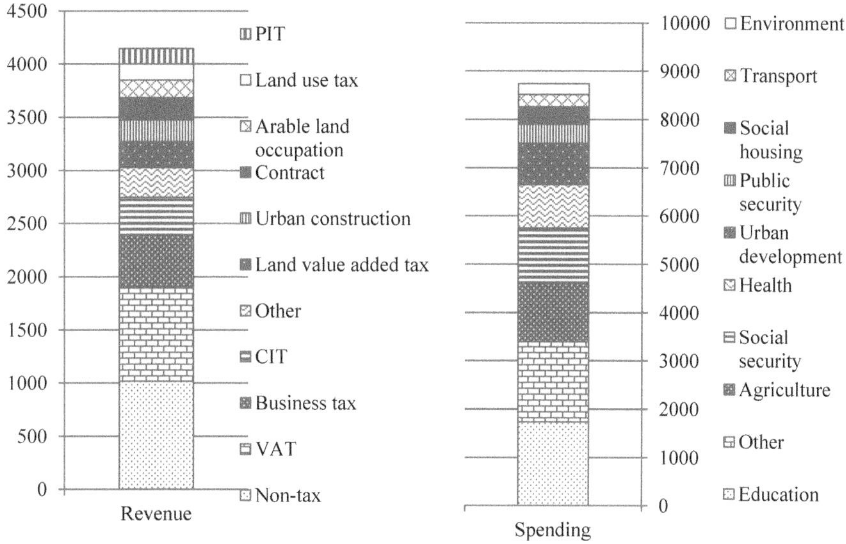

Graph 7. Income and expenditure structure of counties in China in 2016 (billion RNB). Source: own study based on: *OECD Economic Surveys: China 2019*, OECD Publishing, Paris 2019, https://doi.org/10.1787/eco_surveys-chn-2019-en (access: 11/04/2022).

enues from the sale of land rights accounted for up to 40% of total revenues in 2014 (e.g., Chongqing, Anhui, or Zhejiang). However, changes in land sales have slowed the flow of local government revenues in recent years. Other local nontax revenues include fees, charges, penalties, and profits from local state-owned enterprises[89].

Most funds are allocated to education, which accounts for 20% of the budget. It is understandable as counties constitute the level of administration responsible for providing local services, and education is one of the key services. The specificity mentioned above reflects trends in local government spending almost all over the world; in China 21% of the budget is spent on education, especially primary and secondary[90]. Agriculture (14%), social security (14%) and health (10%) also play an important role. The high level of expenditure on agriculture can be explained by the fact that many farmers in their area administer the areas used for agricultural crop or livestock production. However, the areas dependent on agriculture are losing importance, hence the expenditure of counties on ag-

89 Ibid, p. 175.
90 The value applies to 2017; if you add expenditure on higher education (10%), then education as a category in local budgets will reach approximately 31%, far ahead of the second largest position, namely social security (22%). Source: *State and Local Expenditures,* Urban Institute, https://www.urban.org/policy-centers/cross-center-initiatives/state-and-local-finance-initiative/state-and-local-backgrounders (access: 09/11/2021).

riculture is decreasing. Relatively little is allocated to activities related to environmental protection (3%), which can be treated as not paying attention to ecology.

Table 12. Disproportions in per capita income and expenditure at the provincial level by counties in 2016 (in RMB)

Province	Per capita income	Expenditure per capita	GDP per capita	Multiple (expenses / income)
Chongqing	509	2 041	58 502	4.0
Gansu	1 259	7 524	27 643	6.0
Heilongjiang	1 407	5,588	40 432	4.0
Kuangsi	1 516	5 755	38 027	3.8
Jilin	1 752	6 554	53 868	3.7
Shanxi	1 754	5 612	116 562	3.2
Henan	1 830	4 835	42 575	2.6
Tibet	1 921	21 836	35 184	11.4
Qinghai	1,956	13 401	43 531	6.9
Yunnan	1977	7111	31 093	3.6
Hunan	1979	6 233	46 382	3.1
Shaanxi	1 982	6 661	51 015	3.4
Ningxia	2 177	9 254	47 194	4.3
Anhui	2 273	5,300	39 561	2.3
Sichuan	2 288	6 681	35 532	2.9
Hainan	2 293	7 221	44 347	3.1
Hebei	2 460	5 594	43 062	2.3
Guizhou	2 706	8 160	33 246	3.0
Guangdong	3 199	6 395	74 016	2.0
Xinjiang	3 321	10 236	40 564	3.1
Liaoning	3 421	5 309	50 791	1.6
Jiangxi	3 481	7 190	40,400	2.1
Hubei	3,514	6 876	55 665	2.0
Fujian	3 677	6 984	74 707	1.9
Shantung	4 717	5 822	68 733	1.2
Inner Mongolia	5 139	11 120	72 064	2.2
Zhejiang	7 473	9 289	84 916	1.2
Jiangsu	7 628	8 605	96 887	1.1
mean	**1 843**	**7 482**	**68 495**	**4.1**

Table 12 *(Continued)*

Province	Per capita income	Expenditure per capita	GDP per capita	Multiple (expenses / income)
median	2 281	6 779	45 365	3.0

Source: own study based on: *OECD Economic Surveys: China 2019*, OECD Publishing, Paris 2019, https://doi.org/10.1787/eco_surveys-chn-2019-en (access: 11.04.2022); National Bureau of Statistics of China, 2022.

One of the conditions for the provision of public services at a similar level, regardless of the place of residence or birth of citizens, is the maintenance of both income and expenditure per person at the same level. For example, maintaining similar expenditures per person in the field of education, social security or health care allows the provision of these services at a similar level, regardless of whether we are talking about residents of counties located in Tibet or in the Tianjin province. The data show far-reaching disproportions (table 13). This is because the highest per capita income in Jiangsu province (7,628 RMB) is almost fifteen times higher than in the lowest-income province, Chongqing (509 RMB). Similarly, in the case of expenditure, in Tibet (21,836 RMB), it is 11 times that of the Chongqing province (2,041 RMB). Moreover, recent years indicate that the disproportions in both expenditure and revenues between individual producers have tended to increase. It should be noted that the comparison of expenditure and income between individual counties also has some limitations, resulting from differences in prices and labor costs between provinces. The above indicates, however, that despite the analogous financing of individual subnational units (especially counties), it is difficult to talk about the provision of public services of a similar quality at the county level.

There is also a significant difference between the income and expenditure of counties within individual provinces. Nationally, the median income by province in 2016 was 2,843 RMB, and spending was 7,614 RMB; thus, the amount of expenditure was more than two and a half times that of income. Counties, as entities implementing central policies, are in a difficult situation, and the experience of a budget deficit is very common. It may also prove that the funds allocated for the implementation of central policies or other commissioned tasks are insufficient in relation to the expectations of both local government and citizens. Interestingly, significant differences (i.e., more than four times) between expenditure and income most often concern counties located in less developed provinces, e.g., Gansu (GDP *per capita* 27,643 RMB), Qinghai (43,531 RMB), Ningxia (47,194 RMB), i.e., those in which the GDP *per capita index* is lower than the national average (68,495 RMB).

Chapter 3.
Designing the regional development of the People's Republic of China: The challenges of policy formulation and objectives

3.1. Political evolution and Chinese development challenges

The evolution of regional policy is a derivative of the shaping of the PRC's economic policy; it is also an element of the wider economic transformation of the country. Therefore, regional policy is undergoing further changes following the change in the socioeconomic development model. As China develops, it can afford a more sophisticated regional policy (e.g., supporting less developed provinces and human capital in underdeveloped areas, supporting smart city policy). It should be noted that the enhancement of competitiveness and the equalization of development disproportions in the regions are reflected in economic results. Thus, regional policy does not remain merely a complementary public policy to broader economic policy. The results of both these policies, based on the example of China, is beyond doubt.

The shaping of regional policy in the PRC is mainly related to the actions of the central government, which quite effectively controls social processes through a top-down approach. This applies to setting goals, formulating development plans, defining instruments, and ways of achieving goals. This is achieved by the ideological priorities established by the CPC, aimed at focusing attention on the key issues for the Middle Kingdom. Another aspect of setting the goals of regional policy is development planning, although its dimension is different from development planning in democratic states with a free market economy, mainly due to the dominant influence of the state in the economy[1]. As already indicated, the role of the state in the Chinese economy is much greater than, for example, in the free-market economies of western countries. In the PRC, the state not only interferes with market mechanisms, but is also a voluntary organizer of economic

1 Marek Świstak, *O wyższości polityki nad gospodarką i pierwszeństwie mechanizmów rynkowych przed politycznymi. Rola państwa w chińskiej polityce rozwoju regionalnego*, [in:] Hanna Kupś, Maciej Szatkowski, Michał Dahl (ed.), *70 lat Chińskiej Republiki Ludowej w ujęciu interdyscyplinarnym*, Warszawa 2021, pp. 69–82.

space in the face of the forces of supply and demand. This is confirmed by the findings of the literature on the subject, which indicate the role of institutions that have determined the country's development path[2]. This implies much greater expectations towards public institutions in terms of possible catching up in development and building competitiveness in the regional system.

When looking for an answer to the question about the potential elements determining the evolution of regional policy, attention should be paid to the significance of state policy, as well as market mechanisms, analyzed above, as Chinese decision-makers have never come up with a target vision of both regional policy and the socioeconomic model. Even in the period when the planned economy was the most dominant, no target model of regional policy was defined. To a large extent, its shape resulted from the calculation of challenges and possible remedial measures to be applied to overcome them. Among many elements, two seem to be of key importance, that is, the conscious policy of the authorities, often manifested in the formulation of development plans, and market mechanisms operating through more or less unfettered entrepreneurship[3]. In this context, the arguments[4] in favor of the marginalization of planning in the period from the late 1980s and 1990s result from a deliberate decision to admit market mechanisms to the Chinese economy, and thus an element of state policy.

This "growing out of the plan" occurred with the simultaneous stagnation of the planned economy and the emergence of a market dominated economy. There was then an atrophy of some of the features of old-style socialist planning[5], such as the countless mandatory goals to be achieved, the direct allocation of resources by the state, and state control of investment, credit, prices, and foreign trade. During this period, the central government actually reduced its dominant role, handed many powers over economic administration to local authorities, and strengthened the autonomy of private enterprises. However, China's long-term economic planning has retained its continuity, regardless of the fact that the Five-Year Plans from 2 to 5 had no real significance for the government's economic policy at that time. The continuation of the official numbering of the Five-Year Plans shows that they still remain an important instrument of economic policy. It is not without significance that the Five-Year Plans involve a wide range of

2 John Brohman, *Postwar Development in the Asian NICs: Does the Neoliberal Model Fit Reality*, "Economic Geography" 1996, vol. 72, no. 2, pp. 107–130.

3 Bogdan Góralczyk, *Wielki renesans. Chińska transformacja i jej konsekwencje*, Warszawa 2018, pp. 227–248.

4 Barry Naughton, *Growing Out of the Plan: Chinese Economic Reform, 1978–1993*, Cambridge 1995, pp. 309–326; *idem*, *The Chinese Economy: Transitions and Growth*, London 2007, pp. 3–14.

5 Sebastian Heilmann, Oliver Melton, *The Reinvention of Development Planning in China, 1993–2012*, "Modern China" 2013, vol. 39, p. 582.

initiatives, not only in the field of regional policy, such as, for example, supporting entrepreneurship, promoting industrial development, environmental protection, education, and social security.

The key issue in the Chinese model is also the effectiveness of the top-down operation of the hierarchical bureaucracy, which encounters significant problems in the implementation of regional policy. While Chinese bureaucratic structures have mastered activities related to supporting economic growth, activities related to the territorial distribution of resources and supporting competitiveness in underdeveloped areas remain a challenge. Chenggang Xu[6]points out that the fundamental difficulty is the unsolvable problem of motivating officials who have to perform many different tasks, which is hindered by the hierarchical structure of the Chinese administration. In the opinion of the author, the hierarchical system does not work well in administration or research and development institutions, as well as in the judicial system. The above may be an indirect explanation of problems with law enforcement, e.g., in environmental protection. The problem is the motivation to make decisions without the prior approval of the higher administration, which generates many distortions and delays the decision-making process.

Since 1949, China's policy of regional development has evolved many times, which has been accompanied by a shift from a centrally planned economy towards saturation of the socioeconomic system with elements of a free market economy. Over time, not only the system of priorities and the territorial orientation of the policy changed, but also the instruments used. Evolution ran from the classic and ineffective redistribution policy through supporting rapid development (usually unsustainable) to coordinated development. We are talking here, at least in assumption, about a policy that supports redistribution but does not give up on quickly catching up in the development of individual regions. The Chinese experience can be presented as the accumulation of results during successive waves of centralization and decentralization, aimed at more effectively achieving the goals set by the central government. Decentralization, which in addition to the positive effects in the form of greater ability to respond to global and national economic challenges, also brought negative consequences from the point of view of the central authorities. It has contributed to local protectionism, and internal competition at both local and regional levels. From the point of view of a centralized state, this may pose a risk to the country's economic and political future. On the one hand, it stimulates significant regional imbalances, and on the

6 Chenggang Xu, *The Pitfalls of a Centralized Bureaucracy,* "Acta Oeconomica" 2019, vol. 69, no. 1, pp. 1–16.

other hand, it causes political tensions, which may eventually be centrifugal and fail to gain the political approval of the Chinese Communist Party[7].

One of the important instruments for implementing regional policy in China is multiannual planning. It should be noted that the strategic planning system has evolved, as has the country's economic system. In strategic planning in China – apart from a very strong centralization of economic decisions, which manifested itself in the doctrinal hierarchy of plans and the vertical arrangement of connections between various power factors and the prescriptive manner of passing decisions – elements of decentralization appeared. This involved delegating certain powers concerning economic administration to local authorities, taking into account their greater autonomy over enterprises[8]. It was accompanied by a gradually increasing attachment of the driving force of the allocation of production factors to market forces. The current strategic and development plans do not resemble those from the beginning of the PRC, although they still refer to them ideologically.

The evolution of the Five-Year Plans ran from the model of a centrally planned economy to the increasing importance of market mechanisms in the economy. When analyzing the evolution of regional policy, especially regional planning, it should be noted that before China opened up to the world in the late 1970s, the policy discussed here was primarily intended to support economic construction. We are talking about projects related to the country's industrialization – at this stage, attention was focused on the development of large-scale industries. The construction of industrial bases that required comprehensive regional distribution and planning was prioritized and aimed at shaping the internal structure of industrial regional production teams and organizing regional organizations. Consequently, holistic industrial planning of regional construction became the main tenet of regional planning in China during the period of the central planned economy. For example, in the three years leading up to the Second Five-Year Plan, while large-scale infrastructure construction was taking place throughout the country, regional planning was extended to more regions to meet the needs of the situation. Significant internal and external changes in the PRC's regional development environment from the 1990s onwards influenced the transformation of spatial management.

There are three dimensions to this transformation[9]. First, market mechanisms started to be more widely considered as part of the transformation of territorial

7 Wang Shaoguang, Hu Angang, *The Political Economy of Uneven Development: The Case of China*, London- New York, pp. 41–69, 199–216.

8 Sebastian Heilmann, Oliver Melton, *The Reinvention of Development Planning in China…*, p. 582.

9 Wang Qingyun, Shen Bing, Sun Xuegong, Ouyang Hui, Ding Ding, Yu Xiaoli, Gao Shiji, Liu Feng, Liu Weidong, Huang Kun, *EU-China Cooperative Research Program on Regional Policy*,

1953–1957	First FP	Imitation of the Soviet industrial development strategy
1958–1962	Second FP	Policy of the so-called Great Leap Forward
1963–1965	Period of Readjustment	Third Front Construction
1966–1970	Third FP	Cultural Revolution
1971–1975	Fourth FP	Preference for inland regions
1976–1980	Fifth FP	The beginning of reforms, including the so-called four modernizations
1981–1985	Sixth FP	Preparing to open up to the world
1986–1990	Seventh FP	Tiananmen incident in 1989
1991–1995	Eighth FP	Introducing a market economy
1996–2000	Ninth FP	Reform of state-owned enterprises
2001–2005	Tenth FP	Greater integration into the world economy (WTO)
2006–2010	Eleventh FP	Optimization and modernization of the industrial structure, improvement of resource use
2011–2015	Twelfth FP	Environmental protection, social development, industrial restructuring
2016–2020	Thirteenth FP	Use of innovation in development
2021–2025	Fourteenth FP	Innovations, the natural environment, strengthening endogenous development factors

Diagram 8. Evolution of China's regional policy using the example of the Five-Year Plans. Source: Yehua Dennis Wei, *Regional Development in China: States, Globalization and Inequality*, London-New York 2000, p. 194; *The 13th Five-Year Plan for Economic and Social Development of The People's Republic of China (2016–2020)*, announced on December 7, 2016, https://en.ndrc.gov.cn/policyrelease_8233/201612/P020191101482242850325.pdf (access: 11/04/2022); *Five-Year Plans map out China's future development*, https://news.cgtn.com/news/2020-05-15/Five-Year-Plans-map-out-China-s-future-development-QvANs2JxVS/index.html (access: 11/04/2022); John Gittings, *Historia współczesnych Chin. Od Mao do gospodarki rynkowej*, Kraków 2005, pp. 364–368; Scott Morton, Charlton Lewis, *Chiny. Historia i kultura*, Krakow 2007, pp. 332–349.

planning. With the evolution of the market economy, the influence of the market on the allocation of resources became more pronounced and thus its impact on regional planning increased. The operational autonomy of companies increased, capital sources diversified, the planned allocation of production factors gradually transformed into a market-oriented allocation, and most of the planning

2010, pp. 123–124, https://ec.europa.eu/regional_policy/sources/international/pdf/china_study_report_en.pdf (access: 10/04/2022).

related to the region was indicative of these changes. Increasing the importance of the province in regional planning at the expense of the central government required the acquisition of not only planning knowledge but also related skills at the provincial level. Second, physical space, whether regional or urban, was still of interest. Meanwhile, in planning, tasks related to the creation of an environment for development, such as special economic zones, urbanization systems, agglomerations and the integration of rural areas, were of great importance. There is no doubt that the strategy to balance urban and rural development has given new importance to regional planning. Integrating town and countryside has become not only a primary goal of research into regional planning, but also a key goal of government in regulating and controlling regional development. Thirdly, the goals of regional planning have also changed, from simply supporting development towards socially, economically, and environmentally coordinated development. The implementation of these commitments in light of the concept of scientific development promoted in China is undoubtedly a challenge that requires greater effort in the coordination processes in the field of regional development.

3.2. The process of formulating goals: centralized (non)planning

The formulation of development goals takes place through a very extensive planning management system. On the one hand, it results from the scope of the planning in question and, on the other hand, from the multitude of administrative units in the Middle Kingdom. Planning refers not only to the central level, of individual territorial units, but also to areas (sectors) which require appropriate policies or actions to address specific issues. With such an extensive system, dozens of plans, programs, guidelines, and circulars are created. The key factor of success, in addition to coordination, is the coherence of the adopted documents in both territorial and substantive dimensions. Consistency issues come as no surprise when you consider that planning can address issues as detailed as birth rates, cement production, and river clean-up parameters.

According to the opinion of the State Council on strengthening the planning of socioeconomic development from 2005[10], we can distinguish two basic categories of planning, i. e., due to: (1) administrative level, (2) functional dimension. This means that the PRC's planning system includes more or less formalized territorial units, but also covers all the problems deemed significant. Thus, given

10 *Guasuyuan guanyu jiaqiang guomin jingji he shehui fazhan guihua bianzhi gongzuo de ruogan yijian* (国务院关于 加强 国民经济 和 社会 发展 规划 编制 工作 的 若干 意见), http://www.gov.cn/zwgk/2005-10/26/content_84417.htm (access: 10/04/2022).

the administrative levels, the strategic planning system is cascading. It is implemented at the central (national), regional, and local level (e.g., city, commune). However, in the case of planning due to the functional criterion, the following should be indicated:

a) General (equated with sector planning at the central level),
b) Special (targeted at specific areas, including geographic areas e.g., sectors, are the basis for approving large projects, adopting budgets, targeting fiscal spending, and formulating appropriate policies in specific areas),
c) Regional (for special planning, but performed at the provincial level and below this administrative level; refers to sector development planning, areas relevant to a province or part of it).

The plans prepared on the basis of the functional criterion focus on specific development problems, the ones that most often require the implementation of large projects, the financing of which is not sufficient with the resources at the disposal of the local administrative unit. Most often, such initiatives require approval at the central level, i.e., by the State Council. These are also projects that often go beyond the area of one administrative unit, e.g., a county or even a province. Such areas include agriculture, water quality protection, energy, transport, communication, infrastructure construction, use of natural resources, disaster prevention, science and technology, education, culture, health, social security, national defense, industry support, and public utility services. The above is the basis for creating general plans and special plans within a given province (e.g., a special plan for several counties in a province). The developed plans are hierarchical in nature; the lower-level documents must be consistent with the higher-level plans, which directly affects the process of their preparation. Strategies of a lower level, with their priorities, goals, activities, and indicators, must strictly match the strategic documents of a higher level. This means that lower-order plans are a kind of detail of higher-order plans and cannot go beyond the priorities defined in them.

It should be noted that the division of plans adopted according to administrative and functional criteria is not strict, although they are based on a different logic. Thus, they are not two separate planning systems that do not interpenetrate. On the contrary, administrative and functional plans are also subject to coordination due to the fact that they concern economic development or how the Chinese perceive progress. It is an understandable approach because development cannot be treated only from the perspective of administrative units, which are often defined for formal reasons and not *strictly* developmental ones. This approach is also practiced in Europe, for example as part of the EU's regional policy through integrated investments in specific territories[11]. There are certain rules for constructing individual plans. And so, special plans, which must be approved by the State Council, are formulated and implemented by the appropriate organizational units of the NDRC, i.e., at the central level. The prepared macroregional plan (e.g., county or city plan) is submitted by the NDRC in cooperation with the authorities of a given province (county or city) and is implemented after the approval of the State Council[12].

3.2.1. The role of central and regional governments

Both special and regional planning are subordinated to general planning at the central level, which in practice means subordination to the centrally formulated Five-Year Plans. The Five-Year Plans constitute the reference strategy for all other planning documents formulated at the central, regional, and local level. Therefore, all other plans, including special plans, are of a subordinate nature. The necessity to coordinate administrative and functional plans for dozens or even hundreds of such documents is quite a challenge. There is also a requirement to consult the NDRC on all regional and local plans. This also applies to achieving convergence of the plans of a given unit with territorially adjacent units. If neighboring administrative units cannot reach a common agreement, the coordinating role is taken over by NDRC, so as to ensure the consistency of the plans in the territorial dimension. In turn, the NDRC sends the master plans for consultation with the relevant ministries to verify compliance with the special plans. The ministries express their position within 30 days of receiving the draft plan.

The opinion of the State Council of 2005[13] also provides for a partial socialization of the planning process. It indicated that at every level of planning it is necessary to seek the opinions of the relevant ministries of the State Council and relevant authorities, depending on the level of a given plan, as well as the opinions of relevant institutions and individuals. For this purpose, the relevant institutions are obliged to publish draft plans in advance and organize hearings to learn about the opinions of the public. The guidelines of the State Council pay particular attention to taking into account the opinions of special committees of people's congresses of a given level; they do not formulate the same requirement with regard to citizens' representatives. The recommendations of the State Council

11 Marek Świstak, *Polityka regionalna Unii Europejskiej jako polityka publiczna. Wobec potrzeby optymalizacji publicznego działania*, Kraków 2018, pp. 102, 255–256.

12 Guasuyuan guanyu jiaqiang guomin jingji he shehui fazhan guihua bianzhi gongzuo de ruogan yijian (国务院关于加强国民经济和 社会发展规划编制工作的若干意见) op. cit.

13 Ibid.

almost imply an obligation to accept comments submitted by the aforementioned special committees. In the context of consultations, attention is also paid to the special role of experts in giving opinions on draft plans at a given organizational level. Experts at the national, regional, county and commune level must be obligatorily involved in the process of preparing the plans. Experts are required to submit an appropriate report on the presentation of the draft development plan. The consultation requirement does not apply to plans covered by state secrets. *Online* consultations are also conducted, but they are more often used at the provincial level than by central institutions (for example ministries). Online consultation is more of a form of presenting government proposals (e. g., laws, regulations) to the public, rather than an instrument of two-way communication, i. e., waiting for feedback[14].

The most important people in the country, including the prime minister and deputy prime minister responsible for economic affairs, participate in the process of drafting documents such as the preliminary guidelines of the five-year plan and the outline of the five-year plan that follows them. The leaders are supported by a wide group of advisers focused on the Central Finance and Economics Leading Small Group (CFELSG), as well as employees of various departments of the NDRC. It is a select group of economists and economic advisers with a recognized reputation. Due to the fact that these people are somewhat outside the formal system of government, this group retains a certain autonomy and is separated from particular sectoral, regional, and bureaucratic interests. However, it remains close enough to the decision-making process by participating in consultations so that it receives information on the state of the political discussion[15].

Provincial authorities oversee planning at the lower level, such as municipalities, in the same way that the NDRC oversees the preparation of a provincial plan at the central level. As the planning and implementation process develops, goals and responsibilities are assigned to lower-level authorities and individual ministries, who then develop and execute detailed implementation plans. The leading small groups of the NDRC, the so-called interagency panels, coordinate the work of many government bodies on specific issues. At the central level, the leading small groups are usually chaired by a member of the State Council, but the secretariat for the leading small group is one of the NDRC offices, authorizing

14 Steven J. Balla, *Is Consultation the "New Normal?": Online Policymaking and Governance Reform in China*, "Journal of Chinese Political Science" 2017, vol. 22, no. 3, pp. 375–392; Steven J. Balla, Zhoudan Xie, *Online Consultation and the Institutionalization of Transparency and Participation in Chinese Policymaking*, "The China Quarterly" 2021, vol. 246, pp. 473–496.

15 Sebastian Heilmann, *Red Swan: How Unorthodox Policy Making Facilitated China's Rise*, Hong Kong 2018, p. 177.

the office to establish the agenda. The same organizational structure is repeated for provinces and cities. Leading groups are chaired by deputy heads of the territorial units concerned (e. g., provinces, cities), but the staff of these groups often come from local NDRC offices. This means that the central institution maintains far-reaching control over the planning process[16].

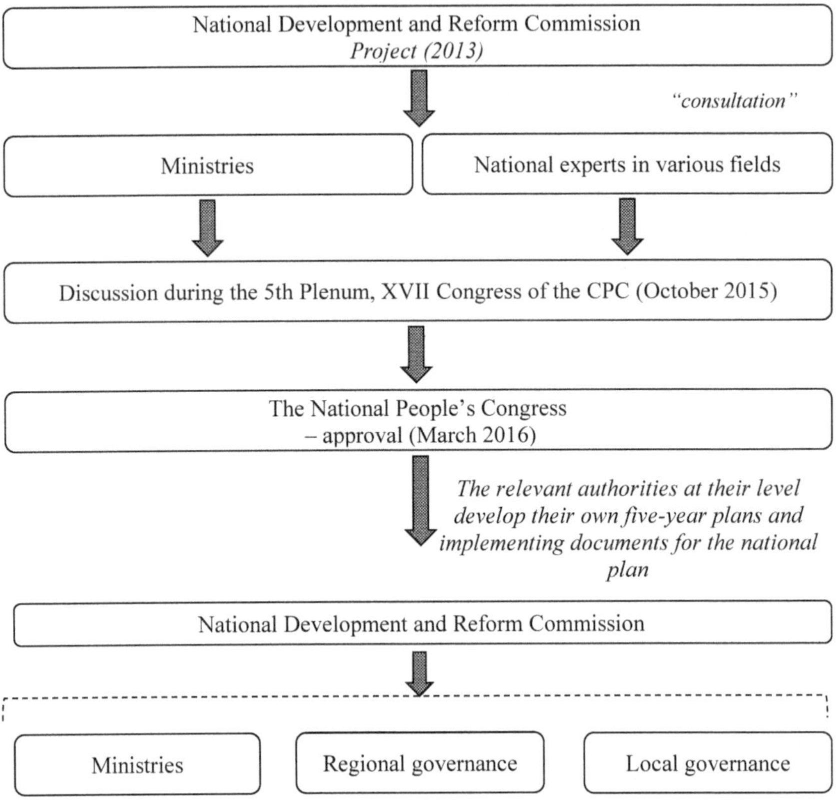

Diagram 9. The process of preparing Five-Year Plans using the example of the 13th Five-Year Plan for 2016–2020. Source: own study.

Planning in a five-year cycle is, above all, the necessity to collect a lot of information, prepare analyses, formulate policies, and then implement and evaluate them. Work on the preparation of a five-year plan usually begins two years before it enters into force, and culminates when the Central Committee announces new guidelines in the plenary session that takes place at the end of the last year of the five-year plan. In the months following approval of the national

16 Sebastian Heilmann, Oliver Melton, *The Reinvention of Development Planning in China, 1993–2012*, "Modern China" 2013, vol. 39, p. 601.

outline, ministries, provinces, and cities publish dozens of thematic special plans that present a first set of practical details on how the main goals of the new five-year plan are to be achieved. But even these documents are not detailed enough to start implementing policies. Relevant institutions such as government offices, the NDRC, and ministries issue many documents, decisions, opinions, programs, explanations, descriptions of methods, in other words, administrative measures, which are to serve the implementation of policy and coordination of various activities at various levels of implementation. They are of considerable importance in the implementation process due to the fact that they indicate specific leading agencies whose task is to coordinate activities, supervise and evaluate individual projects. After the division of tasks, the relevant offices prepare a series of further documents detailing the individual plans, such as "work programs" and "implementation programs". As the level of detail and precision in the scope of the plan's tasks increases, it becomes clearer what is to be achieved and how the plan's implementation will be verified. Documents are developed successively, although the finalization of work on their preparation can take up to two years.

Typically, in the middle of the third year of the implementation of the five-year plans, a formal review takes place at all levels. Thus, in the case of the eleventh Five-Year Plan for 2006–2010, the review began in mid-2008, but its revision was implemented in 2010. The review of five-year plans is also associated with initial research in the field of preparing the next edition of the plan. Thus, a new political cycle of work on the next plan begins. The review is quite politically important as, in addition to collecting information, it also supports the coordination of the entire implementation process.

Table 13. The state planning system in China

Type	**Main goals**	**Management system**	**Legal status**	**Spatial scope**	**Time horizon (years)**
Five-Year Plans	Socio-economic development	Vertical planning framework	Constitution of the PRC	Various levels of administration and their subordinate areas	5
Urban planning	Land development; Physical planning; Economic development	Urban level	The act on urban and rural planning	Urban areas, municipal authorities	15–20

Table 13 *(Continued)*

Type	Main goals	Manage-ment system	Legal status	Spatial scope	Time horizon (years)
Rural spatial planning	Physical land use; Preservation of agricul-tural land	Vertical planning framework	Act on land manage-ment	Various lev-els of ad-ministration and their subordinate areas	15–20

Source: own study based on: Lei Wang, *Spatial Planning and Governance: Literature Review,* [in:] *Changing Spatial Elements in Chinese Socio-economic Five-year Plan: from Project Layout to Spatial Planning,* Singapore 2019, p. 26.

The state system of spatial planning is a kind of hybrid of the legacy of central planning similar to the former Soviet Union and the decentralization solutions of the western countries. Generally speaking, when it comes to planning related to regional policy in China, we have two planning systems, i.e., economic and spatial. Along with the evolution of the planning system, efforts were made to integrate economic and spatial planning at the local level, which, with the high level of centralization of the decisions made, was a major challenge. The effectiveness of planning depends on an appropriate level of coordination. Over time, urban (spatial) planning began to take into account not only a top-down approach, and thus usually centrally made decisions about the location of various development projects, but also decentralization trends. Meanwhile, the integration of economic and spatial planning is necessary due to spatial order. Socioeconomic activities must be related to physical space; spatial planning itself is very difficult to implement, ignoring the economic intentions in a given country[17].

Urban spatial planning as an instrument of regional policy is used in a different way due to the subject of planning. Central authorities see the approval and implementation of appropriate plans as a way to control urban growth. Meanwhile, municipalities use urban planning to facilitate development in their area. This is confirmed by the fact that since the mid-1990s, the planned amount of land for urban development and its distribution in the plans of the central authorities on the one hand, and the municipal authorities on the other, were usually inconsistent[18].

17 Mee Kam Ng, Wing-Shing Tang, *The Role of Planning in the Development of Shenzhen, China: Rhetoric and Realities,* "Eurasian Geography and Economics" 2004 vol. 45, no. 3, pp. 190–211.

18 Yaei Wang, *Institutional reasons of conflicts between master plan and land use plan: causes of land expropriation of local government,* "City Planning Review" 2009, vol. 33, no. 10, pp. 53–59.

The state is a key factor in China's economic development and regional development and is considered essential for growth, transformation, and globalization. It exerts influence through institutions such as the household registration system, work units, and work permits that are periodic in nature. The strength of the Chinese state lies its significant ability to act also in the state-society relationship. Despite some steps towards economic liberalization, land ownership and the selection of human resources remain under state control. The state still largely controls hospitals, educational institutions, state-owned enterprises, and companies. The CPC's monopolistic supervision also extends to the courts and the police. It should be clearly emphasized that the spectacular results in terms of economic growth strengthened the financial strength and investment potential of state institutions[19].

The purpose of development planning at the local level is primarily to strengthen the position of the central government, and in particular the CPC. This is evidenced, in particular, by the hierarchical arrangement of the administration system, where planning follows the pattern of top-down development directives, which should then be implemented at the regional or local level. According to the Chinese authorities, it is about controlling the economy, including market supervision, allocating public resources to support the sustainable and coordinated development of the national economy and social progress. It should be noted that regional planning is not only initiated by the State Council but also reinforced by an appropriately formulated political discourse. The idea of regional planning is also a central part of Hu Jintao's idea of "scientific development". Hence, regional planning can be reduced to top-down orders formulated either under legal regulations or periodic assessments of local administrative staff, which at the regional or local level translate into the obligations of local staff. The above procedure allows for a certain level of negotiation between the local and central authorities, although it is highly regulated. The specificity of regional planning does not come down only to designing the course of such processes as industrialization, development of entrepreneurship, and assigning appropriate resources to these tasks. It consists in planning land use, restructuring the economy, and taking into account social transformation and environmental protection issues. To achieve the assumed goals, many instruments are used, such as the central allocation of resources (including financial resources), and also decentralization of power and economic incentives[20].

19 Yeshua Dennis Wei, *Regional Development in China: Transitional Institutions, Embedded Globalization, and Hybrid Economies,* "Eurasian Geography and Economics" 2007, vol. 48, no. 1, pp. 21–22.

20 Him Chung, *Unequal Regionalism: Regional Planning in China and England,* "Planning Practice & Research" 2015, vol. 30, no. 5, p. 578.

3.3. Beyond growth and social peace: China's regional development priorities

The CPC, which has a power monopoly, plays the most important role in planning social and economic development. The carrier of the directional content is the CPC conventions; the last was the 19th convention in Beijing in 2017. Xi Jinping, chairman of the Central Committee, outlined a vision for the coming years. Such speeches, apart from the propaganda dimension, also take into account the directions of Chinese policy for the coming years, including activities related to socioeconomic development. The president's image of the country is the image of China as a moderately prosperous society. The aim of the speech was to strive for the great success of socialism with Chinese specificity, which, thanks to the work of the Chinese, will contribute to the realization of the Chinese dream and the great revival of the Chinese nation. According to this message, Chinese-specific socialism means a prosperous, strong, democratic, culturally developed, harmonious, and beautiful country.

President Xi Jinping is aware of the country's development problems. He draws attention to the need to combat development imbalances and the growing need to improve the quality of life of the Chinese. At the same time, Xi Jinping emphasizes the need to improve the ability to govern, one of the pillars of which will be the socialist rule of law. Economic development is the key to solving any problem. Moreover, this development must be coordinated, "green" and open. The continuation of state interference in the economy is evidenced by the belief that the market plays a decisive role in the allocation of resources, but the state should play an even more important role. All this, according to Xi, can help advance industrialization, the development of information and communication technologies, urbanization, modernization of agriculture, further globalization of the Chinese economy, and opening up to the world[21].

The above-mentioned speech and other statements by Xi Jinping can be reduced to three dimensions. In the economic dimension, the concern for economic development in all areas is still relevant. This means – as the President expresses – "economic, political, social, and environmental progress"[22]. It can be assumed that these development directions could be signed by any leader of a western state, because it is an exemplification of the internationally accepted

21 Xi Jinping, *Secure a Decisive Victory in Building a Moderately Prosperous Society in All Respects and Strive for the Great Success of Socialism with Chinese Characteristics for a New Era*, Delivered at the 19th National Congress of the Communist Party of China October 18, 2017, s 1, 16, 18 http://www.xinhuanet.com/english/download/Xi_Jinping's_report_at_19th_CPC_National_Congress.pdf (access: 11/04/2022).

22 Xi Jinping, *Innowacyjne Chiny*, Warszawa 2015, p. 59.

concept of sustainable development[23]. In the social dimension, the strategic goal was to build a "moderately wealthy society"[24] by 2021, the 100th anniversary of the establishment of the CPC. A moderately wealthy society was to be achieved, as planned, in 2020, when GDP per capita was to double as compared to 2010[25]. On the other hand, when it comes to the political dimension, one can clearly see the directive to continue following "one's own path"[26], based on specific political and economic solutions in the PRC. At the same time, the leading role of the CPC is inviolable here. The party is the foundation of the political order, which should also be reflected in society because "embarrassment harms the country, while diligence leads to its prosperity"[27]. This, in turn, is to enable the achievement of the strategic goal of a "modern socialist state"[28] by 2049, i.e., the 100th anniversary of the establishment of the PRC. All three dimensions and two strategic goals are to support the main goal, which is "the rebirth of the Chinese nation"[29].

The strategic planning system in China is very complex, consisting of a number of planning documents (Diagram 10). The main instrument, starting in 1949, is the Five-Year Plans, and later the Medium and Long-term Science and Technology Development Programs. These two types of documents constitute the national tools of economic planning at the central level. The central plans coordinate the activities of the central bureaucracy, as well as their local counterparts. They often serve as the basis for similar plans at lower levels of government. In addition, three categories of plans should be distinguished in the planning system: special, macroregional, and local. Interregional macroregional plans are also mapped at the provincial level, between cities and regions, and play an important role in coordinating development goals between different regions. Together, the three types of plan form a complex structure that reflects priorities and shapes the actions of decision makers[30].

---

23 Łukasz Gacek, *Zielona energia w Chinach. Zrównoważony rozwój, ochrona środowiska, gospodarka niskoemisyjna*, Kraków 2015, pp. 30–44.

24 Ibid, p. 54.

25 Ross Granaut, *Mostly Slow Progress on the New Model of Growth*, [in:] Ligang Song, Ross Garnaut, Cai Fang, Lauren Johnston (eds.), *China's New Sources of Economic Growth: vol. 1: Reform, Resources and Climate Change*, Acton 2016, p. 24. Indeed, data analysis confirms the achievement of the goal. For example, it can be shown that China's GDP per capita in 2010 was USD 4,550, while in 2020 it was USD 10,500, see The World Bank, *GDP per capita (current US $) – China*, https://data.worldbank.org/indicator/NY.GDP.PCAP.CD?end=2020&locations=CN&start=1995 (access: 11/04/2022).

26 Xi Jinping, *Innowacyjne Chiny*, op. cit., p. 57.

27 Ibid, p. 62.

28 Ibid, p. 54.

29 Ibid, p. 53.

30 Sebastian Heilmann, Oliver Melton, *The Reinvention …*, op. cit., p. 590.

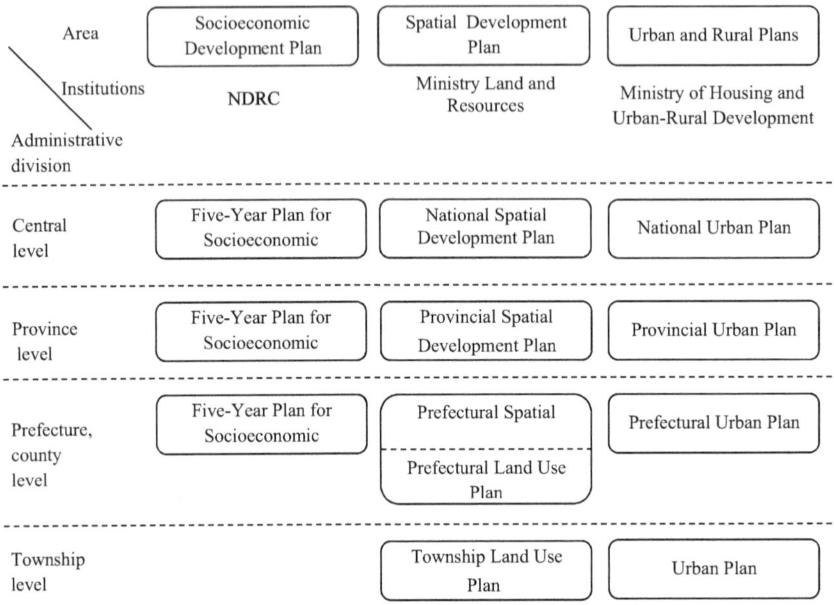

Diagram 10. The place of regional policy in the PRC's development planning system. Source: own study.

Along with the economic transformation of the country, the role of development plans has changed, starting from a propaganda instrument[31], or an element that was supposed to replace the free market[32], and becoming a development policy instrument that constitutes a point of reference in China for creating public policies and actions by state institutions. In other words, the Five-Year Plan is an instrument of social and economic development consisting of a list of goals or guidelines. The current 13th edition of the Plan covers the period 2016–2020. Previous editions (11th and 12th, respectively) covered the years 2006–2010 and 2011–2015. Another strategic document is the Medium- and Long-term Science and Technology Development Programs. Their last edition covers the years 2006–2020, and its objective is to strengthen the innovative capacity of Chinese research and development centers and enterprises[33].

31 In Mao's time, regional planning had two main goals, first, to lead to a relatively quick transition to communism, and second, to contribute to national security. See Suzanne Paine, *Spatial aspects of Chinese development: Issues, outcomes and policies 1949–79,* "The Journal of Development Studies" 1981, vol. 17, no. 2, pp. 133–195.

32 Ashok Dutt, Frank Costa, *An evaluation of national economic planning in the People's Republic of China,* "Geoforum" 1980, vol. 1, pp. 1–15.

33 The State Council, The People's Republic of China, The National Medium- and Long-Term Program for Science and Technology Development (2006–2020), Beijing 2006, https://www.i

3.4. 13th Five-Year Plan for 2016–2020 and its implications

The preliminary draft of the 13th Five-Year Plan for 2016–2020 was announced in April 2013, and the final draft was approved in March 2016 by the NPC. In this context, local plans are more detailed in terms of specific economic goals and projects to be undertaken. Developing local plans is a more socialized process than establishing a central Plan[34]. The structure of the plan's priorities indicates a comprehensive approach to development planning. If we assume that the order of individual parts reflects the degree of importance of the given issues, we may risk the statement that the main development challenges have been identified correctly. Hence, it is not surprising that much attention is paid to innovation as the engine of economic growth. It is nothing new in the contemporary strategic planning of highly developed countries. China is aware that the outcome of the race for economic primacy in the world will occur in the field of innovative solutions that must be carried out in almost every field.

There is no doubt that the vast majority of the 13th Five-Year Plan indicators have been achieved despite the economic effects caused by the COVID-19 pandemic. For example, the goal of doubling the GDP in 2010–2020, which became the basis for the values estimated in the 13th Five-Year Plan, has been achieved. This was made possible due to the strong growth in 2010–2015, even though the percentage target (6.5) was not reached. The overall labor productivity and the added value of the service sector in the economy are among the indicators that have not been achieved (Table 14). Another issue is the coordination of the development policy at the local level and the effectiveness of local authorities' activities[35]. It is especially important to look at the rivalry between the provinces. The Chinese regions use the autonomy given to them to pursue their own pro-innovation policy, which Daniel Cohen also assesses as the result of the provincial governments' aspirations to enrich themselves personally[36].

tu.int/en/ITU-D/Cybersecurity /Documents/National_Strategies_Repository/China_2006.pdf (access: 30/03/2021).

34 Understanding China's 13th Five-Year Plan, http://www.chinabusinessreview.com/understanding-chinas-13th-five-year-plan/ (access: 30/03/2021).

35 Mingxing Liu, Binwen Song, Ran Tao, *Perspective on Local Governance Reform in China*, "China & World Economy" 2006, vol. 14, pp. 16–17.

36 Daniel Cohen, *Prosperity słabości*, Katowice 2011, pp. 181–182.

Table 14. Indicators of the 13th Five-Year Plan for 2015–2020 and implementation (goals and achieved values)

No.	Indicator		Objective		Result		Achieved
			2020	5-year average value	2020	5-year average value	
Economic development							
1.	GDP (trillions of RMB)		> 92.7	> 6.5%	101.6	5.74	Partly Yes
2.	Overall labor productivity (10,000 yuan per person employed)[1]		> 12	> 6.6%	11.7	5.68	No
3.	Urbanization	Permanent city dwellers (%)	60	[3.9] [2]	63.89	[7.79]	Yes
		Registered city dwellers (%)	45	[5.1] [2]	45.4	[5.9]	Yes
4.	Value added of the service sector (% of GDP)		56	[5.5] [2]	54.5	[4.0]	No
Development based on innovation							
5.	Research and development expenditure (% Of GDP)		2.5	[0.4] [2]	2.4	[0.3]	No
6.	Patents for 10,000 people		12	[5.7] [2]	18.8	[9.5]	Yes
7.	Contribution of scientific and technical progress to economic growth (%)		60	[4.7] [2]	60	[4.7]	Yes
8.	Internet access	Households with high broadband access (%)	70	[thirty] [2]	93	[53]	Yes
		Mobile broadband users (%)	85	[28] [2]	> 100	[> 43]	Yes

Table 14 *(Continued)*

No.	Indicator	Objective		Result		Achieved
		2020	5-year average value	2020	5-year average value	
People's well-being						
9.	Increase in disposable income per capita (%)	n / a	> 6.5	n / a	5.6	No
10.	Average length of education by the working age population (years)	10.8	[0.57] 2	10.80	[0.57]	Yes
11.	New employment in cities (million people)	n / a	[> 50] 2	n / a	[53.8]	Yes
12.	Rural population out of poverty (million people)	n / a	[55.75]2	n / a	[55.8]	Yes
13.	Basic retirement insurance (%)	90	[8] 2	> 90.0	[> 8.0]	Yes
14.	Rebuilt flats in derelict urban areas (million flats)	n / a	[twenty]2	n / a	23	Yes
15.	Life expectancy (years)	n / a	[1] 2	77.3	[1] *	Yes
Resources and Environment						
16.	Arable land (million hectares)	124.3	[0] 2	1.24*	[0] *	Yes
17.	Increasing the area newly slated for construction (million hectares)	n / a	[<2.17] 2	n / a	[6,2] *	Yes
18.	Reduction in water consumption per 10,000 RMB of GDP (%)	n / a	[23] 2	n / a	[23.8] *	Yes
19.	Reduction in energy consumption per unit of GDP (%)	n / a	[15] 2	n / a	[13.2] *	No
20.	Non-fossil energy (% of primary energy consumption)	15	[3] 2		[3.3] *	Yes
21.	CO 2 emission reduction per unit of GDP (%)	n / a	[18] 2	n / a	[18.2] *	Yes

Table 14 *(Continued)*

No.	Indicator		Objective 2020	Objective 5-year average value	Result 2020	Result 5-year average value	Achieved
22.	Forest growth	Afforestation (%)	23.04	[1.38] [2]	23.04	[1.38]	Yes
		Forest resources (billion m [3])	16.5	[1.4] [2]	17.56 *	[246] *	Yes
23.	Air quality	Days with good or excellent air quality in cities above the prefecture level (% of the year)	> 80	n / a	82 *	n / a	Yes
		Reduction of PM2.5 particulate matter in cities above prefecture level (%) [3]	n / a	[18] [2]	n / a	[23.1] *	Yes
24.	The quality of surface waters	Class III or better (%)	> 70	n / a	74.9 *	n / a	Yes
		Worse than class V (%)	<5	n / a	3.4 *	n / a	Yes
25.	Total reduction of major pollutant emissions (%)	Chemical oxygen demand	n / a	[10] [2]	n / a	[11.5] *	Yes
		Ammoniacal nitrogen.		[10] [2]		[11.9] *	Yes
		Sulfur dioxide.		[15] [2]		[22.5] *	Yes
		Nitrogen oxide		[15] [2]		[16.3] *	Yes

n / a – data not available.
Remarks:
1. GDP and overall labor productivity shall be calculated using comparable prices, while absolute values shall be calculated using 2015 constant prices.
2. Figures in square brackets are accumulated data from five years.
3. The absence of a target for PM2.5 means that the annual average number exceeds 35 μg / m 3.
* – data from 2019
Source: own study based on: The 13th Five-year Plan for Economic and Social Development of The People's Republic of China (2016–2020), announced on December 7, 2016, pp. 8–10, https://en.ndrc.gov.cn/policyrelease_8233/201612/P020191101482242850325.pdf (access: 30/03/2022), Stiftung Arbeit und Umwelt der IGBCE, *Chinas 14. Fünfjahresplan – Auswirkungen der Umwelt- und Industriepolitik auf die deutsche und europäische Industrie.* Berlin 2022, pp. 14–16, [in:] https://www.arbeit-umwelt.de/wp-content/uploads/Chinas_Umwelt-und-Industriepolitik_StiftungIGBCE.pdf (access: 30/03/2022).

A separate part of the Plan was devoted to supporting the development of individual macroregions, privileged regions, and functional areas. It concerned spatial support for the coordinated development of regions along the north-south and east-west lines of the country. The goals were the orderly flow of production factors, very much needed in the case of the PRC, effective functional land use, fair access to basic public services, and development that was within the scope of the environment and natural resources. The planned measures also applied to the less developed region, mainly those of the west, whilst they would additionally revitalize the north-east. All of this was intended to promote co-ordinated development that would help reduce regional development disparities[37].

Eliminating development disproportions between individual provinces is a major challenge for regional development in a country with such a large population. This is because countries with a high level of centralization suffer from a deficit of an effective system of decision-making, implementation, and information circulation. As in highly developed European countries, also in China, coordination is associated with taking care of the development of various regions of the country, especially those that are lagging behind, for example, in terms of the level of development, infrastructure or access to public services. In democratic countries, it also results from the government's willingness to seek votes from voters living in peripheral areas, usually those that are underdeveloped. They have the same influence on the election of their representatives as the inhabitants of wealthy metropolises. Due to the authoritarian system in the PRC, such calculations do not take place. The authorities are aware of some pressure to improve the living standards of the inhabitants of particular territories, which is important for the legitimacy of the CPC's power. It was assumed that the delimitation of support would take place as part of an unofficial division into economic regions, and not a division into provinces, which is in line with the already formed tradition of territorial management in China.

Therefore, coordination will harmonize the development of the western, north-eastern, and central macroregion with the development of the eastern (coastal) macroregion, which is the leading one in terms of spatial development. The coordination mechanism concerns cooperation, the flows of production factors, access to comparable quality public services for residents, and the establishment of functional zones[38] between individual regions in order to reduce differences in regional development[39]. Technically, it is assumed that a financing

37 The 13th Five-year Plan for Economic and Social Development of The People's Republic of China (2016–2020), announced December 7, 2016, pp. 103–105, https://en.ndrc.gov.cn/policyrelease_8233/201612/P020191101482242850325.pdf (access: 30/03/2022).

38 These are areas which, despite being separate administrative structures of the Middle Kingdom, should be seen as a whole for functional reasons. Examples include areas dependent on the extraction of natural resources, or territorial units based on the development of tourism.

39 The 13th Five-year Plan for Economic and Social Development of The People's Republic of China (2016–2020), op. cit., p. 100.

system will be created that will promote the pairing of development programs of various administrative units. It also involves establishing mechanisms of mutual assistance for the benefit and development of various administrative areas and promoting the creation of zones of common economic development. In the social dimension, one of the coordination challenges is the creation of regional platforms for the exchange of information on services for residents, strengthening interregional coordination in the field of the labor market, employment, and skills support. In addition, there is also the need to develop scientific disciplines and share knowledge resources through the coordinated development of higher education, including vocational education[40]. Interestingly, in order to implement the coordination approach, the authorities envisage the possibility of experimental activities in many areas, e.g., in the form of national comprehensive experimental reform zones.

One of the most important provisions of the 13th Five-Year Plan is not only the support for regions lagging behind in development, but also for areas that were once the subject of revolutionary activity, such as those with a concentration of ethnic minorities, places in extreme poverty, and border places. Reading the Plan leaves no doubt that concern for social peace in these areas involves ensuring the appropriate economic status of their inhabitants. In this context, it was planned to accelerate economic development to significantly raise the standard of living of the population. Actions to achieve this included focusing on the development of alternative industries in areas affected by the depletion of existing resources, e.g., mineral resources, industrial decline, and serious environmental problems. It was proposed to support innovation and the development of alternative manufacturing industries. Therefore, it was necessary to modernize and transform all old industrial bases and mining areas affected by mining damage. Actions were also planned to restore ecologically degraded areas, as well as relocate population for ecological reasons[41].

3.5. 14th Five-Year Plan for 2021–2025: development not only coordinated

The 14th Five-Year Plan is undoubtedly a new installment of the socioeconomic transformation of the PRC. The implementation of the plan determines the execution of the regional development policy. If we take seriously the distribution of emphasis and priorities towards services and modern technologies, there is no doubt that building competitiveness and productivity in less devel-

40 Ibid, p. 110.
41 Ibid, p. 114.

oped regions may change in relation to what the more developed coastal provinces have experienced. On October 29, 2020, during the fifth plenary session of the 19th Congress of the Central Committee of the CPC, the Party leadership's draft proposals for the 14th Five-Year Plan were adopted[42]. On March 11, 2021, the National People's Congress approved the outline of the 14th Five-Year Plan (2021–2025) for the domestic economic and social development of the PRC and the achievement of its long-term goalsby 2035[43]. The document[44] is a next edition of the Five-Year Plan, which in this case focuses on promoting high-quality development in all aspects, including the economy, natural environment, people's well-being, and increasing the importance of the country in the global supply chain. A careful review of the provisions of the 14th Five-Year Plan does not raise any doubt that it is a comprehensive strategy covering many substantive and spatial areas of the PRC's operation. From the perspective of economic policy, special attention should be paid to the economic, social, and political dimensions, although due to the feedback loops between individual areas of influence, the area of security is not without importance in relation to the development of the country as a whole (Table 15). As a reference document for other industry plans prepared by local authorities, it is a reference point for various public policies. Like the last few editions, the 14th Five-Year Plan reflects an approach based on a mixture of a free market and planned economy. Above all, however, it is a manifestation of Chinese pragmatism.

42 Zhongguo gongchandang di shijiu jie zhongyang weiyuanhui di wu ci quanti huiyi gongbao (中国共产党第十九届中央委员会第五次全体会议公报), http://www.gov.cn/xinwen/2020-10/29/content_5555877.htm (access: 30/03/2022).

43 Zhonghua renmin gongheguo guomin jingji he shehui fazhan di shisi ge wu nian guihua he 2035 nian yuanjing mubiao gangyao (中华人民共和国国民经济和社会发展第十四个五年规划 和2035年远景目标纲要), [in:] http://www.gov.cn/xinwen/2021-03/13/content_5592681.htm (acces:s 30/03/2022); Xinua, *Interview: China's 14th Five-Year Plan deserves the world's attention, says scholar,* November 2, 2020, http://www.xinhuanet.com/english/2020-11/02/c_139484868.htm (access: 30/03/2022), Xinua, *Di shisan jie quanguo renmin daibiao dahui di si ci huiyi guanyu guomin jingji he shehui fazhan di shisi ge wu nian guihua he 2035 nian yuanjing mubiao gangyao de jueyi* (第十三届全国人民代表大会第四 国民经济关于会议会议会议和社会发展第十四个五年规划和2035年远景目标纲要的决议), http://www.xinhuanet.com/politics/2021-03/11/c_1127200766.htm (access: 30/03/2022).

44 *Zhonggong zhongyang guanyu zhiding guomin jingji he shehui fazhan di shisi ge wu nian guihua he er ling sanwu nanny yuanjing mubiao di jianyi* (中共中央关于 制定国民经济和社会发展第十四个五年〇和 和 二三五年远景目标 的 建议), http://www.12371.cn/2020/11/04/VIDE1604469480803236.shtml (access: 30/03/2022).

Table 15. Strategic orientation of the 14th Five-Year Plan: main dimensions and domains

Main dimensions			
economic	**social**	**security**	**political**
Main domains			
– innovations, – modern industrial system, – development of the internal market, – digitization, – supporting the development of a socialist market economy, – development of agriculture and rural revitalization, – improving the quality of city development, – coordinated regional development, – promotion of international cooperation (including as part of the Belt and Road initiative)	– social development (education, health care, demography), – supporting the protection of the natural environment (stability of ecosystems, improving the quality of the environment, supporting the so-called green transformation), – strengthening employment activities, – optimization of income redistribution, and social security system	– strengthening national security (military, economic, financial, raw materials, energy, food), – protection of social stability and social security, – modernization of the national defense system and the armed forces, – coordinating the achievements of economic development for national defense	– improving the quality of public services, – strengthening socialist democracy, the rule of law and CPC supervision, – respecting the principle of "one country, two systems" and promoting the unification of the country, – strengthening strategic management, including the leadership role of the CPC and state bodies, – improvement of the development planning system (national, spatial, special, regional) and its implementation, – development of Chinese socialist culture and its impact on the environment

Source: own elaboration based on: *Zhonghua renmin gongheguo guomin jingji he shehui fazhan di shisi ge wu nian guihua he 2035 nian yuanjing mubiao gangyao* (中华人民共和国国民经济和社会发展第十四个五年规划和 2035 年远景目标纲要), [in:] http://www.gov.cn/xinwen/2021-03/13/content_5592681.htm (access: 30/03/2022).

The plan is in many areas a continuation of the activities started in the 13th Five-Year Plan, both in terms of design and priorities in general. What is new is the emphasis placed on the quality of development, and to a lesser extent on the quantitative aspects of economic growth. On the one hand, one can risk the statement that this is only an adaptation to reality, because there is no doubt that the dynamics of economic growth in China is declining year by year. On the other hand, after a period of rapid economic growth, when it was fully accepted that only some people can "get rich"[45], it is time to develop, as the "coordinated" planners put it. Thus, in the declarations of the rulers, it is about quality over quantity; nevertheless, it is also important that the country, where food must be provided for more than 1,400 million people, achieves quantitative production indicators.

Coordination will be concerned with the main challenges of the development of cities, rural areas, regional, economic, and social development, harmonious development of man and nature, and openness to the world. According to the Chinese political elite, the answer to these challenges is to coordinate many public policies at the central level. It will be concern with agricultural policies and the revitalization of rural areas, elimination of development disproportions between urban and rural areas, provision of public services of a similar standard regardless of the place of residence, regional development, and spatial arrangement, for example, the integrated development of Beijing and Tianjin-Hebei, the Yangtze River Delta, and the modernization of Guangdong, Hong Kong, and Macao Bay provinces to build a world-class innovation platform[46]. There is also no doubt that China wants to continue the path chosen previously, increasing its influence both geographically and economically. Therefore, the proposed changes are not breakthrough in nature but constitute a continuation, despite the fact that new accents appear in many areas. They are more geared towards balancing the economy through supply-side reforms, expanding domestic demand, while not sacrificing further economic expansion to the outside world.

The main way to make another leap in development is through innovations[47] and new technological solutions, which is not a major novelty. Currently, almost all highly developed countries treat development in the field of innovation as

45 It meant encouraging the improvement of the material status of some people and regions in the first place. See Cindy Fan, *China's Eleventh Five-Year Plan (2006–2010): From "Getting Rich First" to "Common Prosperity"*, "Eurasian Geography and Economics" 2006, vol. 47, no. 6, pp. 708–723.

46 Guo wei (郭 巍): *Guanche xin fazhan linian, tuidong gao zhiliang fazhan* (贯彻新发展理念，推动高质量发展) https://www.ndrc.gov.cn/xxgk/jd/wsdwhfz/202101/t20210121_1265442.html (access: 30/03/2022).

47 Examples of actions taken to date for innovation include the Made in China Program established in 2015, plans for scientific and technical development, and plans for the development of artificial intelligence. See Łukasz Gacek, *Nowe źródła wzrostu gospodarczego Chin: wiedza i innowacje*, "Roczniki Humanistyczne" 2018, no. XV / 1, pp. 10–14; Ling Li, *China's manufacturing locus in 2025: With a comparison of "Made-in-China 2025" and "Industry 4.0"*, "Technological Forecasting and Social Change" 2018, vol. 135, pp. 66–74; Subin Liengpunsakul, *Artificial Intelligence and Sustainable Development in China*, "The Chinese Economy" 2021, vol. 54, no. 4, pp. 235–248.

key[48], but due to the complexity of the problem, only some countries actually manage to substantially increase the level of innovation. Today, it is a kind of holy grail for governments that want further economic growth[49]. There is no doubt that innovation is one of the variables that influence results and economic growth, also in the regional dimension[50]. However, other factors of development are also important, such as formal institutions, i. e., laws and the legal system of a given country, informal institutions within the broadly understood culture, social capital, human capital, infrastructure and natural resources[51]. In short, innovation, which is a lever for a country or a region, is not only the level of development of this or that industry, but the entire environment understood as an innovative environment. The predominant approach in the 14th Plan is the industry-specific approach, although there is also systemic thinking that reflects complex cause-and-effect relationships.

It is worth paying attention to the areas in which China plans to achieve a high level of excellence and thus gain an advantage over western countries. We are talking about next-generation information technology, biotechnology, new energy sources, new materials, high-end equipment, new electric vehicles, and aviation and marine equipment. The document also mentions the deep integration of the Internet with other industries, including the processing of big data and artificial intelligence, which will facilitate the development of advanced production clusters. The idea is to build emerging, strategic industries as new growth drivers and to support new technologies, new products, new business models, and new forms of business. However, the approach to innovation is not only about building infrastructural conditions for individual industries, e.g., building research and development infrastructure. The PRC also aims to take care of human resources for innovation in the form of supporting talents through science and education. The best laboratories, research and development centers without high-quality scientists cannot contribute to the development of new

48 Jose-Luis Hervás-Oliver, Jose Albors-Garrigos, Sofia Estelles-Miguel, Carles Boronat-Moll, *Radical innovation in Marshallian industrial districts,* "Regional Studies" 2018, vol. 52, no. 10, pp. 1388–1397.

49 Geoff Vigar, Paul Cowie, Patsy Healey, *Innovation in planning: creating and securing public value,* "European Planning Studies" 2020, vol. 28, no. 3, pp. 521–540; Tobias Gössling, Roel Rutten, *Innovation in Regions,* "European Planning Studies" 2007, vol. 15, no. 2, pp. 253–270.

50 William Baumol, *Innovations and growth: Two common misapprehensions,* "Journal of Policy Modeling" 2003, vol. 25, no. 5, pp. 435–444.

51 Robert Putnam, *Bowling Alone: The Collapse and Revival of American Community,* New York 2001; Emmanuel. Mamatzakis, *Public infrastructure and productivity growth in Greek agriculture,* "Agricultural Economics" 2003, vol. 29, no. 2, pp. 169–180; Luuk Klomp, Theo Roelandt, *Innovation performance and innovation policy: The case of the Netherlands,* "De Economist" 2004, vol. 152, no. 2, pp. 365–374.

solutions, products, and services, in other words, contribute to gaining the assumed competitive advantage[52]. This aspect is still a great challenge for the PRC.

Clearly, if China wants to play not a secondary role, but a key role in the world, its development must not only be based on specific industries that demonstrate innovation capacity, but also on geographic areas that have the greatest potential[53]. Cities must continue to act as engines of growth – cities that will be world-class competitively. To achieve this, even greater integration with the global market system is planned, including the development of modern service economy centers. In addition to the appropriate infrastructure, the plans are to develop highly advanced business services, as well as the development of the supply chain, and the development of talents and technologies. In this part, development activities, due to their advancement, can be concentrated only in the most developed agglomerations, such as Shanghai, although the list of competing cities in this respect is much longer. On the occasion of the 14th Five-Year Plan, up to 16 provinces expressed their aspirations to support metropolises of global importance, mainly in the Yangtze River Delta and the Grand Bay Region[54]. Focusing attention on the development of agglomerations with global aspirations will naturally make actions for coordinated development even more difficult.

Another aspect of the concept of coordinated development after 2020 is a strong link between development support and activities for the protection of the natural environment. In practice, resolving environmental and economic conflict is the last thing to be taken into account. So far, the environmental policy strongly promoted by the central authorities has encountered many difficulties at the local level, which means that in some areas the effects are very modest. Hence, the 14th Five-Year Plan includes activities aimed at supporting, apart from the systemic dimension, also the operational provisions, i.e., specific recommendations, as mentioned below. Increasing the involvement of society in pro-ecological activities is certainly a step in the right direction.

52 Zhonghua renmin gongheguo guomin jingji he shehui fazhan di shisi ge wu nanny guihua he 2035 nian yuanjing mubiao gangyao, op. cit.

53 On the importance of *soft power* in Chinese politics, see Rafał Kwieciński, *From "soft power" to China's "smart power"*, [in:] Edward Haliżak, Rafał Ożarowski, Anna Wróbel (eds.), *Liberalizm & neoliberalizm w badaniu polityki zagranicznej państwa i gospodarki światowej*, Warszawa 2016, pp. 99–108.

54 Hu yue shisiwu guihua "zouxiang quanqiu", zhongguo chengshi li "shijie ji" you duo yuan (沪粤十四五规划"走向全球"，中国城市离"世界级"有多远), https://m.thepaper.cn/baijiahao_10856159 (access: 30/03/2022).

3.5.1. A new development model: the dual circulation policy

Focusing on stimulating the internal market does not mean stopping the expansion of the Chinese economy externally. This is confirmed by the so-called dual circulation[55], which includes the mutual strengthening of the domestic and international markets to stimulate long-term and sustainable consumption patterns, and protect against external shocks and instability in the global environment. The first circuit is therefore the internal market (sustainable purchasing power of citizens, creating internal demand), and the second one fulfils the role of supplementing the external market (mainly international trade). The above can be assessed as a relatively passive approach to unpredictability in global markets. In the business sphere, it would be desirable to have a strategy in which new markets are sought or the product range is modernized (mainly in terms of quality). It should be noted that the so-called "dual circulation" policy is not a completely new approach. In this context, the Plan pays attention to the restoration of economic equilibrium.

The financial crisis of 2008 exposed the rapidly developing Chinese economy to a significant decline in economic growth and, at the same time, revealed the fragility of the export-driven economic model. This triggered a shift towards measures to counterbalance economic growth by increasing domestic demand. By observing the policy of the so-called dual circulation, it may be concluded that there is a certain inconsistency among the authorities, since China still wants to open up to the world by promoting free international trade and at the same time strives for economic self-sufficiency. This may lead to the assumption that China is seriously considering a possible scenario of increased competition with the United States when it talks in official documents about the challenges caused by the complex international environment and the associated risks[56]. For the outside world, there may be a reduction in the import of technologically advanced components or other elements of capital goods production. Therefore, there is no doubt that this is a strategy designed to reduce the degree of dependence of the Chinese economy on external threats and to make its further development more dependent on endogenous development factors. According to Chinese planners, the policy of "dual circulation" is to be fostered by[57]:

---

55 Xinhua, *Zhonggong zhongyang guanyu zhiding guomin jingji he shehui fazhan di shisi ge wu nian guihua he er ling sanwu nian yuanjing mubiao di jianyi* (中共中央关于制定国民经济和社会发展第十四个五年规划和二〇三五年五年目标的建议), [in:] http://www.xinhuanet.com/politics/zystj/2020-11/03/c_1126693293.htm (access: 30/03/2022).

56 Ibid.

57 Zhongguo gongchandang di shijiu jie zhongyang weiyuanhui di wu ci quanti huiyi gongbao (受权发布中国共产党第十九届中央委员会第五次全体会议公报), [in:] http://www.xinhuanet.com/2020-10/29/c_1126674147.htm (access: 30/03/2022); Hu Yabei, Zhang Weifu, *Poti*

- strengthening the importance of the domestic market (stimulating internal demand by increasing consumption, investment, stimulating a high level of employment, social security),
- improvement of innovation capacity (science and technology that enables further development based on innovative thought, and not the import of technology from abroad, which is to contribute to the transformation of the industrial base mainly by modernizing the supply chain),
- building a circulation system linking supply, demand, domestic markets (including divided regional markets) and foreign markets to counteract the negative stages of the business cycle (circulation infrastructure, e.g., transport, railways, 5G network, artificial intelligence, fusion between military and civil sectors),
- increasing the coordination of development in city and village (harmonization of development processes, convergence of public governance, including the availability of basic public services),
- improvement of progress in the field of environmental protection (ecological civilization, increase in the quality of life, development of the so-called green technologies and creating demand for them).

Taking into account the average standard of living in China, it seems unlikely that China will be able to largely become independent of exports (goods) and imports of means of production in the next 5 years. This scenario may apply to a specific group of goods, components that the Chinese are not able to produce themselves. Naturally, state-owned investments, e.g., in infrastructure, may strengthen internal demand, but the importance of infrastructure for economic growth (including productivity), also at the regional level, decreases with the increase in equipping the country or individual administrative units with it. Such a policy can contribute to a sharp drop in the efficiency of these investments. Despite the above, there is potential for China to base its development on domestic demand. In 2014–2019, consumption became one of the main driving forces of economic growth; the share of consumption in economic growth amounted to 57.8%, stimulating economic growth by 3.5%[58]. In 2020 alone, the aforementioned indicator was 54.8%, while in the USA it was 82%[59]. The comparison is very far-reaching given the differences in the living standards of the inhabitants of both countries, but it shows the distance that Beijing's political decision makers must

"shisiwu", yi guonei da shichang cujin da xunhuan ((破题 "十四五", 以国内大市场促进大循环), Guangming Network, November 13, 2020, [in:] https://theory.gmw.cn/2020-11/13/content_34365861.htm (access: 30/03/2022).

58 Hu Yabei, Zhang Weifu, op. cit.

59 Data for 2020, The World Bank, *Final consumption expenditure (% of GDP),* [in:] https://data.worldbank.org/indicator/ne.con.totl.zs (access: 30/03/2022).

take into account when implementing the dual circulation model. From the perspective of regional development, the above can be seen as an attempt to overcome the contradiction consisting of the growing need of citizens for increased welfare and better quality of life, and unsustainable development recorded for at least several decades (significant development disproportions).

The above decoupling[60] scenario is possible in the long run as a result of economic rivalry between China and the US. This will determine the PRC development policy[61]. There are many indications that actions toward deglobalization, understood as reducing the degree of interdependence, by reducing China's integration with the world economy, will gain importance as a result of the Chinese-American rivalry. Chinese companies and regions will have to develop new ways to catch up in the technological deception process, solve dependence on foreign suppliers, and avoid being perceived as hostile entities in the host countries and markets. Having an almost unlimited, relatively cheap workforce will be insufficient. Thus, it will be necessary to develop a new economic model with a framework to locate economic activities that do not cross international borders[62].

3.5.2. The regional dimension

The scope of activities included in the 14th Five-Year Plan is very important, because after the Plan is formulated at the central level, it is adapted at the regional level[63]. In the part closely related to regional policy, it is planned to continue activities for coordinated development in the spatial dimension[64]. The

---

60 Hung Tran, Decoupling, Reshoring versus Dual Circulation: Competing Strategies for Security and Influence, Atlantic Council, April 2021, [in:] https://www.atlanticcouncil.org/wp content/uploads/2021/04/Decoupling_Reshoring_versus_Dual_Circulation.pdf (access: 03/30/2023).

61 "Shisiwu": Zhongguo ruhe yingdui bianju ("十四五": 中国如何应对变局), [in:] http://www.xinhuanet.com/politics/2020-10/12/c_1126595127.htm (access: 30/03/2022); Łukasz Sarek *Chiński decoupling – "gospodarka podwójnego obiegu"*, Biuletyn Ośrodka Badań Azji, Centrum Badań nad Bezpieczenstwem Akademi Sztuki Wojennej, 2021, no. 47 / May, pp. 4–6.

62 Michael Witt, *China's Challenge: Geopolitics, De-Globalization, and the Future of Chinese Business*, "Management and Organization Review" 2019, vol. 15, no. 4, pp. 687–704.

63 Consulate-General of The People's Republic of China in Auckland, *CPC unveils proposals for formulating 14th five-year plan, long-range goals*, http://www.chinaconsulate.org.nz/eng/zlgxw/t1829233.htm (access: 30/03/2022).

64 Xinhua, *Xijinping: Guanyu "zhonggong" [zhongyong guonyu zhiding guomin jingji he shehui fazhan di shisige wu nian guihua he er ling sanwu nian yuanjing mubiao di jianyi] de shuoming* (受权发布） 习近平： 关于 制定 国民经济 关于 [中共中央第十四 个 五年规划和二〇三五年远景目标的建议] 的说明),, http://www.xinhuanet.com/politics/leaders/2020-11/03/c_1126693341.htm (access: 30/03/2022); Zhonghua renmin gongheguo guomin jingji he shehui fazhan di shisi ge wu nanny guihua he 2035 nian yuanjing mubiao

main instrument of coordination is the implementation of development activities within the functional area system. One of the manifestations of improvement and implementation is the use of the comparative advantages of different regions to rationalize the flows, and promote effective urbanization while maintaining space protection (e.g., environmental protection infrastructure[65]). I am talking about spatial development, including shaping and locating the main infrastructure, areas of productivity, and public resources. The process of locating agricultural production areas and nature protection areas in order to ensure ecological safety is also important. The plan additionally proposes to focus on the main growth poles, such as central cities and agglomerations, places with the highest potential in the PRC. A new type of urbanization will continue that puts people at the center. The authorities intend to promote urban green building and functional improvement projects, coordinate urban planning, rationally determine the size, population density, and spatial structure of cities, and promote the coordinated development of cities and small towns. Apart from large agglomerations, it is planned to support the main areas of agricultural production, ecologically key areas and places rich in energy resources. In addition to focusing on the coastal (eastern) provinces, revitalization of the western, north-eastern and central provinces is also planned[66].

In the western macroregion, the planned measures can be described as standard, as they focus to a large extent on the further development of infrastructure, development of industries specific to the region, and integration with the "belt and road initiative". For this purpose, a number of large projects are planned, including those aimed at environmental protection. Further actions are planned in the field of fighting poverty and improving quality of life (education, health care). Among the large investments, it is worth paying attention to the industrial district in the Chengdu-Chongqing region, where it is planned to create an economic center and scientific and technical innovation. In provinces located in northeast China, there are plans to reform state-owned enterprises, develop the private sector, and optimize the economic environment. Specific investments include, for example, the construction of the Liaoning economic belt and the Changchun-Jilin-Tumen development pilot zone. The development of economic

gangyao (中华人民共和国 国民经济 和 社会发展第十四 个 五年 规划 和2035年远景目标 纲要), http://www.gov.cn/xinwen/2021-03/13/content_5592681.htm (access: 30/03/2022).

65 An example of the action taken in this respect is the National General Plan for the Protection and Reconstruction of Ecosystems for the years 2021–2035. See Quanguo zhongyao shengtai xitong baohu he xiufu zhongda gongcheng zongti guihua (2021–2035 nian) (全国重要生态系统保护和 修复重大工程总体规划 [2021–2035 年]), pp. 1–2 https://zfxxgk.ndrc.gov.cn/web/fileread.jsp?id=3443 (access: 30/03/2022).

66 Zhonghua renmin gongheguo guomin jingji he shehui fazhan di shisi ge wu nian guihua he 2035 nian yuanjing mubiao gangyao, op. cit.

cooperation between the city of Harbin and Russia is foreseen, as well as the development of winter tourism in cold regions. Central provinces are an area where innovative capacity is to be increased. Provinces are to become the site of advanced production bases. This is to be achieved, among others, by industrial clusters along the Yangtze River, e.g., Beijing-Guangzhou, Lanzhou-Lianyungang and Beijing-Kowloon. To achieve production progress, it is necessary to further expand the metropolitan areas of Wuhan and Changzhutan to make them an important growth pole[67]. The provinces are also areas of agricultural (animal and plant) production, hence the postulate of increasing the competitiveness of agriculture while protecting the natural environment. In this area, it is also focused on improving the accessibility and quality of public services.

The improvement of the transfer payment mechanism, which serves to provide financial support to less developed provinces and peripheral areas, is also assumed. It mainly concerns basic standards for the provision of public services and targeting talents to the area of less developed regions. Importantly, all this is to be possible within the framework of the development of the socialist political system under the leadership of the CPC. The centralization, unification, and determination of the Chinese authorities in achieving their goals remain intact.

The process of planning regional development in China can be summarized as follows. First, in the strategic dimension, development programming belongs to the central authorities and is implemented in the form of nationwide planning, which is then transferred to the regional and local level. Second, both the process of preparing plans and their implementation focuses almost exclusively on the activities of the administration, and the central government uses institutional mechanisms to encourage actions by regions and local governments. Third, the planning process takes little account of the diverse and sometimes pluralistic expectations of regions and local communities, i.e., de facto addressees of regional policy. Harmonization of expectations and, thus, also of actions is enforced by the institutional central authority present at all levels of regional and local development management. Fourth, since the position of the center is dominant, the stimulus to act comes to a lesser extent from regions or local communities and to a greater extent from administrative staff representing the central government, both at the regional and local level. Subnational authorities are overwhelmingly influenced by instruments such as local CPC structures, the system of selection of the cadre, and periodic clerical appraisal. The above observations can be described as adaptive management[68] of regional development,

---

67 Ibid.

68 Sebastian Heilmann, Elizabeth J. Perry, *Embracing Uncertainty: Guerrilla Policy Style and Adaptive Governance in China,* Cambridge 2011, pp. 2–29; Anna Ahlers, *Rural Policy Implementation in Contemporary China: New Socialist Countryside,* Oxon-New York 2014, pp. 13–45.

reminiscent of the principal-agent relationship. In this situation, the expectations and actions of local administrative structures are subject to adaptation. In summary, planning regional development and setting development goals is an instrument of increasing the effectiveness of central government's operation at the local level[69].

69 Him Chung, *Unequal Regionalism: Regional Planning in China and England,* "Planning Practice & Research" 2015, vol. 30, no. 5, pp. 570–586.

Chapter 4.
The main challenges in implementing China's regional policy

4.1. Implementation of development planning

The following sections will deal with the implementation of specific plans and the application of instruments of regional policy, all/many of which are familiar to other countries[1]. Looking at development planning from the Confucianism point of view[2], it can be seen that it is a kind of striving for a certain balance, a desire to control what may disturb peace and social order. Nevertheless, contemporary development planning, as has already been mentioned, refers to the realization of the ideals of a communist state, a state that is able to counteract the negative effects of the laws of supply and demand.

The NDRC plays an important role in the planning process. The Commission has the task of harmonizing various types of proposal, both at the central and regional level. In practice, however, the priorities set by the CPC leadership resonate at the lower administrative levels. This is exemplified by the conferences that are devoted to planning. They are held especially at the end of the year under the auspices of the NDRC and are an opportunity for planners at various administrative levels to meet. Another element ensuring, at least to some extent, two-way communication is the day-to-day administrative activities, which include face-to-face communication such as telephone and in-person visits from provincial and central planning officers. It is also quite typical that individual planning officers know each other personally and try to cultivate good relationships by carrying out their tasks at their administrative level. However, the above-mentioned forms of communication between the center and the regional

1 Christian Hagemann, *EU Funds in the New Member States Party Politicization, Administrative Capacities, and Absorption Problems after Accession*, Cham 2019, pp. 13–39.

2 Jan Wiktor Tkaczyński, *Ustrojowy fenomen Chin w świetle ideowego sporu o wyższości merytokracji nad demokrację i przewadze demokracji nad merytokracją*, [in:] Marek Świstak, Jan Wiktor Tkaczyński (ed.), *Azjatycki model polityki rozwoju społeczno-gospodarczego. Wybrane aspekty w świetle standardów i doświadczeń Unii Europejskiej*, Kraków 2019, pp. 37–63.

level do not ensure that the content of the plans includes appropriate bottom-up demands.

One of the mechanisms by which regional authorities partly influence the agenda of the national regional policy is the so-called "four slices meetings". These are meetings devoted to the development of macroregions, respectively – northeast, northwest, southeast, and southwest – organized at the initial planning stage. The conventions provide an opportunity for provincial governors and other representatives of regional planning departments to exchange views with key decision-makers and planners at the central level. It is possible to discuss the most important development problems that may be included in the next Five-Year Plan. The problem is that such contacts are not promoted in a special way. The public's access to information on the effects of such meetings is very limited. Informal meetings, positions exchanges between central and regional authorities are not transparent, and the official media do not report them in detail[3].

Administrative supervision over the preparation of regional development plans is quite strict. Central planning officials visit the regions. The purpose of the visits is to provide advice and guidance to provincial planners. In recent years, there has been a tendency to professionalize the process by local authorities. Provinces, like central authorities, consult central research institutions (e.g., Academy of Macroeconomic Research, AMR). This procedure, apart from intellectual support, contributes to the harmonization of possible regional development ideas with those adopted at the central level.

Five-year planning at the macrolevel has changed in recent decades, from centralized, closed meetings of party and administrative bodies toward greater consideration of opinions from consultations of various state bodies, and to a lesser extent nonstate and even foreign ones. The Five-Year Plans after 1996 no longer contain long lists of priority investment projects. As a result, the preparation of draft comprehensive Five-Year Plans is much less exposed to lobbying activities within state institutions, as well as to particular sectoral interests. However, this has not eliminated the problem of domestic negotiations and the need to undertake coordination activities. This is because the outline of the Five-Year Plan does not translate immediately into action. It requires extensive detailing of individual issues and thus further negotiations. They concern the assignment of individual obligations and the imposition of specific tasks on individual administrative units[4].

In detail, key policies and special plans are usually drawn up by the local governments or ministries that are directly involved in their implementation.

3 Sebastian Heilmann, *Red Swan…*, op. cit., pp. 179–180.
4 Sebastian Heilmann, Oliver Melton, *The Reinvention…*, op. cit., p. 606.

Although the outline of regional and comprehensive plans provides an important framework, during implementation, various groups such as officials, regional governments, and private interest groups can have their say on the details included within the plans. Central planners must actively cooperate with local administrations implementing policies to ensure that goals, resources, and responsibilities are allocated. The main challenge is to harmonize plans and goals between the different administrative levels. The distribution of funds is naturally very important in this process. After 1993, the harmonization of goals, and thus the distribution of financial resources, is less dependent on top-down directives and relies more on intensive communication between the central and provincial levels. Harmonization of regional and national goals is sometimes the subject of controversy, especially if the regional goals are not as ambitious as desired by the center. If there is a discrepancy, the position of the central government wins more often. By way of example, it is possible to show how the local plan of Shanghai was harmonized with the 11th Five-Year Plan. In 2006 the regional government declared a reduction in energy consumption by 15%, arguing that the region's economy was technologically advanced and energy-efficient; therefore, the reduction to the required 20% was irrational. As a result of the intervention of the NDRC, the regional authorities had to increase the energy savings target to the required 20%. Such an unexpected intervention from the central level automatically had a negative impact on the city's budget. It was not a single case; a similar situation occurred in Guangdong Province[5].

NDRC officials perceive integration with the local administration as a willingness to reach a compromise, e. g., in creating central and local plans. They also see the need to accept greater diversification of the objectives of regional and sectoral plans. However, this implies the need to deviate from the uniform targets due to the diversity at a given administrative level. Despite the open attitude of NDRC officials, the essential element is the achievement of goals. Once the convergence of the plans is complete, their objectives are incorporated into performance criteria (indicators[6]) and contracts, and then remain the same throughout the plan period. This is despite the fact that some deviations are allowed, for example, in the event of a fundamental change in circumstances or identified problems[7].

The analysis of the organization method and the course of the strategic planning process leave no doubt that the plan is not the result of a purely unilateral choice made by the CPC leadership. At the same time, strategic planning in practice, also in the field of regional development, deviates far from the concepts

5 Sebastian Heilmann, *Red Swan…*, op. cit., p. 180.
6 *Wu nanian guihua de lishi jingyan yu zhanwang*, op. cit.
7 Ibid, p. 182.

based on partnership and subsidiarity, mainly due to the limited scope of involving stakeholders in the process and the low transparency of the process[8]. Increasing transparency could threaten the monopoly of the CPC's power. The role of the CPC is still dominant, but the participation of partially pluralistic entities is allowed, in part, because, despite the involvement of many institutions, they are largely state or party entities. In this group, strategic development planning is a series of activities, formulated documents, presented statements, rounds of negotiations, and implementation adjustments. The system shows a high level of centralization, which is confirmed by the CPC's decisions regarding, for example, key development goals. Importantly, this process is to a small extent reflective, conducive to adaptation to the prevailing conditions. However, in a broader sense, a certain degree of authoritarian flexibility can be seen in in how the strategic plans are subsequently implemented.

One of the goals of China's regional policy is to coordinate economic growth at the provincial level, with particular emphasis on the poorer parts of the country. Due to the highly hierarchical structure of political power in China, this process can be described as a kind of nested hierarchy. Central government coordinates, monitors, and authorizes planning at the national and regional level. In this sense, it is a superior unit over the province, which is committed to strictly taking into account not only the established priorities and goals, but also the indicators set at the central level.. The same is true at the provincial level for subordinate units down to the lowest local government level. Therefore, adjusting central priorities to local conditions is very difficult and requires a lot of effort. It is based on direct contacts between officials at various levels and is visible, for example, in permits for the location of special technological development zones and in macroregional planning financed by central government[9]. Beginning in the early 2000s, new forms of contractual macroregional planning have been established between ministries, central institutions, and provincial authorities. Macroregional development programs are a means of regional adjustment of the central regional development policy. Macroregional programs are a continuation of[10] the Western Development Strategy and generally cover more than one province as their prototype. Importantly from a regional perspective, such programs involve

8 On the principles of implementation, including programming of regional policy in the European Union Member States, see Jan W. Tkaczyński, Rafał Willa, Marek Świstak, *Fundusze Unii Europejskiej 2007–2013, Cele -działania-środki*, Kraków 2008, pp. 77–98.

9 Lijing Yang, *Worlds Apart? Worlds Aligned? The perception and prioritization of civil servant values for civil servants from China and the Netherlands,* "International Journal of Public Administration" 2016, vol. 39, no. 1, pp. 74–86.

10 Cindy Fan, Mingjie Sun, *Regional Inequality in China, 1978–2006,* Eurasian Geography and Economics 2008, vol. 49, p. 1.

significant investments in infrastructure and other areas co-financed from the central level[11].

Development plans that go beyond one province are used to define the role of macroregions in the national development strategy. By means of macroregional plans, the central government empowers the regional governments to try (sometimes test) new ways and means to achieve the goals set out in the plans. It is an important instrument from the region's point of view, because, on the one hand, it gives an opportunity to both test and also introduce new elements to the central agenda of the regional policy, and, on the other, it provides additional financial support for the activities implemented under macroregional programs. For example, for macroregional programs for the northern and central provinces, central financial support was complementary, but for macroregional plans of the poorer provinces of West China, it was predominant.

Research[12]shows that local planning officials themselves see macroregional plans as an opportunity to increase political capital, and also to increase flexibility with regard to planning under national Five-Year Plans, as well as legal regulations and executive documents[13]. For example, the Chongqing local government was able to experiment with a possible correction of the *hukou* registration system as part of the Western China development program. However, the consent to experiment is not of a general nature, as exemplified by the coordination of the macroregional strategy planning process. The delegations of the State Council, composed of NDRC officials coming from Beijing, to a large extent monopolize the process of preparing macroregional plans. It is true that local governments are asked to present proposals, statistics, and studies, and are even consulted at the stage of drawing up the plans. Nevertheless, strategies that go beyond one province are often treated as central issues, i. e., tasks that go beyond regional competences. The justification for interference from the central level in this process is the development of an effective division of labor between regional authorities and the need for substantive and regulatory convergence.

Another example of the coexistence of centralism and planning flexibility is the combination of macroregional development with decentralized experimentation, which is referred to as multilevel experimental points. As part of this procedure, the central government, in consultation with regional or local governments, creates areas (special zones) within which activities related to overcoming development problems are carried out; such activities are thus used to demonstrate how other regions might deal with comparable issues. This is a

11 Sebastian Heilmann, Oliver Melton, *The Reinvention …*, op. cit., p. 590.

12 Ibid, p. 592.

13 Xin Ren, *Tradition of the law and law of the tradition: Law, state, and social control in China*, Westport 1997, pp. 3–9.

special solution because it is assumed that the experiences in these zones can be used to shape policy in other parts of the country or introduce national solutions. Under this instrument, it is emphasized that NDRC may use the experience gained in this way, provided that the results are properly checked. These zones include: Shanghai Pudong New Area, Tianjin Binhai New Area, Chengdu, Chongqing City, Wuhan City Circle, Changzhutan City Group, Shenzhen Special Economic Zone, Shenyang Economic Zone. There is also a pilot project for comprehensive tourism reform in Yunnan and a pilot for comprehensive support reform to transform the means of economic development in Zhejiang Province. As part of a comprehensive set of reforms in the provinces, carried out independently at different locations, 21 provinces and municipalities conducted independent pilot projects. More than 70 comprehensive pilot areas have been created in the provinces that support reforms, mainly to eliminate institutional barriers to local economic development and to conduct research on whether the proposed reforms are adequate for local conditions[14].

Designating special zones and the possibility of experimenting are, from the point of view of regional and local authorities, a chance to introduce their own accents to the regional policy to a greater extent, in other words, to increase their freedom to adapt centrally planned regional policy. From the point of view of the authorities, it is an instrument of improvement, optimization not only of planning, but also of policy implementation. It should be noted that, also in this case, the freedom of action of regional and local authorities is subject to rather close coordination with the center. Another important aspect is to take advantage of some kind of competition between the various local authorities. The possibility of forging one's own development path, and in the future, the option of using this experience, including in other administrative units, encourages local authorities to take action in an active manner rather than passively perform the tasks commissioned by Beijing. It should be noted that the combination of planning and experimenting is not a common phenomenon in Chinese regional policy. It has only been used since 1993. This idea appeared in Chinese economic policy with the decision to give the Chinese model of socioeconomic development the character of a socialist market economy[15].

When analyzing the implementation of previous editions of the Five-Year Plans, I will pay attention to three ways of delegating responsibility to solve the

14 Su Min, *Zhongguo duo cengci gaige shidian gay jiben xingcheng,* (中国多层次改革试点格局基本形成), June 8, 2010, https://www.chinanews.com/cj/cj-gncj/news/2010/06-08/2329128.shtml (access: 17/ 11/2021)).

15 Zhang Baijia, *A look at China's policy of reform and openness to the world,* Toruń 2017, pp. 72–78, 102–107.

typical problems of regional policy in China[16]. In development planning, one can notice various modes of governance that are characterized by different logic (Table 16). The command mode governance[17]in China suggests that the central government has quite limited instruments to implement regional policy and focuses almost exclusively on bureaucratic relations. Taking into account the hierarchical method of exercising power, in the implementation of regional policy, there are also methods that are not related purely to bureaucratic efficiency. Thus, it is possible to identify sectors where public and social goods are to be provided through direct funding allocation and administrative oversight. It is the most commonly used management method, where the central authority allocates specific resources, closely monitoring the progress and effects of the implementation of the activities in question. As shown in Table 16, this most often applies to such areas as rail infrastructure, antipoverty programs, and land development. The above appears to be the most centralized bureaucratic procedure by which the implementation of development planning is carried out, because it does not give virtually any freedom to entities that are obliged to take a given action.

Another way to manage the planning and implementation of the policy is contractual planning. Its aim is to motivate lower-level entities (region, local authorities) to implement policy objectives. In this case, specific goals, scope, and performance indicators become the content of the contract. Contracts are usually concluded between central and regional authorities, but also with large enterprises participating in the implementation of state planning. Contracts most often concern such areas as the construction of roads, special technological zones, energy production, hospital reforms, etc. Therefore, these are the areas in which the central government expects grassroots activity not only of local authorities but also of market participants. Although in practice contracts are to some extent imposed on lower-level entities, it should be noted that this is another way to increase the autonomy of lower-level authorities in implementing regional policy. This is because, unlike the direct allocation of funds (obligatory mode), it gives a certain field of negotiation with the central government. Although the planning process under the Five-Year Plans requires the issuance of various types of detail and guidelines, the implementation of the policy by means of contracts allows for the clarification of the parameters of central supervision. We are still dealing here with the principal-agent relationship, i.e., a relationship

16 Sebastian Heilmann, *Economic Governance: Authoritarian Upgrading and Innovative Potential,* [in:] Joseph Fewsmith (ed.), *China Today, China Tomorrow: Domestic Politics, Economy, and Society,* Plymouth 2010, pp. 112–120.

17 Bob Jessop, *The State Past, Present, Future,* op. cit., p. 168.

in which the central authority orders and requires the performance of specific tasks.

Table 16. Modes of governance in Chinese regional development planning

The measure / method of governance	**Mandatory** **Administrative and SOE-based provision of public/social goods**	**Contractual** **Central-regional and government-enterprise cooperation**	**Indicative** **The government induced and market activities**
Allocating-Promotional	Railway construction	Technology development policy	*"Going global"* external investment program
Redistributable	Anti-poverty programs	Rural health care system	Rural income generation
Control	Land use management	Energy industry restructuring	Private / SME sector restructuring

Source: Sebastian Heilmann, *Red Swan…*, op. cit., p. 186.

The third type that can be identified on the basis of the already completed implementation cycles of the Five-Year Plans concerns indicative planning. The indicative type of planning is most often based on government forecasts as to the direction of development of specific areas, e.g., foreign trade, Chinese foreign investments, etc. Here, more persuasive mechanisms are used as compared to the above-mentioned types of management, such as taxes (e.g., information on the reduction of rural taxes, preferences for setting up SMEs in rural areas), indirect incentives (e.g., easier access to bank loans and foreign markets). The purpose of these measures is to stimulate market activities and mobilize resources in sectors considered by the central government to be pro-development[18]. Among all the above-mentioned models of delegating tasks under regional policy, indicative planning gives the best chance of incorporating the bottom-up approach, as long as these objectives have not been included as obligatory in a given sectoral policy, both at a given administrative level and in periodic cadre evaluation. This is the case in terms of indicative planning, as local governments as well as entrepreneurs have greater freedom in making decisions.

18 Sebastian Heilmann, Oliver Melton, *The Reinvention…*, op. cit., pp. 610–611, Sebastian Heilmann, *Red Swan…*, op. cit., p. 186.

4.2. Implementation of regional and macroregional plans

The implementation of regional policy in the PRC consists of undertaking a number of activities, the key of which is the implementation of development plans. As mentioned before, the most important instrument of this type of policy are the next editions of the national Five-Year Plans. In line with the principle of development programming, countless plans are implemented in China that allow resources to be directed toward specific goals. Therefore, in identifying the methods of implementing regional policy in China, it is impossible to be satisfied only with the analysis of central planning and ignore the key aspects of implementing other programs, with particular emphasis on macroregional programs. In this part of the work, attention will be focused on the implementation of selected plans. In order to understand how China's regional policy is shaped it is important to consider the entire process that takes place from the moment a decision is made to the achievement of the planned results.

At the implementation stage, in line with Charles Jones's approach[19], three types of activity are taken into account, i. e., organization, interpretation, and application. The organization is the verification of the extent to which the necessary material, human, and administrative resources have been established. Interpretation, under Chinese conditions, is not only the transfer of legal provisions to administrative and management practice, but also administrative activities, implementation of specific provisions of development plans, adherence to various guidelines, notices, arrangements, and contracts. Due to the complexity of the issues, the factors which affect how the administrative staff operate, including the system of cadre evaluation, are discussed in section 6.2 of this book. And finally, the subject of interest is the application, i. e., the method of delivering specific goods, performing the services assumed in the program, and undertaking other specific activities and instruments. A separate chapter of this work is devoted to the instruments themselves. The diversity of their application in China justifies the above approach and organizes the discussed matter. The universality of the applied regional policy instruments has some limitations because their effects are always derivative not only of the specificity of the instrument, but also of the environment, which consists of the specificity of a given region or country, i. e., legal and political culture, economic situation, and social expectations. Therefore, this section is mainly devoted to the implementation process, which is the result of the interaction of the formal and informal institutional environment.

However, before talking about the implementation process, from the point of view of its shaping path, it is necessary to identify the plans we are dealing with.

19 Charles Jones, *An Introduction to the Study of Public Policy*, California 1984, p. 166.

As indicated above, development planning in China is very complex. The central Five-Year Plans are accompanied by supplementary plans which can be divided into spatial and sectoral plans. Spatial plans are strategic documents for the development of, for example, Chinese macroregions, regions, local territorial units, and functional areas (e.g., the Pearl River area). The importance of the latter lies in the coordination of development as a whole in a given administrative unit or functional area. Sectoral plans are plans devoted to particular industries, areas important from the point of view of the implementation of the central goals of the Five-Year Plans and requiring coordination at the central level. We can mention the energy sector, which is crucial from the point of view of regional competitiveness, including local development. Including sectoral plans in the central plans also results from the political agenda of the CPC, and in particular of its leadership. This is because each of the sectoral plans is accompanied by lively activities related to the formulation of a clear political message (state doctrine) directed not only to society, but above all to cadres, both party and administrative. The formulation of state doctrine is also intended to demonstrate the political unity of the Chinese elite in terms of the directions of activities. Undoubtedly, state doctrine is an instrument used for implementing regional policy. The importance of state doctrine in the implementation of development plans for state structures (central, regional, local) also results from the fact that in the maze of various plans, citizens are not able to orient themselves and officials at appropriate levels are already obliged to do so. It is not just a problem for the Chinese system of implementing development plans and strategies.

The spatial and sectoral plans complement the provisions contained in the Five-Year Plans. As already indicated above, each of the plans must conform to the spirit and letter of the central Five-Year Plans. In other words, the spatial and sectoral plans must be consistent with the implementation of the generally defined goals of the central Five-Year Plans. Moreover, all sectoral plans and some spatial plans require approval at the central level. In the field of regional policy, these are the plans most often adopted by the NDRC. This makes the implementation of plans a very complex process which, as such, requires, first and foremost, an efficient coordination system. Spatial plans, in particular regional and local ones, may also implement the development priorities of individual administrative units. The freedom to create them is quite rationed (as has already been mentioned) due to the fact that at the stage of their formulation, the NDRC standardizes them in accordance with central priorities and principles. Therefore, lower-order spatial plans, especially local ones, only to a small extent reflect the unique development needs of local communities and, to a greater extent, are an instrument for ensuring centrally set regional policy objectives. The list of selected spatial and sectoral plans that accompany the 13th Five-Year Plan is presented in Table 17.

Table 17. Selected spatial and sector plans accompanying the 13th Five-Year Plan

Spatial plans	Sector plans (sectors)
Macroregional (selected examples) - Western Development Plan of January 11, 2017[20], - Promoting the development of the central region of December 26, 2016[21]	- Energy (from December 26, 2016)[22], - Renewable energy (from December 10, 2016), - Development of the rural economy (as of October 27, 2016)[23], - Eliminating poverty (as of September 20, 2016)[24], - Development of meteorology (National Meteorological Development Plan of 23 August 2016)[25], - Desertification in karst areas (as of March 21, 2016)[26], - Development of the coal industry (as of December 22, 2016)[27], - Development of the biological industry (adopted on December 26, 2016)[28], - Construction of the national scientific and technological infrastructure (from December 23, 2016)[29], - Development of crude oil and natural gas production (December 24, 2016)[30], - Use of seawater (as of December 28, 2016)[31], - Wastewater treatment plant and sewage recycling equipment in cities and towns (as of December 31, 2016)[32], - Construction of municipal waste processing plants (from December 31, 2016)[33], - Water saving (as of January 17, 2017)[34], - Use of geothermal energy (adopted on January 23, 2017)[35], - Development of the biogas industry in rural areas (adopted on January 25, 2017)[36], - Development of the food logistics industry (adopted on March 3, 2017)[37], - Development of the national maritime economy (from April 5, 2017)[38], - Prevention and control of water and soil pollution (as of May 25, 2017)[39], - Railway development (as of November 20, 2017)[40].
Regional (selected examples) - Three-year Action Plan for Protecting Beijing's Blue Skies on July 23, 2020)[41], - Heavy Air Pollution Contingency Plan of Beijing Municipality from July 23, 2020, - Regional Plan of Key Investment Projects for Hubei Province in 2018 from February 1, 2018[42], - Shaanxi Province, XIII Five-Year Plan – sports development plan July 19, 2016[43], - Shaanxi Province, XII Five Year Plan – 2016 Environmental Protection[44]	
Local (selected examples) - Spatial development plans in cities, e.g., Beijing Spatial Development Plan[45], - Plan to build a *high-tech* services cluster (Wuhan) of May 31, 2017, - Wuhan's Action Plan for the Integration of Manufacturing and the Internet (2016–2020) of August 17, 2016[46], - 2019 Drinking Water Industry Development in Ankang City of April 19, 2019[47], - Three-year roadmap (2018–2020) to in-depth implementation of the state-owned enterprise reform in Ankang City to accelerate the promotion of high-quality development of December 28, 2018[48], - Three-year roadmap for integrating the city of Chengdu with the Belt and Road Initiative (2019–2021) of September 23, 2019[49], - XIII Five-Year Plan – Environmental Protection of Chengdu on May 17, 2017[50].	

Source: own study.

20 Guojia fazhan gaige wei guanyu yinfa xibu da kaifa "shisanwu" guihua de tongzhi fa gaii xibu [2017] 89 hao) (国家发展改革委关于印发西部大开发"十三五" 规划的通知发改西部 [2017] 89 号), https://zfxxgk.ndrc.gov.cn/web/iteminfo.jsp?id=410 (access: 20/02/2021).

21 Guanyu yinfa cujin zhongbu diqu jueqi "shisanwu" guihua de tongzhi (fa gai diqu [2016] 2664 hao) (关于印发促进中部地区崛起"十三五"规划的通知) (发改地区 [2016] 2664号), [in:] https://zfxxgk.ndrc.gov.cn/web/iteminfo.jsp?id=399 (access: 20/02/2021).

22 Guanyu yinfa nengyuan fazhan "shisanwu" guihua de tongzhi) (fa gai nengyuan [2016] 2744 hào) (关于印发能源发展 "十三五" 规划的通知) (发改能源 [2016] 2744 号), https://zfxxgk.ndrc.gov.cn/web/iteminfo.jsp?id=405 (access: 20/02/2021).

23 Guanyu yinfa [quanguo nongcun jingji fazhan "shisanwu" guihua] de tongzhi (关于印发 [全国农村经济发展 "十三五" 规划] 的通知 (发改农经), https://zfxxgk.ndrc.gov.cn/web/iteminfo.jsp?id=389 (access: 20/02/2021).

24 Guanyu yìnfa quanguo "shisanwu" yi di fupin banqian guihua de tongzhi) (fa gai diqu [2016] 2022 hoo) (关于印发全国 "十三 五" 易地扶贫搬迁规划的 通知) (发改 地区 [2016] 2022号), https://zfxxgk.ndrc.gov.cn/web/iteminfo.jsp?id=387 (access: 20/02/2021).

25 Guanyu yinfa quanguo qixiang fazhan "shisanwu" guihua de tongzhi) (qi fa [2016] 62 hào) (关于印发全国气象发展 "十三五" 规划的通知) (气发 [2016] 62 号), https://zfxxgk.ndrc.gov.cn/web/iteminfo.jsp?id=373 (access: 20/02/2021).

26 Yu yinfa (yanrong diqu shi mo hua zonghe zhili gongcheng "shisanwu" jianshe guihua) de tongzhi (fa gai nong jing [2016] 624 hao) (于印发 (岩溶 地区 石漠化 综合 治理工程"十三五" 建设规划)的通知 (发改农经 [2016] 624号), https://zfxxgk.ndrc.gov.cn/web/iteminfo.jsp?id=353 (access: 20/02/2021).

27 Guanyu yinfameitan gongye fazhan "shisanwu" guihua de tongzhi (fa gai nengyuan [2016] 2714 hao) (于印发 (岩溶地区石漠化综合治理工程 "十三五" 建设规划) 的通知 (发改农经 [2016] 624 号), https://zfxxgk.ndrc.gov.cn/web/iteminfo.jsp?id=400 (access: 20/02/2021).

28 Guanyu yinfa ["shisanwu" shengwu chanye fazhan guihua] de tongzhi (fa gai gao ji [2016] 2665 hao) (关于印发 ["十三 五" 生物产业发展规划] 的 通知 (发 改 高 技 [2016] 2665 号), https://zfxxgk.ndrc.gov.cn/web/iteminfo.jsp?id=404 (access: 20/02/2021).

29 Guanyu yìnfa guojia zhongda keji jichu sheshi jianshe "shisanwu" guihua de tongzhi (fa gai gao ji [2016] 2736 hao) (关于印发国家 重大 科技 基础 设施 建设 "十三 五" 规划 的 通知) (发 改 高 技 [2016] 2736 号), https://zfxxgk.ndrc.gov.cn/web/iteminfo.jsp?id=403 (access: 20/02/2021).

30 Guanyu yinfa shiyou tianranqi fazhan "shisanwu" guīhua de tongzhi) (fa gai nengyuan [2016] 2743 hao) (关于印发石油 天然气发展 "十三 五" 规划的 通知) (发改 能源 [2016] 2743 号) https://zfxxgk.ndrc.gov.cn/web/iteminfo.jsp?id=406 (access: 20/02/2021).

31 Guanyu yinfa [quanguo haishui liyong "shisanwu" guihua] de tongzhi (fa gai huan zi [2016] 2764 hao) (关于印发 [全国海水 利用 "十三五" 规划] 的 通知 (发改环 资 [2016] 2764 号), https://zfxxgk.ndrc.gov.cn/web/iteminfo.jsp?id=401 (access: 20/02/2021).

32 Guanyu yìnfa ["shisanwu" quanguo chengzhen wushui chuli ji zaisheng liyong sheshi jianshe guihua de tongzhi (关于印发 ["十三五" 全国城镇污水处理及再生利用设施建设规划] 的通知), https://zfxxgk.ndrc.gov.cn/web/iteminfo.jsp?id=408 (access: 20/02/2021).

33 Guanyu yìnfa ["shisanwu" quanguo chengzhen shenghuo lese wu hai hua chuli sheshi jianshe guihua] de tongzhi (fa gai huan zi [2016] 2851 hao) (关于印发 ["十三 五" 全国城镇生活 垃圾 无害 化处理设施建设规划] 的 通知 (发改环 资 [2016] 2851 号), https://zfxxgk.ndrc.gov.cn/web/iteminfo.jsp?id=409 (access: 20/02/2021).

34 Guanyu yinfa "jie shui xing shehui jianshe" shisanwu "guihua" de tongzhi (fa gai huan zi [2017] 128 hao) (关于印发 [节水型 社会建设 "十三五" 规划]) 的 通知 (发改环 资 [2017] 128号), https://zfxxgk.ndrc.gov.cn/web/iteminfo.jsp?id=407 (access: 20/02/2021).

35 Guanyu yinfa [di reneng kaifa lìyong shisanwu "guihua"] de tongzhi (关于印发 [地热能开发利用 "十三五" 规划] 的通知),, https://www.ndrc.gov.cn/xxgk/zcfb/ghwb/201702/t20170204_962227.html?code=&state=123 (access: 20/02/2021).

36 Guanyu yinfa [quanguo nongcun zhaoqi fazhan "shisanwu" guihua] de tongzhi (fa gai nong jing [2017] 178 hao) (关于印发 [全国农村沼气发展 "十三五" 规划] 的 通知 (发改农经 [2017] 178号), https://zfxxgk.ndrc.gov.cn/web/iteminfo.jsp?id=413 (access: 20/02/2021).

37 Guanyu yinfa [liangshi wuliu ye "shisanwu" fazhan guihua] de tongzhi (fa gai jingmao [2017] 432 hao) (关于印发 [粮食物流业 "十三五"发展规划] 的通知 (发改经贸 [2017] 432 号), https://zfxxgk.ndrc.gov.cn/web/iteminfo.jsp?id=415 (access: 20/02/2021).

38 Quanguo haiyang jingji fazhan "shisanwu" guihua (全国海洋经济发展 "十三五" 规划), https://zfxxgk.ndrc.gov.cn/web/iteminfo.jsp?id=419 (access: 20/02/2021).

39 Guanyu yinfa danjiangkou ku qu ji shangyou shui wuran fangzhi hi shuitu baochi "shisanwu" guihua de tongzhi (fa gai diqu [2017] 1002 hao) (关于印发丹江口库区及 上游水污染防治和 水土保持 "十三 五" 规划的 通知) (发改 地区 [2017] 1002 号), https://zfxxgk.ndrc.gov.cn/web/iteminfo.jsp?id=14169 (access: 20/02/2021).

40 Guanyu yinfa [tielu "shisanwu" fazhan gui] de tongzhi (fa gai jichu [2017] 1996 hao) (关于印发 [铁路 "十三五" 发展规划] 的 通知 (发改基础 [2017] 1996 号), https://zfxxgk.ndrc.gov.cn/web/iteminfo.jsp?id=430 (access: 20/02/2021).

41 Three-year Action Plan for Protecting Beijing's Blue Skies, http://english.beijing.gov.cn/government/lawsandpolicies/202007/t20200723_1957181.html (accessed: 20/02/2021).

42 Sheng fazhan gaige wei guanyu yinfa hubei sheng 2018 nian sheng ji zhongdian jianshe jihua de tongzhi (省发展改革委关于印发湖北省2018年省级重点建设计划的通知), http://fgw.hubei.gov.cn/fbjd/xxgkml/zdjsxm/zdjsxmqd/201802/t20180209_1012460.shtml (access: 20/02/2021).

43 Shanx and sheng "shisanwu" tiyu shiye fazhan guihua (陕西 省 "十三 五" 体育 事业发展 规划) http://www.shaanxi.gov.cn/zfxxgk/fdzdgknr/ghxx/sswgh/gmjjhshfzgh_2438/201703/t20170321_1662249.html (access: 20. 02. 2021)

44 Shanxī sheng "shisanwu" huanjing baohu guīhua (陕西 省 "十三 五" 环境保护 规划) http://www.shaanxi.gov.cn/zfxxgk/fdzdgknr/ghxx/sswgh/gmjjhshfzgh_2438/201703/t20170320_1662133.html (access: 02/20/2021).

45 Beijing Municipal Commission of Planning and Natural Resources, http://english.beijing.gov.cn/government/departments/202006/t20200627_1932942.html (access: 20/02/2021).

46 Shi renmin zhengfu guanyu yinfa wuhan shi tuijin zhizao ye yu hulianwang ronghe fazhan xingdong jìhua (2016–2020 nian) de tongzhi (市人民政府 关于印发武汉 市 推进 制造业与互联网融合发展行动计划 [2016–2020 年] 的通知), http://www.wuhan.gov.cn/zwgk/xxgk/zfwj/gfxwj/202003/t20200316_973261.shtml (access: 20/02/2021).

47 Ankang shi renmin zhengfu bangongshi guanyu yinfa 2019 nian baozhuang yinyong shui chanye fazhan gongzuo shishi fangan de tong (安康市人民政府办公室关于印发 2019 年包装饮用水产业发展工作实施方案 的通), [in:] http://www.ankang.gov.cn/Content-175443.html (access: 20/02/2021).

48 Ankang shi renmin zhengfu bangongshi guanyu yinfa ankang shi shenru shishi guoqi guozi gaige gongjian jiakuai tujdong gao zhiliang fazhan san nian xingdong fangan (2018--2020 nian) de tong (安康 市人民政府办公室 关于印发 实施国企国资改革市深入加快市 深入资高质量发展三年行动方案 [2018–2020 年] 的通), [in:] http://www.ankang.gov.cn/Content-164371.html (access: 20/02/2021).

49 Chengdu shi renmin zhengfu guanyu yinfa chengdu shi rongru "yidai yilu" jianshe san nian xingdong jihua (2019–2021 nian) de tongzhi (成都市人民政府关于印发成都市 融入"一带一路"建设三年行动计划 [2019–2021 年]的通知) [in:] http://gk.chengdu.gov.cn/uploadfiles/070354020302/2019110615402415.docx (access: 20/02/2021).

50 Chengdu shi huanjing baohu "shisanwu" guihua (成都市环境保护"十三 五"规划), http://gk.chengdu.gov.cn/govInfo/detail.action?id=1637357&tn=2 (access: 20/02/2021).

In the next part, I will focus on the experiences resulting from the implementation of selected macroregional, regional and local programs, including previous editions over the last two decades. An exemplary list is provided in Table 17. Generally speaking, after the approval of numerous development plans, which is most often carried out by the NDRC, the same institution asks, by way of an announcement, provincial, autonomous regions, municipalities, and cities governments directly subordinate to the central government to start implementing the announced plan. Announcements usually contain calls for the adherence to state ideology, the adherence to the goals of a given program, and the strengthening of political leadership in order to implement obligations arising from the plans, which is tantamount to taking organizational measures. Central authorities encourage their subordinate units to introduce innovations to use endogenous potential during implementation activities[51]. The situation is similar with regard to plans of regional and local importance, with the difference that the regional governments announce to their subordinate units the adoption of the plan for implementation.

The NDRC plays an important role in the implementation of development plans, not only from the point of view of the institution's prerogatives (see Point 2.1.2), but also because of the financial resources at its disposal. For 2019 alone, the Commission's total spending was 2,227,189,200 RMB, of which 1,504,617,600 RMB were allocated to public spending related to promoting the development and reform of regional policies. The amount is quite significant, but compared to the annual budgets of the major Chinese cities, it is not impressive. The budget of the capital city oscillates around 697 billion RMB (2019)[52], Wuhan around 267 billion RMB (2017)[53], Shenzhen around 406 billion RMB (2020)[54], and the medium-sized city for Chinese conditions, Kunming (Yunnan province with approximately 4 million citizens) 63 billion RMB (2019)[55]. The amount at the disposal of the NDRC is significant in those areas that are lagging behind in development and, to a lesser extent, highly developed cities. In addition, the transfer of central funds is not the only instrument for financing regional policy.

51 Guasuyuan guanyu xību da kaifa "shisanwu" guihua de pifu (国务院关于西部大开发"十三五" 规划的 批复), https://zfxxgk.ndrc.gov.cn/web/fileread.jsp?id=254 (access: 02/02/2021).

52 The People's Government of Beijing Municipality, http://english.beijing.gov.cn/BeijingInfo/facts/202006/t20200601_1912277.html (access: 20/03/2021).

53 Wuha n Investment Promotion Complaint Center, http://english.wuhan.gov.cn/Investment_1/WIE_12751/202003/t20200316_950597.shtml (access: 20/02/2021).

54 Shenzhen Basics, http://www.sz.gov.cn/en_szgov/aboutsz/profile/content/post_1357629.html (access: 20/02/2021).

55 Kunming's economic aggregate achieved leapfrog growth, https://www.drawfleurdelis.com/2020/kunmings-economic-aggregate-achieved-leapfrog-growth/ (access 20/03/2021).

Within the budget category under public expenditure, the very potential related to strategic planning and implementation by the NDRC is interesting. This institution allocated up to 404,291,800 RMB for this purpose in 2019. The funds enable the coordination and implementation of national economic and social development strategies, medium- and long-term plans, and annual plans, and do not include the costs of the current functioning of the institution. A significant item in the Commission's expenditure is also expenditure on science and technology to the amount of 413 587 500 RMB. These funds are used to carry out various types of applied research in the field of development activities. In recent years, this item has included research on the possibility of cooperating on the Belt and Road (New Silk Road) initiative with individual countries, including China-Japan, China-Great Britain, China-Israel, China-South Korea, China-Germany, China-Norway, China-Austria. Other expenses relate to other tasks (including, for example, housing reform 66,301,800 RMB) and administrative expenses (e.g., social security and employment up to 222,422,400 RMB). The Commission derives its revenues (a total of 2,661,579,700 RMB) from various sources, the most important of which is public funds, i.e., the central budget (1,573,597,910 RMB). This is the pool allocated to the Commission by the State Council for a given year. Another significant source is business income, which amounts to 829,995,800 RMB. Revenue is a consequence of the economic activity carried out, including the auxiliary activity of the Commission. We are talking about the activity of, for example, the NDRC International Cooperation Center, or about the income obtained by a research institute. A separate pool of funds, no longer so significant, is income paid by associates (10,497,500 RMB)[56].

When analyzing NDRC revenues (Graph 8), it should be noted that the level of self-financing is quite high, averaging 31.2%, which is not the norm for this type of agency in other countries. Expenditure related to regional development is generally money coming from the central budget, but doing business makes an important contribution to the Commission's revenues. It is quite symptomatic for the PRC, that an institution performing many tasks, including supervising the implementation of specific plans by public entities and enterprises, itself acts as an entrepreneur. Referring in turn to the expenses of the NDRC, it should be noted that not all funds are spent on activities directly related to regional policy, which results from a wide range of tasks of the institution. The category of public expenditure is definitely funds related to the implementation of regional policy (67.7%). A significant part of this item is activities related to the programming and implementation of plans. The importance of scientific reflection on possible

56 Guojia fazhan gaige wei bumen juesuan [2019 niandu] (国家发展改革 委部门决算 [2019 年度]), July 17, 2020, pp. 11, 13, 50, https://zfxxgk.ndrc.gov.cn/web/iteminfo.jsp?id=17169 (access: 20/11/2021).

solutions to problems in regional policy is the second largest expenditure (18.6%), i.e., science and technology. The remaining activities of the Commission account for around 10% of expenditure.

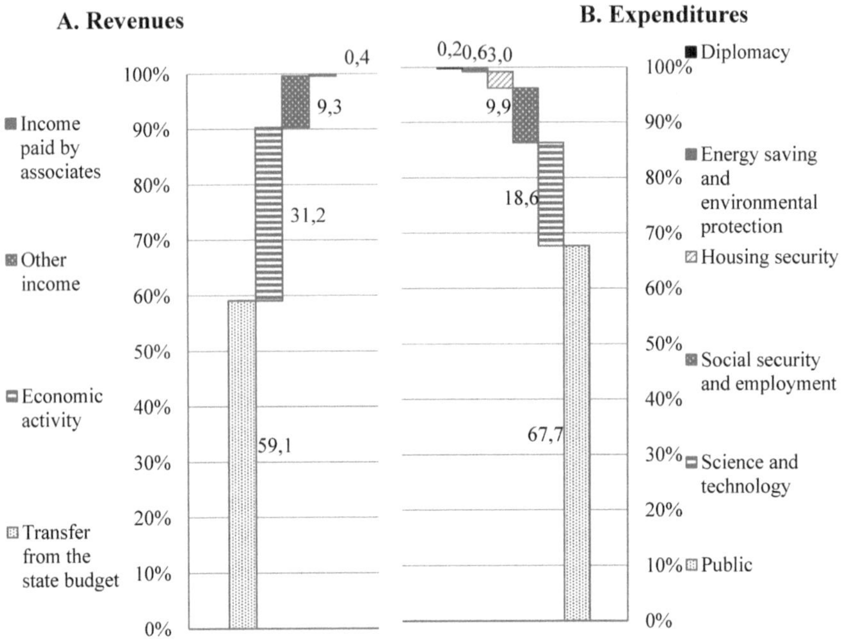

Graph 8. Structure of NDRC revenues and expenditures (2019). Source: own study based on: Guojia fazhan gaige wei boom juesuan (2019 niandu) op. cit., pp. 11, 13, 50.

An extremely important part of the implementation of the regional policy are activities addressed to the central and western provinces of the country. The dynamic development of China, starting from the 1970s, resulted in the dynamic development of the eastern and southern provinces, while the development of the central and western provinces was moderate. Leveling disproportions and creating conditions for competitiveness in less developed regions are the objectives of the regional policy. A clear example of activities in this area is the Western Development Strategy (WDS). This covers activities for the benefit of the western and central regions of China, aimed at balancing development and reducing disproportions, and supporting competitiveness in relation to the eastern provinces. The implementation of the Strategy took place as part of several editions, starting from 2000, and is coupled with the implementation of the Five-

Year Plans, respectively: 10th for 2000–2005[57], 11th for 2006–2010[58], 12th for 2011–2015[59], 13th for 2016–2020[60], currently 14th for the years 2021–2026[61].

WDS belongs to the macroregional strategies / programs / plans implemented in the last two decades, such as the Northeast Revitalization Program, the Pearl River Delta Program, the Yangzi River Delta Program and the Central Regions Program. In Chinese regional policy, this is a relatively new, demanding solution, because there is an even greater need to coordinate actions at the central, regional and local levels. The common denominator of all programs is the acceleration of the development of areas covered by a given program and the fact that their impacts exceed the borders of the provinces. However, the programs can be differentiated according to their duration, specific objectives, and the method of financing. In most cases, the development of such a program involves central funding, but not only this. In developed regions (such as those covered by the Pearl River Delta Program), the implementation of the plan does not always result in an increase in central funding, but always focuses resources on specific goals. Another hallmark of the implementation of macroregional strategies is significant investment, especially in infrastructure, which will be discussed later.

Taking into account the political system of the PRC, macroregional programs are each time subject to central approval under the auspices of the NDRC, which in this process is definitely dominant at every stage of the plan formation. Thus,

---

57 Zhonggong zhongyang guanyu zhiding guomin jingji he shehui fazhan di shi ge wu nanny jihua de jianyi (中共中央 关于 制定国民经济和 社会发展 第十 个 五年 计划 的 建议), http://www.gov.cn/gongbao/content/2000/content_60538.htm; Zhonghua renmin gongheguo guomin jingji he shehui fazhan di shi ge wu nanny jihua gangyao (中华人民共和国国民经济 和 社会 发展 第十 个 五年 计划 纲要), http://www.npc.gov.cn/wxzl/gongbao/2001-03/19/content_5134505.htm (access: 20/11/2021).

58 Released on March 2, 2007, Guasuyuan guanyu xibu da kaifa "shiyiwu" guihua de pifu (国务院关于 西部 大开发 "十 一 五" 规划的 批 复), http://www.gov.cn/gongbao/content/2007/content_549035.htm; https://www.ndrc.gov.cn/fggz/fzzlgh/gjjzxgh/200709/P020191104623124380472.pdf (access: 20/11/2021).

59 Released February 13, 2012, Guasuyuan guanyu xibu da kaifa "shierwu" guihua de pi (国务院关于 西部 大开发 "十二 五" 规划的 批), http://www.gov.cn/gongbao/content/2012/content_2076107.htm (accessed on 17.11.2021); Guasuyuan guanyu xibu da kaifa "shierwu" guihua de pfui guo han [2012] 8 hao (Guasuyuan guanyu xibu da kaifa "shierwu" guihua de pfui guo han [2012] 8 hao (国务院关于西部大开发 "十二五" 规划的批复国函 [2012] 8 号),, http://www.gov.cn/zwgk/2012-02/21/content_2072227.htm (access: 20/11/2021); Xību da kaifa "shierwu" guihua guojia fazhan he gaige weiyuanhui er ling yier nian er yue (西部 大开发 "十二 五" 规划国家发展和 改革委员会二 〇 一 二年 二月),, http://guoqing.china.com.cn/zwxx/2012-02/21/content_24691623.htm (access: 20/11/2021).

60 Released on January 11, 2017, Guanyu yinfa xibu da kaifa "shisanwu" guihua de tongzhi) (fa gai xibu [2017] 89 hao) (西部大开发 "十二五" 规划国家发展和改革委员会二〇一二年二月), https://zfxxgk.ndrc.gov.cn/web/iteminfo.jsp?id=410 (access: 20/11/2021).

61 *China's western development strategy to gain new momentum*, May 28, 2020, http://english.www.gov.cn/policies/policywatch/202005/28/content_WS5ecf2018c6d0b3f0e9498d45.html (access: 20/11/2021).

the implementation of macro-regional plans is also a manifestation of centrally programmed regional policy. The positive aspect of this process of formulating programs is that there is a breakdown in thinking about development in terms of only individual administrative units (especially provinces here). The experiences of regional policies in other parts of the world clearly indicate that certain areas should be looked at not only from the point of view of the existing administrative division, but also from the point of view of the function that a given area performs and the links between the constituent elements of individual areas. The implementation of macroregional programs is also proof of an attempt to overcome the development disproportions of the provinces included in individual macroregions. Although they serve the implementation of centrally planned regional policy, they also provide an opportunity to undertake bottom-up activities accompanying the implementation of macroregional plans. It should be added that the final shape of the plans is also the result of lobbying activities undertaken by local activists, mainly within the CPC (e.g., the Northeast group in the Central Committee at the 3rd Plenum in 1998[62]).

Table 18. Selected macroregional programs

Name of the macro-regional program	Provinces covered by the program
Western Development Strategy – _ *Xibu da kaifa "shiyiw" guihua* (西部 大开发"十一五"规划))	1) Inner Mongolia 2) Guangxi 3) Chongqing 4) Sichuan 5) Guizhou 6) Yunnan 7) Tibet 8) Shaanxi 9) Gansu 10) Qinghai 11) Ningxia 12) Xinjiang
Northeast Revitalization Program – *Dongbei diqu zhenxing guihua* (东北 地区 振兴规划))	13) Liaoning 14) Jilin 15) Heilongjiang 16) Part of Inner Mongolia (since 2007), i.e., Hulunbel City, Xing Unita, Tongliao City, Chifeng City and Xilin Guole League

62 Jae Ho Chung, Hongyi Lai, Jang-Hwan Joo, *"Revive the Northeast" (zhenxing dongbei) Program: Origins, Policies and Implementation,* "The China Quarterly" 2009, no. 197, pp. 110–113.

Table 18 *(Continued)*

Name of the macro-regional program	Provinces covered by the program
Pearl River Delta Program – *Zhujiang sanjiaozhou diqu gaige fazhan guihua gangyao* (珠江三角洲 地区 改革发展 规划 纲 要))[63]	1) Chosen cities Guangdong province (Guangzhou, Shenzhen, Zhuhai, Foshan, Jiangmen, Dongguan, Zhongshan, Huizhou and Zhaoqing City) 2) Hong Kong 3) Macau
Yangzi River Delta Program – *Changjiang sanjiaozhou diqu quyu guihua* (长江 三角洲 地区 区域 规划))[64]	1) Shanghai 2) Jiangsu 3) Zhejiang 4) Anhui
Central Regions Program – *Cujin zhongbu diqu jueqi guihua* (促进中部 地区 崛起 规划))[65]	1) Anhui 2) Shanxi 3) Henan 4) Hubei 5) Hunan 6) Jiangxi

Source: own study based on: *The "Rise of Central China" Plan: Objectives and Impacts with Special Focus on Anhui Province,* Shanghai Flash 2012, issue 4, p. 2, [in:]: https://www.sinoptic.ch/shanghaiflash /texts/pdf/2012/201204_Shanghai.Flash.pdf (access: 20/11/2021), Sebastian Heilmann, Oliver Melton, op.cit., p. 591, Dong Lisheng, *China's Drive to Revitalise the Northeast,* "China Perspectives" 2005, April no. 58, pp. 2–4,

Due to the importance of WDS, a separate sub-section of this subsection is devoted to the strategy. The Northeast Revitalization Program aims[66] to support the revitalization of three peripheral provinces in the northeast of China. The purpose of supporting this area is to implement an approach to development defined as coordinated. It is mainly about revitalizing old industrial bases. Depending on the edition, the program area was slightly modified and so the 2007 edition with a perspective until 2020 covered the provinces of Liaoning, Jilin, Heilongjiang and part of the Autonomous Region of Inner Mongolia, i.e., Hulunbel City, Xing Unita, Tongliao City, Chifeng City and Xilin Guole League, covering a total of 1.45 million $km^{2,}$ with an impact on a population of 120 million inhabitants. As in the case of other strategies of this type, it was assumed that the

63 Zhujiang sanjiaozhou diqu gaige fazhan guihua gangyao (2008–2020) (珠江三角洲 地区 改革发展规划纲要 [2008–2020]), http://www.scio.gov.cn/ztk/xwfb/52/9/Document/1057059/1057059.htm (access: 20/11/2021).

64 Guojia fazhan gaige wei guanyu yinfa changjiang sanjiaozhou diqu quyu guihua de tongzhi (国家发展 改革 委 关于 印发 长江 三角洲 地区 区域 规划 的通知), http://www.gov.cn/zwgk/2010-06/22/content_1633868.htm (access: 20/11/2021).

65 Guasuyuan guanyu cujin zhongbu diqu jueqi "shisanwu" guihua de pifu (国务院关于促进中部 地区 崛起 "十三 五" 规划的 批复), http://www.gov.cn/zhengce/content/2016-12/23/content_5151840.htm (access: 20/11/2021).

66 Dongbei diqu zhenxing guihua ((东北地区振兴规划), http://www.gov.cn/gzdt/2007-08/20/content_721632.htm (access: 20/11/2021).

support would be focused on innovation and institutional reforms. The latter concept covers activities aimed at increasing the efficiency of development management, the entrepreneurship support system, strategic adjustment of the public sector, improvement of the education, health, culture, and sport system, and economic management promoting resource saving and environmental protection (e. g., reducing energy consumption per unit of GDP by approximately 20% on average, annually). The economic goals were related to accelerating the pace of reforms and further opening up the economies of the provinces covered by the program. In this regard, the average annual GDP per capita growth rate of 7.4% was assumed. The plan expected: (1) construction of a production base for the production of advanced devices; (2) development of technologically advanced industries; (3) optimization of the energy industry (building energy security); (4) better use of resources (petrochemical, coal, steel industries); (5) acceleration of the development of the light industry (chemical, pharmaceutical industries); (6) support for agriculture (strengthening the agricultural production base, development of breeding meat animals, organic agricultural products; (7) support for the service sector (logistics, distribution); (8) support for the development of towns and villages (coordination of infrastructure construction in various regions).

The specificity of the Northeast Revitalization Program adopted in 2003 indicates that attention has been focused on reducing disproportions and maintaining social harmony. Generally speaking, the program initially contributed to the economic recovery, i. e., the dynamics of regional development. The annual GDP growth rate of the north-eastern macroregion (i. e., Liaoning, Jilin, Heilongjiang provinces) in 2001–2003 was 9.9%, and after the program was implemented, it increased to 12.9% in 2004–2006, exceeding the national average at the same time by 2.6 percentage points. The share of the north-eastern provinces in China's GDP also slightly increased, i. e., 0.1 percentage point. In terms of the political dimension, there were no major outbreaks of social tensions in the macroregion during the same period. Between 2003 and 2006, the proportion of petitioners in Beijing dropped by 21.4%. The data indicate that the initial effects of the program are declining. The macroregion is an area with problems resulting from the historical shaping of its economy according to the principles of a centrally planned economy (state-owned enterprises)[67]. Changes towards the introduction of market mechanisms to a greater extent were sluggish (restructuring of obsolete industries). These changes were to a small extent accompanied by radical structural changes, and there were also corruption-gen-

67 *Jilin kuai pao beihou de "wang min sudu" (*吉林快跑背后 的"王岷速度") 吉林 快跑背后 的 "王 岷 速度"), http://news.sina.com.cn/c/2007-03-01/095412400380.shtml (access: 20/11/2021); Tony Saich, *Governance and Politics of China*, op. cit., p. 169.

erating phenomena. For illustrative purposes only, in 2005, among the 14 senior provincial and ministerial officials convicted or investigated for corruption in China, five were from the Northeast in 2005. The effect is that the officials themselves admit that the effects are more modest than expected at the beginning of setting up the program[68].

Research by Chinese scholars[69] suggests that the strategy significantly improved regional economic growth and per capita income by increasing GDP and GDP *per capita* by 25.7% and 46%, respectively. The implementation of the program significantly worsened the situation of the regional labor market, i. e., it reduced employment in industry. Furthermore, the strategy did not significantly improve the regional road infrastructure and did not contribute to increasing investment in education or improving social security. Most importantly, it did not have a significant impact on mitigating regional disparities. It should also be noted that, according to research, the effects of the policy are very different in different cities, depending on the size of the cities and their characteristics. Therefore, it is difficult to give an unequivocal answer to the question of whether the Northeast China Revitalization Program achieved its original goals related to the integrated approach. However, it is justifiable to strive to improve the quality of research and development activities and to increase investment in human capital also on the basis of the diversity of urban areas.

The Pearl River Delta program aims[70] to support the development of a part of the Guangdong Province area. Contrary to some other programs, including macroregional ones, here it is planned to support growth poles; therefore, the following are planned: (1) development of modern services such as financial, logistics, IT, business and tourism, outsourcing, development of capital markets; (2) accelerating the development of an advanced manufacturing industry, including the automotive industry (including clusters, international production base), petrochemical, shipbuilding, high-quality equipment production, and nuclear energy; (3) development of technologically advanced industries, (high-tech), development of industrial bases and industrial pacts, processing of large amounts of data, new materials for integrated circuits, next-generation broadband wireless communication, next-generation Internet, biotechnology industries (e. g. stem cells, organisms genetically modified); (4) transformation of traditional industries (textiles, food, building materials; (5) development of modern agriculture, mainly development in the context of increasing its efficiency and pro-ecology, along with the development of the food processing

68 Jae Ho Chung, Hongyi Lai, Jang-Hwan Joo, op. cit., pp. 120–123.

69 Ren Wanxia, Xue Bing, Yang Jun, Lu Chengpeng, *Effects of the Northeast China Revitalization Strategy on Regional Economic Growth and Social Development,* "Chinese Geographical Science" 2020, vol. 30, no. 5, 1 pp. 791–809.

70 Zhujiang sanjiaozhou diqu gaige fazhan guihua gangyao, op. cit.

system); (6) increasing the competitiveness of enterprises; (7) further improvement of infrastructure.

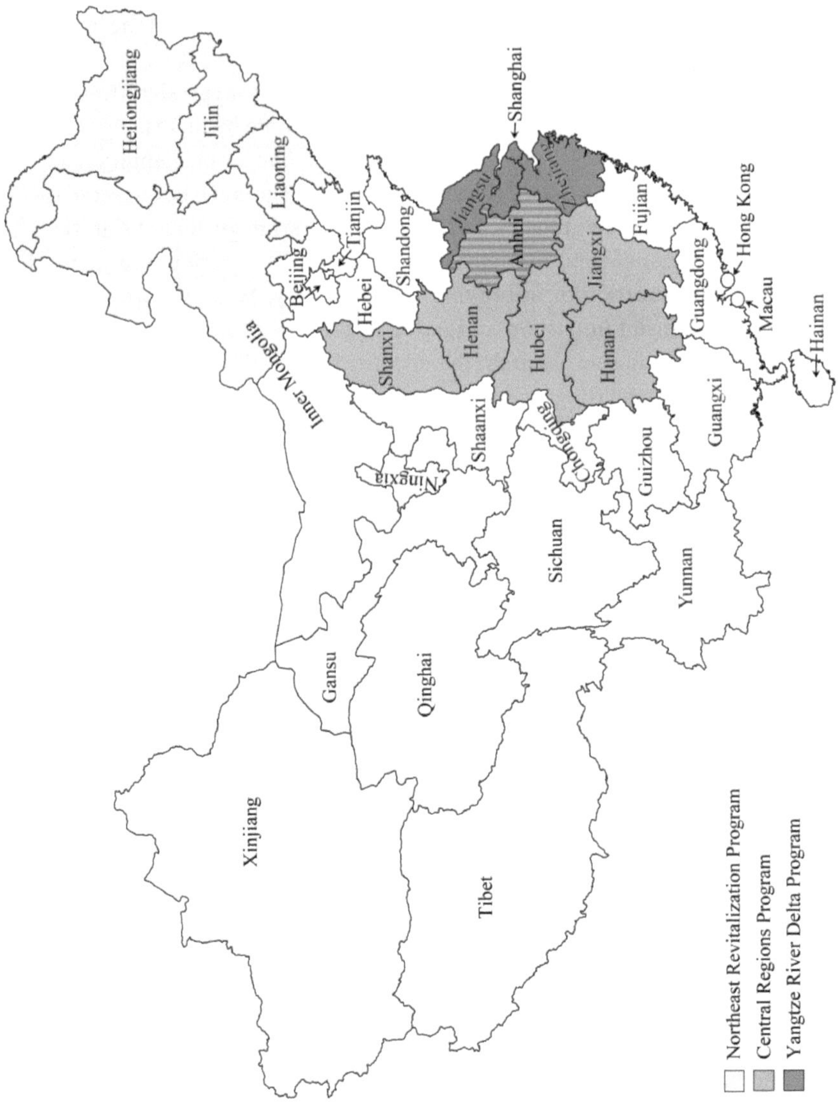

Map 2. Provinces covered by selected macroregional programs. Source: own study

The Yangtze River Delta program covers the provinces of Shanghai, Jiangsu, Zhejiang, and Anhui with a total area of 358,000 km^2. The analysis of basic economic data clearly indicates that the program covers the most competitive and highly developed area of China, which from the economic point of view not only plays a key role in the modernization of the country, but also constitutes a successful model for opening up regional economies to the world. Therefore, the program is not so much aimed at reducing disproportions as integrating the development of the Yangtze Delta area. It is mainly about strengthening the diffusion of development of major centers such as Shanghai, Hangzhou, and Hefei, also toward supporting their functional environment. In this area there are scientific and educational centers, and laboratories of at least national importance. The program zone is characterized by very high innovation potential, exemplified by the number of individuals reaching high positions in the field of research and development, the number of patents submitted, and the intensity of research conducted on a national scale[71]. In principle, this open cooperation, also with the environment (e.g., smaller cities, rural areas) fosters the achievement of synergy and increases efficiency; hence the need to take coordinated actions, e.g., through the Yangtze River Regional Cooperation Office, but also international cooperation platforms. The aspirations of this area to act as a research and business *hub* require further actions to optimize the achieved results, not only on a national but also on an international scale. The implementation of the strategy is to contribute to the development of the Yangtze River Delta as a growth pole and economic showcase of the PRC. All this so that China can participate in global competition and cooperation. The target set for 2025 is related to the economic integration of the Yangtze River delta in the spatial (urban, rural), scientific, technological, infrastructural, environmental, public, and institutional dimensions. By 2025, the difference between the city and the countryside in terms of GDP *per capita* in the central area of the region has been planned to be within the limits of 2.2:1. Development coordination activities should focus on five spheres in which international excellence is planned, namely: (1) finance, (2) trade, (3) shipping, (4) innovation, and (5) technology. The plan also included infrastructure investments in the field of rail transport (including high-speed rail, intercity rail), road, air (modernization of airports) and water transport (ports, port groups), as well as energy infrastructure and environmental construction.

The Central Regions Program (last edition on December 17, 2016) covers provinces with an average level of development if you compare the main macroeconomic indicators. However, at various times the dynamics of GDP growth has been lower than in less developed western provinces. The area of the provinces covered by the program, i.e., Shanxi, Anhui, Jiangxi, Henan, Hubei and Hunan, is 1.028 million km^2, which is 10.7% of the total area of the country. Due

71 *What does the Yangtze River Delta Integration Mean for Businesses in China?*, 17/09/2019, https://www.china-briefing.com/news/yangtze-river-delta-integration-opportunities-incentives-for-businesses-in-china-dual-circulation-strategy/ (access: 20/11/2021).

to natural conditions, including topography and the good quality of the soil, it is a place of significant grain production, a base of energy resources, a base of production, and an integrated transport hub of the PRC[72]. As in the case of other strategies, the aim is to significantly increase the level of economic development. As part of the strategy, it has been assumed that in the long term, food production in this area will increase through the construction of cereal production bases and supporting the modernization of agriculture (including the industrialization of agriculture), and the construction of rural infrastructure. As agriculture significantly interferes with the natural environment, measures are also planned to rationalize the use of energy resources available in the area of the plan (hard coal mines, construction of power grids) and the processing of raw materials. Also, in this case, it is planned to focus on building industrial bases (most often in the form of large urban clusters)[73], increasing innovative capacity and developing technologically advanced branches of industry. Another priority is to optimize transport resources and strengthen the position of the main centers as transport nodes. The development under the program is to be based on urban clusters such as around Wuhan (Hubei province), including the production of modern devices and high-tech products.

4.3. The process of regional policy coordination using the example of the Western Development Strategy

The analysis of individual editions of the WDS leads to the conclusion that the strategies are comprehensive. The layout of priorities can be reduced to areas such as infrastructure, industry, environmental protection, agriculture, and public services. Complementarily, activities aimed at building the mechanisms of competitiveness of 12 provinces included in the WDS, i. e., Inner Mongolia, Guangxi, Chongqing, Sichuan, Guizhou, Yunnan, Tibet, Shaanxi, Gansu, Qinghai, Ningxia and Xinjiang, can also be identified. The last element of WDS implementation is important because international experience shows that the key element is to support endogenous development mechanisms to maintain the dynamics of the phenomena that occurred as a result of external intervention, in this case subsequent editions of the WDS. Only by way of example is it possible to point to the dynamics of growth of investments, which are implemented as long as external public funds are available. And the key is to continue these invest-

72 [Cujin zhongbu diqu jueqi guihua (2016 zhiì 2025 nian)] zhengce jiedu ([促进中部 地区 崛起规划（2016 至2025年）] 政策解读), http://www.scio.gov.cn/34473/34515/Document/1535229/1535229.htm (access: 20/11/2021).

73 Tony Saich, *Governance and Politics of China*, London-New York 2015, p. 169.

ments from a region's own resources. This can occur when an appropriate level of competitiveness is achieved, allowing for the reinvestment of the earnings.

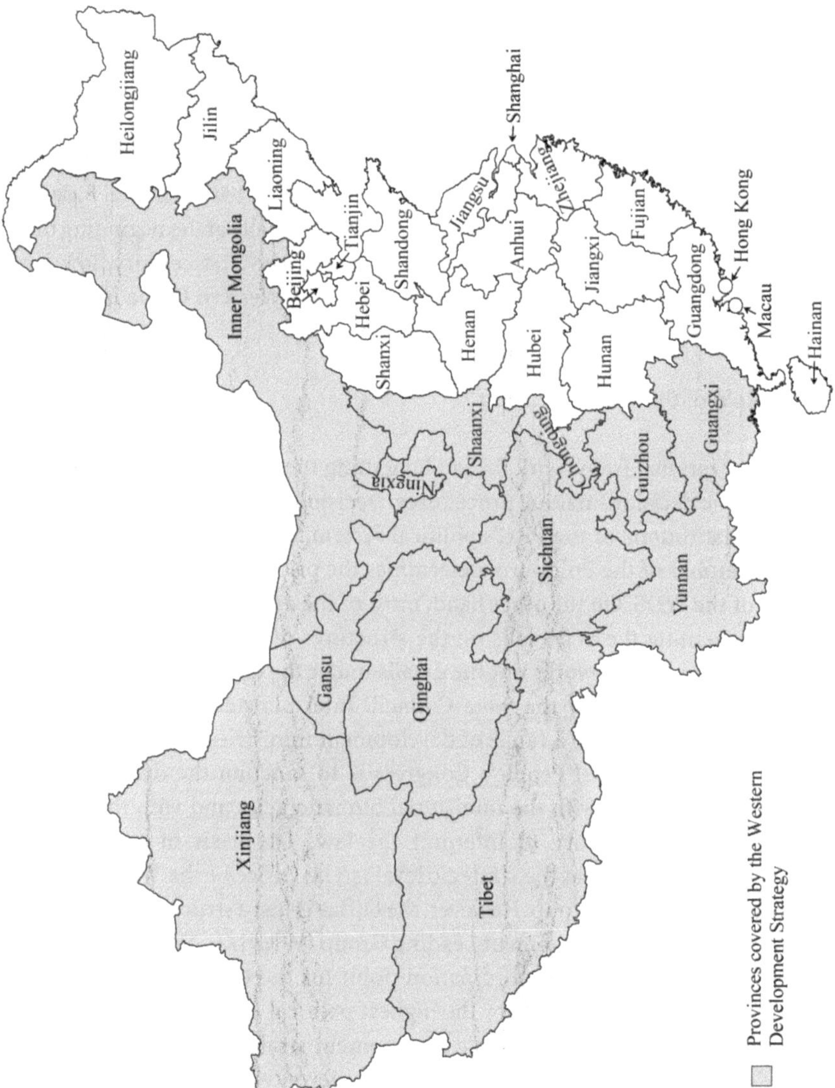

Map 3. Provinces covered by the Western Development Strategy. Source: own study

The specificity of the WDS lies in the fact that from the central level, attempts are made to dynamize economic development, the source of which should be seen in the regional and local system. These observations do not change the fact that the intervention under the WDS, especially in the first editions, focused on investments, mainly in infrastructure. The authorities were convinced that this area had not experienced the industrialization process to the same extent as the provinces of the eastern coast, which was confirmed by the low index of industrial production in this area in relation to the national average. The area of Western China also contains provinces with essential resources for the development of the economy of the whole country, such as oil, gas, coal, rare earth metals, potassium phosphorus, and nonferrous metals. The dispersed and inefficient exploitation of natural resources and the outdated industrial base have led to environmental pollution. If we add to this, especially at the beginning of the strategy implementation, i.e., in the first years of the 21st century, low labor costs, the picture of the limited market potential of Western China is clear.

4.3.1. Role of the Leading Group

The organizational framework for implementing the WDS is based on party and bureaucratic decision-making procedures. Decisions are made by the CPC's elite and key institutions of the PRC's political system. The Secretary General of the CPC, a member of the Politburo, determines the priorities and the basic general outline of the WDS. On the other hand, most of the administrative responsibility for implementing the WDS falls on the structures of the State Council. At this stage, the bureaucracy works out the details under the direction and supervision of the leading organs of the State Council. Interministerial consultations are necessary, which include a range of development ministries. On the other hand, the role of the National People's Congress is to sanction the decisions taken. Implementation rests with the ministerial bureaucracies and with the judiciary insofar as it is necessary to interpret the law. The basis of the WDS implementation structure at the strategic level is The Office of the Western Region Development Leading Group. However, the Office is just a structure that supports the Western Region Development Leading Group (WRDLG). The office plays the role of a high-level central coordination point for the CPC Central Committee and the State Council, that is, for the highest political elites[74].

Thinking about Western China's development strategy was initiated in Jiang Zemin's speech on June 17, 1999, at the Xian conference, in which he first used the phrase *great western development* to describe efforts to boost the development of western provinces under the 10th Five-Year Plan. In 2000 the State Council

74 Gregory T. Chin, *The Politics of China's Western Development Initiative,* [in:] Ding Lu, William Neilson (eds.), *China's West Region Development: Domestic Strategies and Global Implications,* London 2004, p. 139.

established the Western Region Development Leading Group. The leader of this group was Prime Minister Zhu Rongji himself, and Wen Jiabao, Deputy Prime Minister of the State Council, served as deputy head of the group. Following consideration of the proposal and adoption by the National People's Congress, the Office of the WRDLG officially began operating in March 2000, which is considered to be the beginning of WDS implementation. In October 2000, at the fifth plenary session of the XV Central Committee of the CPC, the "Proposals of the Central Committee of the Communist Party on the formulation of the 10th Five-Year Plan for Economic and Social Development" were adopted. The plan emphasizes the implementation of the western region development strategy and the acceleration of the development of the central regions[75].

In addition to the Prime Minister and the Deputy Prime Minister, other members of the Leading Group are the highest officials of the respective ministries, committees and offices[76]. In total, as of August 1, 2018, there are 14 ministers, 6 deputy ministers, and 4 chairmen of national committees. It should be noted that not all working groups have such a high rank, because very often they simply consist of members with the rank of deputy minister at most. The Western Region Development Leading Group[77], along with the Economic Leadership Group, is recognized as one of the most important and influential. Additionally, given the competences of the Leading Group, it is one of the most versatile groups, although its operation is essentially limited to the 12 western provinces. The group also enjoys the status of an advisory body with respect to the Central Committee of the CPC, further enhancing the importance of this group. It should be noted that the Group is not strictly a decision-making body, but its political positions and recommendations influence the final decisions. The decisions of the central government are often based on the recommendations of the Group; in other cases, they are simply a formalization of the position taken by the Group. An important aspect of the Group's functioning is the fact that its competences cover matters of interministerial importance; therefore, it plays a key role in building consensus and coordinating the formal decision-making process. The Group is entitled to review the development strategy, solve the main problems

75 See *Zhonggong zhongyang guanyu zhiding guomin jingji he shehui fazhan di shi ge wu nian jihua de jianyi* (中共中央关于制定国民经济和社会发展第十个五年计划的建议), http://www.cctv.com/news/special/zt1/five/1364.html (access: 20/11/2021).

76 Leading Group for Western Region Development revamped, http://english.www.gov.cn/policies/latest_releases/2018/08/01/content_281476244584930.htm (access: 20/11/2021).

77 Bill Chou, *Government and Policy-Making Reform in China: The Implications of Governing Capacity.* Routledge, 2009, London, New York, p. 65.

related to development planning, and propose appropriate statutory provisions and executive acts[78].

Unlike most working groups, the WRDLG has its own permanent office with permanent staff. The office is tasked with servicing group members; the office receives directives and guidance from higher levels, sets guidelines, collects reports and analyses from research institutes, negotiates with other interested national and industry offices, and reports these activities to the supreme authorities. It also supports the administrative functioning of the Group NDRC, whose organizational structures include the leading group office.

The composition of the Leading Group clearly shows which areas are considered important for the development of the western provinces, i.e., economic and social ministries, but not only these. On the one hand, it is striking that the composition of the group does not include representatives of regional or local governments, which once again confirms the high degree of centralization of development policy directed to the western provinces[79]. On the other hand, the composition of the Group demonstrates the political commitment of the central government to the implementation of the development strategy of the western provinces. Considering the fact that after the adoption of the state budget, individual ministries are the administrators of central funds[80], it is important that the Group includes representatives of institutions that can engage appropriate resources to implement the strategy. We are talking not only about financial resources, but also legal, fiscal, and organizational instruments that seem important in creating a system of preferences for the western provinces covered by the WDS.

The establishment of the WRDLG directly under the auspices of the State Council launched the WDS policy formulation process. The shape of this public initiative is influenced by actors from various levels, also outside the central structure located at the Leading Group level, who try to influence the decisions made both formally and informally. The formal process involves a tender between different levels of bureaucratic institutions; consultation occurs through the Leading Group to build consensus on the impact of the initiative on specific administrations or industries. Any disputes are discussed by other formal bureaucratic bodies (e.g., other working groups)[81]. The informal influence covers a

78 Guasuyuan guanyu chengli guasuyuan xibu diqu kaifa lingdao xiaozu de jueding (国务院关于成立国务院西部地区开发领导小组的决定), http://www.law-lib.com/law/law_view1.asp?id=15782 (access: 20/11/2021).

79 On participation in shaping public policies in China, see Yongshun Cai, *Managed participation in China*, "Political Science Quarterly" 2004, vol. 119, no. 3, pp. 428–432.

80 Bill Chou, *Government and Policy-Making Reform in China…*, op. cit., p. 66.

81 Sebastian Heilmann, Lea Shih, Sandra Heep, *Socialist organizational and ideological features*, op. cit., pp. 72–75.

very diverse repertoire, including personal networks and informal contacts between the ministers and the deputy prime minister. The same is the case with local officials who rely in this situation on personal contacts and links with central officials. Therefore, it can be said that we are dealing here with lobbying, with the difference with the Western countries that in China most of the different interests occur not in the external economic sector, but within the government or in a *quasi* -state structure[82].

Since the WDS covers many areas, it requires making decisions in many sectors, thematic areas, which in turn are managed at the central level by various ministries[83], and these are supervised by the bureaucratic structures subordinate to them. In addition, the WRDLG Office must be as responsive to "external" national interests as other administrative units; industries are interested in a particular aspect of the WDS. Then they become very active in the consultation process. It takes an increasing amount of time to perform this coordination function. If there are disputes at the level of various agencies which cannot be resolved at the level of the WRDLG, the matters are referred according to their merits to the Deputy Director of the NDRC, and sometimes to the Director of the NDRC and the Director of the Leading Group Office, who, while presiding over bureaucratic negotiations, seek to reach an agreement. Due to the rank of the chairman and vice-chairman of the Leading Group, i. e., prime minister and vice-prime minister, their interference concerns only the most important decisions made during the most important meetings of the Leading Group, which means that these people do not engage in daily negotiations[84].

The capacity of the Leading Group Office to coordinate, including conduct political consultations, is quite limited due to the formal powers of individual ministries at the central level. The Office is reliant on soliciting the interest of peripheral units or ministerial units within the central government in order to discharge its responsibilities. As already indicated above, the Leading Group and, on its behalf, the Office have the authority to discuss, negotiate, and coordinate most matters related to the WDS; the Office itself does not have the actual implementation capacity. Such capacities are found in relevant ministries and, due to the specificity of WDS, also in state-owned enterprises operating in sectors important for the WDS, such as energy, transport, telecommunications, construction, and mining. Since the WDS focuses primarily on infrastructure projects, it is reasonable to recall an example from this area.

82 Gregory T. Chin, *The Politics of China's Western Development Initiative*, op. cit., p. 146.
83 About organizational structures of ministries, see: Sebastian Heilmann, Lea Shih, Sandra Heep, *Socialist organizational and ideological features*, op. cit., pp. 80–83.
84 Gregory T. Chin, *The Politics of China's Western Development Initiative*, op. cit., p. 147.

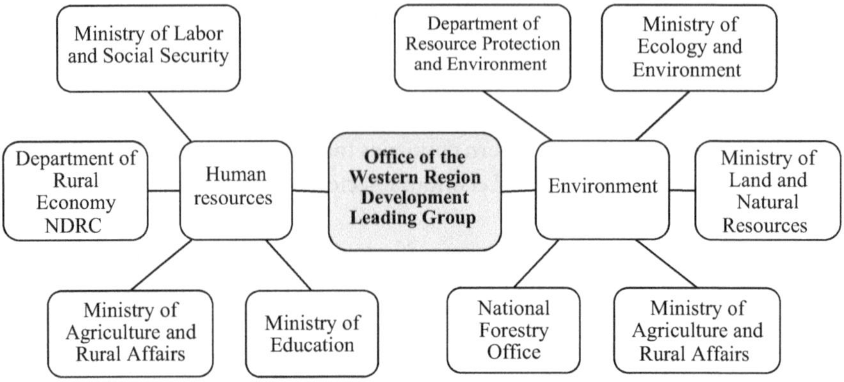

Diagram 11. Coordinating role of the Office of the Western Region Development Leading Group in the implementation of the WDS using the example of the natural environment and human resources. Source: own study based on: Guowuyuan bangong ting guanyu tiaozheng guowuyuan xibu diqu kaifa lingdao xiaozu zucheng renyuan de tongzho, op. cit.; *Zhineng peizhi he nei she jigou*, op. cit.

The ministry responsible for construction controls the spending of government funds allocated to leading infrastructure projects (including in the western regions) approved by the NDRC. Subnational governments are also important in this process, for example, in obtaining funds and administering infrastructure projects in their areas. These are activities in which the WRDLG has no role in day-to-day management. Many infrastructure projects are financed with funds from capital markets (domestic and international), as well as by the relevant departments of the Ministry of Finance (e.g., by issuing bonds) and the Department of Foreign Investments of the NDRC, which are authorized to approve projects. In addition, the WRDLG Office has limited influence over these departments. The situation is similar in other areas, such as the natural environment, energy, and human capital (Diagram 11). In each of these areas, the Office has to negotiate the shape and scope of implemented projects, the resources for which are at the disposal of relevant ministries, departments, or other organizational units[85].

An overview of the coordinating role of the Leading Group Office reveals a fairly broad scope of the decision-making process which is challenging, especially if there is a need to make a quick decision or act on a specific matter. This highly bureaucratic process makes it very difficult to deliver the end product, i.e., a decision resulting from consensus among potentially antagonistic actors. This generates endless activities related to the coordination of meetings, which may lead to an impasse at key moments of the implementation of the WDS. Never-

85 Ibid, p. 148.

theless, what seems to be an obstacle may be an advantage, as it gives an opportunity to increase the representativeness of the final decisions made, where each entity has to partially yield to the demands of others. The search for a balance between various interests at the central level may be important in the process of building the legitimacy of decisions within the WDS.

Implementation challenges include not only fragmented decision-making at the central level, but also coordination efforts at the regional and central levels[86]. Here, the spectrum of attitudes of subnational authorities[87]is very wide: from full acceptance, through clientelism, to local resistance. The most common, however, is the implementation of centrally formulated directives, even at the expense of local needs. Nevertheless, the WDS appears to be a golden opportunity to implement local initiatives to the extent that they fit into the framework of the Strategy. Above all, it is a chance to catch up on development arrears, mainly in terms of infrastructure[88]. Meanwhile, resistance manifests itself in refusing to agree to central instructions. It should be emphasized that subnational officials played an important role in lobbying for the preferential treatment of the West in the context of the growing East-West disparities starting in the early 1990s[89]. In 1995, during meetings related to the 9th Five-Year Plan, leaders from several inland provinces called on national leaders to establish special aid measures and adopt policies to reduce regional inequalities. Regions have repeatedly applied at the national forum (CPC congresses) for assistance to central regions through specific policies, regulations, or investment projects. Therefore, the establishment of the WDS was a response not only to the frustration of regional officials but also to the growing social unrest in the interior of the country. The main issues related to the tension between the center and local government concerned which level of power or actor was the main driver and which was the final arbitrator within the WDS. However, awareness of the existence of objective

86 David Goodman, *The Campaign to "Open Up the West": National, Provincial-level and Local Perspectives*, "The China Quarterly" 2004, vol. 178, pp. 324–331.

87 On the scope of tasks of the Development and Reform Committee in the Sichuan Province, see Sìchuan sheng fazhan he gaige weiyuanhui zhuyao zhize, lingdao jianjie he jigou shezhi (四川省发展和 改革委员会主要职责、领导简介 和 机构设置), 四川省发展 和 改革 委员会主要职责、领导简介和机构设置,), http://www.sc.gov.cn/10462/10778/10876/2020/11/25/ef07e79fbc584644b34476fe6d4974a7.shtml (access: 20/11/2021).

88 Zhiyue Bo, *Governing China in the Early 21st Century: Provincial Perspective*, op. cit., pp. 159–160.

89 Unlike in Western countries, lobbying of the economic sphere played a minor role here, which is symptomatic also in relation to other areas of shaping public policies in the PRC, see: Scott Kennedy, *Comparing formal and informal lobbying practices in China: The capital's ambivalent embrace of capitalists*, "China Information" 2009, vol. 23, no 2, pp. 195–222; Jianxing Yu, Kenichiro Yashima, Yongdong Shen, *Autonomy or Privilege? Lobbying Intensity of Local Business Associations in China*, "Journal of Chinese Political Science" 2014, vol. 19, no. 3, pp. 315–333.

development disproportions between the West and the rest of the country resulted in the reduction of tensions between the central directives and local initiative, both in the context of the administration level and specific industries. An example of this is the subtle resistance of the Shanghai authorities to the centrally promoted policy of encouraging Shanghai developers to invest in the western provinces[90].

4.3.2. The dynamics of the evolution of development priorities

The implementation of the WDS has been planned in such a way as to maximize the impact of the Strategy, at least as intended by the central planners, in the presence of limited resources. Therefore, there was a strategy of targeting support to key geographic areas, also referred to as central zones (*focal belts*), which were to become places of concentrated development. Population density and access to main communication lines, inter alia, were to be taken into account. At the beginning, three areas were designated, that is, (a) delimited by the Qinghai-Lanzhou-Xinjiang line, (b) the upper reaches of the Yangtze River, and (c) the Nanning-Guiyang-Kunming belt. These zones were subject to relatively complex investments, such as infrastructure, environmental, communication, and information technology construction. This solution met local resistance. It was questioned whether designated areas should be supported in view of the existence of other areas where poverty was concentrated. The government, relying on experience from the eastern provinces, in particular special economic zones, and resulting also from the development strategy of the eastern coast, tried to concentrate industry and capital in specific geographic locations, which would further benefit the neighboring areas. Another argument that appeared here was that the designated central zones did not cover a significant part of the areas remaining within the jurisdiction of individual administrative units. A further issue was that decisions on the final location of the zones depended, to a large extent, on personal ties[91] between senior officials from the Leading Group Office, high-ranking CPC leaders, and senior officials from other bureaucratic (e.g., ministerial) units[92].

The main activities of the WDS are based on public intervention in the field of infrastructure investments. The intention of the creators of these investments is to increase the competitiveness of these areas. Generally speaking, investment

90 Gregory T. Ch in, *The Politics of China's Western Development Initiative*, op. cit., p. 151.
91 On the importance of individual factions within the CCP, see Zhiyue Bo, *Balance of Factional Power in China: The Seventeenth Central Committee of the Chinese Communist Party*, "East Asia" 2008, vol. 25, pp. 334–363.
92 Gregory T. Chin, *The Politics of China's Western Development Initiative*, op. cit., p. 157, 160.

projects implemented through the WDS can be reduced to three categories[93]. First, these are projects implemented in western provinces, but that benefit virtually the entire country such as those related to gas transport, the construction of energy transmission networks from the west to the east, and the Qinghai-Tibet railway. Second, these are projects that improve infrastructure conditions in the western region, such as railways, roads, airports, hydroelectric plants, hydrotechnics, and the construction of municipal infrastructure. Third, these are projects that improve the living standards of the inhabitants of the western provinces. This applies, for example, to the network of paved roads at the county level, electricity supply to cities, broadcasting, and television networks at the village level.

The importance of infrastructure in stimulating regional development is under discussion[94]. The discussion can be summarized as follows: Infrastructure is, in most cases, an element necessary to stimulate development, but at the same time insufficient. It is difficult to use even the most innovative research laboratories if you cannot reach them due to the lack or insufficient quality of the transport infrastructure. In fact, it is not about creating (building) this or that infrastructure but about how to use it. Returning to the example of research laboratories, the key is not only to build an object but to equip it with appropriate research equipment. The biggest challenge is to conduct research and development work that will serve to create innovations that determine the competitiveness of the economy, both in the domestic and international market. This, in turn, requires an integrated approach, because here, in addition to human resources, building walls, purchasing equipment, and above all, ideas are needed. Only a comprehensive approach can lead to rational expenditure on infrastructure building and its maintenance.

93 Lin Ling, Liu Shiqing, *Measuring the Impact of the "Five Mega- Projects"*, [in:] Ding Lu, William Neilson (eds.), op. cit., p. 263.

94 Grzegorz Gorzelak, *Fakty i mity rozwoju regionalnego*, "Zarządzanie Publiczne" 2008, no. 4 (6), pp. 78–85.

Table 19. List of priorities of the Western Development Strategy – editions accompanying 11th, 12th, 13th Five-Year Plans in the period 2006–2020

11th 2006–2010	12th 2011–2015	13th 2016–2020
	Infrastructure	
– Construction of highways (including the following sections: Beijing-Kunming, Baotou-Maoming, Qingdao-Yinchuan, Shanghai-Xi'an, Shanghai-Chongqing), expressways; – construction of the main railway lines of supraregional importance; – construction of small airports (e.g., Kangding, Aershan and Yushu) and modernization of airports (e.g., in Xi'an, Urumqi, Xining, Chongqing, Guiyang, Lanzhou); – inland waterways (large infrastructure projects); – pipelines (oil, gas, auxiliary facilities); – water supply, large-scale irrigation systems, construction of retention reservoirs; – IT infrastructure (including broadband network); – construction of the infrastructure of central cities (including public transport, city roads, water supply, sewage, sewage treatment infrastructure, heating, gas network, pipelines, reconstruction of public utility facilities).	– Strengthening the road network (national roads, highways connecting eastern and central provinces, international transport corridors); – civil aviation, construction of the hub and main airports grouped in the north-west, south-west, north and central areas, including regional airports; – water transport; – additional railway lines of supraregional and international importance, including freight transport; – construction of an integrated communication junction in the western macroregion; – transmission networks; – IT infrastructure (telecommunications, radio, television, Internet); – anti-flood infrastructure (retention reservoirs, river regulation).	– Quality of communication buses (elimination of the so-called bottlenecks); – modernization and reconstruction of regional and local (urban, rural) roads, the so-called special roads (port, coastal, tourist); – modernization of the existing railway infrastructure (including that related to the "Belt and Road" initiative); – interoperability of transport infrastructure, civil aviation (new airports, internationalization of existing ones), river navigation (improvement of the trunk of the Yangtze, Wujiang and Jialing rivers, among others), coastal ports; – development of sewage infrastructure; – optimization of energy infrastructure; – modernization of water management infrastructure (protection of water intakes, irrigation system and drinking water supply, flood protection projects in the upper reaches of rivers, including the Yangtze and Yellow River.

Table 19 *(Continued)*

11th 2006–2010	12th 2011–2015	13th 2016–2020
Industry		
- Development of key industries: energy, chemical, mining and processing of mineral resources, metallurgical, advanced technology industries; - development of the processing industry of agricultural, textile and wood products; - development of the tourism industry - fight against poverty (industrialization).	- Modernization of the industrial structure – designation of key economic zones; - modernization towards a modern energy industry (coal, oil, natural gas, wind energy, photovoltaics, nuclear power plants).	- Transformation of traditional industries (including steel and coal); - supporting the development of a modern service industry – logistic service system, home services (cleaning, care for the elderly, health); - high-tech services.
Environmental Protection		
- Conservation of resources and their use; - environmental protection in construction sector; - restoring cultivated forests and meadows; - solutions supporting economic development and environmental protection.	- Strengthening the natural environment (designation of key ecological zones); - coordination and rational use of mineral resources (water, oil, coal, rare earth metals, nonferrous metals); - water quality protection infrastructure; - enhancing pollution control (including emissions).	- Environmental protection (large ecological projects); - improving the environmental compensation mechanism; - promotion of economical use of resources); - restoring grassland, increasing forest cover, establishing nature reserves; - enhancing the protection of the aquatic environment in the mainstems of the Yangtze, Wujiang and Jialing rivers and their tributaries; - promoting recycling, energy savings.

Table 19 *(Continued)*

11th 2006–2010	12th 2011–2015	13th 2016–2020
	Agriculture	
- Adaptation of the agricultural structure (village, processing of agricultural products); - increasing the capacity for agricultural production (industrialization of agriculture, increase in cereal production, agricultural mechanization); - increasing farmers' income (retraining, new competences, migration); - promoting innovation in the agricultural sector; - development of agricultural advisory services.	- Modernization of agriculture (structure); - increasing agricultural subsidies; - increasing agricultural production in selected product categories: tea, silkworms, tobacco and flowers, pigs, promotion of agriculture, forestry; - increasing farmers' income; - rural services.	- Improvement of agricultural infrastructure (including rural local roads, agricultural roads); - support for agricultural production: guarantees of purchase of agricultural products, storage aid; - adjustment of the agricultural structure (adjustment of the type of production to geographical conditions); - promoting food security; - agricultural service system; - innovations in agriculture.
	Public services	
- Improving the provision of public services (development of science and education, including rural education, providing 9-year compulsory education, raising the level of education); - health care system (including hospitals, health centers, health insurance system); - culture and sport	- Development of education, science, supporting talent; - public services (social security system, medical and health services, culture).	- Increasing the supply of public services (education, social security, supporting talent); - revitalization of higher education; - a rural teacher support program; - improving the health of residents.

Table 19 *(Continued)*

11th 2006–2010	12th 2011–2015	13th 2016–2020
	Support of competitiveness	
- Opening up to the outside world: investments from other provinces, foreign direct investment, economic cooperation, foreign trade; - introducing special economic zones; - using loans from international financial organizations and governments.	- Increasing interregional interactions.	- Innovations: supporting the development of the innovation system (investments and financing), building an innovation platform, supporting innovative entrepreneurship; - Urbanization: development of key urban agglomerations, small and medium cities, modernization of urban public infrastructure; - Promotion of public-private partnership.

Source: own work based on: Guowuyuan guanyu xibu da kaifa "shiyiwu" guihua de pifu, op. cit.; Xību da kaifa "shierwu" guihua guojia fazhan he gaige weiyuanhui er ling yier nian er yue, op.cit; Guojia fazhan gaige wei guanyu yinfa xibu da kaifa "shisanwu" guihua de tongzhi fa gaii xibu [2017] 89 hao), op. cit.

The analysis of the priorities of various editions of the WDS shows a certain evolution in almost every field of support. When it comes to transport, the initial goal was simply to build the transport infrastructure (roads, railways, airports) as a response to the infrastructure backwardness of the western provinces. With time, priority was given to the main communication routes, i.e., international, national, and supraregional roads. Currently, transport is also present as one of the main priorities, but activities relate to the improvement of the quality of the transport system, communication buses, and the interoperability of transport systems, i.e., connecting different means of transport (road, rail, air, water). The priorities relate to a greater extent to the construction of such elements of transport infrastructure that are of regional or local importance (e.g., rural roads). Although the WDS still focuses on infrastructure projects, now other priorities have become much more important.

While the 11th and 12th editions of the WDS focused mainly on infrastructure projects, mainly transport, the 13th edition focuses on issues such as the implementation of ecological projects, and increasing the supply and quality of public services. In the context of environmental protection, many investment projects are planned; the change of emphasis should be noted, as it may indicate a correction of the approach to the development of less developed regions (including local administrative units). It is certain that it corresponds to the stage of development of underdeveloped areas, where usually after the stage of equipping them with "hard" infrastructure, initiatives are taken to build competitive advantages. The challenge is that it is impossible to reduce the task to the implementation of individual infrastructure projects, and there is a need for systemic development of local production and service activities, ultimately aimed at building sustainable regional competitive capabilities.

With regard to industry, these were initially priorities related to the construction of key industries, such as energy, chemical, or mining industries. The WDS is now supporting the transformation of traditional industries, such as coal and steel, towards reducing production capacity. Instead, it is proposed to develop industries based on new materials, new energy sources (i.e., mainly renewable), and the biomedical sector. Evolution can also be seen in the case of ecology. In subsequent editions of the EDS, more and more space has been devoted not only to the general protection of the environment but also to the designation of special protection zones, the economical use of resources, and the promotion of energy efficiency and improvement of water quality. The emergence of environmental priorities has been the result of the evolution of national policy in this area and, at the same time, is a response to the significant pollution of the natural environment in the area of western China, including due to the use of outdated production methods.

However, the priority for the development of agriculture in Western China can be reduced to the transformation of the agricultural structure (including migration of the agricultural population to places where there are better farming conditions) and increasing agricultural production, e.g., the production of grains, pigs, but also tea, silkworms, tobacco and flowers. This priority is important for at least three reasons: first, low agricultural incomes are a significant social problem and, at the same time, an element conducive to migration to the southern provinces, where employment conditions are much better. Second, China, with its ever-growing population, is struggling with a shortage of certain groups of agricultural products. Third, the drastic income imbalance among Western China's farmers can, under certain conditions, result in social unrest. Equally important is the support of agricultural advisory services, which determines the improvement of the efficiency of agricultural production. This goal is also intended to promote innovation in the agricultural sector, which is certainly part of the promotion of the demand for possible industrial products in the high-tech field.

Although Table 20 does not fully reflect this, it should be noted that more and more importance is attached (e.g., in the 13th WDS) to access to public services, such as education, higher education, social security and the health care system. Similar to the priority infrastructure, there are construction projects such as schools, hospitals, health centers, and recreational and cultural infrastructure. However, there is no doubt that the center of gravity in the case of individual

WDS editions was placed on the side of investments, mainly in terms of transport infrastructure. However, few provisions refer to the social dimension, building social capital, or human capital. An example is the activities for social exclusion in the WDS edition accompanying the 13th Five-Year Plan. Out of 6 specific objectives in this matter, only 2 relate directly to supporting the development of human resources (e.g., qualifications, competences). We are talking here about the transfer of employment (training aimed at vocational retraining) and education (public financing of basic education, including exemption from fees for vocational and secondary school students). The others concern, for example, the reform of the local economy (e.g., the principle of "one village, one product"), reallocation of the population (e.g., from mountain areas), or social security understood as the modernization of the pension system.

4.4. Implementation of the Western Development Strategy: Between the mandate and the initiative

Within the WDS, development is seen rather in terms of building a variety of infrastructure than as planned socially oriented activities. It is comforting, however, that among the indicators of the implementation of individual editions, more and more refer to the social dimension. And so, in the case of the 11th edition of the WDS, social indicators constituted only 21% of all indicators, while for the 13th edition of the WDS, this value was already 30%. Thus, the social dimension is present, but it is definitely undervalued in relation to *strictly* investment activities. The structure of the WDS reflects a rather traditional approach to development, mainly from the perspective of public investments, whose task is to stimulate the economic situation on the supply side. If, following Manuel Castells[95], we assume that the development takes place in the areas that have the greatest potential (economic, financial, innovative) and the flows of key development factors are decisive, then it can be concluded that the WDS contributes to these flows to a limited extent. This is because, contrary to the assumptions of the strategy, it is difficult to see the comprehensive impact of the plan on a set of interrelated territorial systems, or rather, we can see the focus on individual factors separately. Material investments are treated separately from investments in human resources.

The approach of treating infrastructure as a key development factor is confirmed by the effects of the first years of the implementation of the WDS. Several historic infrastructure investments were started and carried out, which western

95 Manuel Castells, *Społeczeństwo sieci*, Warsaw 2008.

provinces had not experienced before. Between 2000 and 2005, 70 major construction projects were launched, with a total value of 1 trillion RMB. During this period, more than a third of the funds obtained from the long-term treasury bonds issued for construction were allocated to the western regions. In the years 2002–2005, approximately 40% of the funds were allocated to the western macroregion. Funds were mainly allocated to infrastructure; for example, in the years 2000–2005, 220,000 km of roads were built in the western provinces, including 6,853 km of highways; 5,000 km of railway lines have been built and the construction of 10 airports has begun. By 2005, the central government had invested a total of 460 billion RMB in construction projects in the western areas[96]. Between 2000 and 2010, 143 key projects were financed for approximately 2,874.2 billion RMB[97]. As with the instruments used above, the overall focus of the strategy is on infrastructure investments.

When analyzing the method of financing various types of investment projects, it is impossible to ignore the fundamental issue, namely the sources of capital. Table 20 shows that the implementation of the WDS contributed to the targeting of public funds by the government to finance activities in the western provinces, mainly in the field of investments in fixed assets. In the years 2001–2010, the average annual growth rate of the state budget allocated to investments in fixed assets in western China was 30.76% and was significantly higher than in the eastern, central, and northern regions. In addition to financing from the central budget, the implementation of the WDS was supported by funds from national bonds, as well as bonds issued by local authorities with the approval of central authorities. In 2009 alone, western China's provinces issued bonds worth 75 billion RMB[98].

Table 20. Breakdown of the state budget, funds allocated for investment in fixed assets by region (in the years 2000–2010)

Year	Sum domestic (billion RMB)	Regional composition (in %)				
		Eastern China	Central China	Western China	Northeast China	Not classified according to region
2000	159.41	25.56	20.64	25.93	7.25	20.62
2001	205.23	24.46	18.39	25.61	8.82	22.71
2002	253.36	17.80	17.14	34.23	6.84	23.99
2003	210.32	24.40	19.41	38.68	7.92	9.58

96 Shenggen Fan, Ravi Kanbur, Xiaobo Zhang, *China's regional disparities: Experience and policy,* "Review of Development Finance" 2011, no. 1, p. 52.
97 Xu Tian, Xiaoheng Zhang, Yingheng Zhou, Xiaohua Yu, *Regional income inequality in China revisited: A perspective from club convergence,* "Economic Modeling" 2016, no 56, pp. 252–253.
98 Ibid.

Table 20 *(Continued)*

Year	Sum domestic (billion RMB)	Regional composition (in %)				
		Eastern China	Central China	Western China	Northeast China	Not classified according to region
2004	325.50	24.70	20.03	33.61	7.61	14.05
2005	415.50	24.01	19.86	32.84	9.01	14.28
2006	467.20	21.06	21.82	33.13	10.15	13.84
2007	585.71	22.17	24.39	32.12	11.16	10.16
2008	795.48	23.50	24.50	33.08	10.24	8.69
2009	1268.57	21.81	24.46	39.24	9.70	4.79
2010	1467.78	20.64	23.77	41.15	8.70	5.74

Source: own work based on: Lu Zheng, Deng Xiang, *Regional Policy and Regional Development: A Case Study of China's Western Development Strategy,* "Annales Universitatis Apulensis Series Oeconomica" 2013, vol. 15, no. 1, p. 253.

Fiscal transfers to local administrative units of the western provinces played an important role in the implementation of the WDS. Between 2000 and 2005, there was a gradual increase in general transfers to local governments in western China, reaching 404.4 billion RMB during this period, accounting for 52.6% of all transfers[99]. The increase in total transfers (including general transfers and special transfers) also reflected the fact that central government fiscal transfers were directed disproportionately to the western regions. In 1999, 29.01% of the central government's fiscal transfers went to western China, while in 2010 this rate reached 39.42%, indicating a significant upward trend, which was the result of the implementation of the WDS[100]. Total fiscal transfers and subsidies of 500 billion RMB have also been invested in the western areas[101].

The use of fiscal transfers as an instrument aimed at equalizing the incomes of the poorest units of the western provinces was accompanied by changes in the structure of transfer payments[102]. The change of policy resulted from the centralization of the tax system but also from the growing importance of the policy of equalizing the incomes of less developed administrative units of the western provinces. As mentioned earlier, the transfer payment system, which consists of tax credits, special (so-called categorical) payments, and financial (so-called

99 Lu Zheng, Deng Xiang, *Regional Policy and Regional Development: A Case Study of China's Western Development Strategy,* "Annales Universitatis Apulensis Series Oeconomica" 2013, vol. 15, no. 1, p. 251.

100 Ibid.

101 Shenggen Fan, Ravi Kanbur, Xiaobo Zhang, *China's regional disparities:* op. cit., p. 52.

102 Anwar Shah and Chunli Shen, *The Reform of the Intergovernmental Transfer System to Achieve a Harmonious Society and a Level Playing Field for Regional Development in China,* "World Bank Policy Research Working Paper" December 2006, no. 4100, p. 24.

conditional) payments, has changed[103] since the mid-1990s. In the structure of transfer payments, the importance of tax refunds has decreased whilst the importance of the so-called categorical and conditional payments has increased. The tax refund rate decreased from 73.7% in 1995 to 9.1% in 2015. On the other hand, the percentage of categorical payments increased from 11.5% to 51.7% and conditional payments from 14.8% to 39.2% in the same period[104]. The amounts of conditional and categorical payments depend to a greater extent on the political decision of the center, which, with the policy of promoting less developed units, resulted in an increase in the income of these entities.

In addition to financial resources and physical investments, the central government offered western provinces a number of preferences aimed at attracting foreign direct investment and domestic companies. The preferences consisted of, for example, the temporary reduction of the income tax rate to 15% (while the standard one was 30%) for companies operating in preferential industries or, under special conditions, complete exemption from paying it (for peripheral areas). As part of the support for agricultural production, an exemption from agricultural tax was offered for a period of up to 10 years, or, in the case of companies operating in industries promoted by the government, an exemption from import duties and value added tax[105]. Tax preferences were also applied to specific investments located in the provinces covered by the WDS. For example, there were tax exemptions for pilot rural loan cooperatives (in the years 2003–2005), and tax preferences during the construction of the Qinghai-Tibet railway. Almost all types of taxes generated by the project were exempt from payment. For imported equipment used for projects promoted in western areas or in local competing industries, import duties and value-added tax were exempt[106].

The income tax reduction instrument is still used nowadays. In connection with the implementation of subsequent editions of the WDS, the reduction of corporate income tax is expected to be maintained until December 31, 2030. It was agreed to reduce the tax by 15% compared to the basic rate. This applies to enterprises whose main activity is industrial projects specified in the "Directory of Promoted Industries in the Western Region" and whose income from this activity accounts for more than 60% of the total income of the enterprise. The

103 State Council, *Opinions of the State Council on Reforming and Improving the System of Transfer Payment Made by the Central Government to Local Governments,* 27.12.2014, http://lawinfochina.com/display.aspx?id=26568&lib=law (access: 20/11/2021).

104 Yongqiu Wu, Yi Huang, Jing Zhao, Yanping Pu , *Transfer payment structure and local government fiscal efficiency: evidence from China,* "China Finance and Economic Review" 2017 vol. 12, no. 5, p. 2.

105 Shenggen Fan, Ravi Kanbur, Xiaobo Zhang, *China's regional disparities:* op. cit., p. 53.

106 Lu Zheng, Deng Xiang, *China's Western Development Strategy: Policies, Effects and Prospects,* "MPRA Paper" 2011, no. 35201, p. 4.

aforementioned catalog has been established by the NDRC and is subject to updating. If tax authorities have doubts about the fulfillment of the above condition, they are obliged to apply for an appropriate opinion from the NDRC[107].

Financial support for the implementation of the WDS was also provided through financial institutions, mainly state-owned commercial banks. These institutions, as a result of state policy, increased their lending activity for the western regions[108]. At the end of 2010, the loan balance of the China Development Bank reached 1.008 billion RMB, which represented 22.36% of all loans and at the same time shows a significant increase compared to 2001 (17.78%). In addition, the loans launched by the China Agriculture Development Bank aimed at providing financial support for agriculture and industrial development in rural areas reached 336 billion RMB in 2009, which is also a significant increase compared to previous years. Meanwhile, other large banks such as Agriculture Bank of China, China Construction Bank, Industrial & Commercial Bank of China and the Bank of China owned by the state similarly increased their lines of credit to the western regions[109].

The implementation of the WDS through various types of financial instruments has significant limitations. The use of financial support from the central budget, fiscal transfers, bonds or tax exemptions can be applied at a specific time. It is mainly about supporting key development factors, most often equated with the development of infrastructure. Meanwhile, underdeveloped provinces, including local authorities and enterprises, require the creation of long-term mechanisms ensuring the fulfillment of the financial needs of local communities, e.g., small towns, but above all building a relatively sustainable competitiveness. We add that this task is of considerable importance, especially due to the low attractiveness of investment in the western provinces. Taking into account the experience of European countries (e.g., Germany, Italy), the mere provision of various types of infrastructure does not necessarily build a lasting competitive advantage.

Referring to the theory of financial constraints, the authors of which are Joseph Stiglitz and Kevin Murdoch[110], it is worth paying attention to two compatible elements that affect the growth of developing regions in financial terms.

107 Guanyu yanxu xibu da kaifa qiye suodeshui zhengce de gonggao (关于延续西部大开发企业所得税政策的公告), http://www.gov.cn/zhengce/zhengceku/2020-04/28/content_5506990.htm (access: 20/11/2021).

108 Fan Jie, *Western Development Policy: Changes, Effects and Evaluation,* [in:] Y.M. Yeun, Shen Jianfa (eds.), op. cit., pp. 96–99.

109 Lu Zheng, Deng Xiang, *China's Western Development Strategy: Policies, Effects and Prospects,* op. cit., pp. 6–7.

110 Kevin Murdock, Joseph Stiglitz, *Financial Restraint: Towards a New Paradigm,* Working Paper 1995, no. 1355; Huang Yan-hui, *Financial Restraint Theory and its Practices in China,* "Journal of Beijing Technology and Business University" 2014, vol. 29, no. 1, pp. 96–101.

First, appropriate financial regulations; second, appropriate government interventions. In other words, it is necessary to establish a coordinated support system for projects with clear objectives and implementing measures. Using also other research results[111]relating to regional economic and geographic conditions, as well as domestic political measures, which are factors responsible for the development disparities in China, it is worth asking the question whether this system of financial support is optimal.

A cursory overview of the support under the WDS would indicate the concentration of activities also in the area of financial policy, which has already been mentioned in the analysis of the priorities of individual editions of the WDS. However, the financial support system remains ineffective as it cannot meet the multidimensional financial needs at the local level due to three circumstances[112]. First, Western China's residents have lower incomes and lower savings, which is crucial for potential future investments. It is true that savings ratios improve over time, but they are growing much slower than in the rest of the country. Low incomes result in a low savings rate, and this automatically triggers an increased need for external financing (e.g., loans). Furthermore, the economic base, which is based in small towns on agricultural production, generates large credit needs (agricultural activity or extraordinary situations, such as natural disasters). Second, enterprises operating in western China, especially small and medium-sized enterprises, have a problem with obtaining financing due to the high risk of their operations; hence, they ultimately receive small (unsatisfactory) amounts of loans from local financial institutions (e.g., agricultural banks, credit cooperatives). Third, government institutions and agencies with branches in western China responsible for delivering public goods do not pay much attention to the economic efficiency of investments. In the process of supporting, for example, infrastructure, transport, and labor-intensive and capital-intensive enterprises, they are focused on long-term effects. Local government income and expenses were relatively balanced in 1993–2002, while expenses increased more sharply than income in 2003–2011. In this situation, the postulates to optimize the financial support system should not come as a surprise. Hongmei Zhang and Hai Zhu[113]are in favor of increasing financial efficiency, i.e., focusing the financial support system on private enterprises, optimizing and restructuring local industry, supporting product innovations that increase competitive advantage.

---

111 Jan Li, G.H Ran., G.H. Wan, *Interpretation on regional financial development differences in China*, "Economic Research Journal" 2007, no. 5, pp. 42–54.

112 Hongmei Zhang, Hai Zhu, *Study on the Financial Support System for Development of Small Towns in Western China*, [in:] Tai-Chee Wong, Sun Sheng Han, Hongmei Zhang (eds.), *Population Mobility, Urban Planning and Management in China*, Cham, Heidelberg, New York, Dordrecht, London 2015, pp. 320–321.

113 Ibid, pp. 322–323, 325.

Another postulate is the dissemination of cooperative financing, which would be based on cooperation and thus, to a greater extent, would take into account the expectations of local communities. Another proposal is to improve the quality of financial services themselves through greater correlation with local needs, which supports the restructuring of enterprises, as well as improving organizational and marketing skills.

Table 21. Classification of WDS financing sources

Source of funding	Nature of the sources
Fiscal transfers: - tax breaks - general, financial (conditional) - special, so-called categorical	Public, central to subnational authorities
Public Investments: - investments in fixed assets - local investments	 Public, central Public, local
National tax preferences for: - investments (tax exemptions generated by investments) - investors (e.g., tax exemptions for investing companies)	Public, central
Bonds: - governmental - local authorities	Public: - central - local
Financial support system: - credit policy of state-owned banks - foreign banks - private capital - local financial institutions (e.g., rural banks, cooperatives)	 Central, mixed (public-private) Private Local Mixed, public-private

Source: own study.

In summarizing the part concerning the method of financing the WDS, it should be stated that it required the concentration of resources from various sources. Among them, public funds have been decisive, including those at the disposal of the central authorities. The fact that funds from so many different sources have been successfully committed confirms the political importance of the WDS and the centrally implemented policy of coordinated development. Of course, the implementation of such a significant strategy for 12 provinces had to focus on public financing, but the scale of these funds means that public financing is definitely dominant. Among public funds, fiscal transfers and measures aimed at public investment were and still are decisive. Public funding is a clear source of funding but, at the same time, a burden on central and local public finances.

The aforementioned burden on subnational governments is very acute as there is a significant asymmetry between local government spending and revenues. This is because local governments have limited fiscal revenues in relation to expenses and at the same time remain obliged to maintain a high level of expenses also related to the WDS implementation. It is a nationwide problem, but it is especially present in the western regions. Although the expenses of subnational governments are 1.7 times higher than the income in the whole of China, in the case of western provinces it is already 2.44 times (data for 2014). The western China region contributes around 20% to the country's total local fiscal income, while it accounts for 30% of the country's spending. Only in 2011, the fiscal self-sufficiency rate of the western regions (with the exception of Chongqing) was below 50%, and in some less developed areas, this rate was lower than 30%. Although the amount of local fiscal revenues exceeded the amount of central government revenues after 2010, local governments still rely heavily on transfer payments from the central government[114]. Therefore, it is not surprising that local authorities face enormous pressure to implement the WDS. It also proves limited access to capital. It should be further noted that the western part of China bears more fiscal burdens than the national average.

The small investments in human resources in individual editions of the WDS show that, especially in the initial stage of reforms, opening up China to the world was not an important point on the central government's political agenda. The CPC's highest political priority placed social investment in the background. This resulted in a very difficult situation on the labor market from the point of view of the employee. Successive waves of economic liberalization deprived large numbers of workers of job security, thus ensuring the low production costs of the Chinese economy. This does not mean that no action was taken in the social sphere. For example, the WDS also included funds to support development in the social dimension. Investment in education in this macroregion was 15 billion RMB and investment in public health services reached 8 billion RMB during the six-year period 2000–2005[115]. The introduction of a collective health care system in rural areas, which made it easier for the inhabitants of the least developed areas to access primary health care, can be considered to take into account the social dimension. Its impact, due to the low cost recovery (approximately 30%), may raise doubts, but the 80% financial contribution of public institutions (author-

114 Zhiyu Fu, Wenhong Yan, *Promoting the innovation of urbanization system in Western China from the perspective of public finance and taxation,* "China Finance and Economic Review" 2016, vol. 4, no. 4, p. 3, 7.

115 Yao Yang, *The political economy of government policies toward regional inequality in China,* [in:], Yukon Huang, Alessandro Magnoli Bocchi (eds.), *Reshaping Economic Geography in East Asia,* Washington 2009, p. 231.

ities of various levels) allowed it to cover 851 million participants in 2008, which is 91.5% of villagers[116].

Despite significant funds allocated to the implementation of the WDS, the shortage of capital is still a significant factor that limits the development of western China's provinces. The possible closing of the financing gap is difficult, as local authorities are largely dependent on the above-mentioned central funds. The structure of investments in fixed assets confirms a high degree of dependence on domestic political factors and at the same time a marginal share of foreign funds in western provinces in relation to other regions. Due to a lower rate of return on investment and a less attractive investment environment, the provinces covered by the WDS have a problem attracting not only enough foreign capital, but also domestic capital from other Chinese regions (both public and private). Not only that, an outflow of capital can be recorded in the western regions. Data from local statistical years indicate that the ratio of loans to bank deposits in western China is declining year by year. For example, in 1990 it was 125.3%, while in 2010 it was 69.5%. For provinces such as Tibet (23.27%), Xinjiang (56.06%) and Shanxi (60.85%), the rates were well below the average for the western regions[117].

In general, infrastructure projects implemented under the WDS contributed to the improvement of the economic conditions, the quality of life, and, in part, the increase in competitiveness, which is why the importance of the region is systematically improving. However, many of the construction projects that were nationally funded were relatively poorly embedded in the realities of the local economies of the western provinces. If you consider examples of West-East gas or electricity transmission projects, these were projects that brought great benefits to eastern provinces. Most of the contractors, equipment suppliers, and material producers, as well as technical thought, came from outside the western provinces. The role of local entrepreneurship was limited to providing auxiliary materials and making available unskilled labor. The result is that the western provinces have benefited relatively little from these investments and have allocated a lot of their land to them[118]. The current recommendations for supporting the development of the Western provinces focus on supporting innovation, including scientific and technological innovation, and supporting a modern industrial system understood as saturation with information technology in the

116 S. Fan, R. Kanbur, X. Zhang, *China's regional disparities…*, op. cit., p. 52.

117 Lu Zheng, Deng Xiang, *Regional Policy and Regional Development: A Case Study of China's Western Development Strategy*, "Annales Universitatis Apulensis Series Oeconomica" 2013, op. cit., p. 26.

118 Liancheng He, Huiqin Yao, Zhangyong Xu, Lixiong Cai, Shuwei An, *Economic Development in Western China: A Ten-Year Review*, [in:] Huiqin Yao, Zhangyong Xu (eds.), *Redevelopment of Western China*, Singapore 2017, p. 49.

economies of western China. It is mainly about the development of new industries in which information technologies play a key role, such as "Internet plus education", "Internet plus medical care", "Internet and tourism"[119]. Understanding that innovation is currently considered the main growth paradigm, it should be noted that the development of the above-mentioned industries requires skilled workers, and at the same time these areas contribute relatively little to employment in the West. Taking into account the quality of human resources and the supply of qualifications, it should be noted that this does not fully correspond to building the capacity for endogenous and independent growth. The implementation of the above – otherwise accurate – postulates may contribute to the necessity to use external resources, just as almost two decades ago they were used for the implementation of infrastructure construction projects.

The statements above also confirm the experience of several western provinces in the development of advanced technologies. They created the so-called advanced and new technology areas (e. g., Xi'an High and New Technology Area), including numerous science parks, which were to accelerate innovation capacity in the context of limited resources, which were to translate into high-quality development. Indeed, the overall innovation capacity improved significantly, but it should be taken into account that this was done under low initial conditions, which made this type of investment poorly translated into overall national production. Compared to eastern China, innovative industries are still very underdeveloped and have a limited impact on building the regional innovation system. One of the problems that should be noted is the insufficient cooperation between the activities of the research and development sphere and industry. In western provinces, research is carried out in colleges and national institutes, while large companies do not have affiliated research and development institutions. Therefore, research and production are kept separate from each other, so that few test results ultimately lead to a product[120].

The low level of innovation in western provinces can be checked in up to four dimensions. First, the influence of the science and technology sector on overall development is limited. The indicators of scientific potential are low; there are few people involved in science and the number of people engaged in R&D per million inhabitants is low compared to other parts of the country. Second, the quality of the education system is low; there are insufficient conditions for supporting talents, as well as a shortage of competences, i. e., a generally low level of education of the population persists there. Third, the effects of research and

119 Zhonggong zhongyang guasuyuan guanyu xin shidai tuijin xibu da kaifa xingcheng xin gay de zhidao yijian (中共中央 国务院关于 新 时代 推进 西部 大 开发 形成 新 格局 的 指导 意见), http://www.gov.cn/xinwen/2020-05/17/content_5512456.htm (access: 20/11/2021).

120 Liancheng He, Huiqin Yao, Zhangyong Xu, Lixiong Cai, Shuwei An, *Economic Development in Western China: A Ten-Year Review,* [in:] Huiqin Yao, Zhangyong Xu (eds.), op. cit., p. 50.

development activities are unsatisfactory, which is reflected, for example, in the still low number of patents in Western China (252 per million inhabitants in 2019, see Table 22). Fourth, the high-tech and new-tech industry is underdeveloped. Technology companies are underdeveloped, as evidenced not only by the low turnover of these economic entities but also by enterprises' expenditure on R&D. For the western provinces, it is 407 RMB per capita, while for the eastern provinces, it is 1,615 RMB. As a result, this sector, which is important in other parts of the world and even in other Chinese provinces, cannot drive the socioeconomic development of Western China[121]. An example may be the world's leading innovative industries such as artificial intelligence and mass data processing. China is one of the most active countries in this regard; in 2018 the sector was valued at 1,311 billion RMB, which was approximately 60% of investment in the world in terms of artificial intelligence. However, of about 4,000 enterprises, only a few are located in the western provinces[122].

Table 22. Basic indicators of innovativeness of the western provinces in the context of other macroregions (data for 2019)

Indicator	western provinces	central provinces	eastern provinces
Number of R&D employees (per million inhabitants)	779	1 435	3 807
R&D expenditure in industrial enterprises (per capita in RMB)	407	678	1 615
Research projects of enterprises (per million inhabitants)	154	265	724
Number of patent applications (per million inhabitants)	252	450	1 311

Source: own study based on: National Bureau of Statistics of China 2022.

The implementation of the WDS contributed to the dynamization of the phenomena aimed at increasing the level of competitiveness. The economic strength of the western provinces is systematically improving, and the growth rate of the main indicators is higher than for the whole country. The average annual income of urban and rural residents in China and the eastern region increased by more than 10% in 2015, with the regional GDP accounting for 20.1% of the entire

121 Huiqin Yao, Zhangyong Xu, Min Wang, Peng Geng, Kai Li, *Evaluation Report on the Competitiveness of Western Chinese Provinces*, [in:] Huiqin Yao, Zhangyong Xu (eds.), op. cit., p. 148.

122 Deloitte, *Rising innovation in China, China Innovation ecosystem development Report 2019*, September 2019, pp. 30–32, https://www2.deloitte.com/content/dam/Deloitte/cn/Documents/innovation/deloitte-cn-innovation-china-innovation-ecosystem-report-en-191101.pdf (access: 20/11/2021).

country[123]. This did not translate into leveling the disproportions between the western provinces and the rest of the country. Research on the overall economic competitiveness of individual regions leaves no doubt that we are dealing here with a large differentiation among all 31 provinces. If the average level of competitiveness in the country was 39.4 points, then in the provinces covered by the WDS it was only 32.9 points in 2014. It should be added that in some western provinces the results were significantly different from the average (e.g., Tibet 28.3%), and only in one region did the overall competitiveness exceed the average for the whole country (Sichuan 40.1 points)[124].

The situation is gradually changing, i.e., the provinces covered by the WDS increase in some aspects their competitiveness faster than the coastal regions. The same is also true for some macroeconomic indicators. Although the growth dynamics have been higher than, for example, in the eastern provinces during the last two five-year plans, the western provinces are still far from catching up with the national average, not to mention the wealthy eastern provinces. Existing disproportions can be observed in many areas, such as the natural environment, the industrial base, the stage of development, the quality of human resources, the economic openness of a given region, and even the method of public management[125]. The disproportions between the western and eastern provinces may serve as an illustration, and they continue to deepen when we take into account the average GDP per capita or per capita income. This is because the aforementioned GDP per capita difference increased from RMB 31,394 in 2013 to RMB 43,476 in 2018. A similar phenomenon with regard to the provinces covered by the WDS also takes place in relation to the national average, although a smaller scale of the phenomenon can be observed. Therefore, the difference in GDP per capita increased from RMB 11,486 in 2013 to RMB 15,882 in 2018 (Table 23). All this with increased expenses, also from the central budget, in order to improve the economic situation and development opportunities of the poor Western provinces under the WDS.

---

123 Guojia fazhan gaige wei guanyu yinfa xibu da kaifa "shisanwu" guihua de tongzhi fa gaii xibu, op. cit.

124 Jianping Li, Minrong Li, Yanjing Gao, Jianjian Li, Hongwen Su, Maoxing Huang, *China's Provincial Economic Competitiveness and Policy Outlook for the 13th Five-year Plan Period (2016–2020)*, Singapore 2018, pp. 4, 9.

125 Ibid, p. 144.

Table 23. Dimensions of development disparities in the provinces covered by the WDS in the national and intraregional system

Description	GDP per capita – RMB		Income per capita – RMB (city)	
Year	2018	2013	2018	2013
Average for the WDS province	49 371	35 909	33 098	21 878
Average for the eastern provinces[126]	92 848	67 303	46 496	31 183
Average for the PRC	65 253	47 396	37 750	25 279
Difference: PRC – WDS provinces	15 882	11 486	4 653	3 401
Difference: Eastern Provinces – WDS Provinces	43 476	31 394	13 398	9 305
Difference: WDS Mean – Province with the lowest rating	18 035	12 758	9 947	2 005
Multiple (max / min value) for the WDS province	2.1	2.9	1.3	1.3
Standard deviation for the WDS province	11 661	12 342	2 374	1 673
Number of WDS provinces below average	7	8	5	6

Source: own study based on: National Bureau of Statistics of China 2022.

The growing rates of GDP per capita, as well as disposable income per capita in relation to other provinces, e. g., eastern provinces, are accompanied by growing disproportions between the 12 provinces covered by the WDS. The statistical data (Table 23) are ambiguous; there has been a partial increase in the disproportion between WDS provinces in terms of income of city residents and GDP per capita, albeit this includes the extreme results of individual provinces. Comparing the extreme values is not precise enough, but it responds to the postulate of coor-

126 The following provinces were included in the category of eastern provinces for the classification of Chinese official statistics: Beijing, Tianjin, Hebei, Liaoning, Shanghai, Jiangsu, Zhejiang, Fujian, Shantung, Guangdong, and Hainan. National Bureau of Statistics of China 2022.

dinated development, formulated not only within the WDS, but also in individual Five-Year Plans. The main drivers of the development of the WDS provinces are cities and industrial districts, so the differences can be explained by the development of growth poles in accordance with the approach proposed in subsequent editions of the WDS. Time will tell if the development of the poles will spread growth to other, smaller centers as well. It is worth remembering that cities are at different stages of development, which is confirmed by an increase in the standard deviation index for disposable incomes of city residents between 2013 and 2018, that is, from 1,673 to 2,374. This means that the number of regions whose incomes deviate from the average is increasing in all provinces covered by the WDS. It should also be noted that the development disparities, both in terms of GDP per capita and income, are quite significant when comparing the number of provinces with values below the average for all provinces covered by the WDS.

In 12 provinces, nearly half of the city's population does not have an income equal to the average of all WDS provinces. The situation is slightly worse with respect to GDP per capita, where in 2018 7 out of 12 provinces did not reach the average value for all WDS regions. This is another manifestation of the imbalance in the development of individual provinces within the studied group. Consequently, it should be noted that the WDS-covered regions experience high level of development disparities similar to provincial areas in other parts of the country[127]. Similar observations can be made on the basis of the Theil index, which is used primarily to measure economic inequalities (but also other economic phenomena). The indicator based on the real GDP *per capita* of the western provinces increased from 0.031 in 2000 to 0.065 in 2010[128]. It can be noted that for more than two decades of quite intensive support, development disproportions have tended to increase. Therefore, the challenge remains to implement the postulate of sustainable development between the regions, including strengthening coordination. Initial advances in transport investment, followed by environmental projects and integrated industrial planning, did not rule out major imbalances, as demonstrated by the focus on development of major cities while weakening smaller centers. The problem is still the large-scale influx of people to cities and failure to comply with ecological standards, which causes degradation of the urban environment (e.g., air pollution and water scarcity). The overwhelming influence of major cities exacerbates the imbalance in de-

127 Shenggen Fan, Ravi Kanbur, Xiaobo Zhang, *China's regional disparities: Experience and policy*, op. cit., pp. 47–56.

128 Lu Zheng, Deng Xiang, *Regional Policy and Regional Development: A Case Study of China's Western Development Strategy*, "Annales Universitatis Apulensis Series Oeconomica" 2013, op. cit., p. 258.

velopment. Therefore, cooperation is needed at various levels and in various areas, especially between cities and regions[129].

Another issue is the restructuring of industry. In recent years, western provinces have followed the path of restructuring industrial production. This happened, among others, through economic zones and industrial parks. For this purpose, almost every edition of the WDS indicated industries that are key to development (including production). Leading enterprises in the aviation, nuclear, new materials, IT, heavy equipment, automotive and chemical industries have been developed in the Chengdu-Chongqing region; the sugar industry in Guangxi; the tobacco, bio -based and hydropower industries in Yunnan and Guizhou; the aviation and aeronautics, optical, mechanical, and electrical integration, electronics and machinery industries in Xi'an; the non-ferrous metals, rare metals industries in Lanzhou; and the energy, nonferrous and rare earth metals industries in the Hohhot-Baotou-Yinchuan region. The division of labor has been improved, the industrial value chain has been broadened, and market share and competitive efficiency have steadily improved[130]. However, the contribution of the industrial and service sector to employment is low, despite the fact that it contributes significantly to GDP value added. More than half of the workforce is employed in basic industry. In addition, it should be noted that there is a fairly uneven distribution of industries in the western provinces, where most of the industries are located in the Sichuan, Shaanxi, and Guangxi provinces. Other regions have not yet found the right leading industries to give them a comparative advantage. In addition, there are underdeveloped service industries, such as logistics and finance, which cannot cope with the rapid growth of the manufacturing industry. Inefficient resource development has resulted in partial mismanagement and environmental degradation[131].

---

129 Jianping Li, Minrong Li, Yanjing Gao, Jianjian Li, Hongwen Su, Maoxing Huang, *China's Provincial Economic Competitiveness and Policy Outlook for the 13th Five-year Plan Period (2016–2020)*, Singapore 2018, pp. 144–146.

130 Liancheng He, Huiqin Yao, Zhangyong Xu, Lixiong Cai, Shuwei An, *Economic Development in Western China: A Ten-Year Review*, [in:] Huiqin Yao, Zhangyong Xu (eds.), *Redevelopment of Western China*, op. cit., p. 43.

131 Lu Zheng, Deng Xiang, *China's Western Development Strategy: Policies, Effects and Prospects*, "MPRA Paper" 2011, no. 35201, pp. 18–20.

Chapter 5. The importance of selected instruments of regional policy in action

5.1. Public investments as an element of increasing competitiveness and reducing development disproportions

The practice of supporting the competitiveness of regions through the appropriate attitude of public authorities remains unquestionable[1]. We are talking about politics, which can often be reduced to investments that stimulate the development capacity of a given area, i. e., most often spending capital in order to achieve material and non-material benefits. Public investments allow one to build the foundations for the competitiveness of a given territorial unit. This task is most often assigned to both central and subnational (regional, local) authorities. This means that public investments, although they differ in the scope of their impact, still have a common denominator, which is a conscious and deliberate selection of projects and sources of financing. In this sense, individual levels of government act as investors, and therefore it can be inferred that they are empowered to make investment decisions. Taking into account the huge development disproportions between individual regions in the PRC, public investment may be an important instrument for reducing the aforementioned disproportions[2].

As in other areas of public policy, the dominant role of the central government should be taken into account in the case of infrastructure investments. However, the central control of the state has undergone some modification towards multi-level partnerships for the implementation of infrastructure investments. This happened through a series of state regulations. Therefore, local governments were given the right to consider and approve investment projects and the division of tasks between central government and local authorities was determined. Na-

1 Fumitoshi Mizutani, Tomoyasu Tanaka, *Productivity effects and determinants of public infrastructure investment,* "The Annals of Regional Science" 2010, vol. 44, no. 3, pp. 493–521.
2 Kim Andrews, James Swanson, *Does Public Infrastructure Affect Regional Performance?,* "Growth and Change" 1995, vol. 26, no. 2, pp. 204–216.

tional and regional infrastructure investments are the responsibility of Beijing, and local infrastructure investments are the prerogative of local governments. For example, in 2004, by a decision of the State Council, the scope of responsibilities of central government in supraregional projects and projects of national importance was determined. These provisions simplified the system for approving national projects, thus reducing administrative intervention from above. Local governments have also been given a wider range of powers to make investment decisions, and nonstate actors have been given an incentive to participate in infrastructure development. Moreover, local governments of various levels have begun to create many investment companies on their own[3].

The centralization of the political system implies that infrastructure investments were carried out for a long time according to the central development strategy. It consisted, inter alia, of the development of heavy industry (especially until the early 2000s) and striving for the self-sufficiency of individual provinces. Both of the elements indicated had a significant impact on the shape of infrastructure, especially transport equipment. Since the beginning of China's opening up to the world, the sources of financing infrastructure development have been diversified and include the expenses of local authorities, loans from international organizations, and foreign capital. However, the decentralization process that accompanied China's transition to a market economy had a negative impact on infrastructure development at the regional level. On the one hand, local governments, having better information on local conditions and preferences, generally redirected their efforts to meet the demand for public goods. This was especially true for the road network, which was developed in line with local needs, for example, in the eastern provinces. On the other hand, the greater autonomy granted to local governments at every level of the administrative hierarchy had unexpected effects on the level of infrastructure provision, as these authorities paid less attention to transport or telecommunications investments. This was because they were too invested in upgrading industrial capacity. This led to a situation in the early 1990s where infrastructure shortages were also serious, requiring a significant investment effort[4]. Since then, infrastructure investments have been a kind of hallmark of China's socioeconomic transformation.

At the central level, many entities are involved in infrastructure investments. These include the NDRC, Ministry of Finance, People's Bank of China, and industry ministries, including the Ministry of Transport, Ministry of Railways (MOR), Ministry of Housing and Urban and Rural Development, Ministry of

3 Yanyan Chen Jiang Xu, *Infrastructure Investment in China: From Central Monopoly To Multi-Level Partnership*, "Asian Geographer" 2010, vol. 27, no. 1–2, pp. 114.

4 Sylvie Démurger, *Infrastructure Development and Economic Growth: An Explanation for Regional Disparities in China?*, "Journal of Comparative Economics" 2001, vol. 29, no. 1, p. 98.

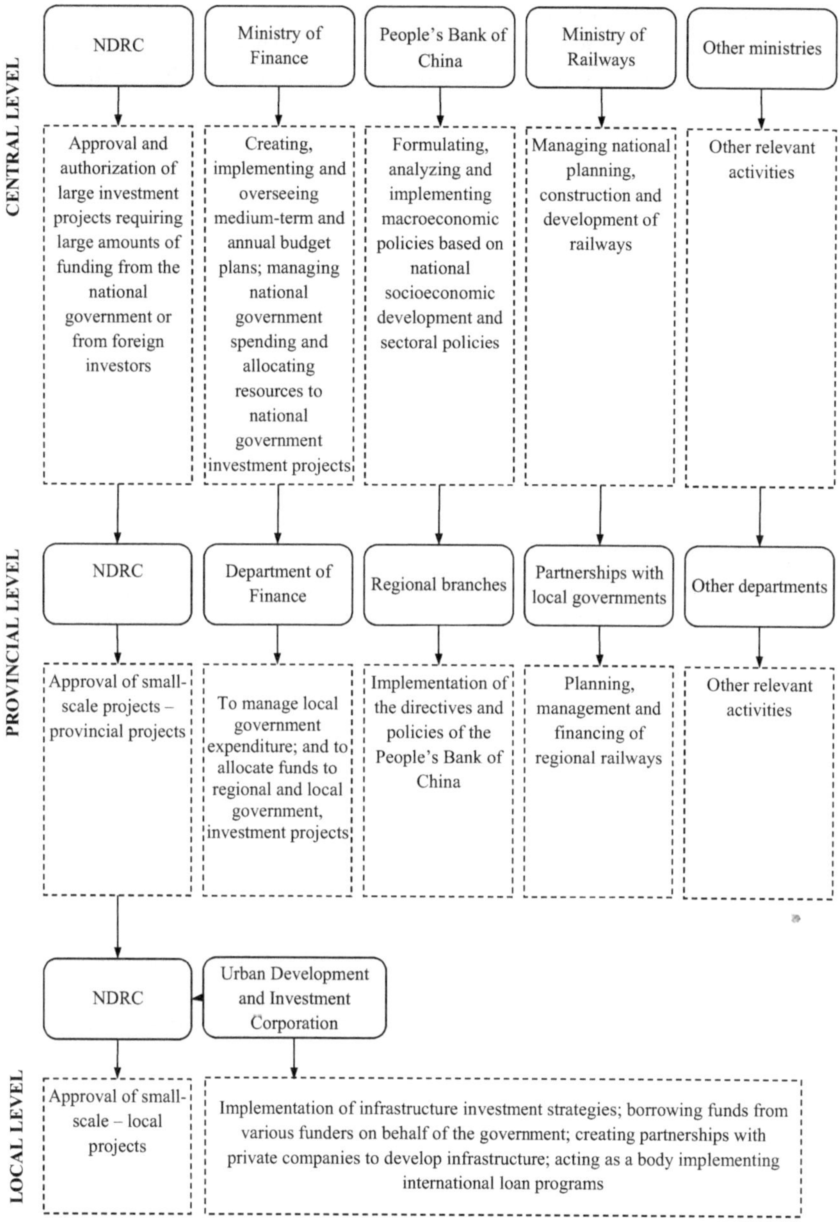

Diagram 12. Institutional structure of infrastructure investments in China. Source: own study based on: Yanyan Chen Jiang Xu, *Infrastructure Investment in China: From Central Monopoly to Multi-Level Partnership*, "Asian Geographer", 2010, vol. 27, no. 1–2, p. 115.

Information Industry, Ministry of Land and Resources, Ministry responsible for Environmental Protection and Ministry of Water Resources. The institutional structure at the regional level is in many respects similar to that at the central level. The Party committee and provincial government representatives make key decisions (e.g., the development and reform committee, the building commission, and other departments related to provincial infrastructure). It should be noted that not all functional institutions are configured at the local level. For example, national rail branches within the MOR are not organized on the basis of provincial jurisdiction. The MOR creates partnerships with territorial authorities as part of corporate schemes. For example, Guangzhou Railway Group (*Guangtie*) was the first railway company in China. It is subject to the MOR but operates as an independent economic entity with its own legal status and is responsible for its own profits and losses. Provincial authorities and large municipalities may have their own project corporations acting as investor representatives, as well as a major shareholder managing the infrastructure at the provincial level, such as the Guangdong Railway Construction Investment Corporation (*Shengtietou*)[5].

It should be noted that infrastructure investment decisions are usually part of socioeconomic and sectoral planning at various levels of government. At the central level, the NDRC plays an important role due to its responsibility to coordinate infrastructure investments. This institution is responsible for approving large investment projects that require support from the central government or foreign investors, as authorized by the State Council. Design approval is a key procedure in the plan-implementation process. The process is based on ensuring that the investment program and public expenditure are in line with the national investment strategy and legislation and that the project meets certain criteria (e.g., economic, social, environmental, and financial). The level of the NDRC's authorization to issue project permits depends on the size of the investment. In general, projects in excess of $7.3 million must undergo a NDRC review and approval process. Smaller projects, such as those of regional importance, are subject to approval by the development and reform committees located in each province[6].

5 Yanyan Chen Jiang Xu, *Infrastructure Investment in China,* op. cit., p. 114.
6 Ibid, p. 115.

Table 24. Investments in fixed assets (excluding rural households) in terms of GDP (in billion RMB)

Type	2017		2012		2007		2001	
	Value	% Of GDP	Value	% Of GDP	Value	% Of GDP	Value	% Of GDP
Central investments	2 586	3	2 376	4	1 316	5	658	6
Local investments	60 579	73	34 109	63	10 429	39	2 341	21
GDP	83 203	100	53 858	100	27 009	100	11 086	100

Source: own study based on: National Bureau of Statistics of China 2022.

Public authorities – central government and local governments – remain very active in investing in physical assets[7]. Central investments are projects carried out by enterprises, institutions, and administrative units that are under the direct direction and management of the State Council and national commissions, ministries, agencies, and large state-owned corporations. Various ministries and departments of the State Council prepare and implement plans through a unified organization or subcommittees that include departments directly under the central government. Due to the vast territory of China, it is not surprising that public investments at the local level many times exceed the value of central investments, e. g., in 2017 they accounted for 95% of the total value. Local investments include construction projects carried out by various institutions under the direct management of regional (province) or local (district, commune, city) authorities. Attention should be paid to the growing importance of local and central investment in relation to GDP. In 2001, local investments amounted to RMB 2,341 billion, which accounted for 21% of GDP, while in 2017 it was already RMB 60,579 billion and accounted for as much as 73% of GDP. This illustrates not only, in a sense, the decentralization of public finances, but also the enormous pressure on local authorities. Taking into account the above-mentioned tendencies, the balancing of development announced by the CPC within the next editions of the Five-Year plans will take place through the actions of regional and local authorities. This, in turn, will put even more pressure on local public finances.

In the last two decades, there have been three main sources of financing fixed assets in the Middle Kingdom (Table 25). The most important source are the so-called own funds, which in 2017 alone accounted for up to 65% of the funds allocated to fixed assets. The data on official statistics show that these are funds

7 Yanqing Jiang, Yunliang Jiang, Jinghai Zheng, *Investment in Infrastructure and Regional Growth in China. Emerging,* "Markets Finance and Trade" 2020, vol. 56, no. 9, pp. 1942–1956.

for investments in fixed assets, received during the reference period by investment units, including the own funds of various enterprises and institutions, or funds obtained from units other than financial funds i. e., funds borrowed from financial institutions (including foreign funds). Since the main executors of investments are subnational governments (regional, local), it should be assumed that a large part in this category will be funds at the disposal of provincial or local governments, and therefore largely public funds. This is another confirmation of the high activity of the authorities in public investments.

Table 25. Sources of financing fixed assets (in billion RMB)

Source	2017		2012		2007		2001	
	Value	% *	Value	% *	Value	% *	Value	% *
Central budget	3 847	6	1 895	5	587	4	254	7
Domestic loans	7 243	11	5 159	14	2 304	15	723	19
Foreign investment	214	1	446	2	513	3	173	5
Own funds	41 770	65	22 779	63	9 137	61	1 891	50
Other	10 894	17	5 682	16	2 539	17	755	20
Total	63 968	100	35 961	100	15 080	100	3 796	100

Source: own study based on: National Bureau of Statistics of China 2022.
* Data are rounded to the nearest percentage.

The enigmatic-sounding item "Own funds" requires some comment in the context of other sources. Own funds are resources derived from fiscal revenues depending on the administrative level, i. e., regional (provincial or local). The participation of subnational governments in the tax was a derivative of successive waves of decentralization and centralization that took place in the PRC, starting from "opening to the world"[8]. Increasing the participation of subnational authorities in local taxes as part of the fiscal decentralization process was a significant incentive for local authorities to generate more income to promote territorial development (including infrastructure investments)[9]. For example, the fiscal reform of 1994 allowed municipalities to collect corporate tax, giving them the opportunity to develop and trade, leading to a revival in building infrastructure and promoting territorial competitiveness to attract potential investors. Since opening up to the world, investment in infrastructure has transformed from an exclusive domain controlled by a central government into a system of negotiation between central and local governments. Functions which before the reforms were exclusively reserved for the central government are now confined to

8 Lin Shuanglin, *How to reform China's fiscal system?*, "China Economic Journal" 2020, vol. 13, no. 1, pp. 62–81.
9 Jean Oi, *Fiscal Reform and the Economic Foundations of Local State Corporatism in China*, "World Politics" 1992, vol. 45, no. 1, pp. 99–126.

a greater extent to local authorities as well as to market players. This has contributed to the emergence of new infrastructure development partnerships. However, the above actions did not lead to a complete retreat of the central government nor to a relaxation of the control functions exercised by Beijing[10].

The second largest source of financing fixed assets is Other, which accounted for 17% of the funds in 2017. These are resources that have not been listed in other items, including funds obtained from natural persons in the form of donations, as well as transferred from other entities. The third largest source of financing fixed assets is Domestic loans (11% in 2017). These are funds borrowed by units implementing investments from banks, but also from nonbank financial institutions. This category also includes measures such as: national loans obtained by higher authorities, national special loans (including loans for coal instead of oil, special loans of workers' mines, etc.), local financial loans organized by special funds, national reserve loans, short-term loans, etc. The analysis of the sources of financing public investments largely indicates the increasing importance of the public finance sector in new investments. Assuming that a large part of the financial sector is state-owned, the involvement of public finances becomes even more visible. It is also worth paying attention to the sharp increase in the value of investments, which almost doubles every 5 years. Authorities, wishing to maintain high economic growth, are taking steps to stimulate the economy. Data from 2012, in the context of data from 2007, indicate high growth, especially in terms of own funds. As a result of the Chinese economic slowdown in 2008, due to the global economic crisis, the authorities in Beijing undertook the implementation of a significant stimulus package for the Chinese economy through additional investments in the area of infrastructure. The question of how long, in 5-year periods, the PRC will be able to almost double its spending on investments in fixed assets remains open.

In the process of opening China to the world, which was associated with the marketization of the Chinese model of socioeconomic development, local governments faced a key challenge. It consisted in attracting to the region or locality not only domestic, but also foreign, capital[11]. If local authorities are treated as a kind of platform for establishing economic contacts, then undoubtedly local government structures are doing quite well. Over the years, they have skillfully used their advantage of having an almost unlimited workforce and low labor costs. Moreover, after several decades of marketization of the Chinese economy, they also have valuable experience. This has positive consequences, for example,

10 Yanyan Chen Jiang Xu, *Infrastructure Investment in China,* op. cit., pp. 109–126.

11 Sandra Poncet, *Inward and Outward FDI in China,* [in:] David Greenaway, Chris Milner, Shujie Yao (eds.), *China and the World Economy,* London 2010, pp. 112–134; Stèphane Dees Foreign, *Direct Investment in China: Determinants and Effects,* "Economics of Planning" 1998, vol. 31, pp. 175–194.

in increasing growth rates, but there are also negative consequences. Officials fighting for investment in their area contribute to the pollution of the natural environment and do not meet the expectations of citizens regarding quality of life. It seems that the tasks of local governments to create appropriate conditions for enterprises, so that they can develop their activities and increase the value of the services or products offered, have been correctly interpreted. However, the general intention to support entrepreneurship, for example, at the local level, is common practice in almost all administrative units in the world. The overall Chinese experience allows us to highlight three aspects that have been successfully implemented by local authorities and have brought success. These include infrastructure, industrial chain coordination, and the establishment of information exchange platforms[12].

Building infrastructure, although it is also a subject of controversy[13], in most development theories, is one of the main recommendations in the form of public investment. However, the scale of Chinese investment in infrastructure has raised many questions and controversies not only among economists but also among policy makers. The question of the importance of infrastructure in the efficiency of private factors of production and total production remains valid in view of the very high activity of the state (including subnational authorities) in building infrastructure. On the one hand, supporters of infrastructure expansion argue that China's infrastructure is underdeveloped and that large-scale investment in it could help China avoid the knock-on effects of the global economic slowdown and further accelerate China's economic growth in the future. On the other hand, opponents of expansion believe that its current resources are already ahead of the real needs of the Chinese economy. There is concern that such a large-scale infrastructure investment plan will not only lead to significant infrastructure underutilization in the economy, but will also increase public sector indebtedness and expose the authorities to significant fiscal risks in the future[14].

12 Ibid, p. 165.

13 Johanes Bröcker, Petit Rietveld, *Infrastructure and regional development,* [in:] Roberta Capello, Peter Nijkamp (ed.), *Handbook of Regional Growth and Development Theories,* Cheltenham, Northampton 2010, pp. 152–181; Alfredo Minerva, Gianmarco Ottaviano, *Endogenous growth theories: agglomeration and transportation costs,* [in:] Ibid, pp. 86–99; David Alan Aschauer, *Is public expenditure productive?,* "Journal of Monetary Economics" 1989, vol. 23, no. 2, pp. 177–200; Sylvie Démurger, op. cit., pp. 95–117.

14 Hao Shi, Shaoqing Huang, *How Much Infrastructure Is Too Much? A New Approach and Evidence from China,* "World Development" 2014, vol. 56, pp. 272–286.

5.1.1. Transport

The activity of public authorities in shaping the Chinese economy after 1978 is noteworthy. Public investment remains an essential element with which to stimulate the accumulation of resources, although recent years also reveal other elements, such as modern technologies. Considering the size and vastness of the PRC, it is a very demanding task. The condition and evolution of many sectors, not only economic, leaves no illusion that the role of public investment, even if it is not unique, is fundamental. The most visible in the Chinese landscape are primarily transport investments (road, rail, water, air). Starting from 1978, a significant challenge in the field of transport was not only the lack of adequate infrastructure, but also the inadequacy of the structure of transport services (planning, implementation, management). Demographic changes (especially the increase in the number of residents in cities), economic development, and population migration made the communication system inefficient and inadequate for current needs. For example, the population of Beijing in the period 1990–2009 increased from 10.8 million to 17.6 million, which, in addition to other phenomena, influenced the traffic load not only in the agglomeration itself, but also in its functional surroundings[15]. At the initial stage of transformation, these were investments in basic infrastructure, with which China was fairly modestly equipped. What is the use of building the best laboratories if industrial or service centers cannot be connected to them? There are suggestions that the PRC will build integrated high-quality infrastructure. If the conditions of the infrastructure are satisfactory, the main challenge will be to optimize its use and to integrate it, including in economic terms.

The implementation of transport investments is a significant financial and organizational effort. With the economic reforms of 1978 and fiscal decentralization in the 1990s, both central and local governments increased investment in various modes of transport. Catching up when it comes to infrastructure, e.g., road infrastructure, is impressive. At the end of 2019, the total length of roads in the country reached 501.25 million km, that is, about 5.4 times more than at the end of 1984. The total length of motorways in 2019 was 1.496 million km, while in 2001 it was only 194,000 km[16], i.e., it grew approximately 7.7 times in 18 years. The rapid development of road infrastructure has significantly improved communication capacity and transport efficiency, accelerated the development of the logistics industry, and promoted the sustainable development of the economy. In 2019, passenger traffic on the country's roads amounted to 885.708 billion km,

15 Zhong -Ren Peng, Daniel Jian Sun, *Qing-Chang Lu, China's Public Transportation: Problems, Policies and Future Prospective to Sustainability*, "Ite Journal" 2012, no. 12, pp. 35–37.

16 National Bureau of Statistics of China 2021.

which is 6.6 times more than in 1984, and the turnover of road cargo amounted to 596.3639 billion km, that is, 113.1 times more than in 1984[17].

The total investment in transportation infrastructure (see Table 26) was RMB 2.777 billion in 2015, almost four times more than in 2005. The largest expenditure was allocated to the development of roads. In 2015, it was RMB 1.641 billion, approximately three times more than in 2005. An even greater increase in expenditure can be recorded in the case of railways (ninefold). In 2020, expenditure on fixed assets in transport amounted to RMB 3.475 billion, of which 2.558 billion were allocated to roads and waterways. This means an increase in spending by 7.1% year on year[18]. In 2014, railway investments in the central and western regions represented 78% of all railway investments. In the central and western regions, 6,747 km of railway lines were commissioned, which is 80% of the lines commissioned at that time. Thanks to the operation of 18 railway projects in the central and western regions, such as the Lanzhou-Xinjiang high speed railway and the Lhasa-Shigatse railway, the length of the Midwest Railway is 70,000 km, covering 62.3% of China, significantly increasing the accessibility rate of high-speed rail in Midwest China[19].

Table 26. Investments in fixed assets in transport infrastructure (in billion RMB)

Type of infrastructure	**2015**	**2005**
Highways	1 651	548
Railways	823	88
Waterways	145	68
Civil aviation	156	21
Total	2 777	726

Source: own study based on: National Bureau of Statistics of China 2022.

For China, transport is a basic strategic industry and an important service sector in the national economy, through which it promotes, at least in principle, sustainable development. At the fifth plenary session of the 19th Central Committee of the CPC in January 2021, it was proposed to accelerate the construction of the transport sector, "based on a new stage of development, implementation of a new

17 [2019 Nian quanguo shoufei gonglu tongji gongbao] jiedu ([2019 年 全国收费公路 统计 公报] 解读), http://xxgk.mot.gov.cn/2020/jigou/glj/202009/t20200928_3471327.html (access: 18/11/2021).

18 2020 Nian jiaotong yunshu jingji xian jiang hou sheng, chixu huifu (2020 年 交通运输经济先降后升持续恢复), http://xxgk.mot.gov.cn/2020/jigou/zhghs/202101/t20210128_3520349.html (access: 18/11/2021).

19 Xiauku Song, Shiguo Wu, Xin Xu., *The Great Change in the Regional Economy of China under the New Normal. The Great Transformation of China*, Singapore 2019, pp. 193–222.

development concept, and building a new development model"[20]. According to Chinese political factors, the transport infrastructure should be an important vehicle for the coordinated development of a modern industrial system, a significant support for the regional coordination development strategy, a guarantee for the overall implementation of rural revitalization, and a significant measure to improve the quality of life of the population.

Representatives of the CPC perceive infrastructure, especially transport infrastructure, mainly through the prism of large infrastructure projects. It should be noted that this thinking is the result of the Chinese mentality and political vision. Nothing better puts reality in order than putting a properly planned and built infrastructure into use, regardless of whether it is a national road, a new railway line, or another airport. The order, as has been known for a long time, is an element of Confucian sociopolitical thought. There is one more circumstance that makes infrastructure so important in contemporary Chinese regional politics. Although strengthening the competitiveness of individual regions may lead to an increase in the importance of particularisms (local, regional), transport is an instrument through which it is possible to connect the main centers of political and economic power with each other. This dilemma, which, let us add, is not only China's experience, seems to be resolved by connecting the country through a series of corridors, including the periphery. Including smaller centers in an extensive network of the most modern infrastructure is a task carried out not only for economic reasons (flow of key goods, including products and services), but also for political reasons. Strengthening the central authority is undoubtedly an important element of the CPC's policy.

Returning to the main conclusions of the fifth plenary session of the 19th Central Committee of the CPC, it should be emphasized that investing in transport infrastructure is an important element of a modern industrial system, a guarantee of maintaining and even modernizing the supply chain in industrial production. The development of modern industries today and in the future will depend on the transport infrastructure. The experiences of the scientific and technological revolution show that they take place alongside and through the transport system. In many areas important to the Chinese economy, the importance of transport is predominant. Moreover, according to official government factors, the construction of transport infrastructure is an important support to improve the quality of life of the population[21].

20 Tang Jin (唐瑾): *Tongchou jiaotong jichu sheshi jianshe zhicheng gao zhiliang fazhan* (统筹交通基础设施建设支撑高质量发展), http://www.ccud.org.cn/article/23416.html (access: 18/11/2021).

21 Tang Jin (唐瑾): *Tongchou jiaotong jichu sheshi jianshe zhicheng gao zhiliang fazhan* op. cit.

There is no doubt that the role of infrastructure, and in particular transport infrastructure, is important in the economic context. In the light of the regional policy, for example, it is about enabling the diffusion of development from large centers to smaller towns. Hence, state policy is aimed at optimizing the layout of land and space and promoting coordinated regional development and new urbanization. Coordination will take place through the implementation of major macroregional strategies, regional development strategies, and major functional area strategies, improvement of mechanisms for shaping coordinated regional development, improvement of new urbanization strategies, and a support system for high-quality development. According to Chinese planners, coordinated development is not only a concept, but a strategy to reduce the regional development gap, optimize spatial distribution, and improve resource space allocation efficiency. This means that public investments, as intended, may concern not only the infrastructure itself, which can be said to be generally available, but the scale of public intervention must be continued on a wider scale and relate to the infrastructure necessary for the development of entrepreneurship. Examples of such activities can be found in the urban clusters and metropolitan areas (e.g., Beijing-Tianjin- Yangtze, River Delta- Yangtze, River Mid-Range-Guangdong, Hong Kong, Macao – Chengyu)[22].

Among the transport investments of the PRC, attention should be paid to railway investments[23]. It is important because, this means of transport is treated as low-emission and therefore environmentally friendly. The results of the research indicate that railway investments in China in the past decade have been a positive stimulus for the economy, and the impact on reducing CO_2 emissions into the atmosphere has been significant. Overall, the economic effects of rail investments in China are achieved primarily through driven demand and production growth, while the contribution to the reduction of rail costs and the increase in rail efficiency has been modest[24]. China's rail policy relates to its overall expansion, rolling stock, tracks, and, above all, extension of high-speed

22 Ibid.

23 Shujie Yao, Fan Zhang, Feng Wang, Jinghua Ou, *Regional economic growth and the role of high-speed rail in China,* "Applied Economics" 2019, vol. 51, no. 32, pp. 3465–3479; Xuehui Yang, Huirong Zhang, Shanlang Lin, Jiaping Zhang, Jianlong Zeng, *Does high-speed railway promote regional innovation growth or innovation convergence?,* "Technology in Society" 2021, vol. 64; Zhenhua Chen, Kingsley E. Haynes, Yulong Zhou, Zhaoxin Dai, *High Speed Rail and China's New Economic Geography: Impact Assessment from the Regional Science Perspective,* Cheltenham, Northampton 2019, pp. 37–82; Marianna Marra, *High speed rail and China's new economic geography: Impact assessment from the regional science perspective,* "Regional Studies" 2020, vol. 54, no. 4, p. 590.

24 Zhenhua Chen, Junbo Xue, Adam Rose, Kingsley Haynes, *The impact of high-speed rail investment on economic and environmental change in China: A dynamic CGE analysis,* "Transportation Research Part A: Policy and Practice" 2016, vol. 92, pp. 232–245.

railways. High-speed rail facilitates movement in urbanized areas. It discharges car traffic, constituting a rational alternative to airplanes, which makes it a much more environmentally friendly solution. The plans envisage connecting approximately 80% of the major Chinese cities by high-speed rail. Hence, a number of investments concern urban transport in the largest Chinese cities, such as Shanghai[25], Wuhan[26], Chengdu[27] and Nanchang[28]. Regional investment projects have also been implemented[29].

China has the longest high-speed rail network in the world (37,900,000 km) and just as much is to be built in the next 15 years. The PRC also plans to build its own Maglev network, called Fixing based on magnetic cushions, with trains moving at speeds exceeding 600 km / h. The first test drives took place in Shanghai in spring 2020, the first train was launched from the port city of Quingdao in July 2021, and the first train is to be put into service in 2025. China also has the longest network of highways – it is already 142,500 km, while the network in the USA, for example, is 108,394 km. Infrastructural achievements are much greater, so China has put into use 6 of the 10 longest bridges in the world, including the longest of them, 164,800 m, connecting Danyang with Kunsham. They also have the 10 longest tunnels in the world. Airport infrastructure also attracts attention. The modern Daxing airport between Beijing and Tianjin, had an estimated construction cost of USD 36 billion. The airport is part of a larger project, i.e., the construction of a *smart city* called Xiongam, where, like eight other mega-projects of this type, solutions based on a green economy, high

25 Guanyu shanghai shi chengshi guidao jiaotong di san qi jianshe guihua (2018–2023 nian) de pifu (fa gai jichu [2018] 1831 hao) (关于上海市 城市轨道交通第三期建设规划 [2018–2023 年])的批复(发改基础 [2018] 1831 号), [in:] https://zfxxgk.ndrc.gov.cn/web/iteminfo.jsp?id=15942 (access: 20/04/2022).

26 Guanyu wuhan shi chengshi guidao jiaotong di si qi jianshe guihua (2019–2024 nian) de pifu (fa gai jichu [2018] 1915 hao) zhengfu xinxi gongkai_zhengwu gongkai-guojia fazhan gaige wei (关于武汉市第四期轨道 轨道建设规划 [2019–2024 年]) 的 批复 (发改基础 [2018] 1915 号 政府 信息 公开 政务公开-国家发展改革 委), https://zfxxgk.ndrc.gov.cn/web/iteminfo.jsp?id=16071 (access: 20/04/2022); Shi fazhan gaige wei guanyu bianzhi 2021 nian shi ji zhengfu touzi jihua he 2021–2023 nian gundong touzi jihua de tongzhi (市发展 改革 委 关于编制2021年市级政府 投资 计划 和2021–2023年滚动 投资 计划 的通知), http://fgw.wuhan.gov.cn/zfxxgk/zfxxgk_4/czzj/czzxzj/202009/t20200914_1477160.html (access: 20/04/2022).

27 Guanyu chengdu shi chengshi guidao jiaotong di si qi jianshe guihua (2019–2024 nian) (关于成都市城市轨道交通第四期建设规划 [2019–2024 年]), https://zfxxgk.ndrc.gov.cn/web/iteminfo.jsp?id=16259 (access: April 20, 2022).

28 Guanyu tiao zheng nanchang shi chengshi guidao jiaotong di er qi jianshe guihua fangan de pifu (关于调整 南昌市 城市 轨道 交通 第二 期 建设 规划 方案 的 批复(发 改 基础), https://zfxxgk.ndrc.gov.cn/web/iteminfo.jsp?id=17547 (access: 20/04/2022).

29 Guanyu yue gangao da wan qu cheng ji tielu jianshe guihua de pifu (关于 粤 港澳 大 湾区 城际铁路建设规划的 批复), https://zfxxgk.ndrc.gov.cn/web/iteminfo.jsp?id=17203 (access: 20/04/2022).

technologies, and artificial intelligence are to dominate. The total investment costs are expected to amount to USD 583 billion[30].

5.1.2. Environmental infrastructure

Investments related to environmental protection are another aspect of public intervention. Building an ecological civilization and sustainable development, as well as integrating economic and social goals with ecological ones, requires not only persuasive actions among society, but most of all the provision of infrastructure elements[31] that will enable the improvement of the quality of the natural environment. Hence the need to build or expand infrastructure based on low-emission solutions and advanced technological innovations, also in the production space. It is also the enforcement of standards in the field of coal-fired power plants, coal-burning boilers, vehicle emissions and air quality[32]. The reduction of air, water, and soil pollution requires specific measures also in the field of appropriate infrastructure. It is similar with regards to increasing the level of wastewater treatment, improving water quality, preventing pollution. China is currently implementing a number of measures to improve the quality of the environment in many areas. One of the most significant systemic instruments is the priority of the Five-Year Plans dedicated to supporting the natural environment.

The implementation of the natural environment support requires, in addition to organizational and legal changes, the implementation of many public investments. As part of the 13th Five-Year Plan, efforts were made to approach the issue in a comprehensive manner; therefore, not all the priorities relating to the improvement of the state of the environment were included in this area, e.g., supporting ecosystems and the environment. Even the authorities admitted that the condition of the natural environment is still unsatisfactory and that the pressure resulting from expectations for economic growth is still very high. They have often dealt with local and even regional pressures on development, while neglecting nature protection[33]. Hence, there is a further need to take systemic

30 Bogdan Góralczyk, *Nowy długi marsz. Chiny ery Xi Jinpinga*, Warszawa 2021, pp. 110–111.

31 Qiong Yang, Xiurong Hu, Yuqing Wang, Ying Liu, Junfeng Liu, Jianmin Ma, Xuejun Wang, Yi Wan, Jianying Hu, Zhaobin Zhang, Xilong Wang, Shu Tao, *Comparison of the impact of China's investment and road investment on the economy and air pollution emissions*, "Journal of Cleaner Production" 2021, p. 293.

32 Jan Wiktor Tkac zyński, Marek Świstak, *Environmental protection in China as a new element of the social and economic development policy model*, [in:] Marek Świstak, Jan Wiktor Tkaczyński (eds.), *Asian model of social and economic development policy. Selected aspects in the light of the standards and experiences of the European Union*, Kraków 2019, pp. 232–233.

33 Zhenhua Chen, Junbo Xue, Adam Z. Rose, Kingsley E. Haynes, op. cit., pp. 232–245.

actions. Not all tasks were achieved to the extent that they were planned. That is why the central authorities have developed several plans and programs until 2035. The analysis of these documents shows that the so far narrowly understood necessity of public intervention is being extended to new areas where there are still lags in terms of the level of environmental protection.

In many regions in the PRC, there is a phenomenon of pressure on economic development, thereby neglecting ecological protection to accumulate the necessary resources to live. In the opinion of the central government, unwise development activities reduce the space of ecological biodiversity. In determining public intervention for environmental protection, it was decided not only to implement particular measures at various levels and in various areas (e.g., air protection), but to regionalize the activities by developing specific construction plans for major national ecosystem protection and restoration projects. An example is the master plan for the protection and restoration of major national ecosystem projects (2021–2035), whose purpose is to designate specially protected areas. This intervention is to be implemented centrally. The implementation of large-scale ecological system protection and renovation projects was mentioned as an important element of the reform in order to implement the report of the 19th Congress of the CPC.

Table 27. List of special construction plans for major national ecosystem protection and restoration projects

No.	Name Plan
1	Plan to build major environmental protection and restoration projects in the Qinghai Plateau Ecological Barrier Area – Tibet (2021–2035)
2	Plan to build major ecological protection and restoration projects in key ecological regions of the Yellow River (including the ecological barrier of the Loess Upland) (2021–2035)
3	Plan to build major environmental protection and reconstruction projects in key ecological regions of the Yangtze River (including the Sichuan – Junnan environmental barrier) (2021–2035)
4	Plan for the construction of large environmental protection and restoration projects in the north-eastern forest belt (2021–2035)
5	Plan to build large-scale environmental protection and northern sand belt reconstruction projects (2021–2035)
6	Plan to build major environmental and restoration projects in southern hilly and mountain areas (2021–2035)
7	Plan to build major environmental protection and coastal rehabilitation projects (2021–2035)
8	Nature reserve construction plan and large projects for the protection of wild animals and plants (2021–2035)

Table 27 *(Continued)*

No.	Name Plan
9	Plan to build large-scale projects for the environmental protection and restoration support system (2021–2035)

Source own work based on: Quanguo zhongyao shengtai xitong baohu he xiufu zhongda gongcheng zongti guihua (2021–2035 nian), op. cit., pp. 42.

The systemic deficiencies identified in environmental protection relate to the control of authority and responsibility. The management system and the coordination and linkage mechanism are yet to be established, and overall planning for ecological conservation and restoration faces greater challenges. Some of the construction goals of green projects and the content of the construction and management measures are important. Some construction projects still struggle to integrate environmental protection requirements (e.g., use of water resources). In addition, the process of providing services still does not take into account respect for natural resources such as soil, light, and heat, native species, and regional ecosystems. Protection of water resources is also quite a challenge. On the one hand, the demand for water in a richer society is growing and on the other, its resources are shrinking. Large-scale overexploitation of groundwater creates an area of groundwater funnels, causing subsidence and seawater penetration, which requires further investment.

Adjusting the investment process by economic entities to the environmental protection requirements is still a serious challenge. Both the market-based investment mechanism and the environmental compensation mechanism still require adjustments, and the lack of appropriate incentives lowers their importance. Therefore, modern civil engineering, taking into account ecological requirements, is based on government investment. Innovative solutions present on the market of the PRC do not adequately take into account the requirements of ecological civilization[34]. Thus, Beijing's decision makers have decided to focus on large environmental protection projects that are to provide a better social environment for pro-ecological activities[35]. These projects (see Table 27) assume the protection of the whole or part of the ecosystems, as well as their revitalization. Their goal is to comprehensively strengthen not only protection, but also rehabilitation works, e.g., forests, meadows, deserts, rivers, lakes, and wetlands.

34 Jan Wiktor Tkaczyński, Łukasz Gacek, *China's environmental policy in terms of European Union standards,* Göttingen 2021. p. 83.

35 Quanguo zhongyao shengtai xitong baohu he xiufu zhongda gongcheng zongti guihua (2021–2035 nian), op. cit., pp. 9–12.

Table 28. List of green industry demonstration databases

No.	Name	Location
1	Tianjin Economic and Technological Development Zone	Tianjin
2	Wu'an Industrial Park	Hebei
3	Gaobeidian Economic Development Zone	Hebei
4	Datong Economic and Technological Development Zone	Shanxi
5	Economic Development Zone of Yitong Autonomous District Manchu	Jilin
6	Fusong Industrial Park	Jilin
7	Caohejing Emerging Technology Development Zone Yancheng District	Shanghai
8	Suzhou National High-tech Industrial Development Zone,	Jiangsu
9	Yancheng Environmental High-tech Industrial Development Zone	Jiangsu
10	Changzhou Economic Development Zone	Jiangsu
11	Wuxing Economic Development Zone	Zhejiang
12	Suichang Industrial Park	Zhejiang
13	Suixi Economic Development Zone	Anhui
14	Fuyang Jieshou High Technology Industrial Development Zone	Anhui
15	Wuhu High-tech Industrial Development Zone	Anhui
16	Fuzhou High-tech Industrial Development Zone	Fujian
17	Fengcheng Circular Economy Industrial Park	Jiangxi
18	High-tech Industrial Development zZone of Dezhou	Shantung
19	Sanmenxia High-tech Industrial Development Zone	Henan
20	Gucheng Economic Development Zone	Hubei
21	Miluo High-tech Industrial Development Zone	Hunan
22	Guangzhou Economic and Technological Development Zone	Guangdong
23	Dongguan Songshan Lake A Technologically Advanced Industrial Development Zone	Guangdong
24	Wuzhou Circular Economy Industrial Park	Guangxi
25	Chongqing Economic and Technological Development Zone	Chongqing
26	Zigong High-tech Industrial Development Zone	Sichuan
27	Qingzhen Economic Development Zone	Guizhou
28	Jinggu Forest Products Industrial Park	Yunnan
29	Xi'an Economic and Technological Development Zone	Shaanxi
30	Golmud Kunlun Economic and Technological Development Zone	Qinghai

Table 28 *(Continued)*

No.	Name	Location
31	Yinchuan High-tech Industrial Development Zone	Ningxia

Source: Luse chanye shifan yidi mingdanmingdan (绿色 产业示范基地 名单), https://www.ndrc.gov.cn/xxgk/zcfb/tz/202101/P020210108597098679981.pdf (access:18/11/2021).

On December 11, 2021, the announcement of the general office of the NDRC on the organization of demonstration bases for the ecological industry was published. The list is a list of bases that are to be demonstrative and, therefore, a kind of model for other units. This means that the authorities managing a given database, at the appropriate time, are obliged to summarize the progress of work, create replicated models of experiences and practices of an exemplary nature. The NDRC and the Ministry of Science and Technology are obliged to exchange experiences and promotional activities in the field of diffusion of developed model solutions on a national scale. Establishing demonstration bases naturally remains the task of the public authorities at the appropriate level, according to the specificity of the unit. The locations of the bases cover mainly the provinces of the more developed east of the country. None of the zones was located in the area of the western macroregion.

5.1.3. Social infrastructure

Social infrastructure also plays a significant role in regional policy, as it includes services such as education, physical and mental health, culture, recreation, and sports programs. It contributes to the sustainable development of cities, scientific and technological strength, and poverty reduction. The main function of social infrastructure is to provide public goods to meet public needs in terms of social activity and to support social development, especially in densely populated cities[36]. With the development of the social economy and rapid urbanization, the requirements of the PRC citizens have shifted from the pursuit of economic growth to a high quality of life. These needs, in terms of being equipped with social infrastructure, also result from dynamic processes related to urbanization; here, the various expectations of middle-class society must be taken into account, such as, for example, the quality of the urban environment[37]. As in the case of

36 Philippa Williams, Barbara Pocock, *Building 'community' for different stages of life: physical and social infrastructure in master planned communities*, "Community, Work & Family" 2010, vol. 13, no. 1, pp. 71–87.

37 Zhanqiang Zhu, Jie Ren, Xuan Liu, *Green infrastructure provision for environmental justice: Application of the equity index in Guangzhou, China*, "Urban Forestry & Urban Greening" 2019, vol. 46, pp. 1–11.

other areas, recent years have also brought significant investment in social infrastructure[38].

The policy in the field of social infrastructure, starting from the Deng reforms, has evolved many times and corresponds to the political priorities of the center and the financial possibilities of the PRC. For example, many primary and secondary schools have been built to promote compulsory education, newly constructed hospitals and medical infrastructure contribute to healthcare, and investments in cultural and sports infrastructure promote physical health. Although these plans and policies have contributed to the improvement of social services, imperfections in public services, such as difficulties in accessing health care, finding a suitable school, or caring for the elderly, are not uncommon. They are the result of the scarcity and regional gaps in social infrastructure, the education system, health care and social care[39]. In the process of urbanization, the demand for urban public goods gradually increases, leading to a deficit in the quantity and quality of original public goods, thus promoting the continuing need for the provision of social infrastructure. Especially in cases of severe scarcity of public goods, it is the responsibility of local authorities to offset (or counteract) this.[40]. Another way in which local authorities are obliged to promote social infrastructure is pressure from above due to the evaluation of clerical cadres. Although the staff appraisal mechanism has been based on economic performance for years, social peace is becoming just as important. From the point of view of state-to-society relations, in the Chinese nomenclature system, social instability due to severe livelihood problems can debase all other achievements in evaluating the official cadre performance[41].

It should be noted that the level of land supply for social infrastructure determines the development of urban areas in the PRC. Insufficient land supply for the needs of social infrastructure causes problems with the provision of social services at an appropriate level. The spatiotemporal provision of land for social infrastructure was investigated based on a 10-year data set of land supply for social infrastructure. The results show that among the three types of social infrastructure, the largest part was made up of educational institutions (73.2% of the entire social infrastructure), health services (12.8%), and cultural and recreational services (12.8%). Between 2007 and 2016, the supply of all types of social infrastructure increased significantly, especially in healthcare facilities. Taking

38 Yuan Gao, Li Tian, Yandong Cao, Lin Zhou, Zhibin Li, Deyi Hou, *Supplying social infrastructure land for satisfying public needs or leasing residential land? A study of local government choices in China*, "Land Use Policy" 2019, vol. 87, p. 1.

39 Ibid.

40 Zan Yang, Rongrong Ren, Hongyu Liu, Huan Zhang, *Land leasing and local government behavior in China: Evidence from Beijing*, "Urban Studies" 2015, vol. 52, no. 5, pp. 841–856.

41 Yuan Gao, Li Tian, Yandong Cao, Lin Zhou, Zhibin Li, Deyi Hou, op. cit., p. 3.

into account the differences in their stage of development, the four economic and geographical regions (i. e., western, central, eastern, and north-eastern) show quite large differences in terms of the supply of land for social infrastructure. The supply of land in this area is closely related to the supply of land for housing construction. The supply of land for healthcare, culture, and sports facilities is not closely related to public demand. This confirms that the government's incentives to capture land income by providing land for social infrastructure are stronger than those to meet the needs of society[42].

5.2. Special Economic Zones as a window to the world of Chinese regions

Special Economic Zones (SEZ)[43] play an important role in the development of the Chinese economy. They were established to develop foreign trade, attract foreign capital, serve as regional centers of growth, and contribute to the modernization of a backward economy. In the course of reforms related to China's opening, the position was developed that SEZ would constitute a window to the world, but at the same time would be different from those zones established in free-market countries[44]. The reason for this solution was that SEZ were only a supplement to the Chinese economy at the beginning of the reforms. China's first experience with SEZ was later used with caution. The authorities wanted to test the solutions to see if the SEZ mechanism could help the country's transformation from a centrally planned economy to a more market-based economy. In addition to attracting foreign capital necessary for development, it was also concerned with the inflow of new technologies and knowledge in the field of management. Capital, technologies, and management know-how were not all; in a short time

42 Ibid, pp. 10–11.

43 For the purposes of this study, it was assumed that SEZ have a defined geographic area, local management, unique benefits and separate customs and administrative procedures. The unique benefits include operating under more liberal laws and economic policies compared to other parts of the country. The concept of SEZ covers a wide range of zones, such as: free trade zones, export zones, industrial parks, free ports, business zones and others. In China, the SEZ refers to a complex of interrelated economic activities and services, rather than a homogeneous activity. Currently you can identify at least 10 types of zones. See: Douglas Zhihua Zeng, *How Do Special Economic Zones and Industrial Clusters Drive China's Rapid Development?*, [in:] Douglas Zhihua Zeng (ed.), *Building engines for growth and competitiveness in China: Experience with special economic zones and industrial clusters*, Washington 2010, p. 4; Xiao Wang, *The Role of Economic Development Zones in National Development Strategies, The Case of China*, Santa Monica-Arlington-Pittsburgh 2013, p. iii.

44 Ingo Liefne, Yehua Dennis Wei, *Introduction: innovation and regional development in China*, [in:], Ingo Liefne, Yehua Dennis Wei (eds.), *Innovation and regional development in China*, New York-London, 2014, pp. 5–7.

the emerging SEZ contributed to the increase in demand for labor, which was not lacking in China. For example, small fishing villages turned into cities and later into metropolises.

SEZ are a well-known instrument of economic and regional policy, applicable in many countries, including highly developed ones[45]. It is worth noting, however, that it does not guarantee success[46]. It appeared in the Middle Kingdom quite late; the first zone was established in 1978; it was located in the eastern part of the Guangdong province. The first four SEZ (Shenzhen, Zhuhai, Shantou, and Xiamen) were established along the southeast coast of China, in the immediate vicinity of Hong Kong and Taiwan, in part to strengthen ties politically with mainland China. Hainan Island was granted SEZ status in 1988. The new Pudong area of Shanghai, which was created in 1990 with the strong support of the central government, acquired extensive special powers and now plays a key role in the Chinese banking sector as well as the stock market. SEZ are formally subordinate to provincial governments, but they have a lot of freedom when it comes to export, taxation and regulation of local markets[47]. It should be mentioned that in the area of the SEZ Shenzhen, the local government issued more than 400 economic ordinances[48] between 1979 and 1990, affecting domestic and foreign trade and investment, and economic legislation.

The location of SEZ in the south-eastern areas of China is proof of the deliberate choice of regional development in China's coastal provinces. The effect of such a regional approach was that a large part of foreign investments were located in the SEZ of the coastal provinces. Between 1979 and 1993, the coastal regions as a whole accepted around 90% of foreign investment, 65% of which was in Guangdong Province. This resulted in an increase in industrial production in the

45 Adam A. Ambroziak, Christopher A. Hartwell, *The impact of investments in special economic zones on regional development: The case of Poland,* "Regional Studies" 2018, vol. 52, no. 10, pp. 1322–1331; Naresh Kumar Sharma, *Special economic zones: Socio-economic implications,* "Economic and Political Weekly" 2009, vol. 44, no. 20, pp. 18–21.

46 It is worth mentioning the program of special industrial zones in Greece. Despite the fact that they were located in less developed regions and instruments encouraging investment were applied, the interest of business turned out to be low and did not contribute to economic growth. The reasons for such a situation include strong administrative control over these areas, and greater profitability of Greek companies functioning in the "gray" zone than those using subsidies from the Greek state (but at the same time remaining under fiscal rigor). As a consequence, high government spending did not bring the expected economic recovery. See Tomasz Grzegorz Grosse, op. cit., pp. 122–123.

47 Dirk Schmidt, Sebastian Heilmann, *Provincial- and municipal-level Governments,* op. cit., p. 87

48 Sebastian Heilmann, *Red Swan …,* op. cit., p. 84.

coastal provinces, together with the SEZ, which accounted for over 50% of China's production[49].

Over time, local governments with SEZ began to take advantage of greater independence in attracting external investors and capital. There was a rivalry between them, described by some as a "murderous fight"[50]. Examples of such activities include waiver of payments by some local governments for land transferred to joint ventures that undertake investments or the reduction of taxes[51]. Generally, representatives of local authorities have learned to remove various administrative and institutional barriers. It was not particularly difficult, because at the beginning, the requirements for running a business were not too high. First, economic results mattered, while environmental protection, employment standards, and other requirements that could not be avoided in developed countries were less important.

As China's reforms progressed, quantitative strategy began to give way to qualitative thinking e. g., creating convincing business models. An example is the city of Chongqing in western China, which is now successfully competing with coastal cities. It owes its success to a business model developed over the years, which consists in creating a platform for optimizing conditions for business entities. This solution, in a nutshell, enables the implementation of two extreme phases of each production activity, i. e., initial and final (logistics supply chain and product marketing).

Taking into account the local competitiveness conditions, SEZ undoubtedly contributed to the use of endogenous development factors by local governments. Increasing labor costs in the East Coast provinces are now shifting manufacturing activities towards the Chinese interior and western provinces. The local governments of the western and central provinces hosting SEZ, despite this process, are still under pressure to create conditions that would increase their attractiveness for investment. The city of Chongqing mentioned above, for example, has introduced a model called "inside and outside", which has managed to make the most of manpower and natural resources. Local human resources were used there, mainly peasants who found jobs in local workplaces in their place of residence. Thanks to this, they could still use public services. Their colleagues, economic migrants, due to the registration system, in this case a rural *hukou,* could not take advantage of this privilege. Local workers also did not have to pay any additional travel costs. This would have been the case had they decided to emigrate to the East Coast regions. The opening of the Chongqing-Xinjiang-

49 Shahul Hameed, *China's Special Economic Zones,* [in:] Swaraj Prakash Gupta (ed.), *China's Economic Reforms: The Role of Special Economic Zones and Economic and Technological Development Zones,* New Delhi 1996, p. 36.

50 Yan Yilong, Bai Gang, Zhang Leyong, Ou Shujun, He Jianyu, op. cit., p. 166.

51 Maria Edin, *Why Do Chinese Local Cadres Promote Growth?* op. cit., pp. 104–105.

Europe railway line was essential for the endogenous development of the city due to which it became possible to export goods abroad, eliminating the problem of lack of access to direct sea freight. The development of the Chongqing Liangjiang SEZ[52], which has become the largest electronics production center in the Middle Kingdom, capable of producing, for example, 40 million laptops a year, is also of great importance for this example.

It should be noted that the economic success of SEZ is the result of actions taken by Beijing on the one hand and local governments on the other. We have already talked about the central government; here we will focus on local structures. Some local governments have developed activities that go beyond simply organizing the good conditions for entrepreneurship. Over time, they became a direct player, participating in the competition, having at their disposal public resources on a free market basis. In such circumstances, they undertake a competitive game in order to attract an external investor. It also happens that they enter into illegal business with dishonest entrepreneurs, and corruption often occurs[53]. This phenomenon has increased with the spread of SEZ. Writing about corruption in the SEZ in the 1980s, Morton and Lewis[54] indicate that children and relatives of Party dignitaries used their contacts and monopolized control over companies. This heightened the frustration of young and educated people who did not have good contacts. In 1987, 150,000 CPC members were punished for abuses of power, and more than 25,000 were removed from the ranks. Despite the negative phenomena, the Chinese governments at various levels (central, local), thanks to the SEZ, are implementing a policy of supporting and developing domestic entrepreneurship. The various instruments that are used in this policy include financial subsidies, loans for people setting up a business, advertising campaigns for domestic companies, and creating business standards[55]. At the beginning of the 20th century, there was an increase in the intensity of using zones as an instrument of regional policy. This resulted in a significant increase in the number of zones in the areas already hosting them, and continued until 2008, before stagnating. As in highly developed countries, the creation of economic development zones in China had positive consequences, which were manifested in for example, an increase in industrial production. Research confirms that, in general, the creation of SEZ stimulates the development process[56].

52 Yan Yilong, Bai Gang, Zhang Leyong, Ou Shujun, He Jianyu, op. cit., p. 168.
53 Ibid.
54 Scott Morton, Charlton Lewis, op. cit., p. 273.
55 Yan Yilong, Bai Gang, Zhang Leyong, Ou Shujun, He Jianyu, op. cit., pp. 170–171.
56 Elisa Barbieri, Chiara Pollio, Francesco Prota, *The impacts of spatially targeted programs: evidence from Guangdong*, "Regional Studies" 2020, vol. 54, no. 3, pp. 415–428.

From the perspective of regional policy, the most significant positive experiences of SEZ lie in the experimental approach and active state policy, along with the simplification of legislation. The policy of supporting SEZ shows strong political commitment and pragmatism on the part of the top leadership of the CPC. To this should be added preferential policies and a fairly wide autonomy of local authorities, considering Chinese conditions. At the local level, some of the most important elements were the participation of local governments in the provision of public goods, the improvement of the external conditions for business, and the formulation of public-private partnerships. To some extent, the success of SEZs in the initial stage of their development was determined by the investment participation of the Chinese diaspora living outside China[57]. Among the positive effects of the SEZ on the economy, the contribution to GDP, increasing the flow of foreign investment, creating new places and attracting advanced technologies to the country should also be mentioned.

Despite the widespread affirmation of the positive effects of SEZ, it is also appropriate to focus on the negative aspects that are of great importance from the point of view of regional policy. It should be remembered that the SEZ were an experiment aimed at increasing production efficiency, as well as a test for the introduction of market mechanisms. The effects of the SEZ-related policy are not unequivocally positive. Negative factors include disproportions in regional development. Initially, decisions about the location of special economic zones covered mainly eastern provinces. At the beginning of the 21st century, they were located in less developed, central, and western provinces. The introduction of SEZ increased disproportions between regions. For example, between 1978 and 1998, Fujian Province (East Coast) saw real GDP grow by 13.9%, while Gansu Province (inland) grew by only 6.7%. In 2000, the 10 provinces with the highest GDP per capita were in the east coast of China[58].

It was disappointing that there was no spillover effect. It was assumed that the faster economic development of the coastal regions would penetrate over time into the central and western regions[59]. On the other hand, the positive impact of SEZ on the development of regions where many zones have been located is unquestionable. Furthermore, regions where SEZ were created earlier brought greater positive economic benefits compared to regions where SEZ were created later. One of the most significant economic impacts of the SEZ on the local

57 Justin Yifu Lin, *Foreword,* [in:] Douglas Zhihua Zeng (ed.), op. cit., p. xiv.

58 Qinghua Zhang, Heng-fu Zou, *Regional inequality in contemporary China,* "Annals of Economics & Finance" 2012, vol. 13, no. 1, pp. 119–143.

59 John M. Litwack, Yingyi Qian, *Balanced or unbalanced development: Special economic zones as catalysts for transition,* "Journal of Comparative Economics" 1998, vol. 26, no. 1, pp. 117–141.

economy was the increase in the level of income and the emerging earning potential of employees in the region.

Several factors can be identified that contributed to the lack of externalities and the increase in regional disparities between Chinese provinces. Regarding the SEZ policy itself, at the very beginning, foreign companies in the first four SEZ received very attractive tax breaks and the possibility of flexible employment. These zones achieved economic success, which increased the inflow of foreign investments. This influx has contributed to the disproportionate development of infrastructure, technology, and human capital in the coastal provinces. Increased management skills and opportunities for economies of scale have created a more attractive social and economic environment for foreign direct investment than in inland provinces[60]. This includes the general economic policy of the PRC. One of the elements was the location of state-owned enterprises, especially large economic entities, which were usually located in coastal regions. The geographical spread of the infrastructure network also strengthened the trend mentioned above. In a situation of partial decentralization of public finances, financially more affluent local authorities (in the area where the SEZ was located) could afford to invest in infrastructure to a greater extent[61].

The uneven development of regions in China also progressed due to the decentralization policy, both budgetary and fiscal of the 1980s [62]. Decentralization is often treated as a positive phenomenon in regional development, as it gives local authorities more opportunities to act and enables the release of grassroots activity (activation of endogenous factors). However, in this case, the decentralization of public finances separated the finances of local and central authorities. Poorer territorial units were more dependent on their own financing, which was very limited in relation to the richer ones. Hence, in the absence of support from the central level, the "vicious circle" mechanism of Gunnar Myrdal was apparent[63], which resulted in an increase in development disproportions between the east and the interior and the west of China. The state policy of special economic zones has paradoxically increased the development disproportions between the western and central regions in relation to the coastal provinces[64]. It has been pointed out that development disparity can be reduced by large in-

60 Belton Fleisher, Haizheng Li, Min Qiang Zhao, *Human capital, economic growth, and regional inequality in China,* "Journal of Development Economics" 2010 vol. 92, no. 2, pp. 215–231.

61 Sylvie Démurger, op. cit., pp. 95–117.

62 Dennis Tao Yang, *What has caused regional inequality in China?,* "China Economic Review" 2002, vol. 13, no. 4, pp. 331–334.

63 It is also referred to as the principle of circular and cumulative causality. See Lloyd G. Reynolds, *Gunnar Myrdal's Contribution to Economics, 1940–1970,* "The Swedish Journal of Economics" 1974, vol. 76, no. 4, pp. 479–497.

64 Crane Bret, Albrecht Chad, Kristopher McKay Duffin, Albrecht Conan, *China's special economic zones,* op. cit., pp. 98–107.

vestments in transport[65] and other infrastructure, improving education, increasing development opportunities in low-income areas, eliminating barriers to migration between different areas, and eliminating tax benefits enjoyed by special economic zones in eastern China. However, mitigating income inequalities can take a long time[66].

5.3. Foreign direct investment in international capital flows: importance for Chinese regions

In today's economy, international capital flows play an increasingly important role, which is of great importance for world trade. Nevertheless, foreign direct investment (FDI) can also be viewed from the perspective of regional policy, i. e., as an instrument to increase regional and even local competitiveness. Investments flowing into a given region may contribute to an increase in production and the creation of new jobs, and thus to increasing its competitiveness. Therefore, they are a desirable element of local and regional development. In this perspective, not only the scale, nature, but also the location of FDI in the Middle Kingdom are important. FDI are treated as long-term, permanent investments. Relations between entities allow one entity established in one country to take control of another entity based in another country[67]. The above investments can take many different forms. We can mention here mergers (of entities from different countries), acquisitions (gaining control over the enterprise), and investments from scratch.

The FDI sector is important for the Chinese economy, as foreign-capital companies account for more than 50% of Chinese exports and 60% of imports. It is estimated that the share of these entities in Chinese GDP in 2004 was 22%. Interestingly, these entities do not have a similarly high share in the Chinese labor market, as they employ only 3% of the available workforce in the country, mainly because their efficiency exceeds the productivity of domestic enterprises in the ratio of 9:1, respectively[68]. This means that the Chinese economy is highly susceptible to fluctuations in foreign investment inflows, which the central authorities are aware of. In recent years, they have called for a more comprehensive basis for economic growth on domestic consumption.

65 S. Yao, Zhaoyong Zhang, *Regional Growth in China Under Economic Reforms*, "The Journal of Development Studies" 2001, vol. 38, no. 2, pp. 167–186.
66 Angus Maddison, *Chinese Economic Performance in the Long Run*, OECD, Paris 2007, p. 22.
67 United Nations, *World Investment Report 2006, FDI from Developing and Transition Economics: Implication for Development*, New York-Geneva 2006, p. 29.
68 John Whalley, Xian XIN, *China's FDI and non- FDI economies and the sustainability of future high Chinese growth*, "China Economic Review" 2010, vol. 21, no. 1, pp. 123–135.

The policy of opening up to foreign trade has also brought a significant influx of capital since the early 1990s. The increase lasted until 2000, after which it decreased slightly due to the Asian crisis. Since China's entry into the World Trade Organization in 2001, it has increased significantly again. It obtained a particularly high value in 2008, when it amounted to USD 108 billion. It is worth noting that at that time there was a crisis in Western economies and an outflow of capital to China. This country has not been hit that hard by the financial crisis. Since 2008, it has experienced relatively steady growth, reaching more than $ 141 billion in 2019 (Figure 9). Thus, China is becoming one of the largest recipients of FDI in the world.

Foreign investors and companies are essential to China's economy, and the Chinese government also recognizes this. Currently, about half a million companies with foreign participation operate in this country. According to official figures, these companies accounted for around 45% of China's foreign trade in 2013, and also created 55 million jobs in the urban economy (about one sixth of all city workers). Since 2000, 8–9% of all global direct investment has gone to China[69]. In recent years, China has stopped being only a recipient of FDI, as economic entities registered in this country invest abroad[70]. Currently, they are very active in Africa.

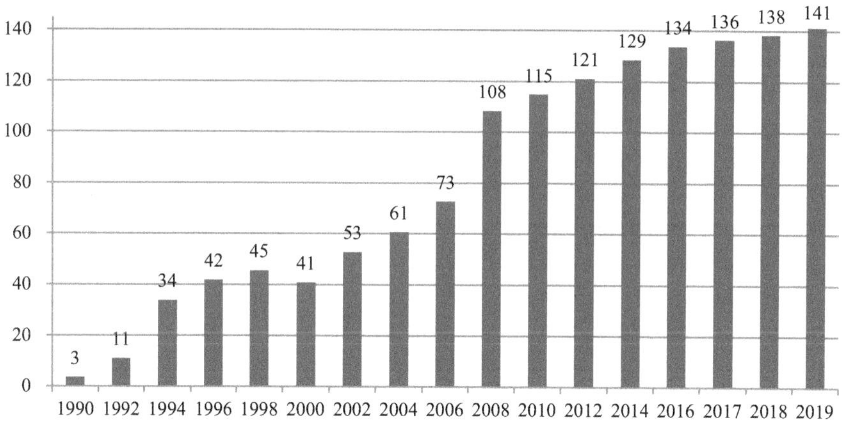

Graph 9. Inflow of foreign direct investment to the PRC in 1990–2018 (billion USD). Source: own study based on: http://unctadstat.unctad.org/wds/TableViewer/tableView.aspx (access: 20/11/2021).

69 Mikko Huotari, Dirk H. Schmidt, Sebastian Heilmann, *Economic globalization and government policy*, [in:] Sebastian Heilmann (ed.), *China's Political System …*, op. cit., pp. 222–223.
70 Changhong Pei, Wen Zheng, *China's Outbound Foreign Direct Investment Promotion System*, Berlin-Heidelberg 2015 pp. 9–18.

The inflow of FDI contributed to economic growth in China and, in the regional dimension, to an increase in the level of competitiveness of some provinces. Therefore, it is worth considering what characteristics of the target investment location determine the specific location of capital and what is the role of the authorities (including regional and local) in attracting foreign capital. The answer to the question of why the capital is located in this province and not another Chinese province is ambiguous[71]. Yingqi Wei, Xiaming Liu, David Parker, Kirit Vaidyas[72] indicate that there is a long-term relationship between the spatial distribution of FDI and the set of regional characteristics. Provinces with a higher level of international trade development, lower wage rates, more R&D workers, higher GDP growth rates, faster infrastructure improvements, faster agglomeration progress, more preferential policies and closer ethnic ties with Chinese living abroad attract comparatively more investment. On the other hand, Canfei He[73] points out that the decision to locate depends more on the costs of obtaining information and the economy of a given agglomeration than on traditional aspects related to costs, such as the level of remuneration. According to this author, FDI is located in multinational cities that are able to minimize the costs of obtaining business information. Therefore, foreign investors prefer the following locations: (a) coastal cities; (b) regional clusters in which other foreign entities already conduct business activities; (c) cities that prefer foreign investors; (d) cities that can have industrial clusters; (e) cities with better infrastructure. Omar Belkhodja, Muhammad Mohiuddin and Egide Karuranga[74] point out that the choice of a specific location is sensitive both to the conditions of the equipment in various cities, regions and economic zones in China, and to the country of origin of the FDI. This is an attempt to explain the significant inflow of FDI from Taiwan. Protection of intellectual property rights, the level of economic development of the agglomeration, investments in education, and the level of regional GDP influence the choice of the location of FDI in the Middle Kingdom.

In summary, it should be noted that the factors identified in individual studies do not coincide. Some elements repeat; others, such as the cost of access to information, is a point noted only in some studies conducted on the same specific research topic. The most frequently mentioned elements include the ex-

71 Leonard Cheng, Yum Kwan, *What are the determinants of the location of foreign direct investment? The Chinese experience,* "Journal of International Economics" 2000, vol. 51, no. 2, pp. 379–400.

72 Yingqi Wei, Xiaming Liu, David Parker, Kirit Vaidya, *The Regional Distribution of Foreign Direct Investment in China,* "Regional Studies" 1999, vol. 33, no. 9, p. 857.

73 Canfei He, *Information costs, agglomeration economies and the location of foreign direct investment in China,* "Regional Studies" 2002, vol. 36, no. 9, p. 1034.

74 Omar Belkhodja, Muhammad Mohiuddin, Egide Karuranga, *The determinants of FDI location choice in China: a discrete-choice analysis,* "Applied Economics" 2017, vol. 49, no. 13, p. 1241.

istence of various types of zone, within which it is possible to conduct business on a preferential basis (e. g., SEZ), infrastructure (e. g., equipment conditions), labor costs, and the level of regional market development. Of course, the above set is not complete. It is also worth noting that among those listed, there are elements that are influenced by the authorities at the national, regional, and local level. Central authorities do not have a direct influence on the location of FDI, but they influence them indirectly through the technical (e. g., infrastructure) and organizational conditions (e. g., access to information on economic activity, SEZ) of business operations.

The distribution of FDI among China's regions remains asymmetric, showing a clear investor interest in the eastern region, especially the fourteen industrial coastal cities and SEZ in Shenzhen, Zhuhai, Shantou, Xiamen, and Hainan. Public policy developed by the Chinese government in the late 1970s created huge differences in regional development between coastal and inland cities, even though statistics show the number of foreign enterprises in inland provinces has increased tenfold. The value of investments increased more than 20 times in the 1990s. FDI examples show that the policy itself can have very different, sometimes unintended, results in different areas[75].

There is no doubt that the inflow of FDI to regional economies is very diversified. From 1978, the main direction of location has been the eastern economic region[76], followed by the central[77] and western regions[78] (Table 29). The disproportions in the inflow of FDI are very significant; in 2019 in the eastern economic region the value was at the level of USD 7,032 billion, more than the total of the other two regions, that is, the central (USD 933 billion) and the eastern (USD 874 billion). The top five provinces that receive the most foreign investment – Guangdong (USD 1,953 billion), Jiangsu (USD 1,173 billion), Shanghai (USD 955 billion), Beijing (USD 599 billion) – are mostly coastal regions and therefore attractive to potential investors. In eastern China, FDI is typically tied to bilateral trade targeting the service industry, the level of industrialization, and the availability of strategic assets in the region[79].

75 John Foster, *Distribution of FDI across China – common policies but differing impacts by region*, "Journal of Chinese Economic and Foreign Trade Studies" 2011, vol. 4, no. 2, pp. 125–138.

76 The following provinces form the eastern economic region: Beijing, Tianjin, Hebei, Liaoning, Shanghai, Jiangsu, Zhejiang, Fujian, Shandong, Guangdong, and Hainan.

77 The Central Economic Region consists of the following provinces: Inner Mongolia, Guangxi, Chongqing, Sichuan, Guizhou, Yunnan, Tibet, Shaanxi, Gansu, Qinghai, Ningxia, Xinjiang.

78 The western economic region includes provinces such as: Shanxi, Jilin, Heilongjiang, Anhui, Jiangxi, Henan, Hubei, Hunan.

79 David W.H. Wong, Harry F. Lee, Simon X. Zhao, Qing Pei, *Region-specific determinants of the foreign direct investment in China*, "Geographical Research" 2020, vol. 58, no. 2, pp. 126–140.

Table 29. Value of investments of foreign capital companies by economic region

Economic region	2019	2018	2017	2012	2002
Value of investments of foreign capital companies (in million USD)					
Eastern	7 032 045	6 351 424	5 693 627	2 568 945	813 249
Central	933 978	786 341	672 737	314 914	86 991
Western	874 003	636 033	532 879	256 736	56 947
Value of investment per capita (in USD)					
Eastern	12 017	10 930	9 862	4,600	1 644
Central	2 138	1 804	1 550	741	2 067
Western	2 289	1 676	1,414	705	159
Percentage increase in the value of investments of foreign capital companies measured year on year					
Eastern	10.7	11.6	35.0	8.5	11.2
Central	18.8	16.9	37.1	9.6	27.8
Western	37.4	19.4	28.2	14.3	8.2

Source: own study based on: National Bureau of Statistics of China 2022, https://data.stats.gov.cn/english/easyquery.htm?cn=E0103 (access: 20/11/2022).

In the central economic region, the following provinces attract the most FDI: Hubei (USD 186 billion), Hunan (USD 184 billion) and Anhui (USD 165 billion). The main advantages of this region are the availability of the domestic market and strategic assets. The lowest value of FDI is consumed by the western provinces, that is, Tibet (USD 2 billion), Qinghai (USD 7 billion) and Guangxi (USD 9 billion). If the FDI inflow is measured by the value of investments, the disproportion between the eastern and western regions is 1:8, while using the investment value *per capita,* the same relationship is at the level of 1:5. Due to a certain variation in the number of inhabitants between individual provinces, it is somewhat complementary to refer to the value of investment per capita of a given economic region.

The above-mentioned factors partially explain the huge disproportions in the location of FDI; however, it should be noted that they are also an effect of the economic policy of the PRC. At the beginning of the transformation process, in the 1980s, the development policy of the eastern provinces was deliberately pursued, in line with the core and periphery theory and the "get rich first" slogans, as has already been mentioned. The diffusion of development toward the west is currently very slow and the activities undertaken so far, mainly public investments in infrastructure, aimed at increasing the inflow of FDI to the western provinces, are characterized by limited effectiveness.

There is no indication that it will be possible to redirect foreign capital to the central or western economic region in the near future to significantly reduce the disproportions. The western economic region has a higher year-on-year growth than the eastern or central economic regions. In 2019, the increase in investments compared to 2018 reached 37.4%, while in central China it was 18.8% and in eastern China slightly more than 10%. The continuous development of the infrastructure of western provinces under various types of support instruments (e.g., the WDS discussed above), and incentives to invest in this area, undoubtedly constitute elements influencing the attraction of foreign capital. However, there is still a long way to go for western provinces to obtain FDI at the level of eastern provinces, such as Guangdong or Jiangsu.

Foreign investors favor provinces of the Chinese coast mainly due to their convenient location and access to the markets of more developed countries[80]. Therefore, large eastern regions benefited much more from foreign investment than the inland regions[81]. It was not only the effect of these decisions of foreign investors, but also of the accompanying capital investments of the government. In 1999–2005, they reached a value of 4,696.7 billion RMB (52.94%), while in the central regions they reached 2,255.1 billion RMB (25.42%), and in the western regions only 1,920.4 billion RMB (21, 65%)[82].

Thus, the structural transformation process of the Chinese economy has triggered various phenomena, such as, for example, the aforementioned migration of people from the countryside to the cities. Authorities in different regions are aware of this problem, so they compete with each other by pursuing a policy of attracting foreign investments, which often leads to fierce competition between them. A positive symptom of this rivalry is the financing of infrastructure development, as well as the introduction of various types of tax reliefs; there are also negative actions of a corrupt nature[83].

It is worth highlighting the impact of FDI on China's regional development and its ability to develop three Chinese economic regions. Research shows that local conditions are among the many factors influencing the attraction of FDI. It is not only about activities aimed at stimulating general economic development (regionally or locally), but above all, the use of local conditions in conjunction with the potential of FDI, which requires the activity on the part of local politicians[84]. From the perspective of building local competitive foundations, the

80 K.C Fung, Hitomi Iizaka, Sarah Tong, *Foreign direct investment in China: Policy, recent trend and impact*, "Global Economic Review" 2004, vol. 33, no. 2, pp. 99–130.
81 Canfei He, *Information Costs, Agglomeration Economies and the Location of Foreign Direct Investment in China*, "Regional Studies" 2002, vol. 36, no. 9, pp. 1029–1036.
82 Yao Yang, *The political economy of government policies toward regional inequality in China*, [in:] Yukon Huang, Alessandro, Magnoli Bocchi (eds.), *Reshaping Economic Geography in East Asia*, World Bank, Washington 2009, pp. 226–227.
83 Daniel Cohen, *Prosperity słabości*, Katowice 2011, pp. 181–182.
84 David Wong, Harry Lee, Simon Zhao, Qing Pei, *Region-specific determinants of the foreign direct investment in China*, "Geographical Research" 2020, vol. 58, no. 2, pp. 126–140.

process of integrating FDI with local businesses is also extremely important. The cooperation of local companies and those with foreign capital does not always bring about positive economic effects at the local level. Examples include the experience of Suzhou City in Jiangsu Province[85] and the Qingdao Development Zone in Shantung Province. They illustrate well the factors of harmonization, FDI policy and the functioning of local entrepreneurship[86]. Importantly, Chinese companies are able to implement the most advanced technology in the world while maintaining low production costs. The sharing of technological resources and managerial skills between domestic and foreign enterprises is of key importance here. This enables R&D and technology transfer to take place through links between local and foreign companies. Local actors benefit from access to the global market through foreign capital. Two aspects are decisive in the local adaptation process: significant local industrial and institutional capacity and the relative advantage of domestic enterprises in accessing a large domestic market. These two elements remain available to a large proportion of Chinese companies.

Local authorities striving for foreign capital are interested not only in investing specific funds but also in creating new jobs and stimulating domestic entrepreneurship. Meanwhile, a big challenge for local communities is the weak rooting of FDI in local economies, which makes the outflow of capital and negligible impact on strengthening local competitiveness likely (susceptibility to economic shocks). Three issues should be noted[87]: technological, structural and institutional. The technological mismatch manifests itself in the technological gaps of local enterprises, the lack of high-class universities, or an adequate level of research and development institutions. Structural issues often concern foreign capital network investment, which not only produces but also has its own suppliers or distributors, and intellectual property protection should also be added. The promotion of FDI by local governments reduces at the same time the resources and support for local enterprises, which should be classified as an institutional problem[88]. For example, if development zones are targeted at foreign enterprises, domestic enterprises have limited access to land for investment. The role of local government policy in making decisions about the location of FDI, although still important, decreases with the growing importance of agglomer-

85 Dennis Wei, *Network Linkages and Local Embeddedness of Foreign Ventures in China: The Case of Suzhou Municipality,* "Regional Studies" 2015, vol. 49, no. 2, pp. 287–299.

86 Jun Yeup Kim, Le-Yin Zhang, *Formation of Foreign Direct Investment Clustering – A New Path to Local Economic Development? The Case of Qingdao,* "Regional Studies" 2008, vol. 42, no. 2, pp. 265–280.

87 Dennis Wei, *Network Linkages and Local Embeddedness of Foreign Ventures in China: The Case of Suzhou Municipality,* op. cit., pp. 296–298.

88 Stefan Kaiser, David A. Kirby, Ying Fan, *Foreign Direct Investment in China: An Examination of the Literature,* "Asia Pacific Business Review" 1996, vol. 2, no. 3, pp. 44–65.

ations, and the range of measures that bring about the harmonization and embedding of FDI in the local economy is quite limited.

5.4. The role of clusters in increasing the competitiveness of enterprises and the regional environment

Clusters are now considered as one of the priority tasks aimed at increasing the competitiveness of not only enterprises, but also the regional environment[89]. When considering the causes of rapid urbanization, or more broadly, the economic development of small Chinese cities and towns, starting from 1978, it is impossible to ignore the role of clusters. The question is: how is it possible that areas deprived of natural resources and significant state investments become modern international urban centers in a few decades? The development of clusters in China naturally includes not only small and medium-sized cities, but also large agglomerations and even small local communities (e.g., villages). The effects of the functioning of clusters over the last few decades leave no doubt that they constitute an instrument for building the competitiveness of regions. Thanks to this instrument, companies or regions gain a competitive advantage and accelerate their development. Such a model did not constitute the mainstream in regional development; although it is well recognized, it still belongs to relatively new development paradigms[90].

Alfred Marshall[91] was one of the first authors to highlight the importance of clusters. He studied the processes of concentration of the branches of production in space and described its main causes (favorable geographical and historical conditions, e.g., decisions and patronage of rulers, migrations of craftsmen). He devoted particular attention to the structure and effects of this concentration. He stated that clusters of companies from related sectors, especially small, specialized craft workshops, offering various products, co-create, together with institutions and the local environment, dynamic economic development. He called this phenomenon of spatial concentration of production (and also services) "industrial districts". In his analysis, Marshall emphasized economies of scale and agglomeration. He also drew attention to the possible unfavorable phe-

89 Magdalena Kogut-Jaworska, *Instrumenty pobudzania rozwoju gospodarczego na obszarach lokalnych,* [in.] Adam Szewczyk, Magdalen Kogut Jaworska, Magdalena Zioło, *Rozwój lokalny i regionalny. Teoria i praktyka,* Warszawa 2011, p. 215.

90 George Marian Isbasoiu, *Industrial Clusters and Regional Development. The Case of Timisoara and Montebelluna,* "MPRA Paper" 2006, no. 5037, pp. 11–14.

91 Alfred Marshall, *Industry and Trade, A study of Industrial Technique and Business Organization; and of Their Influences on the Condition of Various Classes and Nations,* New Delhi 2015, pp. 172–183.

nomenon of dependence of a given location on one industry. The remedy for this would be the operation of many companies from related sectors in the district, offering diversified products. Their ability to reorient themselves and the differences in the production profile would mitigate possible downturns in one industry. Among the classics of the new approach to regional development are Perroux and his concept of growth poles, motor units in which economic growth concentrates. This concept was based on the finding that growth is not uniform and manifests itself in variable intensity – in the form of points and poles.

Michael Porter[92], an American scientist from Harvard Business School, conducting research on the development of the theory of the location of economic activity, formulated and developed the theory of clusters. Today, he is considered to be the creator of the concept of a cluster. According to this author, clusters are a geographical concentration of interconnected specialized manufacturing companies, service providers, suppliers, cooperators, and business environment institutions from specific fields of activity (universities, agencies), which both compete and cooperate with each other. A cluster is an example of the presence of growth poles. The policy associated with their occurrence is a set of activities and instruments used by authorities at various levels to increase the competitiveness of the economy by stimulating the development of existing clusters or creating new ones, mainly at the regional level.

China is dominated by industrial clusters that have a positive impact on local economic growth[93]. These clusters represent a geographic concentration of interconnected companies in a specific field and related institutions. This category often includes financial services providers, educational centers, and various levels of government. These actors are linked by externalities and complementarities of various types. Usually, they are located close to each other. Economic connectivity is at the heart of industrial clusters. They appear in the form of functional and geographic connections. The first are products, services, technologies used, prices; the second is mainly location, processes that make up urbanization or mutual learning. In the context of regional policy, industrial clusters are closely connected with the regional economic system and the structure of industry. These, in turn, depend on many factors, such as the level of regional development, the industrial base, openness to the outside world, opportunities to expand the market, and even historical traditions[94]. The so-called

92 Michael Porter, *The Competitive Advantage of Nations*, London 1990; Michael Porter; *Competitive Advantage, Agglomeration Economies, and Regional Policy*, "International Regional Science Review" 1996, vol. 19, no. 2, pp. 85–90; Michael Porter, *Clusters and the New Economics of Competition*, "Harvard Business Review", 1998, no. 11, pp. 77–90.

93 Douglas Zhihua Zeng, *How Do Special Economic Zones and Industrial Clusters Drive China's Rapid Development?*, "Policy Research Working Paper" 2011, no. 5583, p. 13.

94 Zhu Yingming, *Analysis of Industrial Clusters in China*, Boca Raton 2009, pp. 3–4.

entrepreneurial clusters, those consisting mainly of nonstate funds, create a reduction of income inequalities between cities and rural areas by increasing the incomes of local rural residents.

As already mentioned, the most common clusters are industrial clusters that do not have to be innovative, and their success is due to specialization and the use of the scale effect. Individual regions and cities have specialized in the production of specific goods; they have become the centers for the production of sweaters, socks, children's clothes, toys, underwear, everyday clothes, etc. The Chinese clusters come from specialized cities, associate thousands of specialized small and medium-sized enterprises[95], as well as larger players who work together. Such cooperation naturally favors the formation of clusters in China. Cluster -based rural development was very important in the early stages of industrialization[96] and played a significant role in China's later industrial development. In recent years, local authorities have been using cluster policy more and more consciously[97].

Chinese clusters operate mainly in human resource intensive production sectors. In China, the number of clusters is still growing due to the expansion of industrialized regions and the development of cities. Most industrial clusters are concentrated in coastal provinces such as Zhejiang, Jiangsu, Guangdong, Shantung and Fujian. At the beginning of the 21st century, a quarter of the 404 administrative cities in the Guangdong Pearl River Delta formed approximately 100 clusters of specialized activities (clusters). Zhejiang Province has more than 300 clusters that could be among the world's top ten manufacturing capacity clusters, and over 100 more in the top twenty. These clusters exist in parallel with hundreds of other SEZs (as already mentioned)[98]. Some cities have become famous for having an industrial cluster in their area. Examples include electronic products in Dongguan (Guangdong Province), women's bras and underwear made in Shantou (Guangdong Province), transportation equipment in Shantung, and lighters in Wenzhou (Zhejiang Province)[99].

Clusters are important not only local in stimulating entrepreneurship. They affect the functioning of the regions, and also the entire Chinese economy. The main reason is that a large part of the production of clusters is exported. On the

95 Ruan Jianqing, Zhang Xiaobo, *Finance and cluster-based industrial development in China,* "Economic Development and Cultural Change" 2009, vol. 58, no. 1, pp. 143–164.

96 Susan H. Whiting, *Power and Wealth in Rural China: The Political Economy of Institutional Change,* New York 2006, pp. 5–13.

97 Douglas Zhihua Zeng, op. cit., p. 24.

98 Ibid, p. 25.

99 Anna Jankowiak, *Chinese industrial clusters,* [in:] Bogusława Skulska Anna Jankowiak (ed.) *Innovation Sources of Economies in Eastern Asia,* Wrocław 2012, p. 165; Zuhui Huang, Xiaobo Zhang, Yunwei Zhu, *The role of clustering in rural industrialization: A case study of the footwear industry in Wenzhou,* "China Economic Review" 2008, vol. 19, no. 3, pp. 409–420.

other hand, the impact of clusters on the growth and reduction of inequality is insignificant in highly urbanized regions, especially megacities. The positive effects of cluster movement in China are faced with problems with the freedom to choose the location to start a business, which are related to the limitations of the right to purchase both plots and agricultural land. Besides, entrepreneurial clusters are concentrated only in some regions and do not exist in others. It should also be added that industrial clusters correspond to the administrative areas of local authorities, which distinguishes them from clusters in the USA or Europe[100]. Therefore, their potential to compensate for disproportions between regions is limited.

In recent years, many coastal clusters have begun to move inland, due to rising costs (including labor costs[101]), limited space and the introduction of stringent environmental protection requirements. As a result of this transfer, several clusters were created in the central and western provinces. In some cases, the changes resulted from a deliberate policy of central authorities (e.g., WDS). But such transfers are largely based on market choice, with the government only playing a supporting role. An example is the shoe-producing cluster in Chengdu (Sichuan province), which is the result of the spread of this trend. At the end of 2005, the region had more than 1,200 footwear companies and more than 3,000 affiliated companies that produced more than 10 million pairs of leather shoes per year, accounting for more than 50% of western China's leather footwear exports[102].

The key issue from the point of view of regional policy is related to the challenge of maintaining the level of competitiveness of clusters with the increasing costs of the production factors mentioned above. Here, the central authorities play an important coordinating role, e.g., through the NDRC or other ministries[103]. Chinese clusters maintain their competitiveness mainly because they are able to increase the variety and complexity of their business activities to achieve greater productivity and efficiency. In an export-driven growth model,

---

100 Guo Di, Kun Jiang, Chenggang Xu, Xiyi Yang, *Growth, Inequality and Industrial Clusters in China*, "Journal of Economic Geography" 2020, pp. 1–31.

101 Note the differences in salaries between individual provinces, see China Briefing, *Minimum Wage Levels Across China*, February 22, 2012, https://www.china-briefing.com/news/minimum-wage-levels-across-china (access: 20/11/2021).

102 Douglas Zhihua Zeng, op. cit., p. 27.

103 An example may be the urban cluster development plan in the Beibu Bay for the provinces of Guangdong, Guangxi and Hainan of southern China, or the urban cluster development plan in the Yangtze River Delta. See Guojia fazhan gaige wei zhufang chengxiang jianshe bu guanyu yinfa beibu wan chengshi qun fazhan guihua de tongzhi (国家发展改革委 住房城乡建设部关于印发北部 湾城市群发展 规划的通知), [in:] https://zfxxgk.ndrc.gov.cn/web/iteminfo.jsp?id=414 (access: 18/11/2021); Guanyu yinfa changjiang sanjiaozhau chengshi qun fazhan guihua de tongzhi (关于印发长江 三角洲 城市 群发展规划的 通知), https://zfxxgk.ndrc.gov.cn/web/iteminfo.jsp?id=358 (access: 18/11/2021).

this skill is especially important. In addition to the well-known low cost of labor, many other elements have contributed to the success of Chinese industrial clusters so far. These include, among others[104]:

- increased efficiency and lowered entry barriers through business value chains, production specialization and division of labor,
- effective support for local authorities,
- transfer of knowledge, technology, and skills through links between companies, including state-owned enterprises and foreign companies,
- entrepreneurial spirit and social networks,
- support for innovation and technology from knowledge and public institutions and support from industry associations.

The emergence of bottom-up cluster initiatives since 1978 has been supported by the state's policy as part of China's opening to the world. Maintaining the competitiveness of industrial clusters is also related to the support of local authorities. These activities can be associated with an attempt to shape development in the local and regional dimension; therefore, they should be included in the activities of regional policy. The practice of supporting clusters by substate authorities relates to different stages of their operation. Research shows that cluster initiatives, depending on the stage of development, show different problems and thus different needs. Most often, the support does not appear at first, but at later stages of the cluster's operation. Support, as in other areas related to local development, is multifaceted, focusing mainly on building the business environment, on the one hand, and on counteracting market failure or the so-called external effects, on the other.

Local government support can be broken down into four main elements[105]: (a) infrastructure; (b) regulations and common standards; (c) support for technology, skills and innovation; (d) preferential policies and financial support. In the case of infrastructure construction, we mean not only physical facilities such as roads, bridges, electricity, telecommunications lines, but also a specialized industrial park that facilitates economic activity (e.g., warehouses, docks, logistics centers, etc.). Infrastructure equipment understood in this way helps to build economic bonds, and win suppliers, sellers and buyers; in other words, it stimulates the scale effect[106]. These are specific investments carried out with public funds; for example, the municipal government of Wenzhou (Zhejiang Province) has invested 557 million RMB in the construction of an industrial zone

104 Ibid, p. 28.
105 Douglas Zhihua Zeng, op. cit., p. 30.
106 Belton Fleisher, Dinghuan Hu, William McGuire, Xiaobo Zhang, op. cit, pp. 467–469.

known as the "Chinese capital of footwear"[107]; another example, is the production of cashmere sweaters in Puyuan (Zhejiang Province). The city authorities have invested 580,000 yuan in the construction of the park (with more than 4,300 square meters of space and more than 50 rooms). Local efforts to support infrastructure are also supported by actions implemented through the central government, such as the construction of intercity railways to develop urban clusters in Jiangsu Province[108]. The examples of accompanying central investments indicate a fairly high complementarity of support.

The activity of local governments on regulation consists in improving the services and formal conditions in which clusters operate. Governments establish specific regulations, especially those related to the type of investment, product quality, and standards, to ensure that products manufactured in clusters have a market future. For example, Guangdong Province has introduced investment quality standards in some cities to ensure efficiency, including better use of space and less pollution. Local governments increasingly place an emphasis on technological innovation and the productive modernization of industrial clusters. Taking into account the fact that companies hesitate to invest in innovations and modernization of technologies, the intervention of the authorities seems justified. The positive action of the governments is also the building of appropriate institutions, such as technological innovation centers, the development of industry associations, and the creation of research and development institutes. It is about building an innovative environment that facilitates the flow of knowledge and information between individual entities, including the acquisition of new knowledge (training, tests, certification, inviting foreign partners with specialist knowledge to cooperate).

The last element to be taken into account is the preferential activities of local governments, including financial support. The range of possibilities is very wide; in order to attract suitable enterprises to the clusters, the authorities offer, for example, access to land for production activities, tax exemptions, access to credits and loans, and even financial guarantees. In the Puyuan sweater production cluster, for example, local authorities have established an industrial park

107 Zuhui Huang, Xiaobo Zhang, Yunwei Zhu, *The Formation of Wenzhou Footwear Clusters: How were the Entry Barriers Overcome?*, Invited paper prepared for presentation at the International Association of Agricultural Economists Conference, Gold Coast, Australia, August 2006, pp. 1–13, https://www.researchgate.net/publication/23511448 (access: 18/11/2021).

108 Guojia fazhan gaige wei guanyu jiangsu sheng yanjiang chengshi qun cheng ji tielu jianshe guihua (2019–2025 nian) de pi (国家发展改革 委 关于江苏省 沿江 城市 群 城际铁路 建设 规划 [2019–2025 年] 的 批), https://zfxxgk.ndrc.gov.cn/web/iteminfo.jsp?id=16070 (access: 18/11/2021).

with public funds. In exchange for the investment of well-known brands in the cluster, land, taxes, and credit lines were granted on preferential terms.

Clusters as an instrument of regional policy in China had great potential to increase the competitiveness of individual areas. Their creation was strongly supported by both central and local governments. From a regional policy point of view, the focus on coastal provinces has contributed to their rapid development[109]. Although there is a tendency to relocate clusters to central China, this phenomenon has so far not been significant enough to equalize the development opportunities of residents of the central and western provinces. There are also several challenges related to clustering operations. Many of them were created on the basis of one product per village or one sector per city. At the initial stage of transformation, the aforementioned strategy was adequate to the situation; it allowed the mobilization of rural or urban resources based on comparative advantages (such as, for example, access to an almost unlimited workforce, low labor costs). This has led to a situation in which individual cities or villages strongly compete with each other for the location of clusters. Given the potential threat posed by the decline of the dominant industry, one solution would be to diversify local markets. Therefore, it is justified not so much to continue supporting vertical links within clusters, because these are well-formed, but to support horizontal links. Central government, aware of this threat, has undertaken certain actions, although the results so far cannot be considered fully satisfactory.

5.5. The Belt and Road Initiative as an element of regional development policy

The Belt and Road Initiative (BRI) is undoubtedly an example of public intervention, in which infrastructure plays an important role[110] as a factor of regional development. The concept refers to the historic trade route that connected the PRC with the Middle East and Europe. The route was used by merchants from the third century BC to the 17th century AD; it led through steppes, deserts, and mountains. It was used to transport not only silk but also various iron, paper, gold, and jewelery products. Approximately 12 thousand. km, the road lost its

109 Chi-Han Ai, Hung-Che Wu, Tian-Hang Huang, Rui Wang, *How does knowledge flow in industrial clusters? The comparison between both naturally and intentionally formed industrial clusters in China*, "Asian Journal of Technology Innovation" 2020, published online on November 2, 2020, pp. 2–24.

110 Kalim Siddiqui, *One Belt and One Road, China's Massive Infrastructure Project to Boost Trade and Economy: An Overview*, "International Critical Thought" 2019, vol. 9, no. 2, pp. 214–235.

importance in the middle of the 17th century, after the discovery of the sea route to China[111]. Hence, in western literature, BRI is referred to as the New Silk Road; it is also a reference to the times when China was at the center of events in the world and played a major role in the world economy. Therefore, it is impossible to see the initiative as anything other than a way to stimulate socioeconomic development and ensure the PRC holds a dominant position not only in international trade, but also in the world economy, and thus poses a challenge to the dominant position of the USA.

The vagueness of the assumptions of the Initiative, as well as the extraordinary momentum envisaged of the idea of an alternative connection between China and Europe and the Middle East through a network of transport corridors (land and sea) have not escaped the attention of leaders of various countries and Chinese foreign policy analysts. Many analyses devoted to the Belt and Road Initiative concern its geopolitical importance[112], impact on the regional order[113], consequences for individual countries[114] and international organizations[115], as well as geoeconomics[116]. However, this project is also of great importance in the context of China's internal policies. It is not different with regard to the development of individual Chinese provinces and local structures, whose leaders also

111 Xinru Liu, *The Silk Road in World History*, Oxford 2010, pp. 5–41; Valerie Hansen, *The Silk Road: A New History*, Oxford 2015, pp. 25–53.

112 Lai-Ha Chan, *Can China's Belt and Road Initiative Bulid a Peacful Regional Order? Acquiescence Resistance in South Asia*, [in:] Michael Clarke, Matthew Sussex, Nick Bisley (ed.), *The Belt and Road Initiative and the Future of Regional Order in the Indo-Pacific*, Lanham-Boulder-New York-London 2020, pp. 2–20; Zhiqin Shi, Vasilis Trigkas, *Reconstructing Geography, Power and Politics in the Belt and Road Initiative*, [in:] Alister Miskimmon, Ben O'Loughlin, Jinghan Zeng (eds.), *One Belt, One Road, One Story?: Towards an EU-China Strategic Narrative*, Cham 2021, pp. 67–92.

113 Li Xing, *China's Pursuit of the "One Belt One Road" Initiative: A new World Order with Chinese Characteristics?*, [in:] Li Xing (ed.), *Mapping China's 'One Belt One Road' Initiative*, Cham 2018, pp. 1–28; Ikboljon Qoraboyev, *One Belt, One Road: A Comparative Regionalism Approach*, Yu Cheng, Lilei Song, Lihe Huang, *The Belt & Road Initiative in the Global Arena: Chinese and European Perspectives*, Singapore, 2017, pp. 103–116; Michał Lubina, *From Geopolitical Chance to Security Threat: Polish Public Political Discourse on the One Belt One Road Initiative*, "Polish Political Science Yearbook" 2017, vol. 46, no. 1, pp. 221–238.

114 Ahmed Rashid Malik, *The China-Pakistan Economic Corridor (CPEC): A Game Changer for Pakistan's Economy*, [in:] B.R. Deepak (ed.*), China's Global Rebalancing and the New Silk Road*, Singapore 2018, pp. 69–83.

115 Alister Miskimmon, Ben O'Loughlin, *The EU's Struggle for Strategic Narrative on China*, [in:] Alister Miskimmon, Ben O'Loughlin, Jinghan Zeng (eds.), *One Belt, One Road, One Story?: Towards an EU-China Strategic Narrative*, Cham 2021, pp. 19–44; Zdzisław W. Puślecki, *Światowa Organizacja Handlu i Unia Europejska wobec nowych wyzwań we współczesnym biznesie międzynarodowym*, Warsaw 2021, pp. 196–210.

116 Sijbren de Jong, Willem Th. Oosterveld, Michel Roelen, Katharine Klacansky, Agne Silekaite, Rianne Siebenga, *A road to riches or a road to ruin?: The geo-economic implications of China's new silk road*, Hague 2017, pp. 21–24; Bogdan Góralczyk, op. cit., pp. 378–385.

see it as an opportunity to boost the development of their area. Therefore, it is reasonable to perceive the BRI also as an instrument of regional development policy. Competition concerning participation in the BRI between individual territorial structures says much about how regional policy is shaped, and how traditional hierarchy and centralization is undergoing a certain transformation. A better understanding of the implementation of the new Silk Road project may result in a more accurate assessment of the potential effects of the plan on the international environment, including the countries of the European Union.

The assumption is that the BRI is to be an open and inclusive way to achieve sustainable international development, and political and cultural cooperation on the basis of the peaceful co-existence of independent states. It is an important component of China's "go-out" strategy that has been pursued for over two decades. According to Chinese planners, it is possible through various types of connections, covered by multilateral financial instruments[117]. Among the goals of the initiative is the development of China's global production and trade networks through the development of intercity and logistics infrastructure. The initiative was launched by Xi Jinping in 2013, and its initial geographic scope was based on the Indian Ocean Sea Trail and was later greatly expanded[118]. The BRI nomenclature refers to the land corridors that will connect western China with Europe through Central and South Asia (the Silk Road Economic Belt) and the sea routes that will connect China's southern provinces with Southeast Asia and beyond (the 21st century Silk Route). An important component of the initiative is also the Polar Silk Road[119]. The initiative aims to connect China with the world by sea and land, by developing infrastructure and increasing the capacity for international trade and economic cooperation between countries along the Belt and Road[120]. In order to encourage the participation of other countries in the initiative, it is assumed that the cooperation will be harmonious. This includes the idea of cooperation based on so-called mutual benefits and a vision of action based on

117 Michael Dunford, Weidong Liu, *Chinese perspectives on the Belt and Road Initiative,* "Cambridge Journal. Regions, Economy and Society" 2019, vol. 12, no. 1, pp. 145–167.

118 Shashi Tharoor, *China's Silk Road Revival and the Fears it Stirs are Deeply Rooted in the Country's History,* "New Perspectives Quarterly" 2015, vol. 32, no. 1, p. 19.

119 It is about the interest of the PRC in the management of the Arctic. Attention is drawn here, inter alia, to the need to coordinate individual strategies, national policies, the creation of a network of infrastructure connections and trade development. In the context of intraregional competitiveness, the Chinese authorities are responsible for the need to involve domestic enterprises in the development of infrastructure allowing for the commercial implementation of maritime projects. See Łukasz Gacek, *Współpraca czy rywalizacja: Rosja i Chiny w Arktyce,* "Krakowskie Studia Międzynarodowe" 2018, no. 1 (XV), pp. 151–152.

120 Jihong Chen, Yijie Fei, Paul Tae-Woo Lee, Xuezong Tao, *Overseas Port Investment Policy for China's Central and Local Governments in the Belt and Road Initiative,* "Journal of Contemporary China" 2019, vol. 28, no. 116, pp. 196–21.

common interests and responsibility. The aforementioned vision assumes the implementation of five cooperation priorities (Table 30).

Table 30. Priorities for cooperation under the BRI

Coordination policy:	
– Intergovernmental coordination – Multi-level cooperation agreements – Promoting mutual trust – Building consensus – Strategies and policies for economic development – Joint plans and measures for regional cooperation	
Infrastructure connection:	Undisturbed Trade:
– Construction of infrastructure – Transport regulations – Port cooperation – Sea logistics – Civil aviation – Pipeline safety	– Law enforcement – Standards – Statistics – Supply chain management – Trade liberalization and facilitation – Investment facilitation – Tax – Agriculture – Forestry – Animal breeding – Fisheries and aquaculture – Ocean Sciences – Environmental Protection – Tourism – Mining industries – Generation of energy – Emerging industries
Financial integration:	Exchange of people:
– Currency stabilization, – SWAP and billing – Establishment of a financing institution for the Asian Infrastructure Investment Bank (AIIB), SRF, BRICS New Development Bank (NDB) and the Shanghai Cooperation Organization (SCO) – Strengthen the Interbank Association China – ASEAN and the SCO Interbank Association – Bank loans and credits – RMB bonds – Financial regulation, risk and crisis management	– Cultural exchange – Academic exchange – Staff exchange and cooperation – Media – Exchange and volunteering of young people and women – Tourism – Sport – Disease prevention, treatment and management of epidemic crises – Science and technology – Employment and skills – Entrepreneurship – Social security

- Sovereign wealth funds and commercial equity funds	- Public administration - Political parties and parliaments - City partnership - Non-governmental organizations dealing with education, health care, combating poverty, environmental protection

Source: own study based on: National Development and Reform Commission, Ministry of Foreign Affairs, Ministry of Commerce of the People's Republic of China, *Vision and Actions on Jointly Building Silk Road Economic Belt and 21st-Century Maritime Silk Road,* March 28, 2015, http://cb.mofcom.gov.cn/article/ydyl/201504/20150400930895.shtml (access: 18/11/2021).

From a public investment perspective, infrastructure priority is important. China is proposing to improve the low-carbon environmental and road, rail, air, river, sea, energy, information, and telecommunications infrastructure. Infrastructure development includes not only physical networks, but also the adaptation of technical and institutional standards and management operations. In terms of transport infrastructure, it is about key communication links, removing the so-called transport bottlenecks, modernizing infrastructure, increasing its safety, modernizing traffic management, coordination of transport management, and development of multimodal transport. The initiative relates mainly to international cooperation, but it is impossible to ignore matters related to infrastructure located in individual provinces, which will undoubtedly affect their competitiveness. The government's proactive policy is to increase comparative advantages through targeted investments in hard and, to a lesser extent, soft infrastructure. The implementation of this goal requires the activity of governments of various levels and needs the provision of financing from various sources. Numerous Chinese development banks, as well as other institutional lenders have pledged to support the initiative by undertaking or financing major infrastructure projects[121]. As a result of China's external shift and its impact on global capital, a staggering number of spatial planning patterns have been implemented, including economic corridors, special economic zones, and a vast network of east coast ports[122].

The economic corridors and maritime nodes under the BRI are expected to connect China with developing and developed economies in a way that positions China as a world economic center. The initiative aims to open up new markets

121 Henry Chan, Hing Lee, *The One Belt One Road Initiative – Who's Going to Pay for it?,* [in:] Tai Wei Lim, Wen Xin Lim, Henry Hing Lee Chan, Katherine Hui-yi Tseng (eds.), *China's One Belt One Road Initiative,* London 2016, pp. 169–192.

122 Seth Schindler, J. Miguel Kanai, *Getting the territory right: infrastructure-led development and the re-emergence of spatial planning strategies,* "Regional Studies" 2019, vol. 55, no. 1, p. 47.

and generate demand for Chinese goods with higher added value. China is building industries that are competitive around the world. Unlike Japan's economy in the 1980s, China's economic strength is not due to its technological leadership or regionalized consumer product production networks, but to its comparative advantage through infrastructure and construction development. Dams, highways, electricity generation, and high-speed rail are important attributes of today's China. By highlighting the complementarity of Chinese export *know-how* and the infrastructure needs of developing countries, the BRI offers the Chinese the opportunity to use their huge foreign exchange reserves (China had USD 1.2 trillion in bonds in August 2017)[123].

Many projects are underway, in part because of the fact that Chinese state-owned enterprises proved resilient to the economic crisis in uncertain times. It should be noted that for the purposes of domestic policy, the establishment of an initiative is associated with the need to revitalize Chinese regions and satisfy their economic interests. It is pointed out that the desire to expand infrastructure programs with the help of BRI results from the experience of the long-term financial crisis in 2007–2008. Chinese provinces emerged unscathed from the economic downturn thanks to a USD 586 billion stimulus package that came from local government loans for infrastructure projects. At the beginning of 2010, the funds were spent at the expense of the enormous debt of local governments. At that time, overcapacity exceeded 30% in the iron, steel, glass, cement, aluminum, and energy industries. Many companies located in the east of the country faced a severe profitability crisis, and the return on domestic infrastructure was negative. At the same time, Chinese banks faced a crisis of overaccumulation, with three billion dollars in foreign exchange reserves and diminishing domestic credit prospects. Against this background, the initiative provided an opportunity to use up domestic overcapacity[124].

One of the arguments in favor of the BRI from the perspective of regional policy was the conviction about the need to consolidate the western and south-western provinces. These provinces, thanks to extensive investments in so-called hard infrastructure, were to become the new engines of economic growth, thus stimulating the next phase of Chinese development. The projects of the Belt and Road Initiative would complement the WDS, which produced modest results despite significant fiscal injections, targeted investments, and preferential policy from central government. Competition among provinces to be included in the BRI program was fierce, with regional politicians lobbying to influence the

123 Baogang He, *The Domestic Politics of the Belt and Road Initiative and its Implications*, "Journal of Contemporary China" 2019, vol. 28, no. 116, p. 180.

124 Lee Jones, Jinghan Zeng, *Understanding China's 'Belt and Road Initiative': beyond 'grand strategy' to a state transformation analysis*, "Third World Quarterly" 2019, vol. 40, no. 8, p. 1422.

central government's decision, including the NDRC. Thus, at one of the first national BRI symposiums in December 2013, only 14 provinces were invited[125]. Regions that were not invited to the initiative quickly launched lobbying activities through forums such as the NPC, academia, and the media. The latter, together with scientists, showed historical connections of particular provinces with the location of the ancient Silk Route. The provinces of Shantung and Henan expressed their willingness to actively participate in the construction of the economic belt of the Silk Road, as well as the Sea Silk Road. The first of the provinces mentioned above expressed interest in accelerating the construction of the Jinjiang Yellow River Industry Transfer Demonstration Zone and an active connection with the economic belt of the Silk Road. In turn, the Hubei province authorities were in favor of using the strategic opportunity to build the economic belt of the Silk Road and the Sea Silk Road. The Shaanxi and Henan provinces had intense public discussions about which of them gave rise to the historic Silk Road in their area. Competition in the case of the Sea Silk Road was even tougher. Claims were made by eastern provinces such as Fujian, Jiangsu, Guangdong, and Guangxi. Provinces that did not have strong arguments pointed to the traditional, original geographic location of goods such as porcelain or tea. For example, the provinces of Shantung and Hebei indicated that the cities of Qingdao and Huanghua were the northern starting point of the Silk Route[126]. As a result of the actions taken, the list of provinces covered by the Belt and Road Initiative in the joint communiqué of the NDRC, the Ministry of Foreign Affairs and the Ministry of Trade on March 28, 2015, increased significantly from 14 to 27. This happened despite the fact that some provinces were mentioned indirectly, i.e., for individual cities where the activities were planned to be located.

Table 31. Provinces included in the BRI in 2013 and 2015

Macroregion	Provinces	
	2013 symposium	**2015 communiqué**
Northeast	-	Heilongjiang, Jilin, Liaoning, Inner Mongolia
Northwest	Shaanxi, Gansu, Qinghai, Ningxia, Xinjiang	Shaanxi, Gansu, Qinghai, Sinciang, Ningxia
Southwest	Sichuan, Yunnan, Guangxi	Guangxi, Tibet, Yunnan, Sichuan (listed at city level)

125 *Sheng zheng qiang sichou zhi lu he haishang sichou zhi lu jianshe jiyu* (省争抢丝绸之路 和海上 丝绸之路 建设机遇), https://business.sohu.com/20140214/n394972816.shtml (access:18/11/2021).

126 *Haishang sichou zhi lu bei qidian zai qihang qingdao zheng qiangzhan xian ji* (海上丝绸之路 北 起点"再 起航 青岛正 抢占先机), http://m.dzwww.com/d/news/12081232.html (access: 18/11/2021).

Table 31 *(Continued)*

Macroregion	**Provinces**	
	2013 symposium	**2015 communiqué**
Eastern	Jiangsu, Zhejiang, Guangdong, Fujian, Hainan	Beijing, Fujian, Guangdong, Hainan, Shanghai, Tianjinin, Zhejiang, Shantung (listed at city level)
Central	Chongqing	Chongqing, the following provinces listed at city level: Hunan, Hubei, Henan, Anhui, Jiangxi

Source: own study based on: National Development and Reform Commission, Ministry of Foreign Affairs, and Ministry of Commerce of the People's Republic of China, *Vision and Actions on Jointly Building Silk Road Economic Belt and 21st-Century Maritime Silk Road*, March 28, 2015, op. cit.; Sheng zheng qiang sichou zhi lu he haishang sichou zhi lu jianshe jiyu, op. cit.

One of the most characteristic changes between 2013 and 2015 was the removal of the Jiangsu Province initiative from the project. It was quite a surprise, since it enjoyed the support of Xi. It was previously perceived as a place connecting the land and sea parts of the initiative. Jiangsu provincial officials criticized its removal from the program, mentioned support of Xi, called for its re-inclusion, and when this did not work, published their own plan to implement the initiative in their area in January 2015. Thus, they ignored the fact that the province was omitted by the central authorities. The practice of implementing the New Silk Road shows that almost every province has its own plan for implementing the initiative, including those that have been excluded from it. At the same time, the central government policy is not exclusive. Being removed from the list of provinces covered by the initiative does not mean, according to government officials, that the province cannot use it. Officials emphasized that despite the removal of Jiangsu province from the list, it was still the main area of the Economic Belt of the Silk Road. As a result, all provinces are asked to prepare regional plans for the New Silk Road[127].

The many uncertainties about the geographical scope of the New Silk Road, which was presented in the announcement of 2015, indicate that it is a very general project. An example may be investments that either already started many years ago or new plans that have not been clearly defined so far. Lee Jones, Jinghan Zeng[128] believe that the initiative is a wish list of leading provincial leaders who, having a specific investment plan for their unit, may want to include

127 Yidai yilu bu cunzai quexi shengfen: Jiangsu shi jiaohui dian, difang fangan 10 yue qian chu zi mao qu lian xian pengpai xin (一带一路不存在 缺席省份：江苏是交汇点，地方方案 10 月贸区连线澎湃新), https://www.thepaper.cn/newsDetail_forward_1319660 (access: 20/04/2022).

128 Lee Jones, Jinghan Zeng, op. cit., p. 1423.

it in the new Silk Road package. The communication reflects the different interests and negotiation processes between the central and provincial authorities. The last of the authors mentioned above, using the example of Jiangsu Province, indicates that the regional authorities have the ability to formulate favorable narratives in order to influence the shape of the guidelines for the Belt and Road Initiative formulated by the central government and thus their own goals. This has resulted in a variety of competing, ambiguous, and conflicting political narratives about the BRI in China[129].

After an initial oversight, the richer eastern provinces lobbied to participate in the initiative, which was ultimately a success[130]. Eastern provinces benefited mainly from the maritime part of the initiative when their ports were granted the status of participating in the project. At the provincial level, there is a kind of game of being played with the initiative. As with ministerial priorities, each province has different needs and goals, and long- or underfunded local projects with questionable links to improving commercial connectivity are often included in the initiative. There is no doubt that the use of local policy frameworks and practices can contribute to its successful implementation, although it differs significantly from the originally planned shape[131].

The significant financial resources allocated to the implementation of the BRI arouse competition between provincial governments that would like to receive as many of them as possible. Individual administrative units try to justify the implementation of the Silk Road projects or attract larger investments to their areas. As a result, the initiative is constantly expanding territorially. Competition between Yunnan and Guangxi provinces, which want to act as China's gateway to Southeast Asia[132], is particularly visible. Provincial governments are aware of additional funding opportunities through participation in BRI, as is the case with the WDS. As part of the WDS, Yunnan Province obtained USD 79.4 billion of investments and aid activities from the central government until 2015[133]. This has prompted the governments of the provinces of Yunnan and Guangxi to try to become a gateway to the countries of Southeast Asia.

The main premise for the participation of Yunnan Province in the BRI was its geographical location, that is, the site on the international transport corridor

129 Jinghan Zeng, *Narrating China's belt and road initiative,* "Global Policy", 2019, vol. 10, pp. 207–216.

130 National Development and Reform Commission, Ministry of Foreign Affairs, and Ministry of Commerce of the People's Republic of China, *Vision and Actions on Jointly Building Silk Road Economic Belt and 21st-Century Maritime Silk Road,* March 28, 2015, op. cit.

131 Baogang He, *The Domestic Politics of the Belt…* op. cit., p. 186.

132 Mingjiang Li, *China's Economic Power in Asia: The Belt and Road Initiative and the Local Guangxi Government's Role,* "Asian Perspective" 2019, vol. 43, no. 2, pp. 274–289.

133 Lee Jones, Jinghan Zeng, op. cit., p. 1421.

route connecting China with neighboring Southeast Asian countries, including regional initiatives such as the Greater Mekong Subregion economic cooperation forum (GMS), those undertaken in Indochina, and also cooperation on the Bangladesh-China-India-Myanmar (BCIM) line. Yunnan Province mainly refers to economic and development issues, and to a lesser extent geopolitical ones, such as those in Guangxi Province, as justification for inclusion in the BRI. The provincial governments that aligned with the country's policy of opening up to the outside, including Yunnan's move toward Southeast Asia, led largely to the implementation of their own development goals, visible in previously undertaken initiatives[134]. Examples include the transformation of Yunnan into a moderately prosperous province, green energy development, and the 2012 Yangtze River Economic Belt (YREB) initiative to promote economic integration and environmental development in 11 provinces stretching inland from Shanghai to Yunnan Province.

Including the province in the BRI creates new development opportunities for a peripheral region. In this way, the Yunnan government, while complying with the national goals, have the opportunity to implement their own goals. In the context of regional policy, the BRI creates a new space for bottom-up and top-down interactions between regional governments and central government. Tim Summers[135] notices the influence of the narrative created by Yunnan Province on the final shape of the 2015 communication, that is, the shape of the initiative. The language included was exactly what the discussions of the Yunnan government's provincial policy aimed to achieve. The Center's position on Yunnan's role in the BRI seems to have been shaped by provincial narratives and thus reflects the example of a grassroots provincial agency shaping policy declarations at the national level. This happened alongside the perception of Yunnan province as a region whose interests and actions were not fully consistent with the interests and actions taken at the national level. Examples include paving the way for pipelines through Myanmar, resisting the Kokand conflict in 2009, and Beijing's broader foreign policy goals regarding Myanmar[136]. There is no doubt that the provinces have the possibility of influencing and interpreting central government policy, but they do not have such autonomy as to disregard the policy formulated in Beijing. Lee Jones and Jinghan Zeng believe that the final shape of the BRI, in the context of domestic politics, will be determined by the multi-level struggle for

134 Tim Summers, *Yunnan-A Chinese Bridgehead to Asia: A Case Study of China's Political and Economic Relations with its Neighbors,* Oxford-Cambridge-New Delhi 2012, pp. 83–103.

135 Tim Summers, *The belt and road initiative in Southwest China: responses from Yunnan province,* "The Pacific Review" 2021, vol. 34, no. 2, pp. 206–229.

136 Shahar Hameiri, Lee Jones, Yizheng Zou, *The Development-Insecurity Nexus in China's Near-Abroad: Rethinking Cross-Border Economic Integration in an Era of State Transformation,* "Journal of Contemporary Asia" 2019, vol. 49, issue 3, pp. 473–499.

power and resources between key actors. These include central, regional and local governments, as well as state-owned companies and banks interested in further internationalization of the activities of the Chinese state[137].

Another issue related to the implementation of BRI for the purposes of internal policies, such as regional policy, is the general nature of the concept, which is subject to interpretation. Most of the time, the provincial governments make some clarification. On the one hand, we are dealing with the actions of the central government, which tries to accelerate investments. On the other hand, the general nature of the guidelines means that various types of investment projects can be considered as resulting from the initiative. For example, in 2014, that is, before the 2015 guidelines were issued, the State Council paid USD 94 billion for the initiative. So, there are situations where provinces skillfully try to use BRI for their own purposes. The provinces of Guangxi and Yunnan have acted in this way, trying to take advantage of Xi's favor. Another example is Xinjiang Province[138], where the authorities proposed that the city of Khorgos[139], located on the border with Kazakhstan, be included in the BRI list to implement a project to build a transportation hub (now known as the largest dry port in Central Asia) as part of the Eurasia land bridge. It was not a new proposal, as it had already been proposed in 2005. The same happened with the transcontinental railway linking Xinjiang with Europe, which was entered on the initiative's project list, despite the fact that it was launched in 2012. It is also evident that some infrastructure projects associated with BRI are unjustified from an economic point of view, but due to lobbying activities, mainly by regional and local governments, are implemented (such as the modernization of the second port on the Malay Peninsula)[140].

In the early stage of the implementation of the BRI, public capital, mainly central, regional and local, was responsible for financing a significant part of initiatives motivated by economic reasons. This is confirmed by the database of activities reported for the years 2014–2016[141] developed for the needs of the BRI. Of the 647 reported projects, 305 came from the public sector (i.e., state-owned entities at the central level, state-owned enterprises, ministries and national banks), 364 were contributed by lower-level public entities (subnational, local,

137 Lee Jones, Jinghan Zeng, op. cit., p. 1421.

138 Another issue is the fact that the projects implemented in this region have a strategic impact from the point of view of the authorities in Beijing, and are also considered instrumentally in terms of the challenges to the country's internal security.

139 Henry Ruehl, *The Khorgos Hype on the Belt and Road*, The Diplomat, September 2019, https://thediplomat.com/2019/09/the-khorgos-hype-on-the-belt-and-road/ (access:20/04/2022).

140 Lee Jones, Jinghan Zeng, op. cit., p. 1426.

141 Min Ye, *Fragmentation and Mobilization: Domestic Politics of the Belt and Road in China*, "Journal of Contemporary China", 2019, vol. 28, issue 119, p. 707.

state-owned enterprises, local state-owned banks), and only 78 were submitted by private parties (companies, media associations). The most notable were industry-related activities, including 137 national SOE projects and 108 local SOE projects. The characteristics of complex projects suggest that the main driving force behind RDI projects and programs was the utilization of surplus production in Chinese provinces. The remedy to these problems is the foreign expansion of Chinese enterprises supported by the BRI.

As mentioned above, financing is also applied to infrastructure projects carried out in this area (e.g., the Rails-Highways-Infrastructure project), which were suspended due to the economic downturn and the tightening of lending policy in 2010–2014. These investments were resumed thanks to new BRI funding arrangements; all of the infrastructure projects were closely linked to local authorities, state-owned enterprises and banks[142]. The implementation of national projects as part of the BRI has allowed local governments to replenish the economic situation of loss-making state-owned enterprises. For example, in Jiangxi Province, the local government has established four funds to support companies in the chemical industry. The city of Yulin has committed funds to rescue the unprofitable coal industry as part of the BRI, and in Gangsu Province, the state-owned, loss-making steel producer has received new loans "for globalization" and the purchase of raw materials. Thus, it can be noted that, in the area of infrastructure and financing, the BRI has played an active role in saving some of the declining branches of the local economy[143]. This does not mean that all projects are unjustified from an economic point of view; some of the projects are very beneficial and may revive not only the demand for locally produced goods, but also economic growth in the local and regional system. It should be remembered that internal investments under the BRI are financed not only by the China Development Bank, the Silk Road Fund, foreign funds, but also local Chinese banks and, indirectly, local authorities. The latter, together with the central government, act as loan guarantors or provide their own contribution[144]. This means that in the long run, unsuccessful internal BRI investments may result in an increase in the indebtedness of local authorities and financial institutions.

At this stage, it is difficult to judge the success or failure of the BRI, but it can be seen that the policies of individual provinces can affect centrally planned government programs. This is also possible due to the way the initiative is managed, and divided between various party and state institutions, including the Ministry of Finance, NDRC, Ministry of Trade, and Ministry of Foreign Affairs.

142 Ibid, p. 708.
143 Ibid, p. 709.
144 Ibid.

Each institution is responsible for a separate aspect of the BRI, although all are overseen by a Small Leading Group headed by a chairman with the rank of deputy prime minister. However, it is a relatively weak institution and is not able to efficiently coordinate various government institutions that compete for influence on the shape of the initiative[145].

Governance of the Belt and Road Initiative is also determined by the tensions that occur in the shaping of public policies in China[146]. One dilemma is that between the size of the BRI and the authorities' limited ability to exercise power through control and mobilization, the latter inevitably places an enormous burden on the Chinese bureaucracy. This dilemma points to duality in the operationalization of the BRI, which is at the same time hierarchical and pluralistic with local flexibility. This approach is considered necessary for a functional Chinese bureaucracy, but that does not make it less paradoxical. BRI projects have proved amenable to changes in implementation at the provincial level. Various tensions indicate a fundamental challenge that results from managing such a vast project, or rather loosely related concepts. Moreover, in China's political institutions, it is difficult to identify specific mechanisms to correct potential mistakes made by top leaders[147]. With emerging investments that do not have an economic justification, this can be a great challenge for the PRC.

The evaluation of the BRI from the perspective of building competitiveness or balancing the development of individual regions, at the initial stage of implementation, is very limited. The goals do not mainly concern internal policies, but China's external expansion, and hence a full adjustment to the development challenges of individual regions cannot be expected. However, when implementing such a broad-based investment plan, it seems justified to also set national priorities. Instead, we are dealing with selectively entering regions or individual cities on the list of areas covered by the initiative. This is far from a professional, intentional shaping of regional policy. Residual data on the investments implemented so far indicate that in some cases, especially in peripheral areas, e.g., western provinces, investments will certainly contribute to increasing competitiveness. However, the key decisions will be how to use the infrastructure created in this way, which itself does not necessarily create a development impulse. The emerging discussions regarding the economic viability of individual investments indicate that the question of effectiveness in building internal competitive advantage remains open.

145 Lee Jones, Jinghan Zeng, op. cit., pp. 1427.
146 Elizabeth Economy, *The Third Revolution: Xi Jinping and the New Chinese State*, New York 2018, pp. 20–54.
147 Baogang He, op. cit., p. 194.

Chapter 6. Reflection and adaptation of the regional development policy in China

Regional policy influences phenomena and processes that are of a variable nature. It affects how the needs of citizens are satisfied and how the socio-economic challenges of the PRC are overcome. One of the key aspects of this is the adaptation of solutions applied to emerging challenges and political needs. The main issues of this chapter relate to the reflectivity and adaptability of the regional policy of the PRC. For the purposes of this book, reflection is the application of judgment in creating this public activity and learning is the capability to draw conclusions. This is accompanied by the assumption that the ability to learn is the basis for development, including the development of regional policy[1]. Learning is also a way to temper the increasing complexity of the environment surrounding regional policy. As a result, both learning and reflection at the subnational level can be a mechanism that increases the attractiveness of the region. A limited understanding of how public policies are shaped and how they interact make it difficult to identify good solutions, i.e., practices that can improve the effectiveness of public action.

6.1. Experimentation in the process of optimizing the implementation of regional policy

Optimizing the implementation of public policies in the PRC has been accompanied by many activities related not only to the specific way the country's political system functions, but also to its cultural characteristics. This begins with the central mechanisms of political communication (mainly communications

1 Karol Olejniczak, Jakub Rok, Adam Płoszaj, *Organizacyjne uczenie się i zarządzanie wiedzą – przegląd koncepcji*, [in:] Karol Olejniczak (ed.), *Organizacje uczące się. Model dla administracji publicznej*, Warszawa 2012, pp. 61–107; Karol Olejniczak, Jakub Rok, *Feedback in Public Agencies: A Missing Engine of Organizational Learning?*, [in:] Perrin Burt, Tyrrell Tony (eds.), *Changing Bureaucracies: Adapting to Uncertainty, and How Evaluation Can Help*, London-New York 2020, pp. 17–39.

with a strictly doctrinal overtone, traditions of collective management), involves setting and adjusting political priorities (multiannual planning, setting goals by an appropriately managed personnel system) and leads to the introduction of new activities and policies (most often based on experiments undertaken at a local level). All of these elements are based on the organizational experience of the CPC from 1920 onward. They relate to how public policies were implemented and enforced, and remain rooted in the absence of the principle of checks and balances[2], and the belief that power should be concentrated in the hands of one legitimate entity. The aforementioned uniformity of state power[3] is reflected in two dimensions, that is, constitutional power (the CPC's leading role as enshrined in the Basic Law) and actual power (the CPC's political domination, and its implementation of public policies).

Explaining the implementation of regional policy through the prism of the centralized political system of the PRC is insufficient. From an international comparative perspective, it is intriguing to see how authoritarian institutions[4] and instruments for shaping public policies were adapted after China opened up to the world in the late 1970s. It has been known for a long time that the high level of centralization involved in shaping public policies is burdened with unexpected economic and social consequences. It increases the possible costs of political and economic failure in situations where the attempted solutions are ineffective, and may cause social unrest towards the central government. This is important, as Xi Jinping's rule has contributed to an increase in centralizing tendencies in the shaping of public policies in the PRC[5]. The concentration of power in recent years, especially within the current leadership of the CPC, has been clearly noticeable, affecting both in economic policies and in regional development activities.

One of the instruments ensuring the necessary flexibility, responsiveness and reduction of uncertainty in shaping public policies in China is experimentation.

---

2 It is referred to as the principle of mutual braking and interaction or brakes and balance, and sometimes as the principle of control and balance. This principle applies to the conscious separation (deconcentration) of power between mutually controlling organs. See Andrzej Antoszewski, Ryszard Herbut (eds.), *Leksykon politologii*, Wrocław 2003, p. 321; Andrew Heywood, *Politologia*, Warszawa 2009, p. 203; Rafał Lis, *Zasada hamulców i równowagi a ideały rządów bezpośrednich. Wokół wartości amerykańskiego konstytucjonalizmu*, "Przegląd Sejmowy" 2017, vol. 142, no. 5, pp. 59–72.

3 Andrzej Antoszewski, Ryszard Herbut (eds.), op. cit., p. 150.

4 Xu Chenggang, *The Fundamental Institutions of China's Reforms and Development*, "Journal of Economic Literature" 2011, vol. 49, no. 4, pp. 1076–1151.

5 China File, *What does Xi Jinping's top-down leadership mean for innovation in China?*, September 26, 2016, http://www.chinafile.com/conversation/what-does-xi-jinpings-top-down-leadership-mean-innovation-china (access: 20/11/2021); Shiyu Bo, *Centralization and regional development: Evidence from a political hierarchy reform to create cities in China*, "Journal of Urban Economics" 2020, vol. 115.

It involves trying new ways to solve public problems at the local level and then transferring those that prove effective to the national level. Sebastian Heilmann describes this process as "experimentation under hierarchy", i.e., the adaptation of Chinese public policy through experimentation understood as an unstable but productive combination of decentralized testing of policy instruments with ad hoc central interference resulting in the selective integration of local experiences in public policymaking[6]. Currently, experimentation can be seen in two dimensions: narrower and wider. In the first case, this involves testing the policy, i.e., specific instruments and solutions in order to verify their feasibility and identify the detailed principles of their implementation. The second deals with both testing and the generation of policy to identify new policy options and possible new institutional arrangements. Regardless of the nature of the experiment, very often activities in this area take the form of pilot projects (focusing on a specific issue) or pilot areas (focusing on a specific space, e.g., a township, city, economic, or industrial zone).

In Chinese practice, experimentation is a way to increase adaptability[7] through pilot activities (controlled experiments) carried out by local governments under the supervision of the central government. The level of autonomy of individual territorial structures is of key importance in this process. Administrative units enjoy different levels of autonomy in public policymaking, depending on the policy field, and their economic importance and bargaining power. Autonomy also depends on the contact between regional leaders and decision-makers in Beijing[8]. Based on Table 32, it should be stated that compared to individual administrative units, apart from special economic zones, the experimental zones enjoy a relatively high level of autonomy, especially in areas related to socio-economic development. Obtaining the status of an experimental zone by a given territorial unit is not only a chance for the promotion of local management staff and additional economic incentives, but above all an opportunity to increase autonomy in the field of pilotage. It concerns the possibility of experimenting, which often precedes the establishment of detailed solutions then applied in national politics. Experiments allow the authorities to verify what works in the field and what causes change. They are also a way to try out a variety of methods and processes to discover new solutions. Experiments have a different function

6 Sebastian Heilmann, *From Local Experiments to National Policy: The Origins of China's Distinctive Policy Process,* "The China Journal" 2008, no. 59, pp. 29–30.

7 Shaoguang Wang, *Adapting by Learning: The Evolution of China's Rural Health Care Financing,* "Modern China" 2009, vol. 35, no. 4, pp. 370–404.

8 Dirk Schmidt, Sebastian Heilmann, *Provincial- and municipal-level Governments,* [in:] Sebastian Heilmann (ed.), *China's Political System,* Lanham-Boulder-New York-London 2017, p. 87.

than, for example, conducting observational studies and theoretical analyses because they constitute a direct intervention with verifiable results.

Table 32. Dimensions of autonomy in shaping public policies depending on the administrative unit

Administrative unit	Number	The scope of political power		
		administrative reform	economic development	culture and education
Special administrative regions	2	autonomous	autonomous	autonomous
Directly administered municipalities	4	medium	medium to high*	medium
Provinces	22	medium	low to high*	medium
Autonomous regions	5	low	low to medium*	medium to high
Special zones economic	5	high	high	medium
National experimental zones	4	high	high	medium

* Depending on the fiscal and economic resources available to the individual units.
Source: the present author's own study based on: Dirk Schmidt, Sebastian Heilmann, *Provincial- and municipal-level Governments*, [in:] Sebastian Heilmann (ed.), *China's Political System*, Lanham-Boulder-New York-London 2017, p. 87.

The use of an experimental approach to develop good practices confirms the experience of the PRC administration, which adopted such an approach even before China opened up to the world. Hence, the terms used, such as "model experiment", "experimental point", "model demonstration", "proceeding from point to surface", are part of the political repertoire of Chinese communists. For example, the concepts of an experimental point or model experiment are used to describe the acquisition of experience by doing specific work in one place and then transferring it to the central level of policymaking. The strength of an approach based on an experimental point is to prevent the blind implementation of unknown solutions, since it provides an opportunity for staff to learn something and overcome old habits by trying new solutions previously proven on a small scale[9]. A similar meaning is also attached to the concept of point-to-surface transition, which describes the gradual search for improvement in policymaking, and thus the identification of solutions that can be used in general[10].

Historical experience led Chinese leaders on the eve of economic reforms in the late 1970s to adopt an experimental approach. Deng Xiaoping emphasized that economic reforms (mainly free market) and the opening up of China con-

9 Sebastian Heilmann, *From Local…*, op. cit., pp. 10, 12.
10 Ibid, p. 2.

stituted a "large-scale experiment" that could not be carried out on the basis of textbook knowledge, so vigorous experimentation was required. In this spirit, the establishment of SEZs to support economic development was treated as a kind of experiment. From the moment China opened up to the world, experiments were conducted in the economic sphere and attempts were made to recognize the effectiveness of supply and demand mechanisms was, both in selected geographic areas and in individual industries. Over time, experimentation with economic growth has expanded to other areas. In 1987, the XIIIth Congress of the CPC extended top-down experimentation to non-economic issues: "In implementing reforms, emphasize experimentation, encourage exploration, seek practical interim measures, methods and means, and proceed step by step."[11] The words above were interpreted as an incentive to extend the experiments to the spheres of social management and public services[12], as well as other, not-strictly economic, areas. In 1992, the experimental approach was incorporated into the provisions of the constitution of the CPC – with the proviso that the entire party must bravely experiment with new methods, reviewing new experiences in solving new problems, in order to enrich and develop Marxism in practice[13].

It should be noted that experimentation is currently rationed through the supervision of higher-level authorities over the local authorities implementing it[14]. The role of local authorities boils down to the independent development of a model solution, although the decision to recognize a given solution as a model and suitable for imitation elsewhere in the PRC belongs to the central authorities. In this sense, the use of experimentation to shape public policies in the PRC is a way to achieve the overall goals of centrally established policy. Therefore, top-down experimentation is justified where the central government, acting under its

11 Jianxing Yu, Biao Huang, *Mapping the Progress of Local Government Innovation in Contemporary China,* [in:] Jianxing Yu, Sujian Guo (eds.), *The Palgrave Handbook of Local Governance in Contemporary China,* Singapore 2019, p. 120.

12 The 2018 Jangsu Province Experimental Compulsory Education Curriculum, see Guanyu shishi jiangsu sheng yiwu jiaoyu kecheng shezhi shiyan fanganese luoshi zhong xiaoxue zonghe shijian huodong kecheng keshi de zhidao yijian (关于实施江苏省义务教育课程设置实验方案落实中小学综合课时活动课程指导意见), August 31, 2018, http://www.yangzhou.gov.cn/yangzhou/bmwj/201808/b4b2e9ec3b34436a87faa6038a879698.shtml (access: 11/20/2021).

13 Constitution of The Communist Party of China. Revised and adopted at the 19th National Congress of the Communist Party of China on October 24, 2017, p. 8, http://www.xinhuanet.com//english/download/Constitution_of_the_Communist_Party_of_China.pdf (access: 11/20/2021).

14 Xufeng Zhu, *Mandate Versus Championship: Vertical government intervention and diffusion of innovation in public services in authoritarian China,* "Public Management Review" 2014, vol. 16, no.1, pp. 117–136.

hierarchical powers, selects local authorities as experimental points to test various policy instruments[15].

From the perspective of central government, local governments should be innovative, transparent[16] and conduct effective policy experiments that can be replicated elsewhere[17]. Political experimentation is intended to lead to the creation of "model demonstrations" (*shifan*) and "experimental points" (*shidian*), that is, the formal pursuit of political innovation. In the process of evaluating administrative staff, pressure is intensified to take on the challenges of experimenting at the local level or to copy solutions from those territorial units that are successful or considered to be models. Models are assessed annually by higher level authorities and may influence the political position of leadership at a given level. In addition, lower-level authorities must adhere to the relevant rules and regulations issued by their superiors, e.g., a province or a prefectural city, and any innovative practice is regularly verified as to whether it can be considered a model and further developed. Models and experiments provide the higher-level authorities with information about the direction of the activities of their subordinate units. Hence the key is: resource acquisition, political recognition, and optimal evaluation by higher authorities[18].

Depending on the form of the experiment, the role of regional or local governments in the diffusion of a given solution is slightly different, as is the process of shaping a given policy; a mixture consisting of vertical or horizontal mechanisms may be used[19]. This is significant considering that the choice of a pilot very often depends on the political, practical, and less often, methodological calculations of the central government[20]. We are talking about: (a) experimental regulations (that is, rules defined for trial implementation); (b) experimental points (that is, demonstration models and policy point designs); (c) experimental zones (that is, local areas with wide discretionary powers)[21].

15 Jianxing Yu, Biao Huang, *Mapping …*, op. cit., p. 123.

16 *Guasuyuan bangong ting guanyu quanmian tuiin jiceng zhengwu gongkai white zhunhua guifànhua gongzuo de zhidao yijian guo ban fa* (国务院办公厅关于 全面推进 基层政务公开标准化规范化工作的指导意见国办发), http://www.gov.cn/zhengce/zhengceku/2020-01/08/content_5467526.htm (access: 11/20/2021).

17 Xufeng Zhu, Guihua Bai, *Policy Synthesis through Regional Experimentations: Comparative Study of the New Cooperative Medical Scheme in Three Chinese Provinces*, "Journal of Comparative Policy Analysis: Research and Practice" 2020, vol. 22, no. 4, pp. 320–340.

18 Thomas Heberrer, *Local cadres*, op. cit., pp. 173–174.

19 Youlang Zhang, Xufeng Zhu, *Multiple mechanisms of policy diffusion in China*, "Public Management Review" 2019, vol. 21, no. 4, pp. 495–514.

20 Kilkon Ko, Kayoung Shin, *How Asian countries understand policy experiment as policy pilots?*, "Asian Journal of Political Science" 2017, vol. 25, no. 3, pp. 253–254.

21 Sebastian Heilmann, *Red Swan: How Unorthodox Policy Making Facilitated China's Rise*, Hong Kong 2018, p. 80.

Regarding temporary regulations, their application in China has expanded significantly since the reforms of 1978. Only in 1985 did the national legislature approve a situation in which the central government may issue transitional rules on economic matters. This gave the central government the freedom to issue thousands of interim measures, although formally such measures could be classified as quasi-law. In the years 2001–2006, the share of experimental regulations ranged between 13% and 28%. From 2004 to 2014, the share of experimental economic regulations fluctuated between 17% and 21%. Since 2015, there has been a decline in the issuance of experimental regulations in economic matters, which is associated with a reversal of this policy trend at the highest level. The demonstration models and scoring projects are limited to a specific policy area or economic sector. They are carried out in territorially limited experimental units[22].

However, experimental zones usually constitute geographical units that do not necessarily correspond to a formal administrative division, but which are, due to the conducted experiments, endowed with broad decision-making powers. Actions may relate to the improvement of the administration of economic activity or the promotion of foreign investment as part of testing new policies and new approaches. The solution is used in relation to the so-called special zones; most often they are economic zones, although there are also examples going beyond these strictly economic topics. Establishing experimental zones is not an easy task, as it requires the cooperation of local and regional authorities and, above all, the political will of the government (as discussed below in the case of the Tianjin Binhai New Area). The main challenge is to establish ruling powers that are optimal for the development of a given zone, and at the same time meet the expectations of all centers of government (local, regional, central).

NDRC under the supervision of the State Council in cooperation with the provincial governments systematically combines regional development with decentralized experimentation by establishing a multilevel system of experimental points. In the context of regional policy, we refer to, inter alia, places where experiments related mainly to economic development are undertaken, e. g., special economic zones, but not only these. Such activities are aimed at a diffusion of development by, for example, increasing economic integration in the east-west system of the country. In this approach, experimental points are pilot zones, for example: Shanghai Pudong New Area, Tianjin Binhai New Area, Chengdu, Chongqing City, Wuhan City Circle, Changzhutan City Group, Shenzhen Special Economic Zone, Shenyang Economic Zone. Pilot zones are located in virtually all macroregions, i. e., in the eastern, central, western, and north-eastern provinces (Table 34).

22 Ibid, pp. 83–84.

Table 33. Decentralized experimental schemes as an instrument of regional policy

Selected decentralized special schemes	Area
- Circular economy (based on recycling) - Dissemination of agricultural technology - Integrated urban-rural economic administration - Human resources	Provinces covered by the WDS
Experimental designs, for example: - Land use management - Environmental support funds for rivers - Public hospitals and retirement insurance - Sustainable development of the coal industry regions - Cooperation projects between provinces	Central provinces
- Organizational and technological transformation of the local industrial structure - Economic restructuring based on the city's natural resources - Circulation (recycling oriented) companies and neighborhoods - Issuing loans for SMEs	Northeast provinces
24 experimental schemas plotted and validated, for example: - Administrative reorganization and reform of government investment - Financial market reform - Technological innovation through integrated research and development, - Production bases - Integrated urban-rural administration and land use - Reform of public hospitals	Provinces of the Pearl River Delta program
25 approved experimental designs, for example: - Information industry - Integrated urban-rural administration and land use - Property taxes and environmental taxes - Interprovincial infrastructure and environmental projects - Comprehensive management of lakes and rivers - Local low-carbon economies - Promotion of the private sector	The Yangtze Delta provinces

Source: own study based on: *Zhengfu xinxi gongkai zhinan* (政府 信息 公开 指南), https://zfxxgk.ndrc.gov.cn/web/default.jsp (access: 20/11/2021).

The policy of locating pilot zones should take into account the stage and level of socioeconomic development of a given province and contribute to an increase in economic efficiency. Pilot zones thematically relate to many issues, domains, and industries. These include tourism,, the pilot of a comprehensive economic transformation reform in Yunnan, the civic budget of Zhejiang Province, the social security system in the western provinces, the pilot of the reform of administrative licenses in Tianjin Province, a pilot urban pension scheme in

Liaoning Province, and reducing emissions carbon dioxide in the city of Baoding (so-called low-emission cities)[23]. Pilot studies also relate to issues such as the coordination of urban and rural development, including reform of the property rights system in rural areas and farmers' property incomes[24], the rural health insurance system[25], and building a socialist society or new industrialization, thus covering the main development strategies and the economic reforms of the PRC formulated at the central level.

Table 34. Localization of pilot projects in the main fields by individual macroregion in 2006–2015

Policy area	Northeast Macroregion	Eastern Macroregion	Central Macroregion	Western macroregion
Finance and economy	10	16	10	10
Environment and resource protection	6	9	9	9
Health protection and social security	12	13	13	13
Science, technology, education and culture	4	7	5	5
Agriculture, rural areas	14	15	15	15
Administration	6	8	7	7
Total	36	50	40	39

Source: own study based on: Kilkon Ko, Kayoung Shin, *How Asian countries understand policy experiment as policy pilots?*, "Asian Journal of Political Science" 2017, vol. 25, no. 3, p. 257.

The pilot demonstration zones are intended to focus on overcoming the key problems of economic reforms and are projected to be universal and demonstrative in nature. The role of the NDRC is to coordinate the process across the country. Until 2010, in line with the expectations of the central government and the NDRC, as part of the regional reform, pilot projects were carried out in a total of 21 provinces and townships. More than 70 provincial comprehensive pilot areas have been established to support economic reforms, mainly in the context

23 Xufeng Zhu, *Inter-regional diffusion of policy innovation in China: A comparative case study*, Asian "Journal of Political Science" 2017, vol. 25, no. 3, pp. 274–279.

24 Hongyi Harry Lai, *China's Western Development Program* … op. cit., p. 454.

25 Shaoguang Wang, *Adapting by Learning: The Evolution of China's Rural Health Care Financing*, op. cit., pp. 385–396.

of reducing institutional barriers to local socioeconomic development[26]. The supervision of the NDRC causes the planned national and regional pilot zones to be closely coordinated with each other. When analyzing the substantive scope of the pilot zones, it is impossible to ignore the fact that the central authorities attach great importance to the experimental approach; the variety of areas in which experimental schemes are used, ranging from economic to social or agrarian matters, may be significantly dispersed. Similarly, Chung, Lai, and Joo have commented on the fact that the simultaneous pursuit of multiple regional development patterns in multiple macroregions can undermine most concentrated efforts and political attention because the central government has limited resources[27].

Experimentation can be viewed as a management mechanism through implicit agreements between central and regional governments. It is a kind of granting of powers to shape regional policy at the regional or local level. However, each experiment must comply with national development priorities and adhere to the guidelines for strategic coordination. Although Beijing planners view experimental designs as an instrument to adjust and optimize the planning process, regional decision makers see them as a way to increase policy flexibility and, at the same time, increase their visibility to senior authorities[28]. Thus, the establishment of experimental zones is a contractual mechanism in the implementation of national planning that serves slightly different purposes for national decision-makers, represented, for example, by NDRC officials and representatives of regional or local authorities. Beijing's authorities grant some freedom of action, encouraging experimentation and competition between individual units to solve important implementation problems, including regional policy[29]. Experimentation meets the expectations of regional policymaking from the central level and allows for centralized and selective control, while it enables local authorities to make active, local choice. It also allows for a partial separation of the ideological discussion from the reforms undertaken, assuming that what is the subject of the pilot can be presented on the basis of facts (experiences) as demonstrative.

26 Su Min, *Zhongguo duo cengci gaige shidian gay jiben xingcheng,* op. cit.
27 Jae Ho Chung, Hongyi Lai, Jang-Hwan Joo, *"Revive the Northeast" (zhenxing dongbei) Program: Origins, Policies and Implementation,* "The China Quarterly" 2009, no. 197, p. 125.
28 Xufeng Zhu, *Mandate …,* op. cit., pp. 266–282.
29 Sebastian Heilmann, Oliver Melton, *The Reinvention of Development Planning in China, 1993–2012,* "Modern China" 2013, vol. 39, p. 593.

6.1.1. Tianjin Binhai New Area as an Experimental Zone

The Binhai Area, located only 120 km from Beijing, has significant experience with the creation and operation of experimental zones. The Tianjin Binhai New Area (TBNA[30] has been upgraded to the national experimental zone for the comprehensive framework of this area since 2006[31]. Therefore, the TBNA gained the same status as the Shenzhen Special Economic Zone (from 1980) and the Shanghai Pudong New Area (from 1990) as an area that was intended to become the new growth pole of northern China. The late establishment of the TBNA demonstrates the lack of preferential treatment for the space, despite having comparable advantages in some respects (e.g., location, port access, etc.). The zone area consists of several functional units (Tianjin Economic Development Area, Tianjin Port and Tianjin Port Free Trade Zone), three administrative units (Tanggu District, Hangu District, Dagang District), and parts of two districts (Dongli District, Jinnan District). All units are at the same level of Chinese administrative rank, as is the TBNA Administrative Committee established for the purpose of zone coordination. Currently, the experimental zone covers an area of 2,270 km^{2}, with a coastline of 153 km and a population of 3 million[32].

The Tianjin authorities in the 1990s took steps to establish the area as a free-trade area, which required the approval of the government. However, the proposal was rejected, despite the fact that the previously mentioned Shanghai Pudong New Area was established at that time. In this situation, the Tianjin authorities decided in 1994 to build the TBNA on their own, that is, without significant government preferences. The support obtained from the central government in the form of development loans (2.2 billion RMB) was clearly insufficient. In the first five years of operation, the Shanghai Pudong New Area received twenty-eight times more support than Tianjin Binhai New Area, which clearly shows the preferences of the Chinese regional policy at that time[33].

It should be noted that since the late 1990s, when China launched macroregional support programs such as the WDS, Revitalize Northeast China, and Rise of Central China, Tianjin City was not included; it did not happen until 2005. The Tianjin local government took steps to obtain a preferential policy towards the

30 It is located in the Tianjin administrative area, a city with the status of a province (city with provincial rights), i.e., under the direct management of the State Council, as are Beijing, Shanghai and Chongqing.

31 Zhengfu gongzuo baogao ((政府工作报告) 政府工作报告), http://www.gov.cn/ztzl/2006-03/15/content_227782.htm (access: 20/11/2021).

32 Binhai New Area, http://subsites.chinadaily.com.cn/tianjin/binhai/binhainewarea.html (access: 20/11/2021).

33 Xufeng Zhu, Bing Sun, *Tianjin Binhai New Area: A Case Study of Multi-Level Streams Model of Chinese Decision-Making*, "Journal of Chinese Political Science" 2009, vol. 14, pp. 198–200.

city of Tianjin and the TBNA, but was not inclined to make its area part of a larger concept for the development of the part of China preferred by the central government. In other words, local government advocated the operation of the zone under the auspices of the Tianjin local government, so as to focus on development of the same area. Ultimately, the nationwide concept favored by the central government prevailed, in which the development of the TBNA became part of a wider functional area covering as many as three units, i. e., Beijing, Tianjin, and Hebei. The functional area focuses therefore on the services provided around Bohai Sea. On this basis, in 2006, the area obtained the status of a national experimental zone, which was to be a kind of gateway facilitating the opening up to the world of the northern provinces[34].

Therefore, this approach also takes into account the development of the TBNA in the context of the development of the inland territorial structures, which, without direct access to Bohaj Bay, could benefit from the construction of an international shipping and trade center and associated infrastructure. Correspondingly, the challenge of the TBNA was to optimize port services, including customs clearance and other associated services. Data for 2008 confirm the concept promoted by the central government; 55% of the value of imports and exports from the Tianjin port and more than 66% of the port cargo capacity came from the provinces and inland cities. According to statistics, the integrated customs clearance service center has reduced the processing time of operations from the previous 60 hours to around 2 hours[35]. This means that a model for the development of large ports, large foreign trade, and large logistics has been formed, which was the goal of the central regional policy for this area.

The role of the TBNA is not only limited to port services; it also has great development potential due to the technologically advanced industrial parks, industrial processing zones, and free-trade zones. In late 2009, with the approval of the State Council, the new subprovincial Binhai area was established as the leading county body under the jurisdiction of Tianjin. In September 2013, a new round of management system reform was launched, in line with the so-called large-scale system that flattens and strengthens the bottom-up level. The administrative control management structure and support for functional areas was also established, and the general modernization of cities and streets was in-

34 *Qu qing jieshao* (区情介绍), http://www.tjbh.gov.cn/channels/6254.html (access: 20/11/2021); *Guanyu yinfa tianjin binhai xinqu zonghe peitao gaige shìyan zongti fangan de tongzhi* (关于印发天津 滨海 新区 综合 配套 改革 试验 总体 方案 的 通知), https://www.dongjiang.gov.cn/contents/26/4367.html (access: 20/11/2021).

35 *Tianjin tuijin binhai xinqu zonghe peitao gaige shiyan zongti fanganese shishi* (天津推进滨海 新区综合配套改革试验总体方案实施),), http://www.gov.cn/gzdt/2008-12/01/content_1164813.htm (access: 20/11/2021).

troduced[36]. Since 2016, under the 13th Five-Year Plan, TBNA has been treated as an element of the national coordinated development strategy Beijing-Tianjin-Hebei. The aim of this approach is to deepen and expand the scope of reforms and economic opening, to strengthen the pace of development, and to focus on the functionality of the area[37]. The reforms of development coordination at the TBNA level had a positive effect, although they were an example of significant differences in the perception of the development of this area by local and central governments. The new administrative framework with national support has contributed to the progress of economic reforms[38], including e-government, the use of ICT for business, and improved port logistics[39].

This case study can be summarized in Kingdon's three-stream theory by identifying the key elements of regional policymaking through experimentation. Namely, in order for a public problem to be resolved, there must be three streams: problems, solutions, and political will[40]. The existence of the problem was not a foregone conclusion: while other regions were developing, Tianjin, despite its favorable position, did not show such significant economic growth. However, development problems in other regions, such as western China, meant that attention was focused on areas even more lagging behind in development. The stream of solutions fluctuated according to the policy of preferences of the central government for economic zones or experimental zones, which were positively assessed in the PRC. Detailed solutions, including organizational ones, were already the subject of tension between the center and local authorities. The stream of politics, and thus the will of decision makers, was shaped in an evolutionary manner. Gradually, key political actors were convinced of the concept of preferential support for the TBNA. Apart from formal considerations, the personal relationships of individual leaders played an important role. The stream of political will came as local authorities saw the government's more forward-looking vision that the Tianjin Binhai New Area should be part of wider national regional policy. This meant a slightly different role for the entire Tianjin administrative area. The proof of the success of the actions taken is not only the scale of the impact of the TBNA on other provinces, but also the scale of the

36 *Qu qing jieshao*, op. cit.

37 Tong Li, *Report on the Development of the Tianjin Binhai New Area*, [in:] Yitao Tao, Yiming Yuan (eds.), *Annual Report on the Development of China's Special Economic Zones (2018), Blue Book of China's Special Economic Zones*, Singapore 2019, pp. 195–196.

38 Xufeng Zhu, Bing Sun, *Tianjin …*, op. cit., pp. 208–209.

39 *Binhai seeks new growth momentum*, http://subsites.chinadaily.com.cn/tianjin/binhai/2020-06/23/c_502167.htm (access: 20/03/2021); *Free trade zones buoy work restarts of firms*, http://www.exploringtianjin.com/binhain/2020-04/29/c_489076.htm (access: 20/11/2021).

40 See. John Kingdon, *Agendas, alternatives, and public polices*, New York 1995.

inflow of investments (domestic and foreign)[41], and the volume of goods flowing through the port. It is important to search for optimal solutions (also related to public management), e.g., through subsequent experiments, based on previous experiences.

6.1.2. China (Hubei) Pilot Free Trade Zone

Among the many examples of experimentation activities that will contribute to building a competitive position in the regional system, attention should be paid to the China (Hubei) Pilot Free Trade Zone. The Zone was established by the decision of the State Council in August 2016 to stimulate development in the Hubei Province, particularly in the areas of Wuhan, Fuyang and Yichang[42]. The decision to launch a pilot action was officially made at the central level in March 2017[43]. When establishing the pilot, it was assumed that the Zone will not only contribute to economic development, but will also support innovative solutions. In addition to the activities selected for economic zones, the focus was on innovation in the field of institutional mechanisms[44] in relation to the practices applied in areas outside the zone (taxes, customs, inspections, industry, and trade). The Wuhan agglomeration plays an important role within the zone. Wuhan is focused on the development of the next generation of emerging strategic industries, such as information technology and information services, life and health, intelligent manufacturing and international trade, financial services, modern logistics, inspection and testing, research and development design, electronic commerce, and other modern services.

In November 2018, the implementation of 170 pilot projects was recorded, of which 136 obtained verifiable results, which constitutes 82% of all initiatives taken. The increasingly optimized market environment is gradually gaining recognition among market participants; data show that Wuhan, Fuyang, Yichang – the three large districts of the pilot zone – have recorded a total of 19,657 new business objects, which is evidence of interest in doing business within the zone.

---

41 Zhuoli tuidong chanye youhua shengji, shiti jingji jiiju xiaoying chixu zengqiang (着力推动产业 优化 升, 实体 经济 集聚 效应 持续 增强), [in:] http://www.tjbh.gov.cn/channels/6256.html (access: 20/11/2021); Tong Li, *Report on the Development of the Tianjin Binhai New Area*, op. cit., p. 202.

42 Hubei yi huo pi quanguo di san pi zi mao qu yongbao z mao qu gaige gaodì zai chufa ((湖北已获批全国第三批自贸区拥抱自贸区改革高地再出发), [in:] http://www.hubei.gov.cn/zwgk/hbyw/hbywqb/201609/t20160926_900568.shtml (access: 20/11/2021).

43 China (Hubei) pilot free trade zone, [in:] https://www.china-hbftz.gov.cn/optList.html?cttype=X14 (access: 20/11/2021).

44 Jiannan Wu, Liang Ma, Yuqian Yang, *Innovation in the Chinese public sector: typology and distribution,* "Public administration" 2013, vol. 91, no. 2, pp. 347–365.

Incentives consist mainly in far-reaching administrative facilitations in running a business, the implementation of, inter alia, projects designed to help setting up a business, tax facilitations (automatic tax relief mechanism), simplifications in customs procedures, and public e-services for business. During the period until the end of 2018, the free trade zone became the location of many key industry businesses, including the IT industry, such as Lenovo, Motorola, Xiaomi, and Haikang Weiwei. Science and Technology News Fei has established its second headquarters in Wuhan as a representative of more than 60 well-known high value-added companies. East Lake High-Tech Zone has made investments of more than 200 billion yuan. Aside from the IT sector, the development of electric vehicles has also flourished, as well as the biopharmaceutical industry (investment of approx. RMB 100 million)[45].

The initiative to establish the China (Hubei) Pilot Free Trade Zone came from the authorities of the Hubei province. The Department of Commerce of Hubei Province applied to the national Ministry of Commerce on October 31, 2016, with a request to establish a free trade zone as a pilot zone. A total of more than 200 pilot tasks were planned, covering about 50 provincial level units, but also the cities of Wuhan, Yichang and Fuyang[46]. When developing the initiative, the authorities drew on the experience of other economic zones, especially that located in Shanghai. The establishment of the pilot zone was associated with a fairly detailed definition of tasks that could be carried out by local authorities. Such a detailed catalog of tasks was aimed at strictly targeting the experimental activities. At the same time, despite the rather rigid formal framework, the pilot zone became a unique opportunity to undertake trial activities, which encouraged investments, both domestic and foreign. Therefore, we can identify two types of benefit from the regional perspective. The first one is related to the economic zone that existed before the pilot status was given. The second can be associated with the pilot status itself, which is undoubtedly evidenced by the fact that the provincial authorities themselves asked the central authorities to establish a pilot zone as an experimental area.

The bottom-up initiative to establish the China (Hubei) Pilot Free Trade Zone does not change the fact that national coordination is necessary. This is evidenced by the role of the State Council, and especially the Interministerial Office of the Joint Meeting on Free Trade Pilot Zones, in the process of verifying the experience in granting model status to individual measures (Table 35). Formal

45 *Hubei zi mao shiyan qu: Gaoduan chanya gouzhu fazhan xin shineng* (湖北自贸试验区：高端产业构筑发展新势能),), http://www.gov.cn/xinwen/2018-11/22/content_5342600.htm?zbs_baidu_bk (access: 20/11/2021).

46 *Hubei yi shangbao zi mao qu zongti fangan, sheji wuhan, yichang, xiangyang 3 shi* (湖北已上报自贸区总体方案，涉及武汉宜昌、襄阳 3市), https://www.thepaper.cn/newsDetail_forward_1552821 (access: 20/11/2021).

regulations leave no doubt that it is the central government that decides whether to adopt the developed solutions. Undoubtedly, the management of the pilot project poses a challenge, so the provincial authorities, like the State Council, formulate guidelines for the relevant administrative units (cities, counties and organizational departments of the provincial government) with respect to a number of measures aimed at deepening reforms and innovations (institutional, scientific, technological, industrial)[47].

Table 35. Pilot project using the example of The China (Hubei) Pilot Free Trade Zone

Formal basis	**Announcement of the State Council on the General Plan of the China (Hubei) Pilot Free Trade Zone, March 15, 2007**
Range	China (Hubei) Pilot Free Trade Zone
Area	119.96 km^2, covers three zones: 70 km^2 in Wuhan (including 5.41 km^2 in Wuhan East Lake Integrated Bonded Zone); 21.99 km^2 in Fuyang District (including 0.281 km^2 Puyang Bonded Logistics Center); 27.97 km^2 in the Yichang District
Objective	establishment of a pilot zone, replication, institutional innovation
Tasks	– deepening reforms of the administrative system (optimization of services, decentralization) – establishment and improvement of the social credit system – deepening reforms in the investment process – increasing the use of foreign capital – development of technologically advanced foreign trade platforms – opening the financial sector to the outside – improving the quality of financial services – promoting innovation in science and technology and finance – talent support system – construction of international logistics centers (including activities related to the BRI) – building a service platform for regional development
Forms of activity	institutional opening, generating innovative solutions, coordination (e.g., in the field of industrial development), comprehensive approach

47 *Zhichi zhongguo (Hubei) ziyou maoyi shiyan qu shenhua gaige chuangxin ruogan cuoshi de tongzhi* (支持中国 (湖北) 自由贸易试验区深化改革创新若干措施 的通知)支持中国（湖北） 自由贸易试验区深化改革创新若干措施的通知), [in:] http://www.wehdz.gov.cn/zmq/zcfg_22854/pqzcfg/202102/t20210209_1633195.shtml (access: 20/11/2021).

Table 35 *(Continued)*

Formal basis	**Announcement of the State Council on the General Plan of the China (Hubei) Pilot Free Trade Zone, March 15, 2007**
Management method	- Leading Group for the Promotion of the China (Hubei) Pilot Free Trade Zone – day-to-day Management, Pilot Zone Provincial Agency - the cities in which the zone is located form the Leading Group for the Promotion of the China (Hubei) Pilot Free Trade Zone – day-to-day management, a joint agency established by the cities included in the pilot zone
Supporting institutions	- People's Government of the Province of Hubei - selected cities (supporting) and their administrative units
Verification of experiences	- The Interministerial Joint Meeting on State Council Free Trade Pilot Zones - Hubei Provincial People's Government - Provincial Secretary of the CPC

Source: own study based on: *Guasuyuan guanyu yinfa zhongguo (hubei) ziyou maoyi shiyan qu zongti fangan de tongzhi* (国务院关于印发中国 (湖北) 自由贸易试验区总体方案的通知), http://www.gov.cn/zhengce/content/2017-03/31/content_5182299.htm (access: 04/20/2022); *Guasuyuan guanyu yinfa zhongguo (hubei) ziyou maoyi shiyan qu zongti fangan de tongzhi* (国务院 关于印发 中国(湖北)自由 贸易 试验 区 总体 方案 的 通知), http://www.pkulaw.cn/fulltext_form.aspx?Db=chl&Gid=075ecd80219ce5a0bdfb&keyword&EncodingNitle=0_search (access: 04/20/2022); *Shangwu bu guanyu zhichi zhongguo (hubei) ziyou maoyi shiyan qu jiakuai fazhan ruogan cuoshi de tongzhi* (商务部关于支持中国 (湖北) 自由贸易试验区加快发展若干措施的通知),, http://www.pkulaw.cn/fulltext_form.aspx?Db=chl&Gid=40fadadb43e5f6d4bdfb&keyword=&Encearch_Mame=&EncearchingName=&SearchName=accurate&Search_IsTitle=0 (access: 04/20/2022).

The guidelines provide a detailed catalog of activities that should be "eagerly implemented" at the local level, including activities that traditionally occur in economic zones and those that are actually more for experimentation. A careful examination of the guidelines shows that in the latter case, it is more about innovative solutions than just experimenting, although the former is undoubtedly the result of the latter. In this context, considerable attention is paid to the demonstration value of the solutions practiced (application and replication possibilities). Rather, it is a bit more like a bureaucratic approach, where what is written must be done, but breakthrough innovations do not necessarily come about under these circumstances. The essentiality of this statement is mitigated by the overall economic performance of the entities included in the zone. There is no doubt that from a regional point of view the benefits significantly exceed the costs. In other words, pilot projects are one of the tools to support competitiveness at the regional and local levels.

To summarize this case study of a specific pilot zone, it is important to first note a unique feature of the Chinese political system that, understandably, evolves over time. The rule of economic and partly social issues is much more decentralized[48] than that of administrative and cadre matters. In addition, it should be taken into account that the central government has full powers to interfere in the activities of provincial authorities; it uses its position especially for the purpose of cadre evaluation. Moreover, political signals sent by the central authorities are an important circumstance for conducting experiments, and administrative pressure from the center turns out to be a necessary condition for actions taken at the regional or local level[49]. The central government, observing that the progress in economic liberalization does not result in increasing tendencies of political liberalization, is willing to take risks. Meanwhile, experimentation contributes to the reflectiveness of the system, or at least gives this a formal possibility and provides an opportunity to play various types of games[50], understood as a kind of institutional collective action, where the activity of both parties (government, provincial authorities) depends on the actions of other participants.

The developed solutions are not so much revolutionary organizational innovations as specific simplifications and facilitations. To some extent, they represent a new quality compared to the practices that have been implemented so far. Hierarchical control seems to be safe as it is still quite efficient and one of its instruments is the personnel evaluation system. Experimenting in a limited way increases the freedom of action at the local level in the sense of permanent decentralization, i.e., the delegation of specific powers to the local level. The discussed example confirms the above observations. The experiment could not have been successful if it had not been for the participation of regional authorities, including local authorities, and this is precisely what the circumstances of the experiment allow. On the other hand, there is a threat that experimentation becomes an ordinary practice of public management; after all, as we know from history, the most durable solution is temporary.

---

48 Hon Chan, King Chow, *Public Management Policy and Practice in Western China: Metapolicy, Tacit Knowledge, and Implications for Management Innovation Transfer,* "The American Review of Public Administration" 2007, vol. 37, no. 4, pp. 479–498.

49 Jing Chen, Cui Huang, *Policy Reinvention and Diffusion: Evidence from Chinese Provincial Governments,* "Journal of Chinese Political Science" 2021, March 4.

50 Yu Chen, Anthony Yeh, Yingxuan Zhang, *Political tournament and regional cooperation in China: a game theory approach,* "Annals of Regional Science" 2017, vol. 58, no. 3 pp. 597–622.

6.2. Cadre management as an attempt to eliminate the implementation gap

Similar to other countries, China implements public policies through an administrative apparatus. In a country of 1.4 billion people[51], this requires very extensive bureaucratic structures. Hence, one of the instruments of an effective regional policy is the appropriate cadre management[52]. The concept of cadre in the PRC is very broad, as it refers to all CPC officials and officials serving in administrative institutions, public organizations, and the armed forces, and in particular to persons holding managerial positions. Thus, the term cadre encompasses party leaders and provincial-level units, as well as rural officials and ordinary police officers, so it can certainly be said that it does not refer to a homogeneous group. From 1949, the term cadre has applied to party and state officials remunerated from the state budget[53]. It should be noted that due to a different model of administration than in the West, cadres enjoy authority because they differ from the general mass of society in status. Moreover, from a sociological point of view, they constitute a group which, due to its position, has certain privileges[54].

The modern administration system is similar to the traditional Chinese civil servant hierarchy, was also divided into ranks in the so-called hierarchy *ji*. There were two main categories: civil servant and military servant. Beginning with the Tang Dynasty (618–907), each category was divided into 9 degrees, each of which was divided into 2 classes, higher *(shang)* and lower *(xia)*, for a total of 18 degrees. Each rank had special attributes and rewards. The higher the rank, the greater the privileges and intangible benefits of its holders. Today, administrative staff are commonly referred to as civil servants. According to Art. 2 of the PRC Civil Service Act of 2005, "civil servants" are defined as personnel who perform public duties according to laws and have been included into the state administrative staff with wages and welfare borne by the state public finance. Officially, the public administration has set restrictive standards of action, which can also be found in modern administrations of highly developed countries. It is about

51 Data at the end of 2019, see Zhongguo guojia tongji ju, Zhonghua renmin gongheguo 2019 nian guomin jingji he shehui fazhan tongji gongbao (中国国家统计局,中华人民共和国2019年国民经济和 社会发展统计公报), [in:] http://www.stats.gov.cn/tjsj/zxfb/202002/t20200228_1728913.html (access: 20/11/2021).

52 Jiaqi Liang, Laura Langbein, *Performance Management, High-Powered Incentives, and Environmental Policies in China,* "International Public Management Journal" 2015, vol. 18, no. 3, pp. 346–385.

53 Thomas Heberer, *Local Cadres,* [in:] Jianxing Yu, Sujian Guo (eds.), *The Palgrave…*, p. 157.

54 Wolfgang Drechsler, *Beyond the Western Paradigm: Confucian Public Administration,* [in:] Sara Bice, Avery Poole, Helen Sullivan (eds.), *Public Policy in the "Asian Century" Concepts, Cases and Futures,* London 2018, pp. 25–29.

following the principles of transparency, equality, competition in selecting superiors, basing one's actions on the provisions of law, substantive qualifications, and proceeding with established standards and procedures[55]. If we add to this the slogan of the rule of law with Chinese characteristics promoted in recent years[56], there is no doubt that the formal and legal standards of the administration reflects the good practices of modern administration.

According to the findings of Prof. Wu Jiang, China currently has 1.3 million public institutions operating in various areas, from education, science, health, agriculture, forestry, water management to radio and television broadcasting, publishing press, and others. These institutions employ approximately 30.35 million people. Three-quarters of the employed are workers in education, health care and agricultural technical services, of which about half are employed in the education system[57]. However, the findings of different authors yield different figures for employment in the public sector. The matter is complicated by the fact that the Chinese authorities do not publish updated data on employment in the public sector based on administrative level (see Diagram 13). Estimates[58] indicate that 65.5 million people are employed in the public sector, including 27.4 million people in public service units (in 2008). According to official state statistics, employment in the category of "public management and social organizations" in 2007 was 12.6 million people[59]. The of employees in public institutions is impressive, also because the administration has the ability to influence society, and their interests are not uniform. All this with quite high expectations of ever more efficient public services.

55 The Civil Servant Law of the People's Republic of China, 2005, http://www.asianlii.org/cn/legis/cen/laws/tcslotproc462/ (access: 20/11/2021).

56 It is about applying the idea of the rule of law, understood as obeying the law, which strengthens the CPC's unified leadership in China. According to the Rule of Law Building Plan (2020–2025), the rule of law is to serve economic development, increase security, and improve the CPC's ability to govern the country. This leadership of the CPC is the most basic guarantee of the socialist rule of law. In the operational dimension, it is planned to reform legislative procedures, strengthen control over the administration (including amendments to administrative law), and to modernize, inter alia, Intellectual Property Law, Business Law, Crisis Response Legislation, Local Legislation as well as the Judiciary. These goals are to be achieved by 2035 at the latest. See Zhonggong zhongyang yinfa fazhi zhongguo jianshe guihua (2020–2025 nian) (中共中央印发《法治 中国建设规划 [2020–2025 年]) from January 10, 2021, http://www.gov.cn/zhengce/2021-01/10/content_5578659.htm (access: 20/11/2021).

57 *Ryzykowanie i ingerowanie wymagają dogłębnego rozpoznania,* Liaowang March 17, 2009, translated by Agnieszka Łobacz, [in:] Krzysztof Gawlikowski, Marta Ławacz, Agnieszka Łobasz, Marta Tomczak, Joanna Afek (eds.) *Prasa chińska o przemianach społecznych i kulturowych w początkach XXI wieku,* Warszawa 2020, pp. 299–300.

58 Kjeld Erik Brødsgaard, Chen Gang, *Public sector reform in China: who is losing out?,* [in:] Kjeld Erik Brødsgaard (ed.), *Globalization and Public Sector Reform in China,* Oxon-New York 2014, p. 80.

59 *China Statistical Yearbook 2008,* National Bureau of Statistics of China, pp. 114, 127.

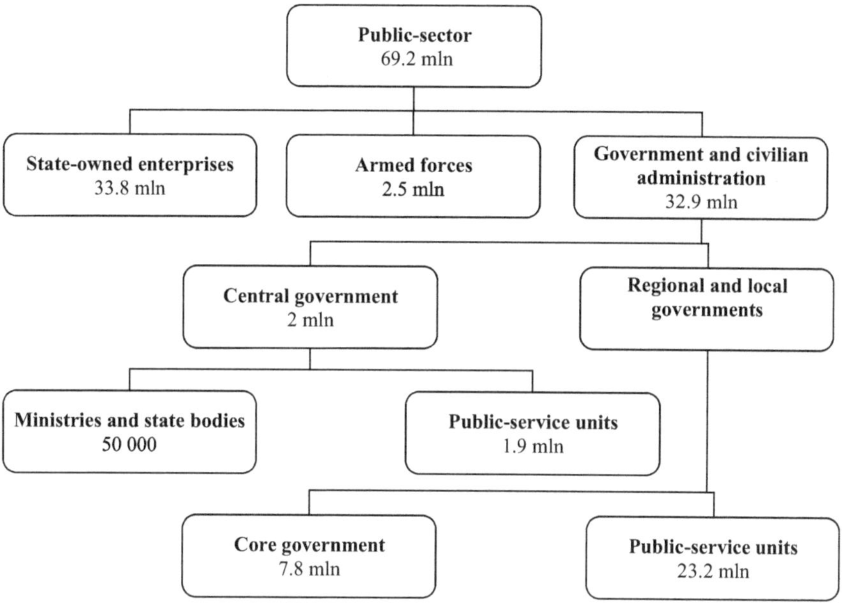

Diagram 13. Distribution of public-sector employees by function and administrative level (2002). Source: own study on the basis of: John P. Burns, *Civil Service Reform in China,* "OECD Journal on Budgeting" 2007, vol. 7, no. 1, p. 60.

In the PRC's political system, the role of the administration in the implementation of public policies is essential as it is a key element of the CPC's control of the implementation of its designated activities. In the implementation of regional policy, the specificity of which consists in the implementation of various tasks in a specific place and time, this role is undoubtedly also played by the local administration. The accuracy of the above is proved by the data showing that approximately 80% of centrally enacted law and 90% of local law are implemented by various types of national administrative structure. The problem is that there are still exceptions in the PRC to the application of law, which is often secondary to the solutions practiced on a microscale; hence, the actions of central government in recent years[60] focus on ensuring the effectiveness of law im-

60 It should be added that the concept of the rule of law was introduced into the Chinese constitution only in 1999, which was associated with China's membership of the WTO in 2001. According to the political programs of that period, the rule of law was to be introduced by 2015. See Zou Keyuan, *Administrative Reform and Rule of Law in China,* "Copenhagen Journal of Asian Studies" 2007, no. 24, pp. 5–32.

plementation, e.g., through the accountability system for its administrative enforcement[61].

China is still governed by a number of administrative laws whose legal status is unclear and/or arbitrary[62]. It is similar with compliance with the law, the transparency of the administration, corruption, and the lack of full independence of the judiciary. Due to these problems, instead of fully achieving the "rule of law", we are dealing with "party power by means of law"[63]. Due to the fact that the rule of law is rather a way to maintain social order of Chinese political socialism, which stabilizes the leading role of the CPC, and does not limit the abuse of public power or protect the fundamental rights of individuals, the law is not the only instrument for implementing public policies, including regional ones. This is evidenced by China's experience with law, preserved in history and culture, which cannot be ignored. If it is recognized that in China the guidelines resulting from Confucianism are widely accepted, the place law holds in Western culture is taken by duties assigned to a given social position. Hence, less attachment is given to legal institutions and greater to local social organizations such as families, and rural and township communities[64]. This makes it all the more reasonable to focus on the functioning of the administration and its evolution in the implementation of regional policy.

Traditionally, one of the instruments by which the implementation of development plans has been motivated is personalized cadre control mechanisms[65]. The functioning of the administration is sustained by the CPC's hierarchical cadre system, which is not without shortcomings as a control tool, but which at the same time is satisfactory in the eyes of most central leaders. This system, let us add, is not optimal, but it is sufficient to keep formal hierarchies and informal networks under control. This is achieved through the management of administrative performance based on staff evaluations, taking into account the goals achieved by officials.

61 *Dazao fa zhongguo liangli mingpian fazhi guojia, fazhi zhengfu, fazhi shehui ti jianshe* (打造法中国亮丽名片法治国家、法治政府、法治社会 -体建设) on November 5, 2020, [in:] http://www.gov.cn/xinwen/2020-11/15/content_5561619.htm (access: 20/03/2021).

62 Stéphanie Balme, *The rule of law in China: On the margins of a bureaucratic and absolutist empire (1978–2014)*, "Revue Francaise d'Administration Publique" 2014, vol. 150, no. 2, pp. 393–413.

63 Zou Keyuan, op. cit., pp. 23–26; Wang Liming, *The Basic Issues concerning the Construction of the Rule of Law in China in the New Era*, "Social Sciences in China" 2020, vol. 41, no. 1, pp. 21–37; Lin Laifan, *The Chinese model of the rule of law*, "Frontiers of Law in China" 2015, vol. 10, no. 40, pp. 657–668.

64 Krzysztof Gawlikowski, *Konfucjański model państwa w Chinach*, Warszawa 2009, pp. 88–89.

65 Hon S. Chan, *Cadre Personnel Management in China: The Nomenklatura* System, *1990–1998*, "The China Quarterly" 2004, no. 179, pp. 703–734; John Burns, *Civil service reform in contemporary China*, "The Australian Journal of Chinese Affairs" 1987, no. 18, pp. 47–48.

The performance measurement system consists in verifying the achievements of officials against the goals previously set. In western democracies, performance management is a technical tool for improving public service delivery. It allows one to generate information on the progress of implementation of public programs in relation to the assumed goals. Due to this, external supervisory institutions as well as citizens have the opportunity to monitor the achieved effects of individual public policies. In this sense, performance measurement can also be seen as a key instrument to promote accountability of public authorities. Meanwhile, in China, the performance-based management system has a slightly different meaning. Since the beginning of the 1990s, it has been primarily an instrument aimed at strengthening the governance capabilities of the Chinese authorities. It is a way to find a balance between dynamic development and social stability. It also results from the awareness of the political elite that the conflict between development and social stability may prevent further growth and undermine the leading role of the CPC. Jie Gao[66] points out that the way performance measurement is performed – from the perspective of often numerical goals – does not adequately address significant management problems and fundamental social and political tensions in Chinese society. The personnel evaluation system established in the early 1990s is thus a *de facto* departure from the tradition of duty and focuses on restrictions and / or awards.

As a consequence, only those parts of development plans that are confirmed in CPC documents and are binding in nature can define the priorities and interests of the subordinate levels of administration. Until the early 1990s, the relationship between the achievement of the goals adopted in the development plans and the evaluation of administrative staff was relatively loose and not systemic in nature[67]. As a result of many reforms of the personnel measurement system, evaluation has become more systematic and begun to include economic aspects as well as social indicators, including both GDP growth and the unemployment rate in a given administrative unit.

Starting in 2006, there has been a breakthrough in the systematic combination of a more integrated set of goals contained in development plans (economic and noneconomic) with evaluation of administrative staff. This was due to the so-called binding targets set at central, national, regional, and local levels. The NDRC planners under the 11th FYP made sure that indicators were clearly defined to facilitate the control of its implementation for both planning bodies and CPC departments. As a result of this, the most important binding priorities

66 Jie Gao, *Governing by goals and numbers: A case study in the use of performance measurement to build state capacity in China,* "Public Administration and Development" 2009, vol. 29, no.1, p. 21.

67 Sebastian Heilmann, Oliver Melton, *The Reinvention …*, op. cit., p. 608.

established in the 11th FYP were included in staff evaluations throughout China. The NDRC officials themselves emphasized[68] that the applied procedure gave a great impulse to the implementation of the key objectives of the 2006–2010 plan. Although national planners communicate binding targets to ensure the implementation of centrally planned objectives, regional and local (including municipal) administrations remain a key link. For example, the municipality of Chongqing[69] has been pursuing goals since 2006 that were partially identical to the national 11th FYP, but also regional-specific goals, as well as goals relevant to the municipality itself. These are environmental, land use, birth control, and healthcare goals. Cadre evaluation[70] was designed to implement not only the binding goals of the five-year plans (benchmarks for staff performance), but also to evaluate the activities undertaken for statistical purposes.

The 11th FYP finally contained 22 goals, of which 8 were binding. The 13th FYP contains 27 goals, 16 of which are binding[71]. The eight binding targets for the 11th FYP were used to assess the performance of local administrative staff; three targets – arable land protection, increasing energy efficiency and reducing pollution – were subject to high-level monitoring in Beijing throughout the plan period. Performance contracts were an instrument through which targets were identified that were binding on officials and sometimes even businesses. The contracts stipulated which of the goals were of veto nature, i.e., failure to achieve them is automatically associated with the lack of professional promotion or other benefits for managerial staff. In this way, the Beijing authorities have decided which goals are primary. This exercise was replicated at the lower levels of the integrated plan evaluation system. Thanks to this system, Beijing has been able to define a small number of high-priority political goals that go far beyond its formal administrative structures[72].

68 Sebastian Heilmann, *Red Swan …*, op. cit., p. 183.

69 Ibid.

70 A similar system of cadre evaluation functions in the higher education system, where the main element is the demonstration of adequate scientific performance by individual researchers. See Ya-Ting Huang, Jian Xu, *Surviving the performance management of academic work: evidence from young Chinese academics*, "Higher Education Research & Development" 2020, vol. 39, no. 4, pp. 704–718. The system of judging staff evaluation introduced in 2011 should also be mentioned. In this system, over 30 indicators are measured that quantitatively measure honesty, efficiency and impact. The system encourages pressure to resolve disputes quickly without being overly angry, and there is a system of praise and rebuke, leading to varying informal responses by law enforcement officials. See Jonathan J. Kinkel, William J. Hurst, *The Judicial Cadre Evaluation System in China: From Quantification to Intra-State Legibility*, "The China Quarterly" 2015, no. 224, pp. 933–942.

71 The 13th Five-year Plan for Economic and Social Development of The People's Republic of China (2016–2020), op. cit., pp. 8–10.

72 Sebastian Heilmann, Oliver Melton, *The Reinvention …*, op. cit., p. 610.

Among the effects of combining personnel evaluation with the achievement of the FYPs goals, the increase in the political status of the NDRC, both at the national and regional level, should be mentioned. NDRC officials played a key role in formulating a goal-based evaluation criterion for clerks based on the binding goals of the FYPs. This is confirmed by the last editions of the plans, in which the documents prepared by the NDRC indicated centralization tendencies in the field of, inter alia, implementation and control of the implementation status of the plans. An example may also be the terminology used that was rejected in the late 1990s, such as "breakdown of plan objectives into individual levels" that reappears in NDRC documents. Interestingly, the above situation is replicated at local government level, where NDRC officials play a similar role in coordinating and approving plans and evaluations on behalf of the region, city, and county government. The binding objectives of the plan and the evaluation of civil servants have therefore become complementary tools of regional policy. This linkage points to the lingering characteristics of China's political economy, radically different from other state-led economies. The linking of cadre assessment and planning is a mechanism resulting from both the command economy and the Leninist party organization. A binding mechanism for human resource planning and evaluation establishes people-based political accountability rather than legal accountability or bureaucratic implementation[73].

The cadre evaluation system allows officials to prioritize public administration tasks. The problem, however, is that the targets have increased over time, so some officials manipulate the data to gain a strategic advantage in the target-based evaluation system. These are unintended consequences of the use of performance indicators for officials, also known as gaming behavior[74]. One of the most frequently cited examples of such a situation is the fabrication of key statistical data on the economy, although not only this[75]. Since the late 1990s, the quality of Chinese statistics has been repeatedly questioned. The deliberate falsification of the value of production by downstream authorities, whose results are assessed in part on the basis of local production growth rates, is an officially recognized fact[76]. Many Chinese and Western authors have questioned the credibility of official real GDP growth rates in some years[77]. Alternative estimates

73 Sebastian Heilmann, *Red Swan …*, op. cit., p. 185.

74 Peter Smith, *On the unintended consequences of publishing performance data in the public sector,* International Journal of Public Administration 1995, vol. 18, no. 2 & 3, pp. 277–310.

75 Albert Park, Sangui Wang, *China's poverty statistics,* "China Economic Review" 2001, vol. 12, no. 4 pp. 384–398.

76 Carsten A. Holz, *China governance project: the institutional arrangements for the production of statistics,* "OECD Statistics Working Paper" 2005, January 19, pp. 4–6.

77 Thomas G. Rawski, Xiao Wei, *Roundtable on Chinese Economic Statistics: Introduction,* "China Economic Review" 2011, vol. 12, no. 4, pp. 298–302; Gerard F. Adams, Chen Yimin, *Skepticism about Chinese GDP Growth – the Chinese GDP Elasticity of Energy Consumption,*

of China's real GDP growth rates suggest growth close to zero in 1998 and 1999 (compared to officially reported 7.8% and 7.2%, respectively) and around half of the original, official, unreviewed real growth rates of 7.1% and 7.3% in 2000 and 2001 respectively. The official 2002 real growth rate is considered incorrect, if not underestimated. The sum of the GDP of individual provinces often exceeds the GDP recorded by the Chinese statistical office[78].

From this book's point of view, both the systemic approach and the bottom-up approach of individual members of the cadre are important. The importance of this issue is raised by the fact that it is on the basis of data generated by the administration that we learn about the state of public policies in the PRC, and it is no different with regional policy. The Chinese official media themselves point to the phenomenon of statistical data falsification. For example, on August 23, 1995, the then Commissioner of the National Bureau of Statistics of China (NBS), pointing to the legitimacy of the amendment to the Act on Public Statistics of 1996[79] stated that "recently the phenomenon of false and misleading reports has spread in some localities and in some units. The danger is great and the impact is very negative."[80] Reports on data falsification then became a standard part of the monthly KBS statistics. The data manipulation reports published there were of two kinds. One presented specific evidence of data falsification, usually related to one local company or local authority. Such hard evidence is relatively rare, and the degree of falsification in a specific case is usually in the single- or two-digit percentage range; comparative data, such as output data for the entire geographic unit, are not shown. The second type of report remained very general, stating that data falsification was taking place, but stating only the standard reasons for its occurrence (achieving growth or other goals and achieving a higher performance rating, but also sloppy survey methods and poor quality of statistical staff).

Returning to the target-based cadre evaluation system in the context of bridging the implementation gap, it should be noted that from the cadre perspective it has a significant impact on the behavior of local administrative personnel. Officials wanting to achieve satisfactory results at all costs tend to play the game, constantly being both under the pressure of punishments and succumbing to the temptation of rewards, in the event of failure or success. Thus, they par-

---

"Journal of Economic and Social Measurement" 1996, vol. 22, no. 4, pp. 231–240; Karen Richardson, *China's Admission of Economic Data Flaws Isn't Likely to Make Fund-Picking Easier,* "Asian Wall Street Journal" 2001, November 22, https://www.wsj.com/articles/SB1006367201710056960 (access 20/11/2021).

78 Carsten A. Holz, *China governance …*, op. cit., pp. 4–6, 9.

79 See *Zhonghua renmin gongheguo tongji fa,* National Bureau of Statistics (中华人民共和国统计 法), http://www.stats.gov.cn/zjtj/tjfg/tjfl/200906/t20090629_8791.html (access: 20/11/2021).

80 Carsten A. Holz, op. cit., p. 7.

ticipate in a kind of data tournament, which motivates them to not report the data accurately enough, the effects of which were mentioned above. The cadre management system is also complicated by the hierarchy of formulated plans, where the supreme authority rarely takes into account local specificities, requiring the achievement of predetermined goals. Implementation at the local level is therefore a product of what the supreme authority expects and what the local authority is actually able to deliver (accomplish)[81].

It is worth paying attention to the reasons why officials play games under the cadre evaluation system. There is no doubt that the games undertaken are of a different nature, but have a common denominator: they make it difficult to actually achieve desired results. With regard to regional policy, they distort the expected goals. Field research conducted by Jie Gao shows significant findings in Shaanxi Province with local officials i. e., local CPC secretaries, leading cadre including members of statistical office staff involved in data collection, and monitoring officials in one of the counties. The findings point to several reasons why local cadres play different kinds of games to show progress in the areas entrusted to their administration[82].

Firstly, it is very common to find that the targets allocated at the local level contradict the situation on the ground. The superior authorities, having received a set of obligatory goals, distribute them, not always taking into account the specificity of their subordinate units. Local authorities, in turn, are obliged to achieve goals that are not adequate for the situation at the local level. An example would be energy efficiency targets in a town with an energy-intensive industry. The strict goals set for energy efficiency to be achieved in a short time are conducive to gaming behavior. In this case, the remedial action of local authorities is simply to temporarily deprive consumers of electricity, which disrupts the functioning of not only households but also enterprises.

Second, the cadre evaluation system establishes collective competition and fosters collusion in the absence of effective means of detecting and punishing the authors of fraudulent reports. The authorities of individual counties evaluate the results of their lower-level units, comparing how well each administration achieved the same goals. Such rivalry leads some township leaders to inflate their statistics. Practices such as fraudulent reporting are emerging in areas where they are difficult to detect. It should also be added that the higher-level authorities do not publish the specific values of the results achieved, but only the order in the ranking, which makes the system's transparency very limited. Particular local authorities do not know what data is reported by other units of the same ad-

81 Jie Gao, *Pernicious Manipulation of Performance Measures in China's Cadre Evaluation System,* "The China Quarterly" 2015, vol. 223, p. 619.

82 Ibid, pp. 631–633.

ministrative level, making it difficult to publicly verify the information presented. There is a tacit agreement of county leaders, which encourages their subordinate officials to play various kinds of game. In fact, provincial officials are in an analogous position in relation to their superior authorities and are also obliged to show progress in achieving goals.

Third, local officials often have to achieve conflicting goals. This is the case where the implementation of one goal often negatively affects the achievement of other goals. Here, in the study area, there was a conflict between economic development and land use. To promote economic growth, local officials use agricultural land to create industrial parks, new roads, and other infrastructure needed to support economic development. As a consequence, the area of land intended for agricultural use is constantly decreasing. Meanwhile, local officials are judged by agricultural production measures, as well as by the targeted expansion of land devoted to agricultural production. As the goals become more demanding, with each passing year it becomes more and more difficult, on the one hand, to increase the area of arable land and, on the other hand, to maintain or increase the scale of industrial production.

Although local authorities are under the control of higher-tier units, creative statistics in the objective-based personnel appraisal system result in unexpected practices in the implementation of particular elements of regional policy. Manipulation most often takes place at the lowest level, i.e., local authorities (e.g. villages), and subsequent levels are already aggregating the collected data and transferring it to the next levels of administration up the hierarchical system – at this stage it is more difficult to manipulate the data. The mechanism of creative accounting can be seen, for example, in relation to the level of income of rural residents. When manipulation occurs, the circumstances of the manipulation are the same in different local government units. Local authorities receive many incentives to inflate incomes, as senior authorities set ambitious goals on which career advancement, financial bonuses, or simply job preservation depend. In the above circumstances, an unauthorized data correction seems to be the best solution[83].

In summary, the cadre evaluation system, created to eliminate the implementation gap of public policies, including regional policies, brings unexpected results. The generally positive procedure of linking some of the objectives of the FYPs with the evaluation of civil servants does not fully produce the desired results. This is because the central supervision imposed on lower-level entities is accompanied by local adaptation activities in the form of various types of games, the purpose of which is to demonstrate the implementation of top-down goals.

83 Maria Edin, *State Capacity and Local Agent Control in China: CCP Cadre Management from a Township Perspective,* "China Quarterly" 2003, vol. 173, pp. 35–52.

The range of behaviors here is very wide and various strategies can be identified among them[84]. One of them is the so-called ratchet effect, i. e. the implementation of the ratios at the minimum acceptable level, in order to prevent the determination of the same ratios at an exorbitant level in the next reporting year. In turn, "noise" is a strategy of demonstrating high activity in order to achieve the set goals. More damaging to the goal of regional policy is "taking shortcuts", that is, doing a sloppy job just to avoid negative evaluation. An example may be the program of building cheap communal flats for rent, which were often not completed in the assumed time and number, and yet the control activities were successfully carried out. Another strategy is the so-called "magic tricks" that consist in the apparent completion of tasks without actually achieving the indicators. The most significant deviation from the achievement of policy objectives is the so-called malicious deviation, where the public interest is sacrificed for personal gain. As part of this strategy, officials are aware of the negative effects of their actions, but do so anyway in order to survive or to excel in their performance assessment.

6.3. Chinese regional policy and the development needs of the PRC: toward mechanisms for assessing the value of public intervention

Evidence-based shaping of public policies, such as regional policy, is desirable because public actions are expected to have positive effects on the target groups at which they are aimed. It is not easy to capture the cause-and-effect relationship between the regional policy intervention and the effects obtained due to the interdependence of factors that influence regional development, both in terms of quantity and quality. A key aspect is the availability of statistical data on the various dimensions of local and regional development. One of the instruments by which an attempt is made to assess the impact of a given policy on the achievement of its goals is evaluation. In China, it covers only a fraction of all research in the field of the functioning of public administration or, more broadly, public policy[85].

Evaluation understood in the western way, i. e., as an assessment of the legitimacy of conducting a given policy, performed in order to possibly correct public actions, is not a very frequent instrument of improving the PRC's policy. This does not mean that policy does not have mechanisms designed to increase

84 Jie Gao, *Governing…*, op. cit., pp. 624–626.

85 Haeil Jung, Ruodan Zhang, *Impact evaluations in South Korea and China*, "Asian Journal of Political Science" 2017, vol. 25, no. 3, p. 328.

the reflectivity and relevance of policy. Evaluation in Chinese public management is practiced in a specific way; its main manifestations can be found in the context of the evaluation system for civil servants. In this context, evaluation can be seen as an assessment of the performance of an organization or person by external experts. Policy evaluations in China appear to be inspired by a mix of neoliberal governance approaches such as new public management (NPM) and national traditions of political leadership, such as the legacy of imperial times and the socialist tradition of personnel evaluation.

Western political systems use evaluations to answer questions that arise in policy formulation, public program design, improvement, and testing effectiveness and efficiency. Therefore, cadre evaluation is a kind of political technique. The assessments are part of the structural system by which the highest authority entities transfer responsibility for policy implementation to their subordinates (most often the administration). Especially in the context of NPM, the center and higher levels of administration use evaluations to withdraw from the daily implementation game and limit it to monitoring evaluation results. Andrew Kipnis[86] called it governance from afar – imposing indirect measures of control and domination on those charged with implementation. The key to this endeavor is to create people who are obedient, hardworking, and responsible by socializing or promoting self-discipline among those who not perceived as ruled, hardworking and responsible[87].

The NPM approach mentioned above and judgments in Chinese political culture lie in the scope and direction of this "soul engineering". Unlike NPM, the moral images of good staff dominate those that promote rational and effective behavior. From the Chinese government's point of view, the assessments are deliberately aimed at adjusting the behavior and increasing the efficiency of the those being evaluated, so they are closer to the traditional norms of the state. This is manifested, for example, in the assessment of leading local cadres using (traditional) features of bureaucratic behavior: *de* (moral quality), *neng* (ability/skills), *qin* (attitude/work diligence), *ji* (achievements) and *lian* (honesty). Therefore, it is not punishment and performance control that are crucial, but a change in attitude and behavior. Power and politics must be internalized[88]. The differences between the NPM and the Chinese evaluation system are seen in the way negative evaluation results are utilized in the administration: they do not necessarily lead to sanctions. Only in extreme cases of inappropriate behavior

86 Andrew B. Kipnis, *Audit cultures: neoliberal governmentality, socialist legacy, or technologies of governing?*, "American Ethnologist" 2008, vol. 35, no. 2, pp. 275–289.

87 Bruno Latour, *Science in Action. How to Follow Scientists and Engineers through Society*, Cambridge 1987, pp. 219–232.

88 Thomas Heberer, René Trappel, *Evaluation Processes, Local Cadres' Behavior and Local Development Processes*, "Journal of Contemporary China" 2013, vol. 22, no. 4, p. 1049.

(usually those that attract the attention of regional or national media) does it act, for example, as a sanctioning mechanism.

The central planning system has very limited effect where guidelines and restrictions targeted at lower administrative structures conflict with the local economic interests of both local clerks and businesses. If certain priorities of the FYPs show synergy with economic priorities or with income growth (for example, the so-called green technologies and their positive impact on the economy), and at the same time the level of their implementation translates into the evaluation of cadre, then their implementation degree is usually satisfactory. This is favored by the integration of human resources management with planning, i.e., the system of cadre appraisal related to the priorities of the FYPs, which is still a major challenge to implement. The above applies in particular to the non-economic goals of the FYPs in a situation where officials have for years been used to achieving economic goals that determined their promotion opportunities. The impact of cadre evaluation on implementing the plans is still relevant. If the achievements in implementing the plan in a given area are difficult to measure, it is easier to conceal failures, making the basis for the clerical evaluation unclear (Table 36).

Table 36. Main elements of cadre evaluation according to the CPCs management and administration regulations (2019)

No.	Dimension	Characteristic
1	Objective	strengthening the leadership of the CPC, controlling, promoting the implementation of policies, increasing the mobilization to action
2	Evaluation criteria	
	Contribution to maintaining socialist political thought	upholding the supreme role of the CPC, supporting state ideologies; supporting the authority of the CPC, observing the political discipline and principles of the CPC, maintaining democratic centralism
	Leadership	ability to exercise leadership powers, implement reforms, innovate, teamwork skills, risk management
	Assessment of the effects of work	verification of the effects of the activities carried out in the following dimensions: economic, political, cultural, social, environmental; counteracting disproportions in development, efficiency, quality of public services
	Refraining from corruption	honesty, discipline and the fight against corruption and its manifestations

Table 36 *(Continued)*

No.	Dimension	Characteristic
3	Evaluating entities	party committees, with a special role as secretaries of party committees, and, if necessary, evaluation teams appointed by them, acting on behalf of the party committees. The process is administered by the staff of the CPC's organizational units
4	Scope of the assessment	staff of the Central Committee of the CPC, the Standing Committee of the National People's Congress, the State Council with relevant ministries, members of party committee offices, working departments, authorities of various levels (including local ones), officials, other state agencies
5	Consequences	professional promotion, higher ranking in the administrative hierarchy, financial and material rewards, penalties, admonitions, relegation
6	How to conduct the assessment	meetings with management at a given level, interviews with staff, research visits, thematic research, on-site observations, inspections
7	Types of grades	ordinary (management), annual, special (evaluation of important special tasks, including urgent and crisis tasks), timely (evaluation of staff within a given term of office)

Source own study based on: Art. 1, 16, 20–26, 40–55, *Zhonggong zhongyang bangong ting yinfa [dang zheng lingdao ganbu kaohe gongzuo tiaolì] (*中共中央办公厅印发 *[*党政领导干部 考核 工作 条例*]), April 2019*, April 2019, http://www.12371.cn/2019/04/21/ARTI1555845144645728.shtml (access: 22/12/2021); *Chen xi zai dianshi dianhua huiyi shang qiangdiao yi gao zhiliang ganbu kaohe jili dan dang zuowei cujin shiye fazhan* ((陈希 在 电视 电话 会议 上 强调 以 高质量 干部 考核 激励 担当 作为 促进 事业 发展), Xinhua , October 23, 2020, http://www.xinhuanet.com/politics/2020-10/23/c_1126650190.htm (access: 20/11/2021).

In relation to the 11th FYP, the officials of the NDRC[89]admitted that they did not have sufficient human resources and means to verify the degree of implementation of the measures at the provincial level. Furthermore, the pressure of central government to implement the priorities of the FYPs has led to a tendency to report mostly positive data and to avoid reporting in areas where progress is not satisfactory, which means that official statistics should be treated with a certain degree of caution[90]. The low credibility of the collected data causes distortions in the very process of official appraisal. Meanwhile, the personnel appraisal system is an essential element by which the achievement of the goals of development plans is promoted. Their effective linkage with priorities increases

89 Sebastian Heilmann, Oliver Melton, *The Reinvention* …, op. cit., p. 614.
90 Ibid, p. 615.

the effectiveness of the implementation of a given priority. The problem is that, in the personnel evaluation, there are more and more evaluation criteria, which often conflict with each other (e.g., economic goals are contrary to the goals of environmental protection). The detailed criteria for assessing cadre[91] are therefore evolving from typically economic factors (income, economic growth) to an increase in the importance of environmental criteria and those related to social security and the provision of public services.

Top-down mobilization is an inherent feature of the implementation of Chinese regional policy, including Five-Year Plans. Through the personnel evaluation instrument, the center tries to influence the shape and scope of policies implemented at the regional or local level. Thus, the assessment is aimed at aligning the preferences and interests of local personnel with the central government's agenda. As already indicated above, the CPC relies on strict control of positions as well as cadre appraisal, but these institutionalized effects do not always work as originally intended. In the past, incentives and punishments have not been a significant determinant of the career path of local mayors, for example. Research into the CPC membership conditions shows that factional ties with various top leaders matter more to provincial leaders than their development performance[92]. The evidence of the effectiveness of the cadre evaluation is the fact that it influences the maximization of revenues by provincial leaders for the benefit of the central government.

If we treat the implementation of the FYPs, including activities in the field of supporting local competitiveness, as determined mainly by the actions of officials, then we need to pay attention to their behavior in the context of personnel evaluation. These behaviors can be defined as the play of various types of games between central authorities and supreme authorities by representatives of local authorities. In this way, it is possible to indicate various effects, including unintended effects, selective policy implementation, data falsification, and concealing problems with the implementation of centrally set goals. Considering the problem of information asymmetry in the party-government hierarchy, local officials exhibit a variety of behaviors that can be described as games. These behaviors take various forms, from mild to disastrous, but most of all, they constitute a form of local adaptation to the requirements set at the level of superior authorities. Contrary to benign gaming behavior, local officials also engage in a variety of disastrous behaviors, including organizing programs and / or concealing the flaws of careless work and data falsification. The prevalence of

91 Chinese Medical Association Publishing House, *Zhonggong zhongyang bangong ting yinfa [dang zheng lǐngdao ganbu kaohe gongzuo tiaoli]* (中共中央办公厅 印发 [党政 领导 干部 考核 工作 条例]), http://www.cmaph.org/zyhsjygjs/889667.jhtml.

92 Litao Zhao, *Mobilization and Irregularity: Volatile Growth of Educational Expenditure in China*, [in:] Jianxing Yu, Sujian Guo (eds.), *The Palgrave…*, op. cit., p. 549.

different gaming behavior among local officials suggests that the cadre evaluation system has limitations in enforcing compliance with the rules, and therefore with policy objectives. When party leaders are aware of the large mismatch between the objective of the policy and actual implementation on the ground, stronger action is often necessary, involving mobilization from above and even more drastic administrative measures[93].

If the economic situation of the world in the perspective of the 14th FYP will abound in many unforeseeable phenomena, which will translate into the results achieved, the decisive factor will be the ability to adjust the political strategy analyzed here to the conditions in which the rulers will act. It is not only about a passive reaction to the existing situation but also about shaping public policies so that action is proactive. In an authoritarian country like China, this can prove to be a big challenge. China cannot be satisfied with economic growth of a few percent, but desires a double-digit value through the implementation of quality reforms.

93 Jie Gao, *Pernicious Manipulation…* op. cit., pp. 618–637.

Conclusion

In order to assess the challenges and effects of China's regional policy, a broad analytical perspective of public policies has been adopted. In this regard, the systemic approach has proved to be particularly appropriate, especially in the context of the process of shaping regional policy. The question of how effective the central planning system in China is, especially in terms of building regional competitiveness, remains valid. In a country with a hierarchical organizational structure, the regional development planning system is one of the most important instruments for implementing regional policy. Although significant progress has been made recently in achieving the goals of the FYPs, failures cannot be ignored. The effectiveness of implementing previous versions of the plans is not less complex. There is no doubt that purely economic goals, in general, have been implemented to the highest possible degree – it is worse with the implementation of other goals, e.g., environmental goals or compensatory measures related to eliminating limited access to resources or improving the quality of human capital in less developed regions. These are redistributive measures aimed at less-valued individuals and social groups, such as health care in the countryside, reforms of the social security system, and some instruments of the labor market policy.

One of the research questions formulated in the introduction concerned the impact of the evolution of the socioeconomic development model on the shaping of the PRC's regional policy. It should be noted that in various periods of the PRC's operation, the authorities took steps to overcome the development trichotomy in the country (western, central, and eastern macroregions). Many strategies and investment plans have been implemented to stimulate the economic growth and living standards of citizens, for example, in the west of the country, in the northeast and central part, as well as in rural areas. From the perspective of the experience of regional policy implemented in other latitudes, the actions of the Chinese authorities can be considered as standard and, to some extent, resulting from the findings of the theory of regional policy, although in many cases errors were also not avoided. The common denominator of these activities was the desire to stimulate the growth and regional development of backward provincial-level units, as well as to improve the quality of life in these areas. The experience of developed countries confirms that apart from investment support, which, although significant, does not determine the increase in competitiveness, social investments are of key importance, mainly in human resources, active labor market policy, and social integration. So far, China has largely followed the path of various types of investments (mainly in infrastructure), which are intended to build the competitiveness of less developed regions. The above strategy contributed to extraordinary infrastructural development, but still without success in terms of economic, social, and spatial cohesion.

There is no doubt that the effects of China's regional development policy can be attributed to state intervention, which is an important element of its model of socioeconomic development. While a similar claim can be made regarding regional policies in countries with a free-market economic model, China is a special case. The so-called state capitalism pays special attention to the state's policy, its institutions, decisions taken, and instruments used. If the above view is considered correct, the role of institutions in determining the country's development path cannot be overlooked. It is about its influence on management processes in a specific space.

The growing expectations of citizens with regard to the state institutions, and more broadly the public sector, result in more attention being paid to the assessment of activities undertaken as part of public management in relation to the observed phenomena that indicate convergence or divergence. Hence, it is impossible to explain the effects of regional policy solely by means of the variable, which is state intervention. Therefore, it turns out to be necessary to refer also to the effects of management, which are a derivative of market mechanisms – mechanisms that are heavily regulated in relation to the PRC depending on the time ranges we analyze. There are no doubts about the findings that the evolution of China's model of socioeconomic development, and especially the saturation of the economy with elements of free market mechanisms resulting in economic growth, affects the effects of regional policy (hypothesis no. 1).

It should be clearly emphasized that this impact is not always positive, as it leads to an increase in development disproportions or intensification of the negative effects of concentration processes. The strong emphasis on quantity since 1978, leaving the qualitative aspects of economic growth aside, is a prime example of this. The emergence of drastic development disproportions is a challenge for the Chinese political elite not only of a socioeconomic nature but above all of a political one, which may undermine social peace, and thus the leading role of the CPC. While at the initial stage of reforms steady economic growth ensured the legitimacy of the system, there is now an expectation of reducing significant development disproportions. The influence of its model of socioeconomic development on regional policy confirms the way the state is involved in the economy. The Chinese state behaves as a voluntary economic actor (deciding on the allocation of resources), a decision-maker (making directional development decisions), and a regulator (adopting regulations concerning, for example, the investment process or environmental protection). In virtually each of the areas, especially in the first one, this is an impact that goes far beyond the models of free-market economies.

After many years of implementing regional policy, the geographical disparities remain significant. As a result, the chances for the development of individual groups of citizens, and even individuals, are radically different depending on the place of residence. Hence the expectation is to level the disproportions between the rich and poor provinces and to build the foundations for competitiveness. The responsiveness of the authorities to the problems resulting from this fact is one of many elements of its legitimacy. The problem is not only academic when we pay attention to the outflow of people from less developed regions to places offering a greater chance of improving the quality of life. Migration puts an excessive pressure on the development of Chinese cities, so that internal migrants are unable to meet their needs fully. These and other socioeconomic problems of the PRC pose little challenge to the CPC and do not undermine its leading role but are to a large extent an obstacle to the implementation of the country's strategic goals in terms of its dominant role in the world. Among the many aspects of this issue, one is beyond doubt: achieving a high level of innovation will not be possible without tackling, for example, the problem of poverty or drastic development disproportions. Although the Chinese government has been pursuing regional policy for many years, the disproportions still pose a challenge not so much to the authoritarian governance system, but to the socioeconomic development of the country as a whole and, in this context, to the achievement of its long-term development goals (hypothesis no. 2).

Conclusions regarding the place of the region and other local authorities in the political system of the PRC leave no doubt that we are dealing with a high level of centralism when it comes to shaping public policies. It is not different in the case of regional policy. The constitutional principles and the political role of the CPC, consisting of a deep penetration of all public institutions, including individual levels of government, make the position of the center very strong. To this should be added the lack of self-governance in a formal sense, since the administration of a given level is subject not only to the supervisory authorities at their administrative level, but also to higher-level units. The senior people's government may overrule the decisions of the lower administration. Particularly significant is the fact that a given level of superior authority may influence the shaping of finances at a lower level of authority. This means that the policy of the State Council and its agencies (e.g., NDRC) plays a dominant role in financial relations. The reluctance to allow political decentralization results from the historical experiences of the PRC, leading to internal particularisms and the development of centrifugal forces, which are considered one of the greatest threats by Chinese political decision makers.

According to the principle of centralism, regional policy is shaped by actions planned from the top. The main instrument of the regional policy defined in this way is multiannual planning. The FYPs are an expression of thinking about development from the perspective of the center, which, while unifying various dimensions of development, takes little account of the local specificity related to the stage of socioeconomic development reached by a given region. This is not only because of constitutional principles but also because of the CPC's role in the Middle Kingdom. The CPC's disciplinary role fosters a top-down approach. In addition, the party ensures central coordination of activities. Thus, local governments have the task of implementing the activities or instruments that are planned at the central level. This often leads to an implementation gap, i.e., the lack of full implementation, due to the fact that the applied measures do not fully match the local specificity. Hence, the hypothesis that Chinese centralism is the main feature of the implementation of regional development activities (hypothesis no. 3) is confirmed.

The findings leave no doubt that the size and complex structure of the government administration determines the effectiveness of policymaking, which determines social stability, progress, and economic development. Although in the PRC we are dealing (de facto) with a one-party authoritarian system, and with it a high degree of top-down central control and initiative, local authorities, including party cadres, have many opportunities to shape, control, or obstruct the implementation of policies including regional policy. Given the sheer size of the country and its potential population, local administrative structures can therefore influence the ability of the entire political system to achieve the desired results. Decentralization in the Chinese political system is present as long as particularisms and centrifugal forces do not begin to dominate, destroying the desired social peace. There are similar manifestations of centralization, which the authorities associate with the expected social peace. They are present to the extent that problems related to the control of the state, including those at the level of local authorities, do not dominate but ensure a minimum level of adaptability.

The relations of the central and subnational authorities in shaping the regional policy reflect the principal-agent relations. In this approach, the central authority delegates certain tasks, and lower-level authorities are obliged to perform them. At the same time, subnational authorities and, in particular, the provinces, due to their powers, perform the role of the superior over the area under their jurisdiction. The role of a principal by subnational authorities is the legacy of the country's transition to an economy model based to a greater extent on market mechanisms. It is not possible to develop the factors of a free market economy only from the central level; the key stakeholder here is subnational authorities (regional and local). The findings made in this book confirm that the hierarchical way of shaping actions for regional development dominates the way of organizing the policy, although it is also possible to identify complementary actions, based on a bottom-up approach, which contribute to the effects of the policy (hypothesis no. 4).

Asymmetric decentralization is also characteristic of China, which can be observed in two dimensions. First, there are certain areas in which it is possible to identify solutions that determine the transfer of competences to a lower level. There are also areas where this process does not take place. Thus, we are dealing with the presence of decentralization elements in the economic dimension, such as fiscal or partially administrative decentralization, but at the same time with the maintenance of control mechanisms in the political dimension, mainly through the CPC. Second, the dimension of asymmetric decentralization is related to the diversification of competences of, for example, provinces in the political, administrative, and fiscal areas. In other words, units representing the same administrative level (e.g., provinces) have different legal, organizational, and factual status. It should be noted that in China, decentralization is not linear, as there are reforms that aim towards (re)centralization, mainly because of the unexpected effects of decentralization. In practice, we never deal with total centralization or with pure decentralization, rather with a mixture of both.

An important point in considering China's regional policy is its adaptability to the challenges faced by the entire country and individual regions. When analyzing the evolution of regional policy and in particular central regional planning, it should be noted that before China opened up to the world in the late 1970s, the policy discussed here was primarily intended to support economic construction (industrialization of the country). From the 1990s, the PRC influenced the transformation of spatial management. Based on the analysis of central planning, it can be concluded that the expected adaptability takes place in most of the provisions of the FYPs: the challenges and general development goals of the Middle Kingdom were accurately defined.

While the general regional policy at the central level responds to the economic challenges of the PRC, there is still a lot to do at the local level, mainly in the context of increasing the powers of local governments to spend funds under macroregional programs. It should also be added that social problems are underestimated at the expense of infrastructure investments, which are treated like the holy grail, and are supposed to be a remedy for any type of socioeconomic backwardness and the resulting consequences. In the confrontation of central and local interests, the former, despite many games undertaken by local authorities, win (hypothesis no. 5).

In the context of adaptability, it is also appropriate to evaluate the most frequently used instruments of regional policy; public investment, special economic zones, foreign direct investment, and clusters constitute the repertoire of both general economic policy and, in a narrower sense, regional policy. In this context, their use undoubtedly contributed to the consistently high economic growth of the country as a whole. However, its assessment from the regional perspective cannot be so unambiguously positive. This is because the use of an instrument at one latitude does not mean that there will be similar positive effects in another region. Looking from the perspective of the last four decades, the use of these tools in such a way as to stimulate the development of the eastern coastal regions in the first place has led to the development disproportions analyzed in this paper, and hence to some problems. Although these disproportions were understandable at the initial stage of the economic transformation of the PRC, they should not constitute the economic landscape of Chinese regions, exposed to the intensification of the effects of concentration and deconcentration – concentration of production and services mainly in the area of eastern provinces and deconcentration in the provinces of central and western China.

The last research question relates to the extent to which the implementation of regional policy is a process in which there is room for reflection and learning about its subject, i.e., regional development. Finally, what is the role of these elements in light of the results of the regional policy? Increasing the effectiveness of implementing public policies in China is accompanied by a variety of activities that derive from the specificity of the functioning of the country's political system, from central mechanisms of political communication, through setting and adjusting political priorities, to introducing new activities and policies. Here, an important role is played by experiments carried out at the local level. Experimenting in the shaping of regional policy may be surprising in the context of the main features of an authoritarian political system in which hierarchy and centralization are at the fore. It turns out that this system tends to take into account also secondary organizational goals articulated by various entities, e.g., national agencies and regions (the so-called fragmentary authoritarianism).

It was identified that experimenting in two dimensions, i.e., testing individual solutions and developing new strategic variants, is particularly important for the regional policy. Participation in pilot projects gives local governments greater discretionary freedom, which is why they are often interested in participating in the process. Experiments often lead to the generation of innovative solutions, also in the sphere of public management. The identified case studies indicate that the solutions developed are not so much breakthrough organizational innovations as specific simplifications and facilitations. To some extent, they represent a new, distinctive quality compared to the practices used so far. At the same time, experimenting in a limited way results in increased freedom of action at the local level (in the sense of permanent decentralization). In the long term, treated as a standard administrative practice, it may lose its importance in formulating model solutions, and thus in terms of adaptability.

Another aspect of reflectivity and learning in the implementation process of regional policy is the cadre evaluation system, the main feature of which is bridging the implementation gap. A review of the principles and criteria indicated that evaluation principles do not take into account the goals and determinants of regional development in an optimal way. From this perspective, the system brings unexpected results. Central supervision imposed on lower-level units is accompanied by local adaptation activities in the form of undertaking various types of games aimed at demonstrating the implementation of top-down goals. The identified actions have a common denominator: local staff, where they are not interested in implementing irrational goals from a local perspective, act to survive or stand out in the evaluation of administrative performance. Furthermore, the lack of public evaluation interventions commonly used in the judgment process makes China's regional policy only partially reflective (hypothesis no. 6).

Based on the study of Chinese authorities' actions aimed at stimulating the competitiveness of less developed regions, it can be concluded that their effects of leveling development disproportions are moderate. In fact, these activities did not unequivocally contribute to reducing the gap between the West and the East, but rather to restoring the development balance of less developed macroregions. The accompanying program slogans, such as the "great development" of the western macroregion, will probably not come true in a short time, but reflect the political weight of the topic of combating development inequalities. Despite their limited effectiveness, such measures should be assessed positively as they provide opportunities (but not guarantees) for further improvement of the regional development policy. If we recognize that the basic dilemma of the policy discussed here is equality or efficiency, then none of these elements gains a clear advantage in relation to the practical regional policy of the PRC. Looking to the future, one thing is certain: reducing regional development disparities in China will be a combination of a pro-market policy and a pro-intervention state policy.

Bibliography

Source Materials

Ankang shi renmin zhengfu bangongshi guanyu yinfa 2019 nian baozhuang yinyong shui chanye fazhan gongzuo shishi fangan de tong (安康市人民政府办公室关于印发 2019 年包装饮用水产业发展工作实施方案 的通), [in:] http://www.ankang.gov.cn/Content-175443.html.

Ankang shi renmin zhengfu bangongshi guanyu yinfa ankang shi shenru shishi guoqi guozi gaige gongjian jiakuai tujdong gao zhiliang fazhan san nian xingdong fangan (2018–2020 nian) de tong (安康 市人民政府办公室 关于印发 实施国企国资改革市深入加快市 深入资高质量发展三年行动方案 [2018–2020 年] 的通), [in:] http://www.ankang.gov.cn/Content-164371.html.

Annual Report 2012, Ping An Insurance. 2012, [in:] https://www1.hkexnews.hk/listedco/listconews/sehk/2013/0327/ltn201303271176.pdf.

Annual Report 2019. Ping An Insurance. 2020, [in:] http://www.pingan.cn/app_upload/images/info/upload/a74ffb10-16be-4415-b9b3-a365225049fe.pdf.

Beijing Municipal Commission of Planning and Natural Resources, [in:] http://english.beijing.gov.cn/government/departments/202006/t20200627_1932942.html.

Chengdu shi huanjing baohu "shisanwu" guihua (成都市环境保护 "十三 五" 规划), [in:] http://gk.chengdu.gov.cn/govInfo/detail.action?id=1637357&tn=2.

Chengdu shi renmin zhengfu guanyu yinfa chengdu shi rongru "yidai yilu" jianshe san nian xingdong jihua (2019–2021 nian) de tongzhi (成都市人民政府关于印发成都市 融入"一带一路"建设三年行动计划 [2019–2021 年]的通知), [in:] http://gk.chengdu.gov.cn/uploadfiles/070354020302/2019110615402415.docx.

China Overtakes the US as the World's Largest Economy, [in:] https://www.iimk.ac.in/libportal/reports/China-Overtakes-US-Worlds-Largest-Economy-White-Paper Euromonitor-Report.pdf.

China Statistics Press, China Statistical Yearbook 2019.

Constitution of The Communist Party of China Revised and adopted at the 19th National Congress of the Communist Party of China on October 24, 2017, [in:] http://www.xinhuanet.com//english/download/Constitution_of_the_Communist_Party_of_China.pdf.

Constitution of the People's Republic of China (full text after amendment on March 14, 2004), http://www.npc.gov.cn/zgrdw/englishnpc/Constitution/2007-11/15/content_1372963.htm.

Dazao fa zhongguo liangli mingpian fazhi guojia, fazhi zhengfu, fazhi shehui ti jianshe (打造法中国亮丽名片法治国家、法治政府、法治社会 -体建设) on November 5, 2020, [in:] http://www.gov.cn/xinwen/2020-11/15/content_5561619.htm.

Dongbei diqu zhenxing guihua (东北地区振兴规划), [in:] http://www.gov.cn/gzdt/2007-08/20/content_721632.htm.

Guanyu chengdu shi chengshi guidao jiaotong di si qi jianshe guihua (2019–2024 nian) (关于成都市城市轨道交通第四期建设规划 [2019–2024 年]), [in:] https://zfxxgk.ndrc.gov.cn/web/iteminfo.jsp?id=16259.

Guanyu shanghai shi chengshi guidao jiaotong di san qi jianshe guihua (2018–2023 nian) de pifu (fa gai jichu [2018] 1831 hao) (关于上海市 城市轨道交通第三期建设规划 [2018–2023年])的批复(发改基础 [2018] 1831 号), [in:] https://zfxxgk.ndrc.gov.cn/web/iteminfo.jsp?id=15942.

Guanyu shishi jiangsu sheng yiwu jiaoyu kecheng shezhi shiyan fangan luoshi zhong xiaoxue zonghe shijian huodong kecheng keshi de zhidao yijian (关于实施江苏省义务教育课程设置实验方案落实中小学综合课时活动课程指导意见), August 31, 2018, [in:] http://www.yangzhou.gov.cn/yangzhou/bmwj/201808/b4b2e9ec3b34436a87faa6038a879698.shtml.

Guanyu tiao zheng nanchang shi chengshi guidao jiaotong di er qi jianshe guihua fangan de pifu (关于调整 南昌市 城市 轨道 交通 第二 期 建设 规划 方案 的 批复), [in:] https://zfxxgk.ndrc.gov.cn/web/iteminfo.jsp?id=17547.

Guanyu wuhan shi chengshi guidao jiaotong di si qi jianshe guihua (2019–2024 nian) de pifu (fa gai jichu [2018] 1915 hao) zhengfu xinxi gongkai_zhengwu gongkai-guojia fazhan gaige wei (关于武汉市第四期轨道 轨道建设规划 [2019–2024 年]) 的 批复 (发改基础 [2018] 1915 号 政府 信息 公开 政务公开-国家发展改革 委), [in:] https://zfxxgk.ndrc.gov.cn/web/iteminfo.jsp?id=16071.

Guanyu yanxu xibu da kaifa qiye suodeshui zhengce de gonggao (关于延续西部 大开发企业所得税 政策 的 公告), [in:] http://www.gov.cn/zhengce/zhengceku/2020-04/28/content_5506990.htm.

Guanyu yinfa [di reneng kaifa lìyong shisanwu "guihua"] de tongzhi (关于印发 [地热能开发利用 "十三五" 规划] 的通知), [in:] https://www.ndrc.gov.cn/xxgk/zcfb/ghwb/201702/t20170204_962227.html?code=&state=123.

Guanyu yinfa "jie shui xing shehui jianshe" shisanwu "guihua" de tongzhi (fa gai huan zi [2017] 128 hao) (关于印发 [节水型 社会建设 "十三五" 规划]) 的 通知 (发改环 资 [2017] 128号), [in:] https://zfxxgk.ndrc.gov.cn/web/iteminfo.jsp?id=407.

Guanyu yinfa [liangshi wuliu ye "shisanwu" fazhan guihua] de tongzhi (fa gai jingmao [2017] 432 hao) (关于印发 [粮食物流业"十三五"发展规划] 的通知 (发改经贸 [2017] 432 号), [in:] https://zfxxgk.ndrc.gov.cn/web/iteminfo.jsp?id=415.

Guanyu yinfa [quanguo haishui liyong "shisanwu" guihua] de tongzhi (fa gai huan zi [2016] 2764 hao) (关于印发 [全国海水 利用 "十三五" 规划] 的 通知 (发改环 资 [2016] 2764 号), [in:] https://zfxxgk.ndrc.gov.cn/web/iteminfo.jsp?id=401.

Guanyu yinfa [quanguo nongcun jingji fazhan "shisanwu" guihua] de tongzhi (关于印发 [全国农村经济发展 "十三五" 规划] 的通知 (发改农经), [in:] https://zfxxgk.ndrc.gov.cn/web/iteminfo.jsp?id=389.

Guanyu yinfa [quanguo nongcun zhaoqi fazhan "shisanwu" guihua] de tongzhi (fa gai nong jing [2017] 178 hao) (关于印发 [全国农村沼气发展 "十三五" 规划] 的 通知 (发改农经 [2017] 178号), [in:] https://zfxxgk.ndrc.gov.cn/web/iteminfo.jsp?id=413.

Guanyu yìnfa ["shisanwu" quanguo chengzhen shenghuo lese wu hai hua chuli sheshi jianshe guihua] de tongzhi (fa gai huan zi [2016] 2851 hao) (关于印发 ["十三 五" 全国城镇生活 垃圾 无害 化处理设施建设规划] 的 通知 (发改环 资 [2016] 2851 号), [in:] https://zfxxgk.ndrc.gov.cn/web/iteminfo.jsp?id=409.
Guanyu yìnfa ["shisanwu" quanguo chengzhen wushui chuli ji zaisheng liyong sheshi jianshe guihua de tongzhi (关于印发 ["十三五" 全国城镇污水处理及再生利用设施建设规划] 的通知), [in:] https://zfxxgk.ndrc.gov.cn/web/iteminfo.jsp?id=408.
Guanyu yinfa ["shisanwu" shengwu chanye fazhan guihua] de tongzhi (fa gai gao ji [2016] 2665 hao) (关于印发 ["十三 五" 生物产业发展规划] 的 通知 (发 改 高 技 [2016] 2665 号), [in:] https://zfxxgk.ndrc.gov.cn/web/iteminfo.jsp?id=404.
Guanyu yinfa [tielu "shisanwu" fazhan gui] de tongzhi (fa gai jichu [2017] 1996 hao) (关于印发 [铁路 "十三五" 发展规划] 的 通知 (发改基础 [2017] 1996 号), [in:] https://zfxxgk.ndrc.gov.cn/web/iteminfo.jsp?id=430.
Guanyu yinfa changjiang sanjiaozhau chengshi qun fazhan guihua de tongzhi (关于印发长江 三角洲 城市 群发展规划的 通知), [in:] https://zfxxgk.ndrc.gov.cn/web/iteminfo.jsp?id=358.
Guanyu yinfa cujin zhongbu diqu jueqi "shisanwu" guihua de tongzhi (fa gai diqu [2016] 2664 hao) (关于印发促进中部地区崛起"十三五"规划的通知) (发改地区 [2016] 2664 号), [in:] https://zfxxgk.ndrc.gov.cn/web/iteminfo.jsp?id=399.
Guanyu yinfa danjiangkou ku qu ji shangyou shui wuran fangzhi hi shuitu baochi "shisanwu" guihua de tongzhi (fa gai diqu [2017] 1002 hao) (关于印发丹江口库区及 上游水污染防治 和 水土保持 "十三 五" 规划的 通知) (发改 地区 [2017] 1002 号), [in:] https://zfxxgk.ndrc.gov.cn/web/iteminfo.jsp?id=14169.
Guanyu yìnfa guojia zhongda keji jichu sheshi jianshe "shisanwu" guihua de tongzhi (fa gai gao ji [2016] 2736 hao) (关于印发国家 重大 科技 基础 设施 建设"十三 五" 规划 的 通知) (发 改 高 技 [2016] 2736 号), [in:] https://zfxxgk.ndrc.gov.cn/web/iteminfo.jsp?id=403.
Guanyu yinfa nengyuan fazhan "shisanwu" guihua de tongzhi) (fa gai nengyuan [2016] 2744 hào) (关于印发能源发展 "十三五" 规划的通知) (发改能源 [2016] 2744 号), [in:] https://zfxxgk.ndrc.gov.cn/web/iteminfo.jsp?id=405.
Guanyu yìnfa quanguo "shisanwu" yi di fupin banqian guihua de tongzhi) (fa gai diqu [2016] 2022 hoo) (关于印发全国 "十三 五" 易地扶贫搬迁规划的 通知) (发改 地区 [2016] 2022号), [in:] https://zfxxgk.ndrc.gov.cn/web/iteminfo.jsp?id=387.
Guanyu yinfa quanguo qixiang fazhan "shisanwu" guihua de tongzhi) (qi fa [2016] 62 hào) (关于印发全国气象发展 "十三五" 规划的通知) (气发 [2016] 62 号), [in:] https://zfxxgk.ndrc.gov.cn/web/iteminfo.jsp?id=373.
Guanyu yinfa shiyou tianranqi fazhan "shisanwu" guīhua de tongzhi) (fa gai nengyuan [2016] 2743 hao) (关于印发石油 天然气发展 "十三 五" 规划的 通知) (发改 能源 [2016] 2743 号) [in:] https://zfxxgk.ndrc.gov.cn/web/iteminfo.jsp?id=406.
Guanyu yinfa tianjin binhai xinqu zonghe peitao gaige shiyan zongti fangan de tongzhi (关于印发天津滨海新区综合配套 改革试验总体方案 的 通知), [in:] https://www.dongjiang.gov.cn/contents /26/4367.html.
Guanyu yinfa xibu da kaifa "shisanwu" guihua de tongzhi) (fa gai xibu [2017] 89 hao) (国家发展改革委关于印发西部大开发"十三五" 规划的通知发改西部 [2017] 89 号), [in:] https://zfxxgk.ndrc.gov.cn/web/iteminfo.jsp?id=410.

Guanyu yinfameitan gongye fazhan "shisanwu" guihua de tongzhi (fa gai nengyuan [2016] 2714 hao) (关于印发煤炭 工业 发展 "十三 五" 规划 的 通知 (发 改 能源 [2016] 2714 号), [in:] https://zfxxgk.ndrc.gov.cn/web/iteminfo.jsp?id=400.

Guanyu yue gangao da wan qu cheng ji tielu jianshe guihua de pifu (关于 粤 港澳 大 湾区 城际铁路建设规划的 批复), [in:] https://zfxxgk.ndrc.gov.cn/web/iteminfo.jsp?id=17203.

Guo wei (郭 巍): Guanche xin fazhan linian, tuidong gao zhiliang fazhan (贯彻新发展理念，推动高质量发展) [in:] https://www.ndrc.gov.cn/xxgk/jd/wsdwhfz/202101/t20210121_1265442.html.

Guojia fazhan gaige wei bumen juesuan [2019 niandu] (国家发展改革 委部门决算 [2019 年度]), [in:] https://zfxxgk.ndrc.gov.cn/web/iteminfo.jsp?id=17169.

Guojia fazhan gaige wei guanyu jiangsu sheng yanjiang chengshi qun cheng ji tielu jianshe guihua (2019–2025 nian) de pi (国家发展改革 委 关于江苏省 沿江 城市 群 城际铁路建设规划 [2019–2025 年] 的 批), [in:] https://zfxxgk.ndrc.gov.cn/web/iteminfo.jsp?id=16070.

Guojia fazhan gaige wei guanyu y infa changjiang sanjiaozhou diqu quyu guihua de tongzhi (国家发展改革 委 关于印发 长江三角洲 地区 区域规划的 通知), [in:] http://www.gov.cn/zwgk/2010-06/22/content_1633868.htm.

Guojia fazhan gaige wei guanyu yinfa xibu da kaifa "shisanwu" guihua de tongzhi fa gaii xibu [2017] 89 hao) (国家发展改革 委 关于印发 西部 大开发 "十三 五" 规划的 通知 发改 西部 [2017] 89 号), [in:] https://zfxxgk.ndrc.gov.cn/web/iteminfo.jsp?id=410.

Guojia fazhan gaige wei zhufang chengxiang jianshe bu guanyu yinfa beibu wan chengshi qun fazhan guihua de tongzhi (国家发展改革委 住房城乡建设部关于印发北部 湾城市群发展 规划的通知), [in:] https://zfxxgk.ndrc.gov.cn/web/iteminfo.jsp?id=414.

Guatachyuan bangong ting guanyu quanmian tuiin jiceng zhengwu gongkai bia zhunhua guifànhua gongzuo de zhidao yijian guo ban fa (国务院办公厅关于 全面推进 基层政务公开标准化规范化工作的指导意见国办发), [in:] http://www.gov.cn/zhengce/zhengceku/2020-01/08/content_5467526.htm.

Guasuyuan guanyu chengli gu persuyuan xibu diqu kaifa lingdao xiaozu de jueding (国务院关于 成立国务院西部地区开发领导小组的决定), [in:] http://www.law-lib.com/law/law_view1.asp?id=15782.

Guasuyuan guanyu cujin zhongbu diqu jueqi "shisanwu" guihua de pifu (国务院关于促进中部 地区 崛起 "十三 五" 规划的 批复), [in:] http://www.gov.cn/zhengce/content/2016-12/23/content_5151840.htm.

Guasuyuan guanyu jiaqiang guomin jingji he shehui fazhan guihua bianzhi gongzuo de ruogan yijian (国务院关于加强国民经济和 社会发展规划编制工作的若干意见), [in:] http://www.gov.cn/zwgk/2005-10/26/content_84417.htm.

Guasuyuan guanyu xibu da kaifa "shierwu" guihua de pfui guo han [2012] 8 hao (国务院关于西部大开发 "十二五" 规划的批复国函 [2012] 8 号), [in:] http://www.gov.cn/zwgk/2012-02/21/content_2072227.htm.

Guasuyuan guanyu xibu da kaifa "shierwu" guihua de pi (国务院关于 西部 大开发 "十二五" 规划的 批), [in:] http://www.gov.cn/gongbao/content/2012/content_2076107.htm.

Guasuyuan guanyu xību da kaifa "shisanwu" guihua de pifu (国务院关于西部大开发 "十三 五" 规划的 批复), [in:] https://zfxxgk.ndrc.gov.cn/web/fileread.jsp?id=254.

Guasuyuan guanyu xibu da kaifa "shiyiwu" guihua de pifu (国务院关于 西部 大开发 "十一 五" 规划的 批 复), [in:] http://www.gov.cn/gongbao/content/2007/content_549035.htm.

Guasuyuan guanyu yinfa zhongguo (hubei) ziyou maoyi shiyan qu zongti fangan de tongzhi (国务院关于印发中国 (湖北) 自由贸易试验区总体方案的通知), [in:] http://www.gov.cn/zhengce/content/2017-03/31/content_5182299.htm.

Guasuyuan guanyu yinfa zhongguo (hubei) ziyou maoyi shiyan qu zongti fangan de tongzhi (国务院关于印发中国 (湖北) 自由贸易试验区总体方案的通知), [in:] http://www.pkulaw.cn/fulltext_form.aspx?Db=chl&Gid=075ecd80219ce5a0bdfb&keyword=&EncodingName=&Search_Mode=accurate&Search_IsTitle=0.

Haishang sichou zhi lu bei qidian zai qihang qingdao zheng qiangzhan xian ji (海上丝绸之路北 起点 "再 起航青岛正抢占先机), [in:] http://m.dzwww.com/d/news/12081232.html.

Hu yue shisiwu guihua "zouxiang quanqiu", zhongguo chengshi li "shijie ji" you duo yuan (沪粤十四五规划 "走向全球", 中国城市离 "世界级" 有多远), [in:] https://m.thepaper.cn/baijiahao_10856159.

Hubei yi huo pi quanguo di san pi zi mao qu yongbao zi mao qu gaige gaodi zai chufa (湖北已获批全国第三批自贸区拥抱自贸区改革高地再出发), [in:] http://www.hubei.gov.cn/zwgk/hbyw/hbywqb/201609/t20160926_900568.shtml.

Hubei zi mao shiyan qu: Gaoduan chanya gouzhu fazhan xin shineng (湖北自贸试验区： 高端产业构筑发展新势能), [in:] http://www.gov.cn/xinwen/2018-11/22/content_5342600.htm?zbs_baidu_bk.

Luse chanye shifan jidi mingdan (绿色 产业 示范 基地 名单), [in:] https://www.ndrc.gov.cn/xxgk/zcfb/tz/202101/P020210108597098679981.pdf.

National Bureau of Statistics of China 2021.

National Bureau of Statistics of China, *China Statistical Yearbook 2018,* [in:] http://www.stats.gov.cn/tjsj/ndsj/2018/indexeh.htm.

National Development and Reform Commission, Ministry of Foreign Affairs, Ministry of Commerce of the People's Republic of China, *Vision and Actions on Jointly Building Silk Road Economic Belt and 21st-Century Maritime Silk Road,* March 28, 2015 [in:] http://cb.mofcom.gov.cn/article/ydyl/201504/20150400930895.shtml.

OECD, OECD Economic Surveys: China 2019, OECD Publishing, Paris 2019, [in:] https://doi.org/10.1787/eco_surveys-chn-2019-en.

OECD / UCLG, *2019 Report of the World Observatory on Subnational Government Finance and Investment – Key Findings,* 2019.

Qu qing jieshao (区情介绍), [in:] http://www.tjbh.gov.cn/channels/6254.html.

Quanguo haiyang jingji fazhan "shisanwu" guihua (全国海洋经济发展 "十三五" 规划), [in:] https://zfxxgk.ndrc.gov.cn/web/iteminfo.jsp?id=419.

Quanguo zhongyao shengtai xitong baohu he xiufu zhongda gongcheng zongti guihua (2021–2035 nian) (全国重要生态系统保护和 修复重大工程总体规划 [2021–2035年]), [in:] https://zfxxgk.ndrc.gov.cn/web/fileread.jsp?id=3443.

Shangwu bu guanyu zhichi zhongguo (hubei) ziyou maoyi shiyan qu jiakuai fazhan ruogan cuoshi de tongzhi (商务部关于 支持 中国 (湖北) 自由贸易试验区 加快发展若干 措施 的通知), [in:] http://www.pkulaw.cn/fulltext_form.aspx?Db=chl&Gid=40fadadb43e5f6d4bdfb&keyword=&EncodingName=&Search_Mode=accurate&Search_IsTitle=0.

Shanxi sheng "shisanwu" huanjing baohu guihua (陕西省"十三五"环境保护规划), [in:] http://www.shaanxi.gov.cn/zfxxgk/fdzdgknr/ghxx/sswgh/gmjjhshfzgh_2438/201703/t20170320_1662133.html.

Shanxi sheng "shisanwu" tiyu shiye fazhan guihua (陕西省"十三五"体育事业发展规划), [in:] http://www.shaanxi.gov.cn/zfxxgk/fdzdgknr/ghxx/sswgh/gmjjhshfzgh_2438/201703/t20170321_1662249.html.

Sheng fazhan gaige wei guanyu yinfa hubei sheng 2018 nian sheng ji zhongdian jianshe jihua de tongzhi (省发展改革委关于印发湖北省2018年省级重点建设计划的通知), [in:] http://fgw.hubei.gov.cn/fbjd/xxgkml/zdjsxm/zdjsxmqd/201802/t20180209_1012460.shtml.

Sheng zheng qiang sichou zhi lu he haishang sichou zhi lu jianshe jiyu (省争抢丝绸之路和海上丝绸之路建设机遇), [in:] https://business.sohu.com/20140214/n394972816.shtml.

Shi fazhan gaige wei guanyu bianzhi 2021 nian shi ji zhengfu touzi jihua he 2021–2023 nian gundong touzi jihua de tongzhi (市发展改革委关于编制 2021 年市级政府投资计划和 2021–2023 年滚动投资计划的通知), [in:] http://fgw.wuhan.gov.cn/zfxxgk/zfxxgk_4/czzj/czzxzj/202009/t20200914_1477160.html.

Shi renmin zhengfu guanyu yinfa wuhan shi tuijin zhizao ye yu hulianwang ronghe fazhan xingdong jihua (2016–2020 nian) de tongzhi (市人民政府关于印发武汉市推进制造业与互联网融合发展行动计划 [2016–2020 年] 的通知), [in:] http://www.wuhan.gov.cn/zwgk/xxgk/zfwj/gfxwj/202003/t20200316_973261.shtml.

State Council, *Opinions of the State Council on Reforming and Improving the System of Transfer Payment Made by the Central Government to Local Governments*, 27.12.2014, [in:] http://lawinfochina.com/display.aspx?id=26568&lib=law.

The 13th Five-year Plan for Economic and Social Development of The People's Republic of China (2016–2020), announced on December 7, 2016, [in:] https://en.ndrc.gov.cn/policyrelease_8233/201612/P020191101482242850325.pdf.

The Civil Servant Law of the People's Republic of China. 2005, [in:] http://www.asianlii.org/cn/legis/cen/laws/tcslotproc462.

The Practice of the "One Country, Two Systems" Policy in the Hong Kong Special Administrative Region, [in:] http://ls.chineseembassy.org/eng/ci/t1164027.htm.

The State Council, The People's Republic of China, The National Medium- and Long-Term Program for Science and Technology Development (2006–2020), Bejing 2006, [in:] https://www.itu.int/en/ITU-D/Cybersecurity/Documents/National_Strategies_Repository/China_2006.pdf.

The World Bank, Final consumption expenditure (% of GDP), [in:] https://data.worldbank.org/indicator/ne.con.totl.zs.

The World Observatory on Subnational Government Finance and Investment, *2019 Edition of the World Observatory of Subnational Finance and Investment, Country Profiles*, [in:] http://www.sng-wofi.org/publications/SNGWOFI_2019_report_country_profiles.pdf.

Three-year Action Plan for Protecting Beijing's Blue Skies, [in:] http://english.beijing.gov.cn/government/lawsandpolicies/202007/t20200723_1957181.html.

Tianjin tuijin binhai xinqu zonghe peitao gaige shiyan zongti fangan shishi (天津推进滨海新区综合配套改革试验总体方案实施), [in:] http://www.gov.cn/gzdt/2008-12/01/content_1164813.htm.

World Bank and the Development Research Center of China's State Council, *China 2030: Building a Modern, Harmonious, and Creative High-Income Society*, Washington 2012.

World Observatory on Subnational Government Finance and Investment, *SNG expenditure by type, % of GDP,* [in:] https://www1.compareyourcountry.org/subnational-government-finance-and-investment/en/1/all/default.

Xību da kaifa "shierwu" guihua guojia fazhan he gaige weiyuanhui er ling yier nian er yue (西部大开发 "十二五" 规划国家发展和改革委员会二〇一二年二月), [in:] http://guoqing.china.com.cn/zwxx/2012-02/21/content_24691623.htm.

Yu yinfa (yanrong diqu shi mo hua zonghe zhili gongcheng "shisanwu" jianshe guihua) de tongzhi (fa gai nong jing [2016] 624 hao) (于印发 (岩溶 地区 石漠化 综合 治理工程"十三五" 建设规划)的通知 (发改农经 [2016] 624号), [in:] https://zfxxgk.ndrc.gov.cn/web/iteminfo.jsp?id=353.

Zhengfu gongzuo baogao ((政府工作报告) 政府工作报告), [in:] http://www.gov.cn/ztzl/2006-03/15/content_227782.htm.

Zhengfu xinxi gongkai zhinan (政府 信息 公开 指南), [in:] https://zfxxgk.ndrc.gov.cn/web/default.jsp.

Zhichi zhongguo (hubei) ziyou maoyi shiyan qu shenhua gaige chuangxin ruogan cuoshi de tongzhi (支持中国 (湖北) 自由贸易试验区深化改革创新若干措施 的通知)支持中国（湖北） 自由贸易试验区深化改革创新若干措施的通知), [in:] http://www.wehdz.gov.cn/zmq/zcfg_22854/pqzcfg/202102/t20210209_1633195.shtml.

Zhineng peizhi he nei she jigou (职能配置与内设机构), [in:] https://www.ndrc.gov.cn/fzggw/bnpz/.

Zhonggong zhongyang bangong ting yinfa [dang zheng lingdao ganbu kaohe gongzuo tiaolì] (中共中央办公厅印发 [党政领导干部 考核 工作 条例]), April 2019, [in:] http://www.12371.cn/2019/04/21/ARTI1555845144645728.shtml.

Zhonggong zhongyang guanyu zhiding guomin jingji he shehui fazhan di shi ge wu nian jihua de jianyi (中共中央 关于 制定国民经济和 社会发展第十 个 五年计划的建议), [in:] http://www.gov.cn/gongbao/content/2000/content_60538.htm.

Zhonggong zhongyang gu persuyuan guanyu jianli jianquan chengxiang ronghe fazhan tizhi jizhi he zhengce tixi de yijian (中共中央国务院关于建立健全城乡融合发展 体制机制和政策体系的意见), [in:] http://www.gov.cn/zhengce/2019-05/05/content_5388880.htm.

Zhonggong zhongyang gu persuyuan guanyu xin shidai tuijin xibu da kaifa xingcheng xin gay de zhidao yijian (中共中央国务院关于 新时代推进西部 大开发 形成新 格局 的指导意见), [in:] http://www.gov.cn/xinwen/2020-05/17/content_5512456.htm.

Zhonggong zhongyang yinfa fazhi zhongguo jianshe guihua (2020–2025 nian) (中共中央印发《法治 中国建设规划 [2020–2025 年]) January 10, 2021, [in:] http://www.gov.cn/zhengce/2021-01/10/content_5578659.htm.

Zhongguo gongchandang di shijiu jie zhongyang weiyuanhui di wu ci quanti huiyi gongbao (受权发布中国共产党第十九届中央委员会第五次全体会议公报), [in:] http://www.xinhuanet.com/2020-10/29/c_1126674147.htm.

Zhongguo gongchandang di shijiu jie zhongyang weiyuanhui di wu ci quanti huiyi gongbao (中国共产党第十九届中央委员会第五次全体会议公报), [in:] http://www.gov.cn/xinwen/2020-10/29/content_5555877.htm.

Zhongguo guojia tongji ju, Zhonghua renmin gongheguo 2019 nian guomin jingji he shehui fazhan tongji gongbao (中国国家统计局, 中华人民共和国 2019 年国民经济和 社会发展统计公报), [in:] http://www.stats.gov.cn/tjsj/zxfb/202002/t20200228_1728913.html.

Zhonghua renmin gongheguo guomin jingji he shehui fazhan di shi ge wu nian jihua gangyao (中华人民共和国 国民经济和 社会发展第十 个 五年计划纲要), [in:] http://www.npc.gov.cn/wxzl/gongbao/2001-03/19/content_5134505.htm.
Zhonghua renmin gongheguo guomin jingji he shehui fazhan di shisi ge wu nian guihua he 2035 nian yuanjing mubiao gangyao (中华人民共和国国民经济和社会发展第十四个五年规划 和2035年远景目标纲要), [in:] http://www.gov.cn/xinwen/2021-03/13/content_5592681.htm.
Zhonghua renmin gongheguo tongji fa (中华人民共和国统计法), [in:] http://www.stats.gov.cn/zjtj/tjfg/tjfl/200906/t20090629_8791.html.
Zhujiang sanjiaozhou diqu gaige fazhan guihua gangyao (2008–2020) (珠江三角洲 地区改革发展规划纲要 [2008–2020]), [in:] http://www.scio.gov.cn/ztk/xwfb/52/9/Document/1057059/1057059.htm.
Zhuoli tuidong chanye youhua shengji, shiti jingji jiiju xiaoying chixu zengqiang (着力推动产业优化升级，实体经济集聚效应持续增强), [in:] http://www.tjbh.gov.cn/channels/6256.html.

Books and Reports

Acemoglu Daron, Robinson A. James, *Why Nations Fail: The Origins of Power, Prosperity and Poverty*, London 2012.
Altshuler Alan, *Bureaucratic innovation, democratic accountability, and politicalred. incentives,* [in:] Alan. Altshuler, Robert. Behn (eds.), *Innovation in American Government,* Washington 1997.
Antoszewski Andrzej, Herbut Ryszard (eds.), *Leksykon Politologii,* Wrocław 2003.
Bankowicz Marek, *Systemy polityczne: podręcznik akademicki. 2, Ustroje państw współczesnych*, Kraków 2020.
Bodde Derk, Morris Clarence, *Law in Imperial China: Exemplified by 190 Ch'ing Dynasty Cases,* Cambridge 1973.
Bogusz Michał, Jakubowski Jakub, *Komunistyczna Partia Chin i jej państwo. Konserwatywny zwrot Xi Jinpinga,* Warsaw 2019.
Braudel Fernand, *Historia i trwanie,* Warsaw 1999.
Bremmer Ian, *The End of the Free Market: Who Wins the War Between States and Corporations?,* London 2010.
Bröcker Johanes, Rietveld Petit, *Infrastructure and regional development,* [in:] Roberta Capello, Peter Nijkamp (eds.), *Handbook of Regional Growth and Development Theories,* Cheltenham, Northampton 2010.
Brødsgaard Erik Kjeld, Gang Chen, *Public sector reform in China: who is losing out?,* [in:] Kjeld Erik Brødsgaard (ed.), *Globalization and Public Sector Reform in China,* Oxon-New York 2014.
Bruno Latour, *Science in Action. How to Follow Scientists and Engineers through Society,* Cambridge 1987.
Cai Fang, *The formation and evolution of China's migrant labor policy,* [in:] Xibao Zhang, Shenggen Fan, Arjan de Haan (eds.), *Narratives of Chinese Reforms: HowDoes China Cross the River?,* Singapore 2010.

Capano Gillberto, Howlett Michael, Ramesh M., *Varieties of governance. Dynamics, strategies, capacities*, London 2015.

Castells Manual, *Network Society*, Warsaw 2008.

Chan Henry, Lee Hing, *The One Belt One Road Initiative – Who's Going to Pay for It?*, [in:] Tai Wei Lim, Wen Xin Lim, Henry Hing Lee Chan, Katherine Hui-yi Tseng (eds.), *China's One Belt One Road Initiative*, London 2016.

Chan Lai-Ha, *Can China's Belt and Road Initiative Bulid a Peacful Regional Order? Acqiuescence Resistance in South Asia*, [in:] Michael Clarke, Matthew Sussex, Nick Bisley (eds.), *The Belt and Road Initiative and the Future of Regional Order in the Indo-Pacific*, Lanham-Boulder-New York-London 2020.

Chandler A. John, *Public Policy and Private Interest: Ideas, Self-Interest and Ethics in Public Policy*, Oxon – New York 2017.

Changhong Pei, Wen Zheng, *China's Outbound Foreign Direct Investment Promotion System*, Berlin Heidelberg 2015.

Chin T. Gregory, *The Politics of China's Western Development Initiative*, [in:] Ding Lu, William Neilson (eds.), *China's West Region Development: Domestic Strategies and Global Implications*, London 2004.

Chołaj Henryk, *China and the world. Contemporary Chinese Economic Model*. Warsaw 2014.

Chou Bill, *Government and Policy-Making Reform in China: The Implications of Governing Capacity*, London, New York 2009.

Cohen Daniel, *Prosperity słabości*, Katowice 2011.

Dargas Marta, *Idee i zasady konstytucyjne chińskiego porządku prawnego*, Warsaw 2017.

Dikun Xie, Ye Chen, (eds), *Chinese Dream and Practice in Zhejiang – Culture*, Singapore 2019.

Dorożyński Tomasz, *Rola polityki Unii Europejskiej w usuwaniu regionalnych dysproporcji gospodarczych. Wnioski dla Polski*, Łódź 2012.

Douglas Zhihua Zeng, *How Do Special Economic Zones and Industrial Clusters Drive China's Rapid Development?*, [in:] Douglas Zhihua Zeng (ed.), *Building engines for growth and competitiveness in China: Experience with special economic zones and industrial clusters*. Washington 2010.

Dunn William N., *Public Policy Analysis*, New York 2015.

Drechsler Wolfgang, *Beyond the Western Paradigm: Confucian Public Administration*, [in:] Sara Bice, Avery Poole, Helen Sullivan (eds.), *Public Policy in the "Asian Century" Concepts, Cases and Futures*, London 2018.

Elizabeth Economy, *The Third Revolution: Xi Jinping and the New Chinese State*, New York 2018.

Feizhou Zhou, Mingzhi Tan, *Relationship between the Central Government and Local Governments of Contemporary China*, Singapore 2017.

Gacek Łukasz, *Zielona energia w Chinach. Zrównoważony rozwój, ochrona środowiska, gospodarka niskoemisyjna*, Kraków 2015.

Garnaut Ross, Song Ligang, Fang Cai, *Reform and China's Long-Term Growth and Development*, [in:] Ligang Song, Ross Garnaut, Cai Fang (eds.), *Deepening Reform for China's Long-term Growth and Development*, Canberra 2014.

Krzysztof Gawlikowski, *The Confucian model of the state in China*, Warsaw 2009.

Góralczyk Bogdan, *Nowy długi marsz. Chiny ery Xi Jinpinga*, Warsaw 2021.

Góralczyk Bogdan, *Wielki renesans. Chińska transformacja i jej konsekwencje,* Warsaw 2018.

Granaut Ross, *Mostly Slow Progress on the New Model of Growth,* [in:] Ligang Song, Ross Garnaut, Cai Fang, Lauren Johnston (eds.), *China's New Sources of Economic Growth: Vol. 1: Reform, Resources and Climate Change,* Acton 2016.

Groenewold Nicolaas, Chen Anping, Lee Guoping, *Linkages Between China's Regions: Measurement and Policy,* Cheltenham-Northampton 2008.

Grosse Grzegorz Tomasz, *Polityka regionalna Unii Europejskiej. Przykład Grecji, Włoch, Irlandii i Polski,* Warsaw 2004.

Guo Qingwang, Jia Junxue, *Structural Reform in China's Regional Governments,* vol. 1, Hong Kong 2013.

Hagemann Christian, *EU Funds in the New Member States Party Politicization, Administrative Capacities, and Absorption Problems after Accession,* Cham 2019.

Halpe Stefan, *The Beijing Consensus: How China's Authoritarian Model Will Dominate the Twenty-First Century,* New York 2010.

Hameed Shahul, *China's Special Economic Zones,* [in:] Swaraj Prakash Gupta (ed.), *China's Economic Reforms: The Role of Special Economic Zones and Economic and Technological Development Zones,* New Delhi 1996.

Hansen Niles, Higgins Benjamin, Savoie Donald, *Regional Policy in a Changing World,* New York-London 1990.

Hansen Valerie, *The Silk Road: A New History,* Oxford 2015.

Heberer Thomas, *Local Cadres,* [in:] Jianxing Yu, Sujian Guo (eds.), *The Palgrave Handbook of Local Governance in Contemporary China,* Singapore 2019.

Heberer Thomas, *Pomiędzy kryzysem a szansą: nowe społeczne wyzwania ze szczególnym uwzględ-nieniem wiejskich Chin,* [in:] Karin Tomala (ed.), *Chiny, Przemiany państwa i społeczeństwa w okresie reform 1978–2000,* Warsaw 2003.

Heilmann Sebastian, *Economic Governance: Authoritarian Upgrading and Innovative Potential,* [in:] Joseph Fewsmith (ed.), *China Today, China Tomorrow: Domestic Politics, Economy, and Society,* Plymouth 2010.

Heilmann Sebastian, Perry J. Elizabeth, *Embracing Uncertainty: Guerrilla Policy Style and Adaptive Governance in China,* Cambridge 2011.

Heilmann Sebastian, *Red Swan: How Unorthodox Policy Making Facilitated China's Rise,* Hong Kong 2018.

Heywood Andrew, *Politologia,* Warszawa 2009.

Hongmei Zhang, Hai Zhu, *Study on the Financial Support System for Development of Small Towns in Western China,* [in:] Tai-Chee Wong, Sun Sheng Han, Hongmei Zhang (eds.), *Population Mobility, Urban Planning and Management in China,* Cham-Heidelberg-New York-Dordrecht-London 2015.

Howlet Michael, *Designing Public policies. Pronciples and instruments,* London-New York 2011

Huang Yasheng, *Capitalism with Chinese Characteristics: Entrepreneurship and the State,* New York 2008.

Jae Ho Chung, *Centrifugal Empire: Central – Local Relations in China,* New York 2016.

Jankowiak Anna, *Chinise industrial clusters,* [in:] Bogusława Skulska Anna Jankowiak (eds.) *Innovation Sources of Economies in Eastern Asia,* Wrocław 2012.

Jessop Bob, *The State Past, Present, Future,* Cambridge-Malden 2016.

Jianping Li, Minrong Li, Yanjing Gao, Jianjian Li, Hongwen Su, Maoxing Huang, *China's Provincial Economic Competitiveness and Policy Outlook for the 13th Five-year Plan Period (2016–2020),* Singapore 2018.

Jianxing Yu, *Introduction: Local* Governance in China-Past, Present, and Future, [in:] Jianxing Yu, Sujian Guo (eds.), *The Palgrave Handbook of Local Governance in Contemporary China,* Singapore 2019.

Jianxing Yu, *Local Governance in China — Past, Present and Future,* [in:] Jianxing Yu, Sujian Guo (eds.), *The Palgrave Handbook of Local Governance in Contemporary China,* Singapore 2019.

Jones Charles, *An Introduction to the Study of Public Policy,* California 1984.

Jong de Sijbren, Oosterveld Th. Willem, Roelen Michel, Klacansky Katharine, Silekaite Agne, Siebenga Rianne, *A road to riches or a road to ruin?: The geo-economic implications of China's new silk road,* Hague 2017.

Kamiński Tomasz, *Sypiając ze smokiem. Polityka Unii Europejskiej wobec Chin,* Łódź 2015.

Kennedy James John, *Rural China: Reform and Resistance,* [in:] William A. Joseph (ed.) *Politics in China: An Introduction,* Oxford 2019.

Kingdon John, *Agendas, alternatives, and public polices,* New York 1995.

Kissinger Henry, *O Chi*nach, Wołowiec 2014.

Klasik Andrzej (ed.), *Strategia konkurencyjna regionu,* [in:] Andrzej Klasik, Florian Kuźnik (eds.) *Zarządzanie strategiczne rozwojem lokalnym i regionalnym,* Katowice 2001.

Kogut-Jaworska Magdalena, *Instrumenty pobudzania rozwoju gospodarczego na obszarach lokalnych,* [in:] Adam Szewczyk, Magdalen Kogut Jaworska, Magdalena Zioło (eds.), *Rozwój lokalny i regionalny. Teoria i praktyka,* Warszawa 2011.

Kołodko Grzegorz, *Czy Chiny zbawią świat?,* Warszawa 2018.

Knoepfel Peter, Larrue Corinne, Varone Frédéric, Michael Hill, *Public policy analysis Bristol,* 2007.

Kraft Michale E., Furlong Scott R., *Public policy. Politics, analysis, and alternatives,* Los Angeles-London-New Delhi-Singapore-Washington 2015.

Kurlantzick Joshua, *State Capitalism: How the Return of Statism is Transforming the World,* New York 2016.

Kwieciński Rafał, *Od "soft power" do "smart power" Chin,* [in:] Edward Haliżak, Rafał Ożarowski, Anna Wróbel (eds.), *Liberalizm & neoliberalizm w badaniu polityki zagranicznej państwa i gospodarki światowej,* Warszawa 2016.

Lawrence V. Susan and Michael F. Martin, *Understanding China's Political System,* [in:] Camelia L. Jacoby (ed.), *China's Political System Features, Institutions, and Leaders,* New York 2014.

Liancheng He, Huiqin Yao, Zhangyong Xu, Lixiong Cai, Shuwei An, *Economic Development in Western China: A Ten-Year Review,* [in:] Huiqin Yao, Zhangyong Xu (eds.), *Redevelopment of Western China,* Singapore 2017.

Liberska Barbara, *Wprowadzenie* [in:] Barbara Liberska (ed.), *Nowa globalna architektura finansowa. W stronę bezpieczniejszego sektora bankowego,* Kraków 2016.

Litao Zhao, *Mobilization and Irregularity: Volatile Growth of Educational Expenditure in China,* [in:] Jianxing Yu, Sujian Guo (eds.), *The Palgrave Handbook of Local Governance in Contemporary China,* Singapore 2019.

Liu Xinru, *The Silk Road in World History,* Oxford 2010.

Maddison Angus, *Chinese Economic Performance in the Long Run,* OECD, Paris 2007.

Malik Rashid Ahmed, *The China- Pakistan Economic Corridor (CPEC): A Game Changer for Pakistan's Economy,* [in:] BR Deepak (ed.*), China's Global Rebalancing and the New Silk Road,* Singapore 2018.

Marshall Alfred, *Industry and Trade, A study of Industrial Technique and Business Organization; and of Their Influences on the Condition of Various Classes and Nations,* New Delhi 2015.

Miskimmon Alister, O'Loughlin Ben, *The EU's Struggle for Strategic Narrative on China,* [in:] Alister Miskimmon, Ben O'Loughlin, Jinghan Zeng (eds.), *One Belt, One Road, One Story?: Towards an EU- China Strategic Narrative,* Cham 2021.

Morton Scott, Lewis Charlton, *China. History and Culture,* Krakow 2007.

Naoyuki Yoshino, Morgan J. Peter, *Central and Local Government Relations in Asia, Achieving Fiscal Sustainability,* Cheltenham-Northampton 2017.

Naughton Barry, *Growing Out of the Plan: Chinese Economic Reform, 1978–1993,* Cambridge 1995.

Naughton Barry, *The Chinese Economy: Transitions and Growth,* London 2007.

North Douglas, *Understanding the process of economic change,* Princeton 2005.

North Douglass. *Institutions, Institutional Change and Economic Performance,* Cambridge 1990.

Olejniczak Karol, Rok Jakub, *Feedback in Public Agencies: A Missing Engine of Organizational Learning?* [in:] Perrin Burt, Tyrrell Tony (eds.) *Changing Bureaucracies: Adapting to Uncertainty, and How Evaluation Can Help,* London-New York 2020.

Olejniczak Karol, Rok Jakub, Płoszaj Adam, *Organizacyjne uczenie się i zarządzanie wiedzą – przegląd koncepcji,* [in:] Karol Olejniczak (ed.), *Organizacje uczące się. Model dla administracji publicznej,* Warszawa 2012.

Pye W. Lucian, *The Spirit of Chinese Politics,* Cambridge, Massachusetts, London 1992.

Peijun Shi, Xuemin Liu, Mingchuan Yang, *Education and Skill Training,* [in:] YM Yeun, Shen Jianfa (ed.), *Developing China's West: A Critical Path to Balanced National Development,* Hong Kong 2004.

Piontek Franciszek, Piontek Barbara, *Teoria rozwoju,* Warszawa 2016.

Porter Michael, *The Competitive Advantage of Nations,* London 1990.

Puślecki Zdzisław W., *Światowa Ogranizacja Handlu i Unia Europejska wobec wyzwań we współczesnym biznesie międzynarodowym,* Warszawa 2021.

Putnam Robert, *Bowling Alone: The Collapse and Revival of American Community,* New York 2001.

Qoraboyev Ikboljon, *One Belt, One Road: A Comparative Regionalism Approach,* [in:] Yu Cheng, Lilei Song, Lihe Huang, *The Belt & Road Initiative in the Global Arena: Chinese and European Perspectives,* Singapore 2017.

Raczkowski Konrad, *Zarządzania publiczne. Teoria i praktyka„* Warszawa 2015.

Ren Xin, *Tradition of the law and law of the tradition: Law, state, and social control in China,* Westport 1997.

Ronghua Shen, Sheng Cao, *Modernization of Government Governance in China. The Great Transformation of China (China's Economic Transformation, Innovation and Development),* Singapore 2020.

Rowiński Jan, Jakóbiec Wojciech, *System konstytucyjny Chińskiej Republiki Ludowej,* Warszawa 2006.

Ryzykowanie i ingerowanie wymagają dogłębnego rozpoznania, Liaowang March 17, 2009, translation Łobacz Agnieszka, [in:] Krzysztof Gawlikowski, Marta Ławacz, Agnieszka Łobasz, Marta Tomczak, Joanna Afek (eds.) *Prasa chińska o przemianach społecznych i kulturowych w początkach XXI wieku*, Warszawa 2020.

Saich Tony, *Governance and Politics of China*, London-New York 2015.

Sandra Poncet, *Inward and Outward FDI in China*, [in:] David Greenaway, Chris Milner, Shujie Yao (eds.), *China and the World Economy*, London 2010.

Schmidt Dirk, Heilmann Sebastian, *Provincial- and municipal-level Governments*, [in:] Sebastian Heilmann (ed.), *China's Political System*, Lanham, Boulder, New York, London 2017.

Shaoguang Wang, Angang Hu, *The Political Economy of Uneven Development: The Case of China*, London-New York 2000.

Shaoguang Wang, Peng Fan, *The Chinese Model of Consensus Decision-Making: A Case Study of Healthcare Reform*, Beijing 2013.

Sheng Yumin, *Economic Openness and Territorial Politics in China*, New York 2010.

Shi Zhiqin, Trigkas Vasilis, *Reconstructing Geography, Power and Politics in the Belt and Road Initiative*, [in:] Alister Miskimmon, Ben O'Loughlin, Jinghan Zeng (eds.), *One Belt, One Road, One Story?*, Cham 2021.

Shuzhong Gu, Meie Xie, Xinhua Zhang, *Green Transformation and Development*, Singapore 2019.

Son Ngoc Chu, Ligang Song, *State Control, Entrepreneurship and Resource Allocation*, [in:] Ligang Song, Ross Garnaut, Cai Fang (eds.), *Deepening Reform for China's Long-term Growth and Development*, Canberra 2014.

Storper Michael, *The Regional World: Territorial Development in a Global Economy*, New York 1997.

Świstak Marek, *Ewolucja chińskiego modelu rozwoju społeczno-gospodarczego w supranarodowej perspektywie Unii Europejskiej*, [in:] Marek Świstak, Jan Wiktor Tkaczyński (eds.), *Azjatycki model polityki rozwoju społeczno-gospodarczego. Wybrane aspekty w świetle standardów i doświadczeń Unii Europejskiej*, Kraków 2019.

Świstak Marek, *O wyższości polityki nad gospodarką i pierwszeństwie mechanizmów rynkowych przed politycznymi. Rola państwa w chińskiej polityce rozwoju regionalnego*, [in:] Hanna Kupś, Maciej Szatkowski, Michał Dahl (eds.), *70 lat Chińskiej Republiki Ludowej w ujęciu interdyscyplinarnym*, Warszawa 2021.

Świstak Marek, *Polityka regionalna Unii Europejskiej jako polityka publiczna. Wobec potrzeby optymalizacji publicznego działania*, Kraków 2018.

Świstak Marek, *Polityka rozwoju społeczno-gospodarczego a wyzwania rozwojowe Chin*, [in:] Marek Świstak, Jan Wiktor Tkaczyński (eds.), *Azjatycki model polityki rozwoju społeczno-gospodarczego. Wybrane aspekty w świetle standardów i doświadczeń Unii Europejskiej*, Kraków 2019.

Szklarska Anna, *Sprawiedliwość w czasach kryzysu*, Kraków 2015.

Szlachta Jacek, *Główne problemy polityki rozwoju regionalnego Polski na przełomie XX i XXI wieku*, [in:] Ryszard Bartoszkiewicz (ed.), *Strategiczne wyzwania dla polityki rozwoju regionalnego Polski*, Warszawa 1996.

Tao Chiu Lam, *The county system and county governance*, [in:] Jae Ho Chung, Tao-chiu Lam (eds.), *China's Local Administration: Traditions and Changes in the Sub-National Hierarchy*, Oxon-New York 2010.

Teets Jessica, Hurst William, *Intoruction and patterns of policy diffusion in China*, [in:] Jessica Teets, William Hurst (ed.), *Local Governance Innovation in China: Experimentation, Diffusion, and Defiance*, Oxon-New York 2014.

Tkaczyński Wiktor Jan, Gacek Łukasz, *China's environmental policy in terms of European Union standards*, Göttingen 2021.

Tkaczyński Wiktor Jan, Świstak Marek, *Encyklopedia polityki regionalnej i funduszy europejskich*, Warszawa 2013.

Tkaczyński Wiktor Jan, Świstak Marek, *Ochrona środowiska naturalnego w Chinach jako nowy element modelu polityki rozwoju społeczno-gospodarczego Państwa Środka*, [in:] Marek Świstak, Jan Wiktor Tkaczyński (eds.), *Azjatycki model polityki rozwoju społeczno-gospodarczego. Wybrane aspekty w świetle standardów i doświadczeń Unii Europejskiej*, Kraków 2019.

Tkaczyński Wiktor Jan, *Ustrojowy fenomen Chin w świetle ideowego sporu o wyższości merytokracji nad demokrację i przewadze demokracji nad merytokracją*, [in:] Marek Świstak, Jan Wiktor Tkaczyński (eds.), *Azjatycki model polityki rozwoju społeczno-gospodarczego. Wybrane aspekty w świetle standardów i doświadczeń Unii Europejskiej*, Kraków 2019.

Tkaczyński Wiktor Jan, Willa Rafał, Świstak Marek, *Fundusze Unii Europejskiej 2007–2013, Cele - działania - środki*, Kraków 2008.

United Nations, *World Investment Report 2006, FDI from Developing and Transition Economics: Implication for Development*, New York-Geneva 2006.

Vanhove Norbert, *Regional Policy: A European Approach*, New York 2018.

Walkowski Maciej, *Chińska strategia rozwoju społeczno-ekonomicznego. Implikacje dla Unii Europejskiej*, Poznań 2018.

Wei Dennis Yehua, *Regional Development in China: States, Globalization and Inequality*, London-New York 2000.

Whiting H. Susan, *Power and Wealth in Rural China: The Political Economy of Institutional Change*, New York 2006.

Williamson John, *Beijing Consensus versus Washington Consensus* [in:] Robert E. Looney (ed.), *Handbook of Emerging Economies*, Yorkshire 2014.

Williamson John, *What Washington Means by Policy Reform* [in:] John Williamson (ed.), *Latin American adjustment: How much has happened*, Washington 1990.

Winiarski Bolesław (ed.), *Polityka Gospodarka*, Warszawa 2006.

Wong Christine, *Overview of Issues in Local Public Finance in the PRC*, [in:] Christine Wong (eds.), *Financing Local Government in the People's Republic of China*, Oxford 1997.

Woś Bolesław, *Rozwój regionów i polityka regionalna w Unii Europejskiej oraz w Polsce*, Wrocław 2005.

Xiao Wang, *The Role of Economic Development Zones in National Development Strategies, The Case of China*, Santa Monica-Arlington-Pittsburgh 2013.

Xiauku Song, Shiguo Wu, Xin Xu., *The Great Change in the Regional Economy of China under the New Normal. The Great Transformation of China*, Singapore 2019.

Xing Li, *China's Pursuit of the "One Belt One Road" Initiative: Anew World Order with Chinese Characteristics?*, [in:] Li Xing (ed.), *Mapping China's 'One Belt One Road' Initiative*, Cham 2018.

Yan Yilong, Bai Gang, Zhang Leyong, Ou Shujun, He Jianyu, *China's Great Way. The Communist Party of China and Chinese Socialism*, Toruń 2018.

Yang Yao, *Political economy causes of China's economic success* [in:] Ross Garnaut, Ligang Song, Cai Fang (eds.), *China's 40 Years of Reform and Development: 1978–2018*, Acton 2018.

Yang Yao., *The political economy of government policies toward regional inequality in China,* [in:] Yukon Huang, Alessandro Magnoli Bocchi (eds.), *Reshaping Economic Geography in East Asia,* Washington 2009.

Yang Zhong, *Chinese township government: between a rock and a hard place,* [in:] Jae Ho Chung, Tao-chiu Lam (ed.), *China's Local Administration: Traditions and Changes in the Sub-National Hierarchy,* Oxon-New York 2010.

Yanrui Wu, Ning Ma and Xiumei Guo, Growth, *Structural Change and Productivity Gaps in China's Industrial Sector,* [in:] Ligang Song, Ross Garnaut, Cai Fang (eds.), *Deepening reform for China's long-term Growth and development,* Canberra 2014.

Yu Jianxing, Huang Biao, *Mapping the Progress of Local Government Innovation in Contemporary China,* [in:] Jianxing Yu, Sujian Guo (eds.), *The Palgrave Handbook of Local Governance in Contemporary China,* Singapore 2019.

Zhang Baijia, *A look at China's policy of reform and openness to the world,* Toruń 2017.

Zhenhua Chen, Kingsley E. Haynes, Yulong Zhou, Zhaoxin Dai, *High Speed Rail and China's New Economic Geography: Impact Assessment from the Regional Science Perspective,* Cheltenham, Northampton 2019.

Zhu Yingming, *Analysis of Industrial Clusters in China,* Boca Raton 2009.

Zybała Andrzej, *Państwo i społeczeństwo w działaniu. Polityki publiczne wobec potrzeb modernizacji państwa i społeczeństwa,* Warszawa 2013.

Articles

Acemoglu Daron, Johnson Simon, Robinson James, *Institutions as the Fundamental Cause of Long-Run Growth,* "NBER Working Paper" May 2004, no. 10481.

Acemoglu Daron, Johnson Simon, *Understanding institutions,* "Journal of Political Economy" 2005, vol. 113, no. 5.

Adams F. Gerard, Chen Yimin, *Skepticism about Chinese GDP Growth – the Chinese GDP Elasticity of Energy Consumption,* "Journal of Economic and Social Measurement" 1996, vol. 22, no. 4.

Ahlers L. Anna., Schubert Gunter, *Effective Policy Implementation in China's Local State,* "Modern China" 2015, vol. 41, no. 4.

Ai Chi-Han, Wu Hung-Che, Huang Tian-Hang, Wang Rui, *How does knowledge flow in industrial clusters? The comparison between both naturally and intentionally formed industrial clusters in China,* "Asian Journal of Technology Innovation" 2020, Published online: November 2, 2020.

Ambroziak A. Adam, Hartwell A. Christopher, *The impact of investments in special economic zones on regional development: The case of Poland,* "Regional Studies" 2018, vol. 52, issue 10.

Andrews Kim, Swanson James, *Does Public Infrastructure Affect Regional Performance?,* "Growth and Change" 1995, vol. 26, issue 2.

Aschauer David Alan, *Is public expenditure productive?,* "Journal of Monetary Economics" 1989, vol. 23, no. 2.

Axel Dreher, Fuchs Andreas, *Rogue Aid? An Empirical Analysis of China's Aid Allocation,* "The Canadian Journal of Economics" 2015, vol. 48, no. 3.

Balla Steven J., *Is Consultation the "New Normal?": Online Policymaking and Governance Reform in China,* "Journal of Chinese Political Science" 2017, vol. 22, no. 3, pp. 375–392.

Balla Steven J., Zhoudan Xie, *Online Consultation and the Institutionalization of Transparency and Participation in Chinese Policymaking,* "The China Quarterly" 2021, vol. 246.

Balme Stéphanie, *The rule of law in China: On the margins of a bureaucratic and absolutist empire (1978–2014),* "Revue Francaise d'Administration Publique" 2014, vol. 150, issue 2.

Barbieri Elisa, Pollio Chiara, Prota Francesco, *The impacts of spatially targeted programs: evidence from Guangdong,* "Regional Studies" 2020, vol. 54, issue 3.

Barkley L. David, *Evaluations of Regional Competitiveness: Making a Case for Case Studies,* "The Review of Regional Studies" 2008, vol. 38.

Bartolini Stefano, Sarracino Francesco, *The Dark Side of Chinese Growth: Declining Social Capital and Well-Being in Times of Economic Boom,* "World Development" 2015, vol. 74.

Belkhodja Omar, Mohiuddin Muhammad, Karuranga Egide, *The determinants of FDI location choice in China: a discrete-choice analysis,* "Applied Economics" 2017, vol. 49, no. 13.

Bo Shiyu, *Centralization and regional development: Evidence from a political hierarchy reform to create cities in china,* "Journal of Urban Economics" 2020, vol. 115.

Bottazzim Laura, Peri Giovanni, *Innovation and spillovers in regions: Evidence from European patent data,* "European Economic Review" 2003, vol. 47.

Bradsher Keith, *China Asks Other Nations Not to Release Its Air Data.* New York Times, 5 June 2012, https://www.nytimes.com/2012/06/06/world/asia/china-asks-embassies-to-stop-measuring-air-pollution.html?r=0.

Broadman Harry G., Sun Xiaolun, *The Distribution of Foreign Direct Investment in China,* "World Economy" 1997, vol. 20.

Brohman John, *Postwar Development in the Asian NICs: Does the Neoliberal Model Fit Reality,* "Economic Geography" 1996, vol. 72, no. 2.

Brombal Daniele, *Accuracy of environmental monitoring in China: Exploring the influence of institutional, political and ideological factors,* "Sustainbility" 2017, no. 9.

Burns John, *Civil service reform in contemporary China,* "The Australian Journal of Chinese Affairs" 1987, no. 18.

Burns P. John, *Civil Service Reform in China,* "OECD Journal on Budgeting" 2007 vol. 7, no. 1.

Cai Yongshun, *Managed participation in China,* "Political Science Quarterly" 2004, vol. 119, no. 3.

Chan Hon, Chow King, *Public Management Policy and Practice in Western China: Metapolicy, Tacit Knowledge, and Implications for Management Innovation Transfer,* "The American Review of Public Administration" 2007, vo. 37, no. 4.

Chan S. Hon, *Cadre Personnel Management in China: The Nomenklatura* System, 1990–1998, "The China Quarterly" 2004, no. 179.

Chen Jihong, Fei Yijie, Lee Tae-Woo Paul, Tao Xuezong, *Overseas Port Investment Policy for China's Central and Local Governments in the Belt and Road Initiative,* "Journal of Contemporary China" 2019, vol. 28, issue 116.

Chen Jing, Huang Cui, *Policy Reinvention and Difusion: Evidence from Chinese Provincial Governments,* "Journal of Chinese Political Science" 2021, published March 4, 2021 (electronic version).

Chen Ling, Naughton Barry, *An Institutionalized Policy-making Mechanism: China's Return to Techno-Industrial Policy,* "Research Policy" 2016, vol. 45, no. 10.

Chen P.J. Charles., Zengquan Li, Xijia Su, Zheng Sun, *Rent-seeking incentives, corporate political connections, and the control structure of private firms: Chinese evidence,* "Journal of Corporate Finance" 2011, vol. 17, issue 2.

Chenggang Xu, *The Fundamental Institutions of China's Reforms and Development,* Journal of Economic Literature 2011, vol. 49, no. 4.

Chenggang Xu, *The Pitfalls of a Centralized Bureaucracy,* "Acta Oeconomica" 2019, vol. 69, issue 1.

Chung Him, *Unequal Regionalism: Regional Planning in China and England,* "Planning Practice & Research" 2015, vol. 30, no. 5.

Chung Ho Jae, Lai Hongyi, Joo Jang-Hwan, *"Revive the Northeast" (zhenxing dongbei) Program: Origins, Policies and Implementatio,* "The China Quarterly" 2009, no. 197.

Danlu Bu, Chenyu Zhang, Philip T. Lin, Fang Hu, *Political uncertainty, institutions and accounting conservatism: evidence from the provincial leader turnover in China,* "Spanish Journal of Finance and Accounting" 2020, vol. 49, issue 4.

Dees Stèphane, *Foreign Direct Investment in China: Determinants and Effects,* "Economics of Planning" 1998 vol. 31.

Démurger Sylvie, *Infrastructure Development and Economic Growth: An Explanation for Regional Disparities in China?,* "Journal of Comparative Economics" 2001, vol. 29, issue 1.

Deng, Yongheng, Randall Morck, Jing Wu, Bernard Yeung, *China's pseudo-monetary policy,* "Review of Finance" 2015, vol. 19, issue 1.

Dennis Tao Yang, *What has caused regional inequality in China?,* "China Economic Review" 2002, vol. 13, no. 4.

Di Guo, Jiang Kun, Xu Chenggang, Yang Xiyi, *Growth, Inequality and Industrial Clusters in China,* "Journal of Economic Geography" 2020, vol. 20.

Dong Lisheng, *China's Drive to Revitalise the Northeast,* "China Perspectives" 2005, April no. 58.

Duan Haiyan, Jing Vivian Zhan, *Fiscal Transfer and Local Public Expenditure in China: A Case Study of Shanxi Province,* "China Review" 2011, vol. 11, no. 1.

Dunford Michael, Liu Weidong, *Chinese perspectives on the Belt and Road Initiative,* "Cambridge Journal of Regions, Economy and Society" 2019, vol. 12, issue 1.

Dutt Ashok, Costa Frank, *An evaluation of national economic planning in the People's Republic of China,* "Geoforum" 1980, vol. 1.

Edin Maria, *State capacity and local agent control in China: CCP cadre management from a township perspective,* "China Quarterly" 2003, vol. 173.

Fan Cindy, *China's Eleventh Five-Year Plan (2006–2010): From "Getting Rich First" to "Common Prosperity",* "Eurasian Geography and Economics" 2006, vol. 47, no. 6.

Fan Cindy, Sun Mingjie, *Regional Inequality in China, 1978–2006,* "Eurasian Geography and Economics" 2008, vol. 49.

Fleisher Belton, Haizheng Li, Min Qiang Zhao, *Human capital, economic growth, and regional inequality in China,* "Journal of Development Economics" 2010 vol. 92, issue 2.

Foster John, *Distribution of FDI across China – common policies but differing impacts by region,* "Journal of Chinese Economic and Foreign Trade Studies" 2011, vol. 4, no. 2.

Fukuyama Francis, *What is governance?,* "Governance: An International Journal of Policy, Administration, and Institutions" 2013, vol. 26, issue 3.

Fulong Wu, *The global and local dimensions of place-making: remaking Shanghai as a world city,* "Urban Studies" 2000, vol. 37, issue 8.

Fung K.C., Iizaka Hitomi, Parker Stephen, *Determinants of US and Japanese Direct Investment in China,* "Journal of Comparative Economics" 2002, vol. 30, no. 3.

Fung K.C., Iizaka Hitomi, Tong Sarah, *Foreign direct investment in China: Policy, recent trend and impact,* "Global Economic Review" 2004, vol. 33, issue 2.

Gacek Łukasz, *Nowe źródła wzrostu gospodarczego Chin: wiedza i innowacje,* "Roczniki Humanistyczne" 2018, no. XV / 1.

Gao Jie, *Governing by goals and numbers: A case study in the use of performance measurement to build state capacity in China,* "Public Administration and Development" 2009, vol. 29, issue 1.

Gao Jie, *Pernicious Manipulation of Performance Measures in China's Cadre Evaluation System,* "The China Quarterly" 2015, vol. 223.

Geping Rao, Wang Zhenmin, *Hong Kong's 'One Country, Two Systems' Experience under the Basic Law: two perspectives from Chinese legal scholars,* "Journal of Contemporary China" 2007, vol. 16, issue 52.

Goodman David, *The Campaign to "Open Up the West": National, Provincial-level and Local Perspectives,* "The China Quarterly" 2004, vol. 178.

Gorzelak Grzegorz, *Fakty i mity rozwoju regionalnego,* "Zarządzanie Publiczne" 2008, no. 4 (6).

Gössling Tobias, Rutten Roel, *Innovation in Regions,* "European Planning Studies" 2007, vol. 15, no. 2.

Groh Peter Alexander, Wich Matthias, *Emerging economies' attraction of foreign direct investment,* "Emerging Markets Review" 2012, vol. 13, issue 2.

Guthrie D, *Between markets and politics: organizational responses to reform in China,* "American Journal of Sociology" 1997, vol. 102.

Ha-Joon Chang, Grabel Ilene, *Reclaiming development from the Washington consensus,* "Journal of Post Keynesian Economics" 2004, vol. 27.

Hall Peter, Taylor Rosemary CR, *Political science and the three new institutionalisms,* "Political Studies", 1996, vol. 44, no. 5.

Hao Shi, Shaoqing Huang, *How Much Infrastructure Is Too Much? A New Approach and Evidence from China,* "World Development" 2014, vol. 56.

He Canfei, *Information Costs, Agglomeration Economies and the Location of Foreign Direct Investment in China,* "Regional Studies" 2002, vol. 36, issue 9.

He Baogang, *The Domestic Politics of the Belt and Road Initiative and its Implications,* "Journal of Contemporary China" 2019, vol. 28, no. 116.

Heberer Thomas, *Representation in a context across political orders and the Chinese case,* "Journal of Chinese Governance" 2019, vol. 4, issue 4.

Heberer Thomas, Trappel René, *Evaluation Processes, Local Cadres' Behavior and Local Development Processes,* "Journal of Contemporary China" 2013, vol. 22, issue 4.

Heilmann Sebastian, *From Local Experiments to National Policy: The Origins of China's Distinctive Policy Process,* "The China Journal" 2008, no. 59.

Heilmann Sebastian, Melton Oliver, *The Reinvention of Development Planning in China,* 1993–2012, "Modern China" 2013, vol. 39.

Henry Wai-chung Yeung, *Local politics and foreign ventures in China's transitional economy: the political economy of Singaporean investments in China,* "Political Geography" 2000, vol. 19, issue 7.

Herr Hansjoerg, *Underdevelopment and unregulated markets: why free markets do not lead to catching-up,* "European Journal of Economics and Economic Policies-Intervention" 2018, vol. 15.

Hervás-Oliver Luis Jose, Albors-Garrigos Jose, Estelles-Miguel Sofia, Boronat-Moll Carles, *Radical innovation in Marshallian industrial districts,* "Regional Studies" 2018, vol. 52, no. 10.

Him Chung, *Unequal Regionalism: Regional Planning in China and England,* "Planning Practice & Research" 2015, vol. 30, no. 5.

Holz A. Carsten, *China governance project: the institutional arrangements for the production of statistics,* "OECD Statistics Working Paper" 19 January 2005.

Holz A. Carsten, *The quality of China's GDP statistics,* "China Economic Review" 2014, vol. 30.

Hongbin Li, Li-An Zhou, *Political turnover and economic performance: the incentive role of personnel control in China,* "Journal of Public Economics" 2005, vol. 89, issue 6–7.

Hongbin Li, Li-An Zhou, *Political turnover and economic performance: the incentive role of personnel control in China,* "Journal of Public Economics" 2005, vol. 89, issues 9–10.

Hongyi Harry Lai, *China's Western Development Program: Its Rationale, Implementation, and Prospects,* "Modern China" 2002, vol. 28, no. 4.

Hu Aidi, Schmitt Valérie, *China,* International Labor Organization 2017, https://www.usp2030.org/gimi/ShowCountryProfile.action;jsessionid=D41r8zQbPIpXhYXtNn2R2rJBr72l_7jtDhXGRY0Hxo959?SIid=234gUs?SIid=234.

Huang Yan-hui, *Financial Restraint Theory and its Practices in China,* "Journal of Beijing Technology and Business University" (Social Sciences) 2014, vol. 29, no. 1.

Hudson Bob, Hunter David, Peckham Stephen, *Policy failure and the policy-implementation gap: can policy support programs help?,* "Policy Design and Practice" 2019, vol. 2, no. 1.

Hu Yabei, Zhang Weifu, Poti "shisiwu", yi guonei da shichang cujin da xunhuan ((破题"十四五"，以国内大市场促进大循环), Guangming Network, 11/13/2020, https://theory.gmw.cn/2020-11/13/content_34365861.htm.

Hung Tran, Decoupling / Reshoring versus Dual Circulation: Competing Strategies for Security and Influence, Atlantic Council, April 2021, https://www.atlanticcouncil.org/wpcontent/uploads/2021/04/Decoupling_Reshoring_versus_Dual_Circulation.pdf.

Huovari Janne, Aki Kangasharju, Aku Alane, *Constructing an Index for Regional Competitiveness,* "Pellervo Economic Research Institute, Working Paper", vol. 44, Helsinki, 2001.

Isbasoiu Marian George, *Industrial Clusters and Regional Development. The Case of Timisoara and Montebelluna,* "MPRA Paper" 2006, no. 5037.

Jean Oi, Fiscal *Reform and the Economic Foundations of Local State Corporatism in China,* "World Politics" 1992, vol. 45, no. 1.

Jelonek W. Adam, *Asian values – as a political platform and subject of sociological research,* "Asia and the Pacific" 2004, vol. 7.

Jiangang Peng, Jing He, Zhangfei Li, Yu Yi, Groenewold Nicolaas, *Regional Finance and Regional Disparities in China,* "Australian Economic Papers" 2010, vol. 49, no. 4.

Jiannan Wu, Liang Ma, Yuqian Yang, *Innovation in the Chinese public sector: typology and distribution,* "Public administration" 2013, vol. 91, issue 2.

Jianxing Yu, Kenichiro Yashima, Yongdong Shen, *Autonomy or Privilege? Lobbying Intensity of Local Business Associations in China,* "Journal of Chinese Political Science" 2014, vol. 19, no. 3.

Jianxing Yu, Lin Li, Yongdong Shen. *Rediscovering intergovernmental relations at the local level: The devolution to township governments in Zhejiang Province,* "China Review" 2016, vol. 16, issue 2.

Jianxing Yu, Xiang Gao, *Redefining decentralization: Devolution of administrative authority to county governments in Zhejiang province,* "Australian Journal of Public Administration" 2013, vol. 72, issue 3.

Jinping Xi, *Secure a Decisive Victory in Building a Moderately Prosperous Society in All Respects and Strive for the Great Success of Socialism with Chinese Characteristics for a New Era,* Delivered at the 19th National Congress of the Communist Party of China October 18, 2017, http://www.xinhuanet.com/english/download/Xi_Jinping's_report_at_19th_CPC_National_Congress.pdf.

Jones Lee, Zeng Jinghan, *Understanding China's 'Belt and Road Initiative': beyond 'grand strategy' to a state transformation analysis,* "Third World Quarterly" 2019, vol. 40, issue 8.

Jun Yeup Kim, Le-Yin Zhang, *Formation of Foreign Direct Investment Clustering – A New Path to Local Economic Development? The Case of Qingdao,* "Regional Studies" 2008, vol. 42, issue 2.

Jung Haeil, Zhang Ruodan, *Impact evaluations in South Korea and China,* "Asian Journal of Political Science" 2017, vol. 25, no. 3.

Kaiser Stefan, Kirby David A., Fan Ying, *Foreign Direct Investment in China: An Examination of the Literature,* "Asia Pacific Business Review" 1996, vol. 2, no. 3.

Kam Wing Chan, Li Zhang, *The Hukou system and rural urban migration in China: Processes and changes,* "The China Quarterly" 1999, vol. 160.

Kanbur Ravi, Zhang Xiaobo, *Fifty Years of Regional Inequality in China: a Journey Through Central Planning, Reform, and Openness,* "Review of Development Economics" 2005, vol. 9, no. 4.

Karen Jingrong Lin, Xiaoyan Lu, Junsheng Zhang, Ying Zheng, *State-owned enterprises in China: A review of 40 yearsof research and practice,* "China Journal of Accounting" Research 2020 vol. 13, issue 1.

Kennedy Scott, *Comparing formal and informal lobbying practices in China: The capital's ambivalent embrace of capitalists,* "China Information" 2009, vol. 23, no 2.

Keyuan Zou, *Administrative Reform and Rule of Law in China,* "Copenhagen Journal of Asian Studies" 2007, no. 24.

Kinkel J. Jonathan, Hurst J. William, *The Judicial Cadre Evaluation System in China: From Quantification to Intra-State Legibility,* "The China Quarterly" 2015, no. 224.

Kipnis Andrew B., *Audit cultures: neoliberal governmentality, socialist legacy, or technologies of governing?*, "American Ethnologist" 2008, vol. 35, issue 2.
Klein Lieselotte, *The European Community's Regional Policy*, "Built Environment" 1981 vol. 7.
Klomp Luuk, Roelandt Theo, *Innovation performance and innovation policy: The case of the Netherlands*, "De Economist" 2004, vol. 152, no. 2.
Knight John, Shi Li, *Unemployment duration and earnings of re-employed workers in urban China*, "China Economic Review" 2006 vol. 17, no. 2.
Ko Kilkon, Shin Kayoung, *How Asian countries understand policy experiment as policy pilots?*, "Asian Journal of Political Science" 2017, vol. 25, no. 3.
Laifan Lin, *The Chinese model of the rule of law*, "Frontiers of Law in China" 2015, vol. 10, no. 40.
Lei Wang, *Spatial Planning and Governance: Literature Review*, [in:] *Changing Spatial Elements in Chinese Socio-economic Five-year Plan: from Project Layout to Spatial Planning*, Singapore 2019.
Leonard Cheng, Yum Kwan, *What are the determinants of the location of foreign direct investment? The Chinese experience*, "Journal of International Economics" 2000, vol. 51, no. 2.
Li Jan, Ran G.H., Wan G.H., *Interpretation on regional financial development differences in China*, "Economic Research Journal" 2007, no. 5.
Li Ling, *China's manufacturing locus in 2025: With a comparison of "Made-in-China 2025" and "Industry 4.0"*, "Technological Forecasting and Social Change" 2018, vol. 135.
Li Tong, *Report on the Development of the Tianjin Binhai New Area*, [in:] Yitao Tao, Yiming Yuan (eds.), *Annual Report on the Development of China's Special Economic Zones (2018), Blue Book of China's Special Economic Zones*, Singapore 2019.
Liang Jiaqi, Langbein Laura, *Linking anticorruption threats, performance pay, administrative outputs, and policy outcomes in China*, "Public Administration" 2018, vol. 97, issue 1.
Liang Jiaqi, Langbein Laura, *Performance Management, High-Powered Incentives, and Environmental Policies in China*, "International Public Management Journal" 2015, vol. 18, no. 3.
Liengpunsakul Subin, *Artificial Intelligence and Sustainable Development in China*, "The Chinese Economy" 2021, vol. 54, no. 4.
Liefne Ingo, Wei Yehua Dennis, *Introduction: innovation and regional development in China*, [in:] Ingo Liefne, Yehua Dennis Wei (eds.), *Innovation and regional development in China*, New York London, 2014.
Lis Rafał, *The principle of brakes and balance and the ideals of direct government. Around the Values of American Constitutionalism*, "Przegląd Sejmowy" 2017, vol. 142, no. 5.
Litwack John M., Qian Yingyi, *Balanced or unbalanced development: Special economic zones as catalysts for transition*, "Journal of Comparative Economics" 1998, vol. 26, no. 1.
Liu Mingxing, Song Binwen, Tao Ran, *Perspective on Local Governance Reform in China*, "China & World Economy" 2006, vol. 14.
Lo Shiu Hing, *Comparative political systems: The cases of Hong Kong and Macau*, "Journal of Contemporary Asia" 1995, vol. 25, no. 2.

Lu Zheng, Deng Xiang, *China's Western Development Strategy: Policies, Effects and Prospects,* "MPRA Paper 2011", no. 35201.

Lu Zheng, Deng Xiang, *Regional Policy and Regional Development: A Case Study of China's Western Development Strategy,* "Annales Universitatis Apulensis Series Oeconomica" 2013, vol. 15, no. 1.

Lubina Michał, *From Geopolitical Chance to Security Threat: Polish Public Political Discourse on the One Belt One Road Initiative,* "Polish Political Science Yearbook" 2017, vol. 46, no. 1.

Majid Nomaan, *The great employment transformation in China,* International Labor Organization 2015, https://www.ilo.org/wcmsp5/groups/public/±ed_emp/documents/publication/wcms_423613.pdf.

Mamatzakis Emmanuel, *Public infrastructure and productivity growth in Greek agriculture,* "Agricultural Economics" 2003, vol. 29, no. 2.

March James G., Olsen Johan P., *Institutional Perspectives on Political Institutions,* "Governance" 1996, vol. 9, issue 3.

Marra Marianna, *High speed rail and China's new economic geography: Impact assessment from the regional science perspective,* "Regional Studies" 2020, vol. 54, no. 4.

Mee Kam Ng, Wing-Shing Tang, *The Role of Planning in the Development of Shenzhen, China: Rhetoric and Realities,* "Eurasian Geography and Economics" 2004, vol. 45, issue 3.

Mertha Andrew, *China's 'Soft' Centralization: Shifting Tiao / Kuai Authority Relations,* "The China Quarterly" 2005, vol. 184.

Min Ye, *Fragmentation and Mobilization: Domestic Politics of the Belt and Road in China,* "Journal of Contemporary China", 2019, vol. 28, issue 119.

Minarcíková Eva, *EU-China cooperation on regional policy,* "Perspectives in Science" 2016, vol. 7.

Minerva Alfredo, Ottaviano Gianmarco, *Endogenous growth theories: agglomeration and transportation costs,* [in:] Roberta Capello, Peter Nijkamp (eds.), *Handbook of Regional Growth and Development Theories,* Cheltenham, Northampton 2010.

Mingjiang Li, *China's Economic Power in Asia: The Belt and Road Initiative and the Local Guangxi Government's Role,* "Asian Perspective" 2019, vol. 43, no. 2.

Minjia Chen, Yongnian Zheng, *China's Regional Disparity and Its Policy Responses,* "China & World Economy" 2008, vol. 16, no. 4.

Minjia Chen, Yongnian Zheng, *China's Regional Disparity and Its Policy Responses,* "China & World Economy" 2008, vol. 16, no. 4.

Mizutani Fumitoshi, Tanaka Tomoyasu, *Productivity effects and determinants of public infrastructure investment,* "The Annals of Regional Science" 2010, vol. 44, no. 3.

Murdock Kevin, Stiglitz Joseph, *Financial Restraint: Towards a New Paradigm,* Working Paper 1995, no. 1355.

Nair Sreeja Howlett Michael, *Meaning and power in the design and development of policy experiments,* "Futures" 2016, vol. 76.

Naughton Barry, *Is China Socialist?* "Journal of Economic perspectives" 2017, vol. 31, no. 1.

Paine Suzanne, *Spatial aspects of Chinese development: Issues, outcomes and policies 1949–79,* "The Journal of Development Studies" 1981, vol. 17, no. 2.

Park Albert, Wang Sangui, *China's poverty statistics,* "China Economic Review" 2001, vol. 12, no. 4.

Pauly Mark, *Income Redistribution as a Local Public Good,* "Journal of Public Economics" 1973, vol. 2.

Pei Li, Yi Lu, Jin Wang, *Does flattening government improve economic performance? Evidence from China,* "Journal of Development Economics" 2016, vol. 123.

Porter Michael, *Clusters and the New Economics of Competition,* "Harvard Business Review", 1998, November.

Porter Michael, *Competitive Advantage, Agglomeration Economies, and Regional Policy,* "International Regional Science Review" 1996, vol. 19, no. 2.

Qinghua Zhang, Heng-fu Zou, *Regional inequality in contemporary China,* "Annals of Economics & Finance" 2012, vol. 13, no. 1.

Qingyun Wang, Bing Shen, Xuegong Sun, Hui Ouyang, Ding Ding, Xiaoli Yu, Shiji Gao, Feng Liu, Weidong Liu, Kun Huang, *EU – China Cooperative Research Program on Regional Policy,* 2010, https://ec.europa.eu/regional_policy/sources/international/pdf /china_study_report_en.pdf.

Qingzhi Huan, *Regional Supervision Centers for Environmental Protection in China: Functions and Limitations,* "Journal of Current Chinese Affairs" 2011, vol. 40, issue 3.

Qiong Yang, Xiurong Hu, Yuqing Wang, Ying Liu, Junfeng Liu, Jianmin Ma, Xuejun Wang, Yi Wan, Jianying Hu, Zhaobin Zhang, Xilong Wang, Shu Tao, *Comparison of the impact of China's investment and road investment on the economy and air pollution emissions,* "Journal of Cleaner Production" 2021, vol. 293.

Quade Elizabeth, *The Logic of Anticorruption Enforcement Campaigns in Contemporary China,* "Journal of Contemporary China" 2007, vol. 16, issue 50.

Ramasamy Bala, Yeung Matthew., *The Determinants of Foreign Direct Investment in Services,* "World Economy" 2010, vol. 33.

Ravi Kanbur, Xiaobo Zhang, *Fifty Years of Regional Inequality in China: A Journey Through Central Planning, Reform, and Openness,* "Review of Development Economics" 2005, vol. 9, issue 1.

Rawski G. Thomas, Wei Xiao, *Roundtable on Chinese Economic Statistics: Introduction,* "China Economic Review" 2011, vol. 12, no. 4.

Reyes Aroche Fidel, *The death of development theory: From Friedrich von Hayek to the Washington consensus,* "Journal o f Post Keynesian Economics" 2018, vol. 41.

Reynolds G. Lloyd, *Gunnar Myrdal's Contribution to Economics, 1940–1970,* "The Swedish Journal of Economics" 1974, vol. 76, no. 4.

Roger Gordon Wei Li, *Chinese enterprise behavior under the reform,* "American Economic Review" 1991, vol. 81, no. 2.

Ruan Jianqing, Zhang Xiaobo, *Finance and cluster-based industrial development in China,* "Economic Development and Cultural Change" 2009, vol. 58, issue 1.

Sarek Łukasz, *Chinese decoupling – "dual circulation economy",* "Bulletin of the Asia Research Center, Security Research Center of the Academy of Martial Arts", 2021, no. 47 / May.

Schindler Seth, Kanai Miguel J., *Getting the territory right: infrastructure-led development and the re-emergence of spatial planning strategies,* "Regional Studies" 2019, vol. 55, no. 1.

Schmidt Dirk H., Heilmann Sebastian, *Provincial- and municipal-level governments,* [in:] Sebastian Heilmann (ed.), *China's Political System,* Lanham, Boulder, New York, London 2017.

Schubert Gunter, Heberer Thomas, *Continuity and change in China's "local state developmentalism"*, "issues & Studies" 2015, vol. 51, no. 2.

Shah Anwar, Shen Chunli, *The Reform of the Intergovernmental Transfer System to Achieve a Harmonious Society and a Level Playing Field for Regional Development in China,* "World Bank Policy Research Working Paper", December 2006, no. 4100.

Shahar Hameiri, Lee Jones, Yizheng Zou, *The Development-Insecurity Nexus in China's Near-Abroad: Rethinking Cross-Border Economic Integration in an Era of State Transformation,* "Journal of Contemporary Asia" 2019, vol. 49, issue 3.

Shapiro Daniel, Yao Tang, Xuejing Cathy Ma, *Mode of Entry and the Regional Distribution of Foreign Direct Investment in China,* "Journal of Chinese Economic and Business Studies" 2007, vol. 5, issue 3.

Sharma Kumar Naresh, *Special economic zones: Socio-economic implications,* "Economic and Political Weekly" 2009, vol. 44, no. 20.

Shenggen Fan, Ravi Kanbur, Xiaobo Zhang, *China's regional disparities: Experience and policy,* "Review of Development Finance" 2011, no. 1.

Shiuh-Shen Chien, *Economic Freedom and Political Control in Post-Mao China: A Perspective of Upward Accountability and Asymmetric Decentralization,* "Asian Journal of Political Science" 2010, vol. 18, issue 1.

Shiuh-Shen Chien, *Local responses to globalization in China – a territorial restructuring process perspective,* "Pacific Economic Review" 2008, vol. 13, issue 4.

Shuanglin Lin, *How to reform China's fiscal system?,* "China Economic Journal" 2020, vol. 13, issue 1.

Shujie Yao, Fan Zhang, Feng Wang, Jinghua Ou, *Regional economic growth and the role of high-speed rail in China,* "Applied Economics" 2019, vol. 51, no. 32.

Shuming Bao, Gene Hsin Chang, Sachs D. Jeffrey, Wing Thye Woo, *Geographic Factors and China's Regional Development under Market Reforms, 1978–1998,* "China Economic Review" 2002, vol. 13, issue 1.

Siddiqui Kalim, *One Belt and One Road, China's Massive Infrastructure Project to Boost Trade and Economy: An Overview,* "International Critical Thought" 2019, vol. 9, no. 2.

Siqin Kang, Jiangnan Zhu, *Do People Trust the Government More? Unpacking the Distinct Impacts of Anticorruption Policies on Political Trust,* "Political Research Quarterly" 2021, vol. 74, issue 2.

Smith Graeme, *Measurement, promotions and patterns of behavior in Chinese local government,* "The Journal of Peasant Studies" 2013, vol. 40, issue 6.

Smith Peter, *On the unintended consequences of publishing performance data in the public sector,* "International Journal of Public Administration" 1995, vol. 18, issue (2 & 3).

Summers Tim, *The belt and road initiative in Southwest China: responses from Yunnan province,* "The Pacific Review" 2021, vol. 34, no. 2.

Soo Francis, *China and Modernization: Past and Present. A Discussion,* "Studies in Soviet Thought" 1989, vol. 38, no 1.

Tharoor Shashi, *China's Silk Road Revival – and the Fears it Stirs – are Deeply Rooted in the Country's History,* "New Perspectives Quarterly" 2015, vol. 32, no. 1.

Trzciński Krzysztof, *Czym jest stabilność polityczna państwa?,* "Przegląd Politologiczny" 2015, no. 2.

Vigar Geoff, Cowie Paul, Healey Patsy, *Innovation in planning: creating and securing public value,* "European Planning Studies" 2020, vol. 28, no. 3.

Wang Liming, *The Basic Issues concerning the Construction of the Rule of Law in China in the New Era,* "Social Sciences in China" 2020, vol. 41, issue 1.
Wang Shaoguang, *Adapting by Learning: The Evolution of China's Rural Health Care Financing,* "Modern China" 2009, vol. 35, no. 4.
Wang Yaei, *Institutional reasons of conflicts between master plan and land use plan: causes of land expropriation of local government,* "City Planning Review" 2009, vol. 33, issue 10.
Wanxia Ren, Bing Xue, Jun Yang, Chengpeng Lu, *Effects of the Northeast China Revitalization Strategy on Regional Economic Growth and Social Development,* "Chinese Geographical Science" 2020, vol. 30, issue 5.
Wardęga Joanna, *Unequal modernization and transformations of the social structure in the People's Republic of China,* "Krakow International Studies" 2015, year 12, no. 3.
Wei Dennis Yeshua, *Regional Development in China: Transitional Institutions, Embedded Globalization, and Hybrid Economies,* "Eurasian Geography and Economics" 2007, vol. 48, issue 1.
Wei Dennis, *Network Linkages and Local Embeddedness of Foreign Ventures in China: The Case of Suzhou Municipality,* "Regional Studies" 2015, vol. 49, issue 2.
Whalley John, Xian XIN, *China's FDI and non-FDI economies and the sustainability of future high Chinese growth,* "China Economic Review" 2010, vol. 21, issue 1.
William Baumol, *Innovations and growth: Two common misapprehensions,* "Journal of Policy Modeling" 2003, vol. 25, issue 5.
Williams Philippa, Pocock Barbara, *Building 'community' for different stages of life: physical and social infrastructure in master planned communities, Community,* "Work & Family" 2010, vol. 13, issue 1.
Williamson John, *Beijing Consensus versus Washington Consensus,* https://relooney.com/NS3040/Washington-Consensus-Chapter.pdf.
Witt Michael, *China's Challenge: Geopolitics, De-Globalization, and the Future of Chinese Business,* "Management and Organization Review" 2019, vol. 15, no. 4.
Wong Christine, Karplus J. Valerie, *China's War on Air Pollution: Can Existing Governance Structures Support New Ambitions?,* "The China Quarterly" 2017, vol. 231.
Wong David, Lee Harry, Zhao Simon, Pei Qing, *Region-specific determinants of the foreign direct investment in China,* "Geographical Research" 2020, vol. 58, no. 2.
World Foresight Forum, *The Beijing Consensus: An alternative approach to development,* April 2011, issue brief no. 2, https://hcss.nl/sites/default/files/files/reports/WFF02_issue_Brief_The_Beijing_Consensus02.pdf.
Xu Tian, Xiaoheng Zhang, Yingheng Zhou, Xiaohua Yu, *Regional income inequality in China revisited: A perspective from club convergence,* "Economic Modeling" 2016, no. 56.
Xuehui Yang, Huirong Zhang, Shanlang Lin, Jiaping Zhang, Jianlong Zeng, *Does high-speed railway promote regional innovation growth or innovation convergence?,* "Technology in Society" 2021, vol. 64.
Xufeng Zhu, Bing Sun, *Tianjin Binhai New Area: A Case Study of Multi-Level Streams Model of Chinese Decision-Making,* "Journal of Chinese Political Science" 2009, vol. 14.
Xufeng Zhu, *Inter-regional diffusion of policy innovation in China: A comparative case study,* "Asian Journal of Political Science" 2017, vol. 25, no. 3.

Xufeng Zhu, *Mandate Versus Championship: Vertical government intervention and diffusion of innovation in public services in authoritarian China,* "Public Management Review" 2014, vol. 16, no. 1.

Yang Lijing, *Worlds Apart? Worlds Aligned? The perception and prioritization of civil servant values for civil servants from China and the Netherlands,* [in] "International Journal of Public Administration" 2016, vol. 39, no. 1.

Yanqing Jiang, Yunliang Jiang, Jinghai Zheng, *Investment in Infrastructure and Regional Growth in China. Emerging,* "Markets Finance and Trade" 2020 vol. 56, no. 9.

Yanrui Wu, *Is China's economic growth sustainable? A productivity analysis,* "China Economic Review" 2000, vol. 11, issue 3.

Yanyan Chen Jiang Xu, *Infrastructure Investment in China: From Central Monopoly to Multi-Level Partnership,* "Asian Geographer", 2010, vol. 27, no. 1–2.

Yao S., Zhang Zhaoyong, *Regional Growth in China Under Economic Reforms,* "The Journal of Development Studies" 2001, vol. 38, issue 2.

Ya-Ting Huang, Jian Xu, *Surviving the performance management of academic work: evidence from young Chinese academics,* "Higher Education Research & Development" 2020, vol. 39, issue 4.

Ying Zhang, *Analysis of the history and current status of country-to-district-transformation,* "Legal System and Society" 2016, vol. 24.

Yingqi Wei, Xiaming Liu, Parker David, Vaidya Kirit, *The Regional Distribution of Foreign Direct Investment in China,* "Regional Studies" 1999, vol. 33, no. 9.

Yinqiu Lu, *Local Government Financing Platforms in China: A Fortune or Misfortune?,* IMF Working Papers 2013 vol. 13, issue 243.

Yongqiu Wu, Yi Huang, Jing Zhao, Yanping Pu, *Transfer payment structure and local government fiscal efficiency: evidence from China,* "China Finance and Economic Review" 2017 vol. 12, no. 5.

Youlang Zhang, Xufeng Zhu, *Multiple mechanisms of policy diffusion in China,* Public Management Review 2019, vol. 21, no. 4.

Yu Chen, Anthony Yeh, Yingxuan Zhang, *Political tournament and regional cooperation in China: a game theory approach,* "Annals Regional Science" 2017, vol. 58, no. 3.

Yu Jianxing, Lin Li, Yongdong Shen, *Rediscovering Intergovernmental Relations at the Local Level: The Devolution to Township Governments in Zhejiang Province,* "China Review" 2016, vol. 16, issue 2.

Yuan Gao, Li Tian, Yandong Cao, Lin Zhou, Zhibin Li, Deyi Hou, *Supplying social infrastructure land for satisfying public needs or leasing residential land? A study of local government choices in China,* "Land Use Policy" 2019, vol. 87.

Zabielskis Peter, *Environmental Problems in China: Issues and Prospects.* [in:] Zhidong Hao, Sheying Chen (eds) *Social Issues in China. International Perspectives on Social Policy, Administration, and Practice,* vol. 1, New York 2014.

Zan Yang, Rongrong Ren, Hongyu Liu, Huan Zhang, *Land leasing and local government behavior in China: Evidence from Beijing,* "Urban Studies" 2015, vol. 52, no. 5.

Jinghan Zeng, *Narrating China's belt and road initiative,* "Global Policy", 2019, vol. 10.

Zeng Zhihua Douglas, *How Do Special Economic Zones and Industrial Clusters Drive China's Rapid Development?,* 'Policy Research Working Paper' 2011, no. 5583.

Zhanqiang Zhu, Jie Ren, Xuan Liu, *Green infrastructure provision for environmental justice: Application of the equity index in Guangzhou, China,* "Urban Forestry & Urban Greening" 2019, vol. 46.

Zhenhua Chen, Junbo Xue, Adam Rose, Kingsley Haynes, *The impact of high-speed rail investment on economic and environmental change in China: A dynamic CGE analysis,* "Transportation Research Part A: Policy and Practice" 2016, vol. 92.

Zhiyu Fu, Wenhong Yan, *Promoting the innovation of urbanization system in Western China from the perspective of public finance and taxation,* "China Finance and Economic Review" 2016, vol. 4, no. 4.

Zhiyue Bo, *Balance of Factional Power in China: The Seventeenth Central Committee of the Chinese Communist Party,* "East Asia" 2008, vol. 25.

Zhiyue Bo, *Economic performance and political mobility: Chinese provincial leaders,* "Journal of Contemporary China" 1996, vol. 5.

Zhiyue Bo, *Governing China in the Early 21st Century: Provincial Perspective,* "Journal of Chinese Political Science" 2002, vol. 7.

Zhong-Ren Peng, Jian Sun Daniel, *Qing-Chang Lu, China's Public Transportation: Problems, Policies and Future Prospective to Sustainability,* "Ite Journal", May 2012.

Zhu Xufeng, Bai Guihua, *Policy Synthesis through Regional Experimentations: Comparative Study of the New Cooperative Medical Scheme in Three Chinese Provinces,* "Journal of Comparative Policy Analysis: Research and Practice" 2020, vol. 22, no. 4.

Zhuo Chen, Zhiguo He, Chun Liu, *The Financing of Local Government in China: Stimulus Loan Wanes and Shadow Banking Waxes,* "ADBI Working Paper Series" 2018, no. 800.

Ziyin Zhuang, Wei Zou, *Gonggong zhichu neng fou cujin jingji zengzhang* (公共 支出 能否 促進 經濟 增長), "Guanli Shijie (管理 世界)" 2003, Tiji (体积) 7.

Zuhui Huang, Xiaobo Zhang, Yunwei Zhu, *The role of clustering in rural industrialization: A case study of the footwear industry in Wenzhou,* "China Economic Review" 2008, vol. 19, no. 3.

Zuhui, Xiaobo Zhang, Yunwei Zhu, *The Formation of Wenzhou Footwear Clusters: How were the Entry Barriers Overcome?,* Invited paper prepared for presentation at the International Association of Agricultural Economists Conference, Gold Coast, Australia, August 2006, [in:] https://www.researchgate.net/publication/23511448.

Web Documents

[2019 Nian quanguo shoufei gonglu tongji gongbao] jiedu ([2019 年 全国收费公路 统计公报] 解读) [in:] http://xxgk.mot.gov.cn/2020/jigou/glj/202009/t20200928_3471327.html.

[Cujin zhongbu diqu jueqi guihua (2016 zhiì 2025 nian)] zhengce jiedu ([促进中部 地区 崛起 规划（2016 至2025年）] 政策解读), [in:] http://www.scio.gov.cn/34473/34515/Document/1535229/1535229.htm.

"Shisiwu": Zhongguo ruhe yingdui bianju ("十四五"： 中国如何应对变局), [in:] http://www.xinhuanet.com/politics/2020-10/12/c_1126595127.htm.

2020 Nian jiaotong yunshu jingji xian jiang hou sheng, chixu huifu (2020 年 交通运输经济先降后升持续恢复), [in:] http://xxgk.mot.gov.cn/2020/jigou/zhghs/202101/t20210128_3520349.html.

Alvaredo Facundo, Chancel Lucas, Piketty Thomas, Saez Emmanuel, Zucman Gabriel, *World inequality report 2018*, [in:] https://wir2018.wid.world/files/download/wir2018-full-report-english.pdf.

An Overview of Spatial Policy in Asian and European Countries, [in:] http://www.mlit.go.jp/kokudokeikaku/international/spw/general/china/index_e.html.

Binhai New Area, [in:] http://subsites.chinadaily.com.cn/tianjin/binhai/binhainewarea.html.

Binhai seeks new growth momentum, [in:] http://subsites.chinadaily.com.cn/tianjin/binhai/2020-06/23/c_502167.htm.

Capital Trade Incorporated, An Assessment of China's Subsidies to Strategic and Heavyweight Industries, [in:] https://www.uscc.gov/sites/default/files/Research/AnAssessmentofChina'sSubsidiestoStrategicandHeavyweightIndustries.pdf.

China (Hubei) pilot free trade zone, [in:] https://www.china-hbftz.gov.cn/optList.html?cttype=X14.

China Briefing, *Minimum Wage Levels Across China*, 22.02.2012, [in:] https://www.china-briefing.com/news/minimum-wage-levels-across-china.

China File, *What does Xi Jinping's top-down leadership mean for innovation in China?* September 26, 2016, [in:] http://www.chinafile.com/conversation/what-does-xi-jinpings-top-down-leadership-mean-innovation-china.

China's western development strategy to gain new momentum, May 28, 2020, [in:] http://english.www.gov.cn/policies/policywatch/202005/28/content_WS5ecf2018c6d0b3f0e9498d45.html.

Chinese Medical Association Publishing House, *Zhonggong zhongyang bangong ting yinfa [dang zheng lǐngdao ganbu kaohe gongzuo tiaoli]* (中共中央办公厅 印发 [党政 领导 干部 考核 工作 条例]), [in:] http://www.cmaph.org/zyhsjygjs/889667.jhtml.

Consulate-General of The People's Republic of China in Auckland, *CPC unveils proposals for formulating 14th five-year plan, long-range goals*, [in:] http://www.chinaconsulate.org.nz/eng/zlgxw/t1829233.htm.

Deloitte, *Rising innovation in China, China Innovation ecosystem development Report 2019*, September 2019 [in:] https://www2.deloitte.com/content/dam/Deloitte/cn/Documents/innovation/deloitte-cn-innovation-china- innovation-ecosystem-report-en-191101.pdf.

Free trade zones buoy work restarts of firms, [in:] http://www.exploringtianjin.com/binhain/2020-04/29/c_489076.htm.

https://stat.gov.pl/obszary-tematyczne/rachunki-narodowe/rachunki-regionalne/wstepne-szacunki-produktu-krajowego-brutto-w-przekrój-regionow-w-2018-roku,8,2.html.

https://stat.gov.pl/obszary-tematyczne/rachunki-narodowe/rachunki-regionalne/wstepne-szacunki-produktu-krajowego-brutto-w-przekrój-regionow-w-2018-roku,8,2.html.

https://www.ndrc.gov.cn/fggz/fzzlgh/gjjzxgh/200709/P020191104623124380472.pdf.

Hubei yi shangbao zi mao qu zongti fangan, sheji wuhan, yichang, xiangyang 3 shi (湖北已上报自贸区总体方案，涉及武汉宜昌、襄阳 3市), [in:] https://www.thepaper.cn/newsDetail_forward_1552821.

Jilin kuai pao beihou de "wang min sudu" (吉林快跑背后 的 "王岷速度") 吉林 快跑背后 的 "王 岷 速度"), [in:] http://news.sina.com.cn/c /2007-03-01/095412400380.shtml.

Kunming's economic aggregate achieved leapfrog growth, [in:] https://www.drawfleurdelis.com/2020/kunmings-economic-aggregate-achieved-leapfrog-growth.

Leading Group for Western Region Development revamped, [in:] http://english.www.gov.cn/policies/latest_releases/2018/08/01/content_281476244584930.htm.

Liang Xiang, *Dramatic Changes,* Beijing Review 1986, no. 8, 24 February, [in:], http://www.bjreview.com/Special_Reports/2018/40th_Anniversary_of_Reform_and_Opening_up/Now_and_Then/Shenzhen/201806/t20180622_800133456.html.

Liu Qin, *Clear as mud: how poor data is thwarting China's water clean-up,* China Dialogue, May 18, 2016, [in:] https://www.chinadialogue.net/article/show/single/en/8922-Clear-as-mud-how-poor-data-is-thwarting-China-s-water-clean-up.

OECD Economic Surveys: China 2005, 2005, [in:] https://read.oecd-ilibrary.org/economics/oecd-economic-surveys-china-2005_eco_surveys-chn-2005-en#page82.

Ping An Insurance Group, [in:] https://www.forbes.com/companies/ping-an-insurance/#8856a605c7b0.

Richardson Karen, *China's Admission of Economic Data Flaws Isn't Likely to Make Fund-Picking Easier,* Asian Wall Street Journal 22 Nov. 2001, [in:] https://www.wsj.com/articles/SB1006367201710056960.

Ruehl Henry, *The Khorgos Hype on the Belt and Road,* The Diplomat, September 2019, [in:] https://thediplomat.com/2019/09/the-khorgos-hype-on-the-belt-and-road.

Chinese Communist Party website, *Zhonggong zhongyang guanyu zhiding guomin jingji he shehui fazhan di shisi ge wu nian guihua he er ling sanwu nian yuanjing mubiao di jianyi* (中共中央关于 制定国民经济和社会发展第十四个五年〇和 和 二三五年远景目标 的 建议), [in:] http://www.12371.cn/2020/11/04/VIDE1604469480803236.shtml.

Shenzhen Basics, [in:] http://www.sz.gov.cn/en_szgov/aboutsz/profile/content/post_1357629.html.

Sìchuan sheng fazhan he gaige weiyuanhui zhuyao zhize, lingdao jianjie he jigou shezhi (四川省发展和 改革委员会主要职责、领导简介 和 机构设置), 四川省发展 和 改革 委员会主要职责、领导简介和机构设置, [in:] http://www.sc.gov.cn/10462/10778/10876/2020/11/25/ef07e79fbc584644b34476fe6d4974a7.shtml.

Su Min, *Zhongguo duo cengci gaige shidian gay jiben xingcheng* (中国多层次改革试点格局基本形成), June 8, 2010, [in:] https://www.chinanews.com/cj/cj-gncj/news/2010/06-08/2329128.shtml.

Tang jin (唐瑾): Tongchou jiaotong jichu sheshi jianshe zhicheng gao zhiliang fazhan (统筹交通基础设施建设支撑高质量发展)唐瑾：统筹 交通 基础 设施 建设 支撑高质量发展), [in:] http://www.ccud.org.cn/article/23416.html.

The "Rise of Central China" Plan: Objectives and Impacts with Special Focus on Anhui Province, Shanghai Flash 2012, issue 4, [in:]: https://www.sinoptic.ch/shanghaiflash/texts/pdf/2012/201204Shanghai.Flash.pdf.

The People's Government of Beijing Municipality, [in:] http://english.beijing.gov.cn/BeijingInfo/facts/202006/t20200601_1912277.html.

The World Bank, [in:] https://databank.worldbank.org/data/reports.aspx?source=2&series=NY.GDP.MKTP.CD,NV.AGR.TOTL.ZS,NV.IND.TOTL.ZS,NV.IND.MANF.ZS,NV.SRV.TETC.ZS,NV.SRV.TOTL.ZS#.

The World Bank, *GINI index – China,* [in:] https://data.worldbank.org/indicator/SI.POV.GINI.

Understanding China's 13th Five-Year Plan, [in:] http://www.chinabusinessreview.com/understanding-chinas-13th-five-year-plan.

Urban Institute, *State and Local Expenditures,* [in:] https://www.urban.org/policy-centers/cross-center-initiatives/state-and-local-finance-initiative/state-and-local-backgrounders.

What does the Yangtze River Delta Integration Mean for Businesses in China?, 17/09/2019, [in:] https://www.china-briefing.com/news/yangtze-river-delta-integration-opportunities-incentives-for-businesses-in-china-dual-circulation-strategy.

World inequality report 2018, Written and coordinated by: Facundo Alvaredo, Lucas Chancel, Thomas Piketty, Emmanuel Saez, Gabriel Zucman, [in:] https://wir2018.wid.world/files/download/wir2018-full-report-english.pdf.

Wu nian guihua de lishi jingyan yu zhanwang (五年规划的历史经验与 展望), [in:] http://www.china-cer.com.cn/shisiwu/2020050810.html.

Wuhan Investment Promotion Complaint Center, [in:] http://english.wuhan.gov.cn/Investment_1/WIE_12751/202003/t20200316_950597.shtml.

Xinhua Chen xi zai dianshi dianhua huiyi shang qiangdiao yi gao zhiliang ganbu kaohe jili dan dang zuowei cujin shiye fazhan (陈希 在 电视 电话 会议 上 强调 以 高质量 干部 考核 激励 担当 作为 促进 事业 发展), October 23, 2020, [in:] http://www.xinhuanet.com/politics/2020-10/23/c_1126650190.htm.

Xinhua, *Xijinping: Guanyu "zhonggong [zhongyong guonyu zhiding guomin jingji he shehui fazhan di shisige wu nian guihua he er ling sanwu nian yuanjing mubiao di jianyi] de shuomíng* (受权发布） 习近平： 关于 制定 国民经济 关于 [中共中央第十 四 个 五年 规划和二〇三五年远景目标的建议] 的说明), [in:] http://www.xinhuanet.com/politics/leaders/2020-11/03/c_1126693341.htm.

Xinhua, *Zhonggong zhongyang guanyu zhiding guomin jingji he shehui fazhan di shisi ge wu nian guihua he er ling sanwu nian yuanjing mubiao di jianyi* (中共中央关于制定国民经济和社会发展第十四个五年规划和二〇三五年五年目标的建议), [in:] http://www.xinhuanet.com/politics/zystj/2020-11/03/c1126693293.htm.

Xinhua, 混合 所有制经济已占 40% 5–10 年后将达到 80%, November 25, 2003, [in:] http://news.southcn.com/china/zgkx/200311250786.htm.

Xinua, *Di shisan jie quanguo renmin daibiao dahui di si ci huiyi guanyu guomin jingji he shehui fazhan di shisi ge wu nian guihua he 2035 nian yuanjing mubiao gangyao de jueyi* (第十三届全国人民代表大会第四 国民经济关于会议会议会议和社会发展第十四个五年规划和2035年远景目标纲要的决议), [in:] http://www.xinhuanet.com/politics/2021-03/11/c_1127200766.htm.

Xinua, *Interview: China's 14th Five-Year Plan deserves world's attention, says scholar,* November 2, 2020, [in:] http://www.xinhuanet.com/english/2020-11/02/c_139484868.htm.

Yidai yilu bu cunzai quexi shengfen: Jiangsu shi jiaohui dian, difang fangan 10 yue qian chu zi mao qu lian xian pengpai xin (一带一路不存在 缺席省份：江苏是交汇点， 地方方案 10 月贸区连线澎湃新), [in:] https://www.thepaper.cn/newsDetail_forward_1319660.

Zhonggong zhongyang guanyu zhiding guomin jingji he shehui fazhan di shi ge wu nian jihua de jianyi (中共中央关于制定国民经济和社会发展第十个五年计划的建议), [in:] http://www.cctv.com/news/special/zt1/five/1364.html.

Zhonghua renmin gongheguo guomin jingji he shehui fazhan di shisi ge wu nian guihua he 2035 nian yuanjing mubiao gangyao (中华人民共和国国民经济和社会发展第十四个五年规划和 2035 年远景目标纲要), [in:] http://www.gov.cn/xinwen/2021-03/13/content_5592681.html.